On Words and Sounds

On Words and Sounds:
A Selection of Papers from the 40th PLM, 2009

Edited by

Kamila Dębowska-Kozłowska
and Katarzyna Dziubalska-Kołaczyk

CAMBRIDGE
SCHOLARS
PUBLISHING

On Words and Sounds:
A Selection of Papers from the 40th PLM, 2009,
Edited by Kamila Dębowska-Kozłowska and Katarzyna Dziubalska-Kołaczyk

This book first published 2011

Cambridge Scholars Publishing

12 Back Chapman Street, Newcastle upon Tyne, NE6 2XX, UK

British Library Cataloguing in Publication Data
A catalogue record for this book is available from the British Library

ISBN (10): 1-4438-3161-1, ISBN (13): 978-1-4438-3161-1

TABLE OF CONTENTS

PREFACE

The present volume *On Words and Sounds* is a collection of selected papers from PLM2009. The Poznań Linguistic Meeting (PLM) is an annual general linguistics conference that continues the tradition of the Polish-English contrastive conferences started by Jacek Fisiak in 1970. The new name "Poznań Linguistic Meeting" and profile were introduced in 1997 by Katarzyna Dziubalska-Kołaczyk when she took over as the Head of the Organising Committee. The Meetings are organised by the School of English, Adam Mickiewicz University, Poznań.

The book consists of fifteen articles, each of which can be read separately or in relation to others. The book will definitely appeal to the academic readership interested in the linguistic disciplines such as: phonetics and phonology, morphology, syntax, sociolinguistics, pragmatics and clinical linguistics. Collectively, the contributions investigate the interrelationships among those disciplines as well as between language and music. The central aim for the scholars was to explore PLM2009 leitmotif 'Variants, Variability, Variation' and show that the complete study of language involves diversified frameworks often rooted in the interdisciplinary approaches. This book aims at bringing together scholars aware of the need to merge individual linguistic disciplines and to provide comprehensive models for the study of the complexity of language.

—Kamila Dębowska-Kozłowska and Katarzyna Dziubalska-Kołaczyk, Editors

THE SPEECH-TO-SONG-ILLUSION REVISITED

SIMONE FALK
LUDWIG-MAXIMILIANS-UNIVERSITY, MUNICH, GERMANY
AND TAMARA RATHCKE
UNIVERSITY OF GLASGOW, UNITED KINGDOM

Abstract

The present study investigates the boundaries of speech and song from an acoustic-perceptual perspective. Using the speech-to-song illusion as a method, we tested rhythmic and tonal hypotheses in order to find out whether acoustic characteristics can cue the perceptual classification of a sentence by German listeners as sung or spoken. First, our results show that, despite individual differences, the speech-to-song illusion is a robust perceptual phenomenon comparable to those known in visual perception. Second, the experiment revealed that acoustic parameters – especially tonal structure – facilitate the perceptual shift from speech to song pointing to an acoustically guided decoding strategy for speech- vs. song-like signals.

1. Introduction

The question whether music and language should be considered as modular entities or share common resources and processes has been hotly debated in recent discussions (Peretz and Coltheart 2003, Patel 2008, Peretz in press). Concerning brain modularity, the phenomenon of song is especially intriguing as it obviously combines musical and linguistic structures. The existence of musical speech or music with words seems *per se* to corroborate the hypothesis of at least some shared domains (Patel in press). Nevertheless, the idea that singing might be exclusive to a language- or music-specific module and that during singing "music may act as a parasite of speaking" or vice versa has also been discussed (Peretz 2003, in press).

With respect to this controversy, it is worth taking a closer look at the mechanisms and acoustic premises guiding the perceptual conceptualisation of speech as opposed to song. In particular, we are interested in a perceptual phenomenon – the 'speech-to-song-illusion' (see Deutsch 1995, Deutsch et al. 2008) – that provides some evidence that an acoustic signal can be perceived both as speech and song.

1.1 An auditory illusion: speech-to-song

The illusion arises when a spoken utterance is presented in a loop so that the same prosodic structure with its speech-related characteristics is repeated over and over again. Surprisingly, listeners tend to perceive a shift from speech to song during the course of repetitions when they are told to judge the phrase as song- or speech-like. Unlike most visual illusions, this auditory effect seems to be unidirectional, i.e. once perceived as sung, a phrase cannot be perceived as spoken again (Deutsch 1995). So far, the illusion has only been studied with English listeners using a single English phrase (*(but they) sometimes behave so strangely*) which was originally spoken in context by the author herself (Deutsch 1995).

In an experiment by Deutsch et al. (2008), subjects listened 10 times to this phrase. After each repetition, they were asked to judge the phrase on a five-point-scale as speech or song. Unfortunately, the depiction in Deutsch et al.'s report only compares the judgments after the first and last presentation of the stimulus. This leaves the question open if the perceptual shift occurs abruptly at some point in the loop or if it is rather a continuous process. Additionally, it has been reported that the acoustics of the looped stimulus had to be unchanged since slight transposition of pitch or random permutation of syllables blocked the illusion (Deutsch et al. 2008). The speech-to-song illusion seriously challenges a strictly modular view of speech and music processing. In a modular architecture (Peretz and Coltheart 2003), the information available in the acoustic input is sent to task-specific modules that specialise in different sorts of input features for further processing. This implies that acoustic characteristics would predetermine if the incoming signal was processed in either music- or speech-related modules. The speech-to-song-illusion poses a problem since the acoustics of the same input can be perceived and processed both as speech and song without changing the incoming signal. Therefore, Deutsch et al. (2008) – while adhering to the modular concept – proposed that the same input activated separate pathways of speech versus song processing during the task. They also concluded that the perception of a phrase as speech or song could not be determined by specific music- or speech-like acoustic properties.

1.2 On the acoustics of speech vs. song

There are mainly two core features – pitch and rhythm – which are shared by both speech and music. However, these features are structured in a music/language-specific way, i.e. rhythm and pitch are associated with different acoustic instances depending on which medium/style they represent.

As far as pitch is concerned, scalar structure is said to be one of the most prominent musical features that speech generally lacks (Krumhansl 2005). Scalar structure in Western tonal music is represented by two scales, the major and the minor. For each of them, several tonal intervals are precisely defined in their tonal relationships and each deviation from these intervals is perceived as dissonant (Schellenberg and Trehub 1996). There is no such strict system of allowed tonal intervals in speech. The scaling of pitch targets and their intervals can vary considerably, the variation being conditioned phonetically (e.g. Lieberman and Pierrehumbert 1984), phonologically (e.g. Niebuhr 2007) or by discourse functions like grade of prominence (e.g. Ladd and Morton 1997). Furthermore, f0-trajectories of speech are characterised by f0-movements with variable slopes (t'Hart, Collier and Cohen 1990) whereas temporal stability of f0-targets is typical of pitch events in music (Zatorre et al. 2002). These differences are illustrated in Fig. 1 showing a German sentence (*Im Herbst bricht sich das Licht im bunten Laub*, English: 'In autumn, light is refracted by colourful leaves.'), which was both spoken and musically interpreted by the first author. As shown in the left-hand panel, the f0-trajectory of the sung phrase looks like a staircase leading up and down as it is formed by several f0-levels of equal intervals (seconds) whose number roughly corresponds to the number of syllables in the phrase. In contrast, f0-trajectories of the spoken phrase shown in the right-hand panel contain a series of falling and rising movements which vary in their slopes and intervals.

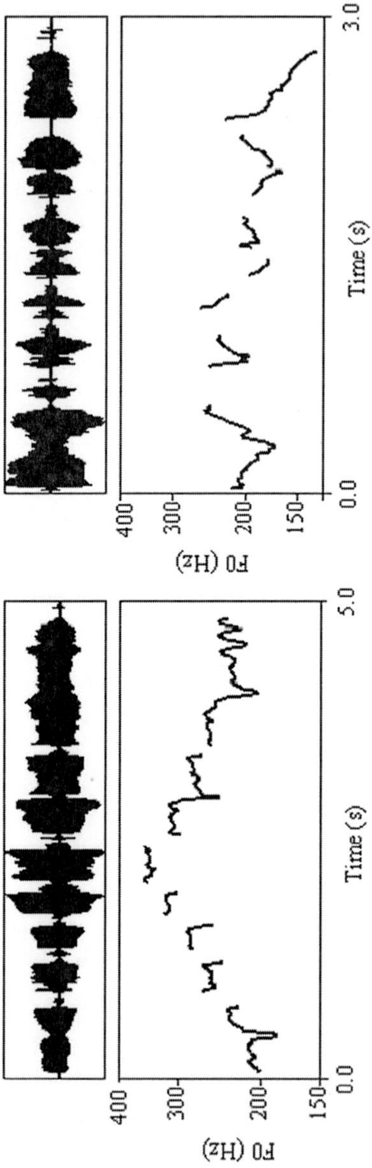

Figure 1: Waveforms and f0-trajectories of the sung (left-hand panel) and spoken (right-hand panel) German utterance "Im Herbst bricht sich das Licht im bunten Laub" (see text). F0 is scaled logarithmically.

Rhythm can be defined as the patterning of accentuation and grouping in sequences of events which systematically recur in time (e.g. Arvaniti 2009, Clarke 1999). As far as grouping is concerned, a composition of segments organised in syllables is widely agreed to be the smallest rhythmical unit of speech (Cutler 1991). In contrast, intervocalic intervals were assumed to constitute the smallest rhythmic units in song (Sundberg 1989). The predominance of intervocalic to syllabic chunking in song is demonstrated in Fig. 2, comparing both possibilities on the same sung German phrase *Schneeflöckchen, Weissröckchen, wann kommst du geschneit* (taken from a Christmas song; in English: 'Little snowflake, little white skirt, when will you appear to come down to earth'). As pointed out in Fig. 2, there is a tendency towards equal temporal spacing when segments of a sung phrase with equal note durations are arranged as intervocalic intervals but not as syllables: the mean of syllabic duration *dur (*S) is 0.47 sec with a standard deviation of 0.16 sec, whereas the mean of intervocalic intervals *dur(ii)* is 0.45 sec with a standard deviation of only 0.10 sec. Related to the temporal structure, isochrony has been widely discussed in both speech and music. However, speech patterns widely failed to show any isochrony in production (see Arvaniti 2009, Nolan and Asu 2009 for a critical overview), whereas temporal patterns in music are generally structured in a more systematic, isochronous way (metrically bounded music: e.g. Cooper and Meyer 1960, Drake and Palmer 1993).

Against the background of considerations given above, the English phrase used by Deutsch et al. (2008) was remarkable with respect to its tonal make-up. First of all, the phrase-final interval of 8 semitones (st) constitutes a minor sixth which is a well-defined consonant musical interval. Furthermore, besides some micro-prosodic f0-perturbations induced by consonants (Lövqvist et al. 1989), there are several relatively plain f0-stretches during the course of the sentence (especially the level-like production of the phrase-final word *strangely)*, which rather relates to the sung than to the spoken example in Fig. 1. Hypothetically, the coincidence of relatively stable f0-trajectories and the harmonic interval in phrase-final position may have facilitated the occurrence of the speech-to-song illusion as reported in Deutsch et al. (2008).

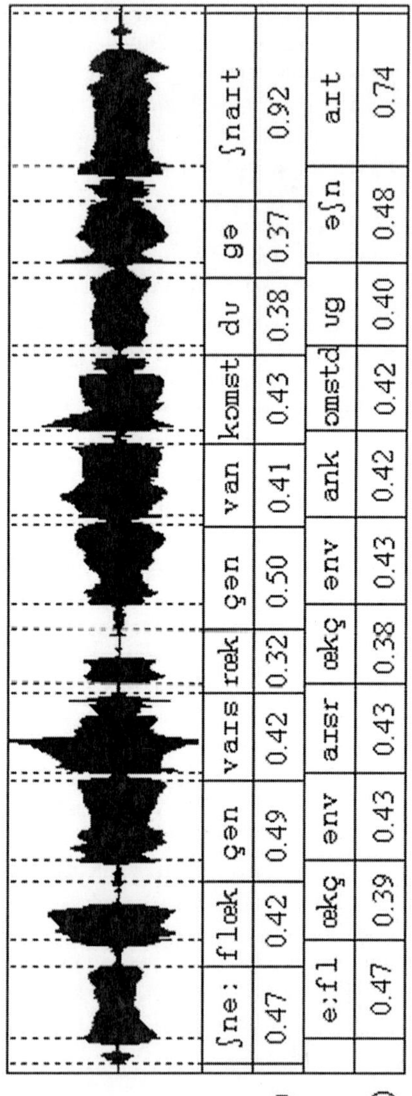

Figure 2: Labels and durations of syllables (S) as opposed to intervocalic intervals (ii) of the German phrase *Schneeflöckchen, Weissröckchen, wann kommst du geschneit* sung by an amateur female singer.

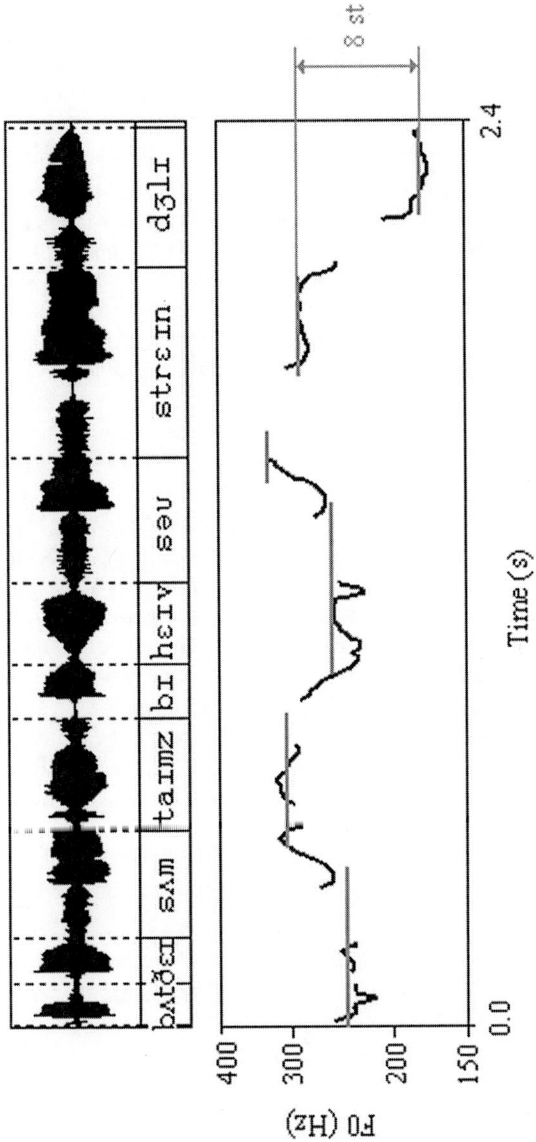

Figure 3: Waveform, syllabic labelling and f0-trajectory of the English phrase *but they sometimes behave so strangely* used in the illusion experiment by Deutsch et al. (2008). See text for more details.

1.3 Musicality: external factors of illusion perception

As we know from speech and music pathology, there is a certain autonomy between song on the one hand and speech perception and production on the other. For one thing, there are aphasic subjects with severe expressive speech pathology who are still able to sing (Warren et al. 2003, Mogharbel et al. 2005/2006, Peretz et al. 2004a). On the other hand, there are acquired or congenital amusics who can perform quite normally in speech-prosody related tasks (Peretz and Hyde 2003, Hyde and Peretz 2004). Congenital amusia is a multiple-faceted music processing deficit which affects the ability to, for example, judge if two melodies are the same or different, detect when music is out of key, produce pitch intervals and/or recognize what should be familiar tunes from their culture (Ayotte et al. 2002, Dalla Bella et al. 2009). The core deficit in this disorder concerns pitch processing, therefore individuals with this deficit are also called tone-deaf in the literature (Foxton et al. 2004, Hyde and Peretz 2004).

However, a deeper link between the processing of melodic and intonational pitch is also discussed (Patel et al. 1998, Nicholson et al. 2003). Patel et al. (1998) studied two individuals with acquired amusia subsequent to cortical brain damage. The salient finding from this study was that for both amusics, performance in a linguistic intonation task was very similar to performance in a tone sequence task, suggesting shared processing of melodic contours across the two domains.

Besides pathological cases, there is some evidence that music education can positively influence the subjects' ability to differentiate intervals of varying range (see t'Hart 1981). For these reasons, we decided (1) to take into consideration musical training and (2) to perform a subtest of the Montreal Battery of Evaluation of Amusia (MBEA, Peretz et al. 2003) in order to assess whether some subjects could be at risk to be congenitally tone-deaf.

2. Perception experiment

2.1 Hypotheses

In contrast to Deutsch et al. (2008), we generally assume that acoustic properties of a given signal do play a role in inducing a perceptual shift from speech to song (the *Main Hypothesis*). As discussed in 1.2, the stimulus used for the original illusion task has inherently been optimal in its tonal layout to generate the effect. Therefore, we are going to explore whether and which acoustic features of a stimulus are better than others in inducing the shift from speech to song. More precisely, we hypothesise that two sets of signal-related features can account for (1) the fact that the auditory illusion emerges and (2) how rapidly it occurs within a loop.

The *Tonal Hypothesis* assumes that the perceptual shift is predominantly induced by tonal properties of a spoken utterance, namely:

(1.a) *Target stability:* If the tonal make-up of a sentence has more stable tonal targets, the shift will occur earlier compared to a sentence with unstable targets.

(1.b) *Interval structure:* If the tonal properties of a sentence involve scalar relationships of music, the shift will occur more easily.

In contrast, the *Rhythmic Hypothesis* assumes that the shift is primarily facilitated by rhythmic factors such as:

(2.a) *Accentual regularity:* If accented syllables are more regularly spaced, the shift will occur earlier compared to a non-regular distribution of accents since temporal regularity of beats increases the perception of a strong rhythm.

(2.b) *Segmental grouping:* Temporal grouping of segments into intervocalic intervals of same length will lead to an earlier shift from speech to song in contrast to a syllabic grouping of segments.

2.2 Method

2.2.1 Materials and test stimuli

With respect to the *Rhythmic Hypothesis* (2.a), two sentences were chosen as experimental materials (***bold*** = accented):

Im ***Re**gal liegen* ***Na**del und* ***Fa**den.* (English: 'There are needle and twine on the shelf.')
Im ***Gar**ten blühen heute* ***Klee*** *und* ***Mohn**.* (English: 'Today, clover and poppy are blooming in the garden.')

Spoken with broad focus, accents appear regularly in the first sentence, constituting a kind of anapest (two weak units are followed by a strong beat) as opposed to the second sentence where there is no such regularity. However, both sentences have 10 syllables and 3 accents in a broad focus.

Four sentences were added to serve as fillers (see 2.2.2). All sentences were read by a female speaker of Standard German and recorded in a sound-isolated booth at the Institute of Phonetics and Speech Processing in

Munich. All durational and f0-manipulations were done using *Praat* (Boersma and Weenink 2001). Typical f0-values of the speaker as well as her intonation patterns produced in both test utterances were used as the basis for creating tonal stimuli. To implement the tonal target stability hypothesis (1.a), f0-contours between relevant f0-targets were either kept stable or changed gradually with respect to segmental landmarks. Regarding the tonal interval structure hypothesis (1.b), we implemented the perfect fifth (interval of 7 semitones, st) twice in the signal: once as an ascending interval at the first pitch-accent and again as a descending interval at the last pitch-accent of the sentence. The interval in the speech-like condition was set to 5.5 st which should not be interpreted in terms of music scale. A top and base-line declination of 0.5 st was applied to pitch-accented and unaccented syllables. Fig. 4 compares f0-trajectories of stimuli created for both test sentences: (1) music-like stimuli with scalar structure and stable f0-targets are indicated by black lines, whereas (2) speech-like stimuli with non-scalar relationship between f0-targets and gradually changing f0-contours are shown by grey lines.

To test the temporal grouping hypothesis (2.b), the sentences had to be chunked into syllables as well as into intervocalic intervals. Due to schwa reduction in both test sentences (in /liːgən/, /blyːən/ and /faːdən/), distinguishing 10 rhythmic units for both conditions proved difficult. We decided to consider phrase-medial reduced forms as single rhythmic units, i.e. [liːgn], [blyːn] and phrase-final [faːdn̩] as two different units (see Tables 1 and 2). This decision was made with respect to the finding that phrase-final rhythmic units tend to have additional duration when compared to phrase-medial units (e.g. Lehiste 1973). As shown in Table 1, intervocalic intervals all had equal duration. In contrast, in the speech-like condition (Table 2), unaccented syllables were shorter than accented ones, as is usually the case in speech (e.g. Beckman and Edwards 1990). In each sentence, duration of the final rhythmic unit accounted for final lengthening. The total length of every test sentence was 1.85 sec. Note that there were some small deviations from these target values as manipulations were done manually.

The duration and tonal make-up of the filler stimuli were also manipulated in order to establish a homogenous experimental signal. Four rhythmic and/or tonal interpretations were created for each of the four fillers. The procedure described above resulted in 16 test stimuli (2 sentences x 2 durations x 2 f0-contours x 2 f0-ranges) and 16 filler stimuli (4 sentences x 4 interpretations). Each of the 32 stimuli was looped with 10 repetitions and a 0.4 sec pause between them. Note that the pause within the loop used in Deutsch et al. (2008) was twice as long as the pause implemented in our stimuli. During pilot sessions, a shorter pause seemed to support the illusion effect.

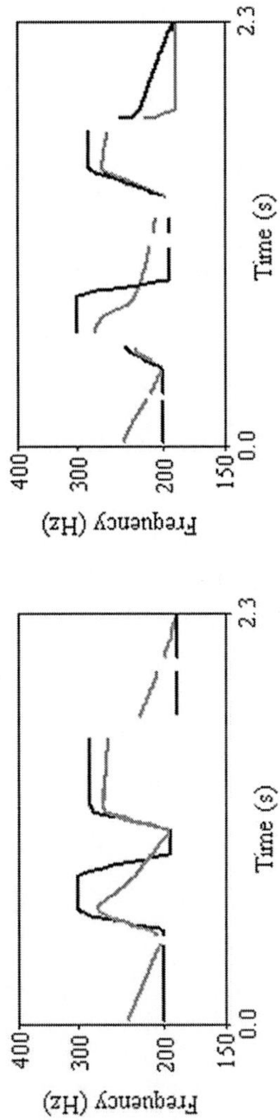

Figure 4: F0-trajectories of the music-like tonal structure (black lines) and the speech-like tonal structure (grey lines) in the test sentence *Im Regal liegen Nadel und Faden* (left-hand side) as opposed to the test sentence *Im Garten blühen heute Klee und Mohn* (right-hand side).

Table 1. Chunking and duration of intervocalic units (in sec, song-like condition 2.b). Capitals: pitch-accented vowels.

Units	imr img	eg Art	All nbl	ignn ünh	Ad eut	el ekl	undf E	Ad undm	n On	Total
Duration	0.20	0.20	0.20	0.20	0.20	0.20	0.20	0.20	0.25	1.85

Table 2. Chunking and duration of syllabic units (in sec, speech-like condition 2.b). Capitals: pitch-accented vowels.

Units	im	re	gAl	lign	nA	del	und	fA	dn	Total
Duration	0.15	0.15	0.25	0.15	0.25	0.15	0.15	0.35	0.25	1.85
Units	im	gAr	tn	blün	heu	te	klE	und	mOn	Total
Duration	0.15	0.25	0.15	0.15	0.15	0.15	0.25	0.15	0.45	1.85

2.2.2 Filler stimuli

The fillers were pairs of sentences with syntactic and rhythmic structure similar to the target test sentences, but they differed from those semantically, morpho-phonologically and partly with respect to the number of pitch accents. The following sentences served as fillers (***bold*** = accented):

Die ***Rin****der kann man nicht* ***fin****den.* (English: 'You cannot find the cows.')
Die ***Kin****der soll man nicht* ***bin****den.* (English: 'You should not take possession of your children.')
Im ***Himmel sin****gen die* ***En****gel.* (English: 'In heaven, angels are singing')
Im ***Stall quen****gelt der* ***Ben****gel.* (English: 'In the barn, the baby boy is whining')

The fillers were manipulated both tonally and rhythmically resulting in 16 additional stimuli (4 sentences x 4 manipulations). Rhythmical manipulations were applied randomly to the four sentences and comprised varying lengthening grades of intervocalic intervals, syllables or whole phrases. For each sentence, two stimuli with level-like and two stimuli with contour-like tonal make-ups were included.

2.2.3 Procedures

The total of 32 stimuli was divided into two sets, each containing 8 test and 8 filler sentences in order to keep test duration as short as possible and to prevent subjects from hearing sentences with the same semantic content too often, i.e. no more than four times. Each test started with three practice sentences among which we presented the original English stimulus (Deutsch 1995) and two German practice sentences. For the test phase, 16 stimuli were pseudo-randomised using one randomisation list per subject. Randomisation was guided by the following rules: (1) the test always started with a filler sentence and (2) between two test sentences with the same semantic content, at least two other (test or filler) sentences always intervened.

The subjects' task was to listen to the looped stimuli and to press a button as soon as they had the impression that the signal was no longer a spoken phrase, but had song or music-like qualities. Interestingly, we observed an effect the instruction had on the perception of the illusion during pilot sessions: if subjects' attention was not called to the potential shift from an auditory impression of a spoken phrase to that of a sung phrase, they tended to report cases of verbal transformations (Warren 1961, see section 3 of this paper) or perceived some changes in prosodic structure of the looped stimuli. At this point, formation of the illusion reflects the main perception principle attested for both visual and auditory modalities being dependent on expectation and experience (see Hawkins 2009 for an overview).

After each trial, subjects had to confirm whether they really had perceived a change in the signal or not. Subsequently, they were asked to solve a simple mathematical equation. This was done to interrupt the test phase, to distract subjects' attention and to clear working memory load from sound imprints induced by massive repetition of the previously heard stimulus. After the main test phase, subjects additionally performed the scale subtest of the MBEA (Montreal Battery of Evaluation of Amusia, Peretz et al. 2003). In this test, subjects had to compare musical phrases (i.e. tone sequences that differ in one pitch relationship or not) and to judge them as "same" or "different". This test was included as we expected an influence of the subjects' musical expertise on their ability to perceive the illusion more easily. Additionally, we obtained self-reported musical capacity with scores ranging from 0 (non-musical at all) up to 10 (very musical).

The last task of the experimental session was to judge the quality of the non-repeated stimuli as spoken or sung (singing/speaking-style rating task). The subjects were asked to listen to the complementary set of test and filler sentences (only one presentation per stimulus) and to decide on a seven point scale whether stimuli were spontaneously perceived as clearly/ quite/ rather spoken (1-3) or rather/ quite/ clearly sung (5-7); unclear cases were to receive the label 4. All tests were run on computer using DMDX software (Forster and Forster 2003). Auditory signals were presented via Sennheiser head-phones of good quality. The session lasted about 25 min.

2.2.4 Subject sample

In total, 62 native speakers of German (13 m, 49 f) aged between 19 and 46 (mean age: 24 years) participated in the experiment. 52 subjects reported having some experience with music (singing or playing an instrument). On average, these subjects had started musical training at the age of 8 and continued for about 7 years. The rest of the sample (10 subjects) had no music education. Each subject was tested separately. The sample was divided into two groups (30 and 32 subjects). Each group was tested once using one of the stimuli sets (set 1 or set 2). The data for test stimuli from set 1 consisted of 30 judgments for each stimulus in the illusion task and 32 decisions in the singing/speaking-style rating task, whereas for set 2, there were 32 judgments for each stimulus in both tasks.

2.3 Results

2.3.1 Tonal versus rhythmic cues

Overall, in filler and test stimuli, 60 out of 62 subjects experienced a shift from speech to song. Regarding the test stimuli alone, 59 out of 62 perceived the shift. The perception of the shift seems to be quite robust: in the test stimuli, 41 subjects (66 %) reported a shift in more than 50 % of the items. Fig. 5 gives an overview of the results showing the percentage of perceived illusions dependent on the four experimental factors. As predicted by our *Main Hypothesis*, acoustic characteristics did influence the overall perception of the illusion. In favour of the *Tonal Hypothesis*, tonal cues – in particular target stability – had the strongest effect on the perception of the illusion: stimuli with stable targets and interval structure were more likely to evoke the illusion than stimuli with unstable targets and without scalar relationships. Surprisingly, rhythmic factors did not show any obvious effects. Stimuli with regular pitch-accent distribution induced slightly more occurrences of the illusion, whereas stimuli with equal duration of intervocalic intervals were more likely to suppress rather than to facilitate the illusion, which was in contrast to our prediction (see 2.b). Repeated measures ANOVA performed with four independent factors (*target stability, interval structure, accentual regularity, segmental grouping*) and dependent variable being the number of perception shifts revealed significant results only for *target stability* (F=8.5 and p<0.01) and for the interaction *target stability* * *accentual regularity* (F=12.6 and p<0.001). As shown in Fig. 6, the illusion was most often perceived in stimuli with stable targets and accentual regularity whereas it was least often reported for stimuli lacking these two characteristics.

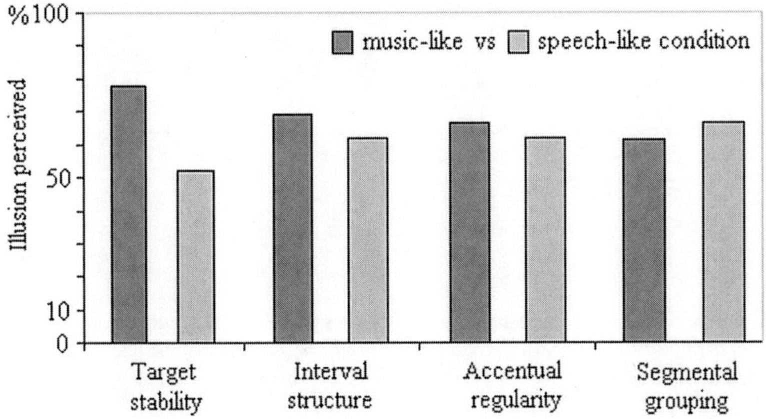

Figure 5: Percentage of perceived speech-to-song shifts dependent on the four experimental factors (averaged for two stimuli sets).

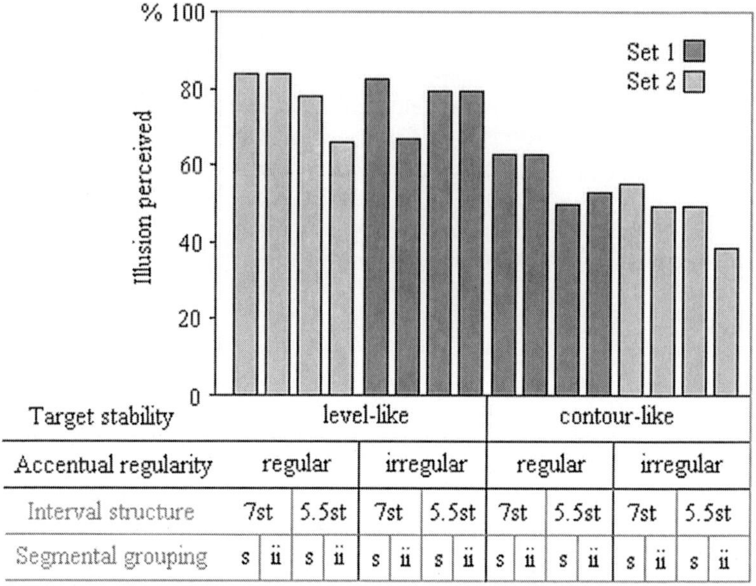

Figure 6: Percentage of perceived speech-to-song shifts for each test stimulus (n_1=30 for set 1, n_2=32 for set 2). Test factors are presented with respect to their potential to induce the illusion (in descending order from top to bottom).

Table 3 presents the frequency of perception shifts during the course of ten repetitions (1-10) compared to the frequency of failed illusion averaged for all stimuli. Note that a similar pattern of judgment distribution was observed for each experimental condition. According to repeated measures ANOVA, no significant differences were caused by the four tested factors, i.e. in contrast to our predictions, acoustic characteristics of the stimulus did not 'slow down' or 'speed up' the occurrence of the illusion, but rather contributed to the overall rate of perception shifts. Obviously, there was some variation in the speed of perception shift in our subject group (Median: 4th repetition). However, the illusion was mostly perceived during the third repetition of the stimulus in all conditions.

Table 3: Frequency of judgements (no illusion perceived vs. illusion reported during the 1-10 repetition) dependent on the four test factors (music-like *m-l* or speech-like *s-l*).

Factor		*No Ill.*	*Repetition*										*Sum*
			1	*2*	*3*	*4*	*5*	*6*	*7*	*8*	*9*	*10*	
Target stability	m-l	55	11	30	54	33	28	10	11	8	5	3	248
	s-l	117	3	14	27	22	18	15	11	8	4	9	248
Interval structure	m-l	77	8	24	45	30	27	13	11	4	4	5	248
	s-l	95	6	20	36	25	19	12	11	12	5	7	248
Accentual regularity	m-l	79	9	26	46	24	26	8	11	9	5	5	248
	s-l	93	5	18	35	31	20	17	11	7	4	7	248
Temporal grouping	m-l	93	5	17	35	31	20	14	12	9	4	8	248
	s-l	79	9	27	46	24	26	11	10	7	5	4	248
Mean		*86*	*7*	*22*	*40.5*	*27.5*	*23*	*12.5*	*11*	*8*	*4.5*	*6*	*248*

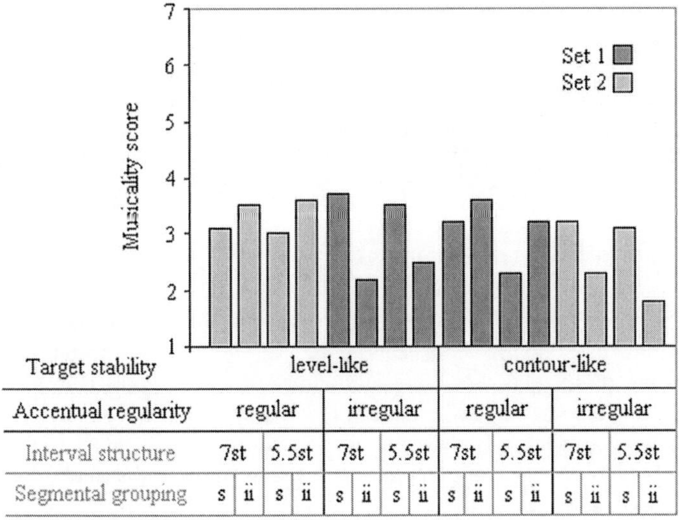

Figure 7: Mean scores for each test stimulus in the singing/speaking-style rating task (n_1=30 for set 1, n_2=32 for set 2). Test factors are presented with respect to their potential to induce the illusion (in descending order from top to bottom, as in Fig. 6).

Concerning the singing/speaking-style rating task (see Fig. 7), there is no correlation between the rating score of a stimulus and its potential to induce the illusion obtained in the illusion test. Obviously, perception of the illusion during the main test cannot be considered an artefact of stimuli acoustics, it being too song-like from the start. Overall, the test stimuli were judged as rather spoken (score range: 1.5-4, averaged score 3). Repeated measures ANOVA with four independent factors (*target stability, accentual regularity, interval structure, segmental grouping*) and dependent variable being the score from the singing/speaking style task revealed no significant effects for any of the test factors. Thus, we could assume that all our test stimuli are perceived more or less equal in their speech and song-like quality. One of the filler sentences received a relatively high score in the style rating task (*quite sung*: mean 5.2, median 6). This stimulus had stable targets and was lengthened with a factor of 1.6 to the original sentence (*Im Stall quengelt der Bengel*, see 2.2.2). Interestingly, this stimulus was not better in inducing the illusion (75% of cases) than the test stimuli with relatively low style rating scores (3-4 scale points, see Fig. 7; for overall illusion perception in 80-85% of the cases, see Fig. 6). In contrast, one test stimulus with intervocalic intervals, non-scalar structure, irregular accentual timing and non-stable targets received the lowest style rating score of about 1.5 and evoked the least number of perceptual shifts (under 40 %). In sum, we can assume that the illusion is more likely to occur as soon as the acoustics of a stimulus are somehow ambiguous between speech and song – as given in most of the test stimuli. Stimuli in which acoustics were too song-like did not facilitate perception of the illusion, but stimuli with too speech-like features did weaken the probability of the shift.

2.3.2 Individual perception patterns

The inter-individual ranking of stimuli presented above (Fig. 5) was also intra-individually consistent. Fig. 8 shows how often subjects (grouping of subjects was done by number of shifts reported in the eight test stimuli they heard) experienced the illusion on average in the two most often and two least often perceived stimuli per set. It can be seen that subjects with a low perception rate of the shift in the test stimuli (1 of 8, 2 of 8, 3 of 8) perceived it at least in one of the two stimuli that were perceived most often by the whole group of subjects. Additionally, in these subject groups, the shift was rarely perceived in the two least often perceived stimuli on the set. Furthermore, subjects who heard the illusion more often in the overall set of test stimuli, also heard it earlier in the looped test stimuli (n=62, negative correlation between mean number of illusion occurrences per subject and mean number of repetitions, R^2=-0.6, p<0.001).

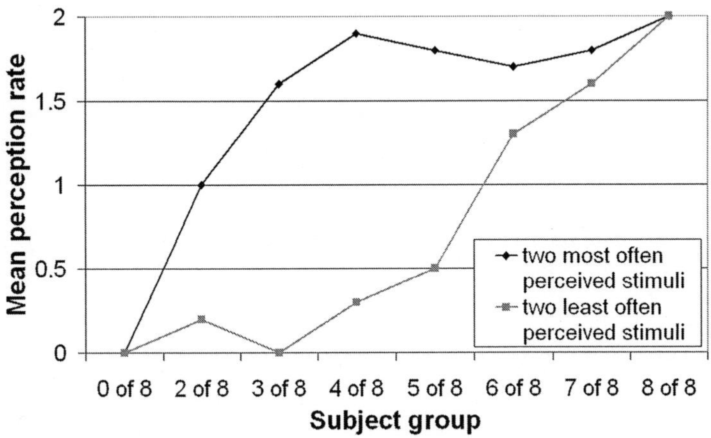

Figure 8: Mean perception rate of the two inter-individually most (black) and least (grey) often perceived stimuli.

Concerning musicality, averaged MBEA-values of subjects with versus without musical education differed significantly (p<0.01; t=3.25) showing that musicians were more sensitive to tonal changes (mean score 25 out of 30 points) than non-musicians (mean score 23 out of 30 points). However, there was no significant correlation between obtained MBEA-values and the number of illusion occurrences reported for the test stimuli nor did MBEA-scores correlate with the tendency to perceive the speech-to-song shift earlier or later in the loop. Overall, 7 subjects performed worse than the cut-off score (22) in the MBEA scale subtest, one performed on the level of the average of amusics as reported in Peretz et al. (2003). However, all of those subjects reported to hear the shift in 50 to 100 % of the test stimuli. Thus, we conclude that the scale subtest of the MBEA was not sensitive to predict the individual performance pattern of subjects in the illusion test.

3 Discussion

Our study confirms that the speech-to-song-illusion as described for an English sentence (Deutsch 1995, Deutsch et al. 2008) is robustly perceived by listeners of (at least) another intonation language, as we have demonstrated that the illusion emerges (1) in German and (2) with various sentences and manipulated speech.

In general, the results support our *Main Hypothesis*: acoustic properties of the signal did influence the perception of the illusion, and especially the overall frequency of its occurrence. So far, the study has mainly supported the *Tonal Hypothesis* since target stability significantly facilitated occurrence of the illusion. In contrast, the results were less clear in terms of the *Rhythmic Hypothesis*. We can assume that the latter's phonetic implementation was not powerful enough to yield prominent effects in this study. However, we cannot claim that our conception of rhythm was completely wrong as we observed a significant interaction between target stability and accentual regularity. Temporal regularity of accents seems to be a secondary cue which supports the perception of the illusion. Isochronous spacing between pitch accents – i.e. an exact "beat" structure – may induce an even stronger effect and should be tested in a further experiment.

Concerning the segmental grouping condition (2.b) we encountered some problems specific to German vowel reduction processes: test sentences with schwa-elision (see 1.4) led to difficulties in chunking of intervocalic intervals. As we know, vowels in speech differ from vowels in song depending on voice register, the latter exposing more peripheral qualities in lower registers that are also used in speech (Sundberg 1987, Falk 2007). Thus, vowel reduction or undershoot in speech could have been constraining perception of the illusion. Further testing with stimuli sentences lacking schwa-vowels will shed more light on this question.

The study has shown that there were individual differences in the perception of the illusion since some subjects heard the illusion more often (and sometimes earlier) in the loop than others. In general, intra-individual performance followed the inter-individual ranking of stimuli but the study did not reveal a basis for explanation of individual performance patterns. So far, we could not find a link between the performance pattern in the illusion test and performance in the MBEA scale subtest. A different battery for assessing musical abilities might be better suited to capture individual differences in the perception of the illusion.

Interestingly, when subjects did perceive a shift, they were most likely to experience it during the third repetition within the loop. This effect was also quite robust for all experimental conditions. As reported for some optical illusions (as e.g. Necker Cube or Rubin Vase, Gregory 1971)[1] or other auditory illusions like Auditory Stream Segregation (Bregman and Campbell 1971), a certain amount of time – or even a verbal instruction – is usually needed until re-interpretation of the originally perceived image/signal is possible and a perceptual shift occurs. We assume that the repetitive structure of the signal triggers a pattern matching process in the listener that results in a strong impression of the acoustic features of a signal. This might be similar to production processes in a speech cycling task with the result "[...] that a higher level dynamic emerges within which the timing of subordinate processes are constrained" (Cummins and Port 1998).

In the verbal domain, several effects induced by massive repetition of verbal stimuli have been reported in the literature, i.e. "semantic satiation" (Smith 1984), "syntactic fatigue or satiation" (e.g. Francom 2009) and "verbal transformation" (e.g. Warren 1961, Ditzinger et al. 1997). These processes might share common grounds with the speech-to-song illusion as they create a situation in which the linguistic and grammatical meaning stepwise lose their importance. "Semantic satiation" is achieved by massive repetition of a word, during which subjects are experiencing a feeling of "detachment" of meaning during the course of repetition. In a spreading activation network model, semantic satiation is explained as an over-activation of the target word node which consequently fatigues and hinders the access of the meaning of the word. Thereby, phonological neighbour nodes in the lexicon become more and more available to the extent to which the target word node becomes satiated/ over-activated, leading to "verbal transformations". This term refers to the fact that subjects report hearing phonological similar words (e.g. *face, space, paste* instead of *pace*) during the repetition cycle (McKay et al. 1993). However, Pilotti et al. (1997) conducted an experiment showing that repetition of the same word in different speakers' voices blocked the satiation effect. The authors therefore conclude that the observed effect is less due to semantic satiation than to early acoustic adaptation to the signal (Eimas and Corbit 1973). This is an interesting parallel to the speech-to-song illusion where the variation of the tonal or rhythmic make-up of the given phrase within the loop blocked the illusion as well (cf. Deutsch 1995, Deutsch et al.

[1] Both Necker Cube and Rubin Vase are ambiguous drawings which allow two interpretations of foreground vs. background. A three dimensional wire-frame drawing of a cube does not show which is in front and which is behind when two lines cross. Similarly, a picture of a white hourglass-shaped vase against dark background is schematic and its shape is formed like two profiles facing each other.

2008). Another parallel to the findings of our experiment is that at least 3 to 4 repetitions are necessary before semantic satiation is observed (Pilotti et al. 1997). In our study the perceptual shift from speech to song also occurred most often during the third repetition. These parallels give rise to further research questions: Is semantic satiation a relevant process to the speech-to-song illusion or are both the effect of an earlier acoustic analysis process? How will differences in semantic and syntactic complexity affect the perceptual shift from speech to song? If there is underlying semantic satiation in the speech-to-song illusion, can we observe also the reverse process of song-to-speech by re-semantisation e.g. by instruction to concentrate on aspects of the meaning of the sentence?

Finally, our results do not allow direct conclusions about the modular or non-modular nature of speech and song processing. However, the fact that some acoustic properties of the signal in our experiment facilitated song perception better than others could point to a decoding strategy relying on specific acoustic cues to rate the "song-likeness" or "musicality" of a signal. Furthermore, it seems plausible that the decoding includes a re-evaluation of the acoustic structure at early stages of processing. Through the establishment of a recurrent pattern, the loop becomes a rhythmically structured event in which the specific melodic and rhythmical properties of the signal may become more and more salient to the listener until they dominate the perceptual impression. After the overall acoustic pattern has been "carved out" by the listener, it is free to be re-evaluated as a plausible or non-plausible musical event. Some aspects of the acoustics – as target stability – seem to be more powerful to cue musical interpretation which in the end leads to the perception of song instead of speech. This points in the direction of a modular approach, but more empirical evidence is needed to explore this issue.

4 Conclusions and open questions

The present study has shed some light on the processes underlying the speech-to-song illusion. First of all, we have demonstrated that the perceptual shift was robustly perceived by a group of German listeners in a variety of sentences and that the occurrence of the shift was influenced by the acoustic make-up of the stimuli. The results suggest that a certain ambiguity in the acoustics of a signal may be necessary to induce the shift. The most potent cue to the speech-to-song illusion in this experiment was tonal structure (stability of tonal targets), but we also found a certain potential of rhythmic properties to influence the perceptual shift. This is an issue that will be investigated in further experiments by exploring in more detail which rhythmic properties are most specific to speech as opposed to music.

Secondly, we provided evidence that individual differences in the perception of the speech-to-song illusion exist. Regarding this domain, the study has, however, opened more questions for empirical investigation than it was able to answer and which should be further investigated, i.e. what enables some subjects to perceive the illusion more easily than others? Can subjects switch between speech and song perception of the same stimulus or will the speech-to-song illusion stay unidirectional? Finally, we assume that semantic satiation is a process that could be facilitating the perceptual shift from speech to song. Is it a prerequisite for the perceptual shift to take place or is it the result of the acoustic pattern matching process induced by massive repetition? This is also left to further studies on the speech-to-song-illusion.

References

Arvaniti, Amalia. 2009. "Rhythm, timing and the timing of rhythm." *Phonetica* 66: 46-63.

Ayotte, Julie, Isabelle Peretz, and Krista Hyde. 2002. "Congenital amusia. A group study of adults afflicted with a music-specific disorder." *Brain* 125: 238-251

Beckman, Mary, and Jan Edwards. 1990. "Lengthening and shortening and the nature of prosodic constituency". In *Papers in laboratory phonology I,* edited by J. Kingston and M. Beckman, 152-178. Cambridge: University Press.

Boersma, Paul, and David Weenink. 2001. "Praat, a system for doing phonetics by computer." *Glot International 5*: 341-345.

Bregman, Albert. S., and Jeffrey Campbell. 1971. "Primary auditory stream segregation and perception of order in rapid sequences of tones." *Journal of Experimental Psychology, 89: 244-249.*

Clarke, Eric F. 1999. "Rhythm and timing in music." In *The psychology of music*, edited by Diana Deutsch, 473-500. New York, London, Paris, San Diego: Academic Press.

Cooper, Grosvenor, and Leonard B. Meyer. 1960. *The rhythmic structure of music*. Chicago: University of Chicago Press.

Cummins, Fred, and Robert F. Port. 1998. "Rhythmic constraints on stress timing in English." *Journal of Phonetics 26* (2): 145-171.

Cutler, Anne. 1991. "Linguistic rhythm and speech segmentation." In *Music, language, speech and brain*, edited by Johan Sundberg, J.,

Lennart J. Nord, and Rolf Carlson, 157-166. Macmillan: Houndsmills and London.

Dalla Bella, Simone, Jean-François Giguère, and Isabelle Peretz. 2009. "Singing in congenital amusia." *Journal of the Acoustical Society of America* 126 (1): 414-424.

Deutsch, Diana. 1995. *Musical illusions and paradoxes.* CD: Philomel Records.

Deutsch, Diana, Rachael Lapidis, Trevor Henthorn. 2008. "The speech-to-song-illusion." *J. Acoust. Soc. America* 124*:* 2471.

Ditzinger, D., B. Tuller, and J.A.S. Kelso. 1997. "Temporal patterning in an auditory illusion: the verbal transformation effect." *Biological Cybernetics* 77: 23-30.

Drake, Carolyn, and Caroline Palmer. 1993. "Accent structures in music performance." *Music Perception* 10 (3): 343-378.

Eimas, Peter. D., and John D. Corbit. 1973. "Selective adaptation of linguistic features detectors." *Cognitive Psychology* 4: 99-109.

Falk, Simone. 2007. "Speech clarity in infant-directed singing: an analysis of German vowels." In: *Proceedings of the XVI. ICPhS Conference, Saarbrücken, 6. - 10. August 2007*, 1525-1528.

Forster, Ken I., and Jonathan Forster. 2003. "DMDX: A windows display program with millisecond accuracy." *Behavior Research Methods, Instruments, and Computers* 35 (1): 116-124.

Foxton, J.M., J.L. Dean, R. Gee, Isabelle Peretz, Timothy D. Griffiths. 2004. "Characterization of deficits in pitch perception underlying 'tone deafness'." *Brain* 127(4): 801-810.

Francom, Jerid C. 2009. *Experimental Syntax: exploring the effect of repeated exposure to anomalous syntactic structure – evidence from rating and reading tasks.* Unpublished Dissertation, University of Arizona.

Gregory, R.L., 1971. "Visual illusions." In *Image, object and illusion,* edited by R. Held, 48-58. San Francisco: Freeman.

't Hart, Johan 1981. "Differential sensitivity to pitch distance, particularly in speech." *Journal of the Acoustical Society of America,* 69: 811-821.

t'Hart, Johan, Rene Collier, and Antonie Cohen. 1990. *A perceptual study of intonation: an experimental-phonetic approach to speech melody.* Cambridge: University Press.

Hawkins, Sarah. 2009. Phonological features, auditory objects, and illusions. *Journal of Phonetics* 38 (1): 60-89.

Hyde, Krista L., and Isabelle Peretz. 2004. "Brains That Are out of Tune but in Time." *Psychological Science* 15: 356-360.

Krumhansl, Carol L. 2005. "Musikalische Bezugssysteme." In *Allgemeine Musikpsychologie* edited by Thomas H. Stoffer and Rolf Oerter. Berlin, 267-306. New York: de Gruyter.

Ladd, D. R, and R. Morton.1997. "The perception of intonational emphasis: Continuous or categorical?" *Journal of Phonetics* 25: 313–342.

Lehiste, Ilse. 1973. "Rhythmic units and syntactic units in production and perception." *Journal of the Acoustical Society of America* 54 (5): 1228-1234.

Lieberman, Mark, and Janet Pierrehumbert. 1984. "Intonational invariance under changes of pitch range and length." In *Language Sound Structure*, edited by A. Arnoff and R. Oehrle, 157-233. Cambridge, MA: MIT Press.

Lövqvist, Anders, Thomas Baer, Nancy S. McGarr, and Robin S. Story. 1989. "The cricothyroid muscle in voicing control." *Journal of the Acoustical Society of America* 85 (3): 1314-1321.

MacKay, D. G., G. Wulf, C. Yin, and L. Abrams. 1993. "Relations between word perception and production: New theory and data on the verbal transformation effect." *Journal of Memory and Language* 32: 624-646.

Mogharbel, C., G. Sommer, W. Deutsch, M. Wenglorz, and I. Laufs. 2005/2006. "The vocal development of a girl who sings but does not speak." *Musicae Scientiae*, 235-258.

Nicholson, Karen G., Shari Baum, Andrea Kilgour, Christine K. Koh, K. G. Munhall, and Lola L. Cuddy. 2003. "Impaired processing of prosodic and musical patterns after right hemisphere damage." *Brain and Cognition* 52: 382-389.

Niebuhr, Oliver. 2007. "The signaling of German rising-falling intonation categories - The interplay of synchronization, shape, and height." *Phonetica 64*: 174-193.

Nolan, Francis, and Eva L. Asu. 2009. "The pairwise variability index and coexisting rhythms in language." *Phonetica 66:* 64-77.

Patel, D. Aniruddh. 2008. *Music, language and the brain.* Oxford: University Press.

—. In press. "Language, music, and the brain: a resource-sharing framework." In *Language and Music as cognitive systems,* edited by Patrick Rebuschat, Martin Rohrmeier, M., John Hawkins, and Ian Cross. Oxford: University Press.

Patel, D. Aniruddh, Isabelle Peretz, Mark Tramo, and Raymonde Labreque. 1998. "Processing Prosodic and Musical Patterns: A Neuropsychological Investigation." *Brain and Language* 61: 123–144.

Peretz, Isabelle. In press. "Music, language and modularity in action." In *Language and Music as cognitive systems,* edited by Patrick Rebuschat, Martin Rohrmeier, M., John Hawkins, and Ian Cross. Oxford: University Press.

Peretz, Isabelle, Anne Sophie Champod, and Krista Hyde. 2003. "Varieties of musical misorders: The Montreal battery of evaluation of amusia." *Annals of the New York Academy of Sciences* 999: 58-75.

Peretz, Isabelle, and Max Coltheart. 2003. "Modularity of music processing." *Nature neuroscience* 6: 688-691.

Peretz, Isabelle, Lise Gagnon, Sylvie Hébert, and Joel Macoir. 2004. "Singing in the brain: Insights from cognitive neuropsychology." *Music Perception* 21(3): 373-390.

Peretz, Isabelle, and Krista Hyde. 2003. "What is specific to music processing? Insights from congenital amusia." *Trends in Cognitive Sciences* 7(8): 362-367.

Pilotti, Maura, John S. Antrobus, and Martin Duff. 1997. "The effect of presemantic acoustic adaptation on semantic 'satiation'." *Memory and Cognition* 25 (3): 305-312.

Schellenberg, E. Glenn, and Sandra E. Trehub. 1996. "Natural music intervals. Evidence from infant listeners." *Psychological Science* 7 (5): 272-277.

Smith, Lee C., 1984. "Semantic satiation affects category membership decision time but not lexical priming." *Memory and Cognition* 12, 483-488.

Sundberg, Johan. 1987. *The science of the singing voice.* Illinois: Northern Illinois Press.

—. 1989. "Synthesis of singing by rule." In *Current directions in computer music research,* edited by Max V. Mathews, and John R. Pierce, 45-55. Cambridge: MIT Press.

Warren, J.D., J.E. Warren, N.C. Fox, and E.K. Warrington. 2003. "Nothing to say something to sing: primary progressive dynamic aphasia." *Neurocase* 9: 140-155.

Warren, Richard M. 1961. "Illusory changes of distinct speech upon repetition: The verbal transformation effect." *British Journal of Psychology* 52, 249-258.

Zatorre, Robert J., Pascal Belin, and Virginia B. Penhune. 2002. "Structure and function of auditory cortex: music and speech." *Trends in cognitive Science* 6: 37-46.

OCCASIONAL SINGERS SING MORE PROFICIENTLY WHEN MEMORY LOAD IS REDUCED

MAGDALENA BERKOWSKA
AND SIMONE DALLA BELLA
UNIVERSITY OF FINANCE AND MANAGEMENT, WARSAW, POLAND

Abstract

In this study singing proficiency in occasional singers was examined when memory demands are reduced by asking participants to sing on a syllable as compared to singing with lyrics. Fifty occasional singers were asked to sing well-known melodies from memory (e.g., "Brother John") and to imitate these melodies after they were presented at a slow tempo. The melodies were sung with lyrics and on the syllable /la/ in two separate conditions. Sung renditions were analyzed with an acoustically-based method yielding objective measures of pitch and temporal accuracy. The results revealed increased accuracy on both the pitch and the time dimensions (e.g., lower deviation from the notated intervals and lower temporal variability) when occasional singers produced melodies on the syllable /la/ as compared to singing with lyrics. This was observed both when participants sang from memory and when they imitated melodies at a slow tempo. Moreover, occasional singers performed more in tune and more in time when they imitated the melodies than when they sang them from memory. Enhanced performance when memory load is reduced (i.e., when singing on a syllable) can result from improved memory retrieval of musical information. Moreover, focusing attention selectively on melodic information, without needing to remember lyrics, may remarkably increase accuracy in producing pitch intervals. Reduced temporal variability when singing on a syllable is probably the consequence of producing the same linguistic unit as compared to different syllables when singing with lyrics (i.e., with different articulation times likely increasing temporal variability).

Introduction

Singing, a natural activity for humans, is a universal form of vocal expression which is widespread in our culture. Yet, most believe that individuals without musical training are unable to carry a tune. This general belief is not confirmed by recent evidence, showing that occasional singers can sing proficiently in tune and in time, provided that they perform at a slow tempo (Berkowska and Dalla Bella, 2009[a]; Dalla Bella, Giguère, and Peretz, 2007; Dalla Bella and Berkowska, 2009). Furthermore, occasional singers are as proficient as professional singers (i.e., they sing in tune and in time), when producing a well-known melody (e.g., "Happy Birthday") at a slow tempo (Dalla Bella et al., 2007), and exhibit accurate memory for the initial pitch and tempo of popular songs (Bergeson and Trehub, 2002). Still, some individuals in the general population exhibit major difficulties in sung performance (i.e., "poor singers" or "tone deaf individuals"). They represent approximately 10-15% of the general population (e.g., Dalla Bella et al., 2007; Pfordresher and Brown, 2007; Wise and Sloboda, 2008). Poor singing has been often treated as the result of impoverished pitch perception (Ayotte, Peretz, and Hyde, 2002; Foxton et al., 2004; Hyde and Peretz, 2004). However, perceptual deficits are not the only factor which can bring about deficient vocal performance. Inaccurate sensorimotor integration can lead to poor-pitch singing. Moreover, one of the potential causes of poor singing may be linked to a faulty memory system (Dalla Bella, Giguère, and Peretz, 2009; Wise and Sloboda, 2008; for reviews, see Berkowska and Dalla Bella, 2009[b]; Pfordresher and Brown, 2007). The role of memory in singing proficiency was examined in the present study.

In previous studies occasional singers were asked to sing from memory melodies with lyrics (Dalla Bella et al., 2007; Dalla Bella and Berkowska, 2009; see Berkowska and Dalla Bella, 2009[b], for a review). This task is quite demanding in terms of memory, requiring the retrieval of musical information (i.e., pitches and durations) as well as of linguistic information (i.e., the lyrics). To assess the potential effect of memory load on singing proficiency, here we examined singing proficiency in occasional singers asked to sing on a syllable (i.e., with reduced memory demands) as compared to singing with lyrics.

Method

Participants

Fifty occasional singers (15 males and 35 females), mostly university students at the University of Finance and Management in Warsaw, aged between 19 and 39 years (M = 25.1 years), with 12.3 years of general education on average, and without formal musical training, took part in the study.

Materials and procedure

The participants performed a *Familiar melody production task* (hereafter referred to as Production task) and a *Familiar melody repetition task* (hereafter referred to as Repetition task). In the Production task participants sang from memory three familiar melodies on the syllable /la/ (i.e., "Brother John", "Jingle Bells", "Sto lat"), and, in a separate condition, the same melodies with Polish lyrics. In this task participants chose the most comfortable tempo and the initial pitch of their performance. In the Repetition task participants produced the same melodies with lyrics and on the syllable /la/, which were imitated at a given slow tempo as indicated by a metronome. Before the presentation of the melody the metronome was sounded for 4 beats to indicate the tempo ("Brother John", 96 beats/min, quarter note inter-onset interval (IOI) = 625 ms; "Jingle Bells", 125 beats/min, quarter-note IOI = 480 ms; "Sto lat", 80 beats/min, quarter-note IOI = 750 ms). The melody was presented twice with the metronome; the participants imitated the melody right afterwards after the metronome was switched off. Each melody was presented within participants' vocal range.

Measures of Singing Proficiency

The measures of singing proficiency were computed using an acoustically-based method (for a thorough description, see Dalla Bella et al., 2007, 2009). Estimates of pitch heights and time onsets obtained with acoustical analyses served to compute the following measures of accuracy on the pitch and time dimensions.

Pitch Dimension Variables

Pitch interval deviation is the size of the pitch deviations from the notation obtained by averaging the absolute difference in semitones between the produced intervals and the intervals prescribed by the notation. Small deviation refers to high accuracy in relative pitch.

Number of pitch interval errors is the number of errors in the production of musical intervals as compared to the notation. An error is scored when the produced interval is larger or smaller than one semitone as compared to the notated interval.

Initial pitch deviation (only for the Repetition task) indicates the amount of pitch transposition (i.e., absolute pitch difference in semitones between the first note of the melody to be imitated and the first note of the produced melody).

Time Dimension Variables

Temporal variability is the amount of time deviation obtained by computing the coefficient of variation of the quarter-note IOIs (i.e., the Standard Deviation of the IOIs divided by the mean IOI). Small temporal variability indicates high accuracy in relative duration.

Number of time errors is the number of errors in the production of note durations. An error is scored when the produced note is at least 50% longer or shorter than the duration predicted from the preceding note, as prescribed by the notation.

Tempo deviation (only for the Repetition task) is the amount of tempo change (i.e., absolute difference in percent of the quarter-note IOI between the tempo of the melody to be imitated and the tempo of the produced melody).

Results and Discussion

All participants were able to produce complete performances (300 in the Production task and 300 in the Repetition task). For both tasks, the measures of pitch and time accuracy were averaged across the three melodies. Means and variability of pitch and time accuracy when participants sang with lyrics and on a syllable are illustrated in Table 1. For each measure of pitch and time accuracy common to the two tasks, separate 2 (task) x 2 (condition) repeated-measures ANOVAs were run by taking Task (Production vs. Repetition) and Condition (with lyrics vs. on /la/) as the within-subject factors. As can be observed, occasional singers were more accurate in both pitch and time dimensions when they sang on a syllable than when they sang with lyrics. Occasional singers departed less from the notation when they sang on a syllable than when they sang with lyrics. This was observed in both tasks, as revealed by pitch interval deviation (for the Production task (*t(49)* = 5.13, *p* < .001); for the Repetition task (*t(49)* = 3.96, *p* < .001)), (see Figs. 1 and 2). In both tasks similar results were obtained when we examined pitch interval errors, (for the Production task (*t(49)* = 5.05, *p* < .001); for the Repetition task (*t(49)* = 3.19, *p* < .01)), (see Figs. 3 and 4). A similar advantage when singing on a syllable as compared with singing with lyrics was observed on the time dimensions, as attested by temporal variability for the Production task (*t(49)* = 3.13, *p* < .05). It was not significant for the Repetition task (*t(49)* = 1.33, *p* = n.s.); similar results were obtained for the number of time errors in both tasks (for the Production task (*t(49)* = 0.98, *p* = n.s.); for the Repetition task (*t(49)* = 0.03, *p* = n.s.).

Table 1. Mean and variability of pitch and time accuracy computed for performances with lyrics and on /la/, in the Production task and in the Repetition task.

	Production task		Repetition task	
	Lyrics	La	Lyrics	La
Variable	*M* (SE)	*M* (SE)	*M (SE)*	*M* (SE)
Pitch dimension				
N. of pitch interval errors	4.0 (0.4)	3.0 (0.3)	3.1 (0.4)	2.4 (0.3)
Pitch interval deviation (semit.)	0.57 (0.03)	0.48 (0.03)	0.50 (0.02)	0.41 (0.02)
Initial pitch deviation (semit.)	-	-	1.6 (0.2)	1.5 (0.2)
Time dimension				
N. of time errors	0.9 (0.04)	0.8 (0.06)	0.6 (0.04)	0.7 (0.10)
Temporal variability (CV IOIs)	0.20 (0.01)	0.18 (0.01)	0.16 (0.01)	0.15 (0.01)
Tempo deviation (% of the IOI)	-	-	5.5 (0.4)	6.3 (0.5)

In addition, participants were more accurate on the pitch dimension when they imitated melodies at a slow fixed tempo (i.e., in the Repetition task) than at the faster spontaneous tempo (i.e., in the Production task) as indicated by pitch interval deviation ($F(1,49) = 13.75$, $p < .001$), and by the number of pitch interval errors ($F(1,49) = 18.90$, $p < .001$). On the temporal dimension, participants were similarly more accurate in the Repetition task than in the Production task, as revealed by temporal variability ($F(1,49) = 43.82$, $p < .001$), and by the number of time errors ($F(1,49) = 15.52$, $p < .001$).

To sum up, the present study provides evidence that singing accuracy on both the pitch and the time dimensions is enhanced when memory load is reduced. Improving performance can result from enhanced memory retrieval of music information. When linguistic information is reduced, it is likely that participants can focus selectively on pitch heights and time durations during singing, thus leading to higher accuracy. This effect contrasts with what is observed in amusic individuals, who had less difficulties to sing with lyrics than when singing on a syllable (Dalla Bella et al., 2009). In sum, these results indicate that memory is an important factor affecting both pitch and temporal accuracy in sung performance. The extent to which faulty memory retrieval can alone lead to inaccurate singing in absence of other disorders (such as inaccurate auditory-motor integration) deserves further enquiry.

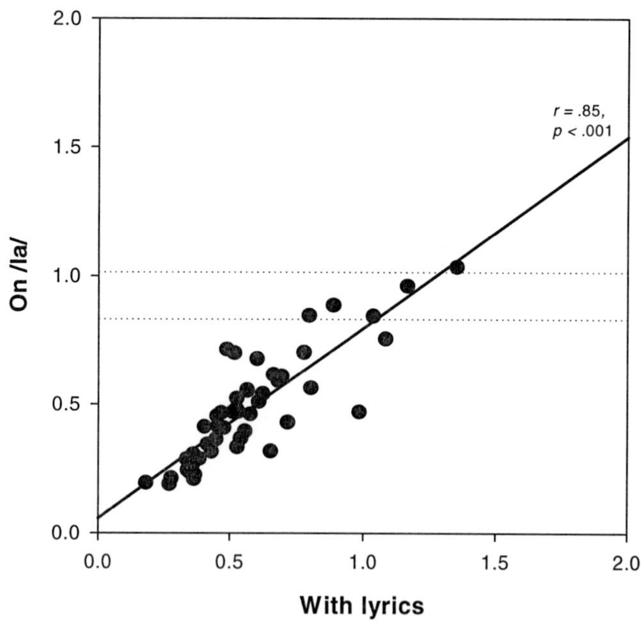

Figure 1. Singers' individual performances (pitch interval deviation in semitones) in the Production task.

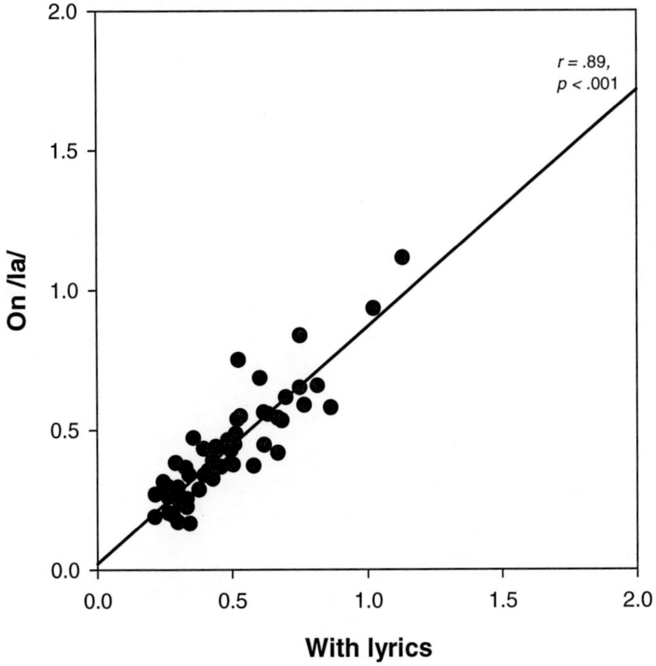

Figure 2. Singers' individual performances (pitch interval deviation in semitones) in the Repetition task.

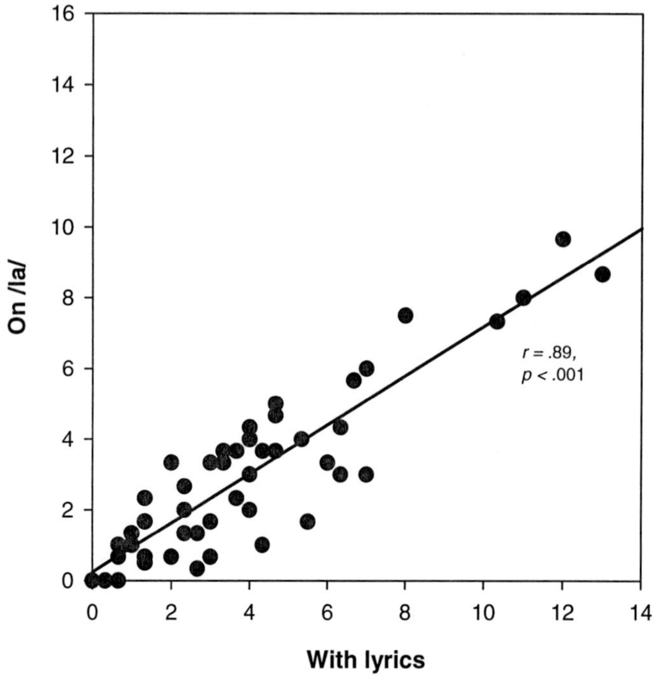

Figure 3. Singers' individual performances (no. of pitch interval errors) in the Production task.

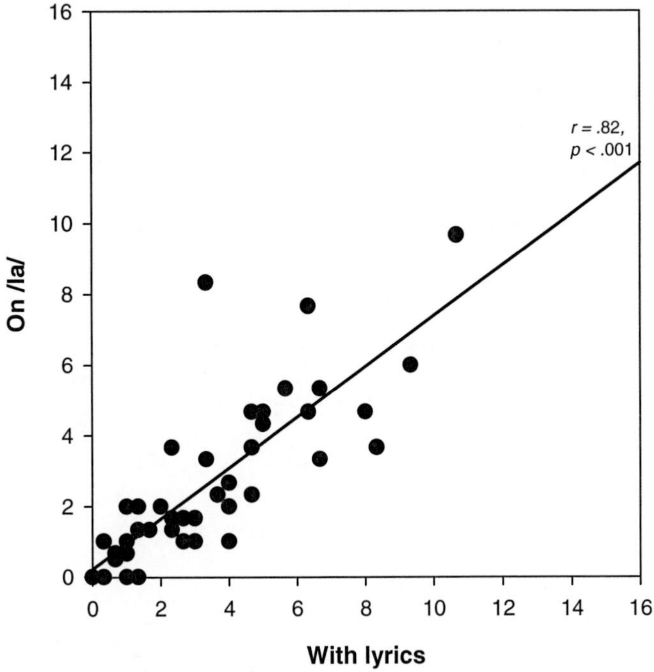

Figure 4. Singers' individual performances (no. of pitch interval errors) in the Repetition task.

References

Ayotte, J., Peretz, I., and Hyde K. 2002. "Congenital amusia: A group study of adults afflicted with a music-specific disorder." *Brain,* 125(2): 238-251.

Bergeson, T.R., and Trehub, S.E. 2002. "Absolute pitch and tempo in mothers' songs to infants." *Psychological Science, 13:* 72-75.

Berkowska, M., and Dalla Bella, S. 2009a. "Reducing linguistic information enhances singing proficiency in occasional singers." *Annals of the New York Academy of Sciences,* 1169: 108-111.

—. 2009b. "Acquired and congenital disorders of sung performance: A review." *Advances in Cognitive Psychology*, 5: 69-83.

Dalla Bella, S., and Berkowska M. 2009. "Singing proficiency in the majority: Normality and "phenotypes" of poor singing." *Annals of the New York Academy of Sciences, 1169*, 99-107.

Dalla Bella, S., Giguère, J-F., and Peretz I. 2007. "Singing proficiency in the general population." *Journal of The Acoustical Society of America,* 121: 1182-1189.

—. 2009. "Singing in congenital amusia." *Journal of the Acoustical Society of America*, 126 (1): 414-424.

Foxton, J.M., Dean, J.L., Gee, R., Peretz, I. and Griffiths, T.D. 2004. "Characterization of deficits in pitch perception underlying "tone deafness". *Brain,* 127: 801-810.

Hyde, K.L. and Peretz, I. 2004. "Brains that are out of tune but in time." *Psychological Science,* 15: 356-360.

Pfordresher, P.Q. and Brown S. 2007. "Poor-Pitch in the absence of "Tone Deafness." *Music Perception,* 25: 95-115.

Wise, K.J. and Sloboda J.A. 2008. "Establishing an empirical profile of self-defined 'tone deafness': Perception, singing performance and self assessment." *Musicae Scientiae,* 12: 3-23.

INTERACTION BETWEEN STRUCTURE AND MELODY: THE CASE OF KABYLE[1] NOUNS

SAMIR BEN SI SAÏD
UNIVERSITE DE NICE

Abstract

The fact that phonological objects can be present in the lexical root but absent from the surface realization is yielded by the restricted pattern of the syllabic space: the structure does not offer enough space to all the melodic items to be associated and realized on the surface level.
The Kabyle external plural presents some vowels which are not present in the singular form, e.g. iddəw "monkey" → idd<u>a</u>w-n "monkeys", iccər "nail" → acc<u>a</u>r-n "nails", iccəw "horn" → acc<u>i</u>w-n, ittəw "big eye"→ att<u>i</u>w-n "big eyes" (-n is the suffix of plural). As they cannot be predicted, these vowels should belong to the root and they are absent in the singular form because of the templatic restriction. My proposal is that the singular form in Kabyle nouns may be constrained by the size of the structure, i.e. in Kabyle language the interpretation of the melody is constrained by the structure.

Introduction

Phonological objects can be present in the lexical root but absent from the surface realization, as was shown in phonological studies, as early as the 1980s. Indeed, it has been demonstrated that floating consonants can exist as shown by Encrevé for the French liaison phenomenon (Encrevé 1988), as well as floating vowels in the behaviour of the Czech initial vowel suffixes _ov or _ity (cf. Markéta Ziková and Tobias Scheer 2009). It has also been argued that some tones can behave in the same way and

[1] Kabyle Berber (also called *Taqbaylit*) is spoken in Northern Algeria

hence be characterized as floating items (Hyman, Larry and Maurice Tadadjeu, 1976). The fact that such objects may float is yielded by the restricted pattern of the syllabic space. As a consequence, we can say that the structure can block the pronunciation of the melodic material. i.e. the structure does not offer enough space to all the melodic items to be associated and realized on the surface level.

I will argue here that the Kabyle external plural may be explained by the same pattern. It is to be noted first that in Kabyle, nouns are to be considered as templatic since the interpretation of the melody is constrained by the structure and because a given melody may not automatically be associated with the same structure. In this context, I will show that the melodic items corresponding to the external plural do belong to the lexical entry but are not phonetically realized in the singular form because of the template restriction.

First, I will introduce some aspects of the Kabyle morphophonological system. Then, I will show that some melodic items can be absent in the singular form but present in the plural. In section III and IV, I will explain why the Kabyle morphophonological system behaves this way and present my analysis relying on a templatic approach.

I. Background: aspects of Kabyle phonology and morphology

(1) Syllable structure

I take as the basis of this study the framework of Government Phonology in general, and the *CV model* in particular. In the latter, syllabic structure consists of a sequence of light open syllables: a non-branching onset (C) is followed by a non-branching nucleus (V) (Lowenstamm 1996).
A final consonant, a closed syllable, a branching onset, a geminate and a long vowel are represented as under (1) below (Lowenstamm 1996, Scheer 2004):

(1)

```
Final        Closed syllable  Branching    Geminate     Long vowel
consonant                      onset
 C  V        C V C V          C V C V      C  V  C  V   C  V  C  V
 |           | | |            |   | |       \      /        \      /
 r    #      b a r            b   r a          b                a
```

(2) Kabyle plural

There are two types of plurals in Kabyle[2]: The external plural, called "-n plural", characterized by the suffixation of –n to the singular form (iθβir → iθβir-n "pigeon"). The second is called internal plural or "A plural". It is characterized by a modification of the quality of the stem vowels, as well as by the appearance of an *A* in the last vocalic position (aγanim → iγunam "reed").

It is to be noted that the alternation of the initial vowel singular → plural occurs in 97% of nouns (Basset 1945). It is probably a prefixed (unproductive?) article which however cannot be dissociated from the root. This alternation plays no role in the demonstration below.

(3) Vowel system

On the surface, the vocalic system of Kabyle is made of three peripheral vowels and schwa.

i u

a

Regarding schwa, its occurrence is predictable in Kabyle, and the sequences |əCV| and |Cə#| are alien sounds. As described by Chaker (1983), the schwa occurs in the following environments:

(2)

a. between two word-final consonants C__C# e.g. /izəm/
b. between C1 and C2 of a C1C2C3V cluster C1__C2C3V e.g. /idəflan/
c. between a consonant and geminate C__CxCx: e.g. /adəbbuz/

In a sequence of consonants, the schwa alternates with zero and is inserted from right to left from the last consonant:

a. iʃəlqəm « lip »

---

[2] In this paper I focus only on the external plural.

b. iʃləqmən « lips »

II. Presence vs. absence of melodic items in external plural formation

The external plural may contain segments that are absent in the singular (Ben Si Saïd 2009a, 2009b).

(3)

item absent in singular	Singular	Plural	Gloss
a	uʃʃən	uʃʃan-n	fox
	iδmər	iδmar-n	side of the chest
	alwəs	ilwsa-n	brother-in-law
i	iʃʃəw	aʃʃiw-n	horn
	$\text{itt}^{ʕ}\text{əw}$[3]	$\text{att}^{ʕ}\text{iw-n}$	big eye
	iʃrəw	aʃriw-n	green vegetable
u	amrar	imurar	cord
	aδrar	iδurar	Mountain
j	aβəqqa	aβəqqaj-n	slap
	agurbi	igurbij-n	shack
	aɟuδu	aɟuδuj-n	tip

[3] ʕ is the symbol of a pharyngealized consonant.

w	aɣənʒa	iɣənʒaw-n	spoon
	aməçsa	iməçsaw-n	shepherd
	ifêr	afriw-n	wing
θ	alma	alma θ -n	grassland
	ajəfki	ijəfki θ -n	milk

Under (3), the alternating items that appear in the plural cannot be predicted: they must be piece and parcel of the lexical representation of the root. For reasons to be developed below, they do not appear in singular forms.

III. Why are some melodic items absent in the singular?

Table (4) shows different behaviors with respect to the singular/plural pattern. Let us observe the plural formation of different noun classes and the appearance of new items in the plural forms.

(4)

	Cluster	Singular	Plural	Gloss
a.	VCCVC	aɹraw	iɹraw-n	gathering
		aʃwaw	iʃwaw-n	scarf
		aʕlaw	iʕlaw-n	wool blanket
b.	VCCC	inʃəw	anʃiw-n	feather
		iddəw	iddaw-n	monkey
		iʃʃəw	aʃʃiw-n	corn

c.	VCC	iləs	ilsaw-n	tongue
		uδəm	uδmaw-n	face
		iʃʃ[4]	aʃʃiw-n	name

(a) illustrates the behavior of the noun class presenting VCCVC clusters: these only show the adjunction of the plural suffix /n/. The VCCC noun class exemplified in (b) shows the appearance of a vowel in the V2 position. In (c), we can see that the VCC noun class presents the appearance of a vowel as in (b) but also the adjunction of a /w/ element.

IV. Templatic analysis

1 Templates

Templates are a fixed sequence of CV positions that are associated with a morpho-semantic value. The melodic material of the lexical items must comply with this skeleton when it instantiates the morpho-semantic value at hand (McCarthy 1979, Lowenstamm 2003). In Arabic there are 15 verbal forms and each form is constrained by its template. Table (5) shows the template of Form I (perfective active):

(5)

	Root	Template Forme I	Forme I	Gloss
a.	rsm	C1VC2VC3	rasam	to draw
	frq	C1VC2VC3	faraq	to separate
	drs	C1VC2VC3	daras	to study
b.	md	C1VC2VC3	madad	to lengthen
	hb	C1VC2VC3	habab	to love
	sm	C1VC2VC3	samam	to poison

We observe under (5.a), that a sane root (trilateral) filled the template, but when the root is bilateral (5.b), the second consonant must spread on C3-Position to satisfy the template.

[4] iʃʃ is the inter-speaker's variation of iʃʃəw

2 Peripheral vowels

I adopt the hypothesis that peripheral vowels are underlyingly long in Kabyle: melodic material associated with a single position appears as schwa or zero (cf. Bendjaballah 1995, 1999, Ben Si Saïd 2009b for Kabyle and Lowenstamm 1991 and Bucci 2009 for other languages).

(6)

```
C  V  C  V      C  V  C  V      C  V  C  V        CV
   \     /         \     /         \     /          |
     A               I               U          A/I/U/Ø
    [a]             [i]             [u]          [ə]/Ø
```

In her analysis of Kabyle verbs, Bendjaballah (2001) argued that the positive preterit contains an underlying /i/ which surfaces only in the negative form as shown in (7) below:
(7)

```
Positive preterit                 Negative preterit

C  V  C  V  C  V                  C  V  C  V  [nC  V]  C  V
|     |  |  |                     |     |  \       /   |
x     d  i  m                     x     d      i       m

   xdəm                                   xdim
```

According to the analysis of Bendjaballah, the negative form offers an empty CV to the template of the positive form and the [i] of the preterit negative *xdim* is the result of the propagation of an underlying /i/ to the [nCV] unit. This implies that the /i/ is already present in the positive form but it does not access to two V positions. Consequently it can not surface as a full vowel.

3. Analysis

I propose in Ben Si Saïd (2009b) that the external plural template is made of 7 [CV] units. The singular is also templatic but it does not impose a uniform size on all singular nouns. However, the singular is organized into 17 noun classes:

Examples: class 1: VCC: izəm : 4 CV-template
class 2: VCCC: aδfəl: 5 CV-template
class 8: VCCVC: argaz: 6 CV-template

Besides, I suggest that vowels that are absent in the singular but present in the plural (for examples, see table 3) are melodically present though associated to a single position in the singular. Also, the reason why some stem-final consonants are not pronounced in the singular is explained by the fact that they are floating. Examples from (4) are thus analyzed in the following way: plural formation is regular iff:

1. all material that appears in plural forms is considered as a lexical ingredient of the root.
2. peripheral vowels are underlyingly long.
3. all external plurals are made of 7 CV units.

(8)

a. all melodic items are associated with the skeleton:

singular: VCCVC:
6CV-template

```
C V C V C V C V C V  C V
  \   / |   | \   /  |
    A   ʝ   r   A    w
```

aʝraw "gathering"

plural: 7CV-template

```
C V C V C V C V C V C V C V
  \   / |   | \   / |   |
    I   ʝ   r   A   w   n
```

iʝraw-n

Under (a), in the singular, the melody is not constrained by the structure. We can observe that all melodic items find a site on the skeleton to be associated with. The output [aʝraw] does not differ from the input /aʝraw/.

b. V2 is associated to one V-position:

singular: VCCC: 5CV-template

```
C V C V C V C V C V
  \   / |   | | |
    I   n   ʃ I w
```

inʃəw "feather"

plural: 7CV-template

```
C V C V C V C V C V C V C V
  \   / |   | \   / |   |
    A   n   ʃ   I   w   n
```

anʃiw-n

Under (b), we see that we have the same quantity of melodic items as under (a) but the template is smaller (one CV less). That's why V2 is associated with one V-position, and realized as schwa on the surface. The input /inʃiw/ gives /inʃəw/ as an output.

c. V2 is associated to one V-position and the final-consonant is floating

singular: VCC: 4CV-template

```
C V C  V  C  V C V
  \    /  |    | |
    I     l    s A w
```

iləs "tongue"

plural: 7CV-template

```
C V C  V  C  V C V C  V  C  V  C  V
  \    /  |    | \    /  |     |
    I     l    s    A    w     n
```

ilsaw-n

Under (c), there are two CV units less than in (a) though with the same melody. As a consequence, V2 is associated with only one vocalic position and the last consonant [w] floats.

It is to be noted that the variation observed between different regions or according to the age of the speakers can be explained as follows:

- diatopic variation: /iβarδi / "chest" can be realized [iβarδi] or [iβərδi]→ We see that in the second rendition, the V2 vowel is lost with regards to the first rendition.
- age variation: /ajawaw/, for people who live in West of the Kabyle region, can be pronounced [ajawaw] or [ajawa] → we see that depending on the age of the speakers the last consonant is or is not pronounced.

Conclusion

To summarize, I show that some lexically present items of roots do not surface in the singular because the template of their singular class does not provide enough space. I also show the uniformity of plural template for all external plurals which are made of 7 CV units. I also propose that the interpretation of the melody is a function of the structure. Finally, the diachronic and diatopic scenario that we can deduce is that Benveniste's "économie du langage" also concerns templates. The nouns analyzed in (8) may originally have been associated to the same skeleton although (8b and c) lost a piece of their structure: some melodic items are always present in the lexicon but cannot surface. To finish, I suggested that the realization of melodic items is subject to diatopic and inter-speaker variation.

References

Basset, André.1945. "Sur la voyelle initiale en berbère." la *Revue Africaine*, 82-88.

Bendjaballah, Sabrina. 1995. *Aspects du système verbal du berbère (Kabyle).* DEA Dissertation,Université de Paris 7.

Bendjaballah, Sabrina. 1999. "Trois figures de la structure interne des gabarits: activité morphologique du niveau squelettal des representations phonologiques en berbère, somali et béja." PhD dissertation, Université de Paris 7.

Bendjaballah, Sabrina. 2001. "The Negative Preterite in Kabyle Berber." *Folia Linguistica* 34 (3-4): 185-223.

Ben Si Saïd, Samir. 2009a. Association under grammatical control: the external plural agent A in Kabyle Berber. Paper presented at GP Round Table, Budapest, 25 April.

—. 2009b. *La formation du pluriel en kabyle.* MA thesis. Université de Nice.

Bucci, Jonathan. 2009. *Réduction vocalique et partage en coratin.* MA thesis. Université de Nice.

Chaker, Salem. 1983. *Un parler berbère d'Algérie (syntaxe)*, Aix-en-Provence, Publications of Université de Provence.

Encrevé, Pierre 1988. *La liaison avec et sans enchaînement: phonologie tridimensionnelle et usages du français.* Paris: Seuil.

Hyman, Larry and Maurice Tadadjeu. 1976. "Floating tones in Mbam-Nkam." In *Southern California Occasional Paper in Linguistics 3*, edited by Larry M. Hyman, 57-111. Los Angeles: Department of Linguistics, University of Southern California.

Lowenstamm, Jean. 1991. "Vocalic length and syllable structure in Semitic." In *Semitic Studies in Honor of Wolf Leslau on the Occasion of his 85th Birthday*, edited by A.S. Kaye, Wiesbaden: Harrassowitz.

—. 1996. "CV as the only syllable type." In *Current trends in Phonology: Models and methods*, edited by J. Durand and B. Laks, 419-441. Salford: Manchester.

—. 2003. "A propos des gabarits." *Recherches Linguistiques de Vincennes* 32:7-30.

McCarthy, John J. 1979. "Formal problems in Semitic phonology and morphology." PhD dissertation, MIT.

Scheer, Tobias. 2004. *A Lateral Theory of Phonology Vol.1: What CVCV, and why should it be?* Berlin: Mouton de Gruyter.

Ziková, Markéta and Tobias Scheer 2009. "Havlík vs. Lower: Slavic vowel-zero alternations and a unified phase theory." Paper presented at Formal Description of Slavic Languages (FASL 18), Cornell University, Ithaka, 15-17 May.

L1 AND L2 PROCESSES IN SPEAKERS WITH SENSORINEURAL HEARING LOSS

MARTA MARECKA
AND MONIKA POŁCZYŃSKA
ADAM MICKIEWICZ UNIVERSITY, POZNAŃ

Abstract

Individuals with Sensorineural Hearing Loss (SNHL) have impaired perception and production of speech sounds. They perceive sounds with a higher detection threshold, their perception of sound frequencies and resolution is limited, and the intensity of dynamic range of sounds is narrowed (Boothroyd 1984; Moore 1995; Jürgens, Brand and Kollmeier 2009). In particular, individuals with SNHL have problems with the perception and production of sibilant sounds (Pittman and Stelmachowicz 2000; Halpern and Tobin 2008). This is especially true in languages which have many sibilant phonemes, e.g. Polish. Polish has twelve sibilants that are articulated in relative proximity. In our previous study (Marecka and Połczyńska 2009) we found that Polish individuals with SHNL frequently produce sibilants with an off-shot leading to a general merger of sibilant phonemes. We proposed to name this process 'sibilant imprecision'. We also observed that individuals with SNHL frequently centralise vowels. This process might be caused by the fact that vowels lack tactile cues that are present in the production of, for example, stop consonants that are produced relatively well by the SNHL population. We hypothesise that individuals with SNHL should apply more processes in the second language (L2, English) than in the first language (L1, Polish), especially if proficiency level of L2 is low. At the same time, we expect that the two most common processes used by Polish individuals with SNHL – sibilant centralisation and vowel centralisation – should be used with a similar frequency of occurrence in L1 and L2. We investigated three native speakers of Polish (two females and one male) with SNHL. There was one subject (S1) with moderate SNHL and two with profound SNHL (S2 and

S3). S1 acquired SNHL at the age of 7 months, whereas S2 and S3 suffered from congenital SNHL. The average age of the participants was 24,6 years (SD=3,39). The L2 proficiency level was assessed with *The Clinical Test of Proficiency in English as the Second Language* (Połczyńska 2009). S1 was a pre-intermediate speaker, S2 an intermediate and S3 an elementary. The subjects performed thc *Polish Dysarthria Test* (Połczyńska-Fiszer and Pufal 2006) and *English as the Second Language Test in Dysarthria* (Połczyńska 2009). Their speech was recorded, analysed acoustically with PRAAT, and transcribed. The results show that the subjects used on average 17.6 types of phonological processes in L1 and 27 types of processes in L2. As expected, among these processes, two were applied particularly frequently by all the subjects: sibilant centralisation (the process constituted 29% of all the processes applied in L1 and 29% in L2) and vowel centralisation (29% of all the processes applied in L1 and 26% in L2). We found that proficiency level affects the frequency and number of occurrences of processes in L2. S1 and S3, who were much less proficient in their L2 than S2, had more processes in L2. The results also indicate that the participants used significantly more processes in word-medial position, which is less cognitively salient than in word-initial and word-final positions (55% of occurrences in L1 and 46% in L2).

Introduction

Sensorineural Hearing Loss (SNHL) is a perceptual disorder that involves damage to the cochlea, the auditory nerve or the central nervous system (Bystrzanowska 1963, Moore 1995, Pruszewicz 2003). It changes the perception of sounds in numerous ways. Firstly, the dynamic range of sounds is lowered in SNHL individuals and their hearing threshold (detection threshold of sounds) is raised, which means that quieter sounds are not perceived (Moore 1995, Halpern and Tobin 2008). The detection threshold is usually especially high for high frequency sounds (Bystrzanowska 1963, Jürgens, Brand and Kollmeier 2009). Moreover, SNHL impairs the perception of frequencies. The resolution of frequencies is poorer and some frequencies are not perceived at all (Moore 1995). This affects the perception of speech to a great extent. Especially segmental features of speech are problematic for SNHL speakers because the minor differences in frequencies between the segments are at times very difficult to detect. This is due to the fact that it is in general more difficult to perceive the differences in frequency than, for instance, in intensity. Sounds in which those differences in frequency are not very salient, such as sibilants, are especially difficult to perceive for SNHL speakers (Boothroyd 1984, Halpern and Tobin 2008).

The problems with aural perception of speech segments often lead to considerable speech impairment in SNHL individuals who use oral languages for communication. Obviously, this does not mean that speakers cannot compensate for auditory impairment by using tactile and kinaesthetic cues (the position of articulators in the speaker's mouth) to learn the articulation of particular segments and to control their vocal performance. On the contrary, the study of Nasir and Ostry (2008) makes the claim that hearing impaired people can compensate for their lack of auditory feedback by using tactile cues. Steffens et al. (1994) demonstrated that tactile cues can be important for speech development of young SNHL children and that reinforcing these cues can help eliciting more speech-like vocalisation in those children. However, even in spite of the aforementioned compensatory strategies, speech impairment is evident in most SNHL individuals communicating with an oral language.

The speech segments that are commonly affected by this impairment are those which offer little tactile feedback (such as vowels), as well as sibilants, which are practically imperceptible to many SNHL individuals (as has been already mentioned, the perception of high frequency sounds is especially limited). In the case of sibilants the perceptual difficulty is particularly salient, since it usually cannot be alleviated with an appropriate hearing aid. Most aids do not amplify very high frequencies that provide a cue for recognising a sibilant sound (Boothroyd and Medwetsky 1992). Distortions of vowels have been reported in previous studies by Richardson (1993), Huttenen (2001), Vick et al. (2001), Lane et al. (2007), and Ménard et al. (2007). The first two papers also mention problems with sibilants. The difficulties with perception and production of sibilant sounds in SNHL have been the subject of research conducted by, for instance, Lane and Webster (1991), Matthies et al. (1994), Pittman and Stelmachowicz (2000), Kosky and Boothroyd (2001) and McGarr et al. (2004). Sibilant distortions are particularly visible in languages that posses a high number of sibilant phonemes. For example, Polish comprises 12 sibilants produced in three places of articulation, located in close proximity[1]. The contrast between the Polish dental /s/, alveolar retroflex /ʂ/ and alveolo-palatal /ɕ/ is much less salient (both in terms of frequency differences and tactile cues that these segments provide) than the English

[1] The whole set contains three voiceless fricatives, three voiced fricatives, three voiceless affricates and three voiced affricates, articulated in the dental, alveolar and palato-alveolar place of articulation (Gussmann 2007).

/s/ – /ʃ/ contrast. In the study by Marecka and Połczyńska (2009) performed on three SNHL speakers of Polish, problems with the production of sibilants were the most salient ones, although difficulties with the production of vowels were also very frequent.

The study in question analysed phonological processes applied by SNHL individuals. The authors employed two theoretical sister frameworks: (1) Natural Phonology (NP) (Donnegan and Stampe 1979, Dziubalska-Kołaczyk 2002, Dziubalska-Kołaczyk 2004) and (2) Phonology as Human Behaviour (PHB) (Tobin 1997, Tobin 2009). According to these theories, speakers strive to acquire maximum communicative value in their utterances with minimum effort and therefore they apply phonological processes in their speech. Phonological processes are speech errors which involve simplifications of speech sounds that are difficult to articulate. The processes are applied in first language (L1) acquisition (Stampe 1969) and in disordered speech (Dressler and Dziubalska 1995, Połczyńska-Fiszer and Pufal 2006, Połczyńska 2009, Tobin 2009). The idiosyncratic processes used by disordered speakers mirror the perceptual or articulatory difficulties of these speakers (Tobin 1997). NP and PHB divide the processes into (1) *Substitutions* (fronting, stopping, spirantisation, etc.), the most communicative processes, (2) *Assimilations* (prevocalic voicing, devoicing, etc.) and (3) *Changes in the syllable structure* (consonant deletion, consonant cluster reduction, etc.), the most radical and least communicative processes.

In the study by Marecka and Połczyńska (2009), two phonological processes that were most salient were sibilant imprecision and vowel centralisation. Sibilant imprecision is an idiosyncratic substitution process applied by SNHL speakers, in which sibilants are produced with an articulatory off-shot leading to a merger of those sounds. Vowel centralisation is a process in which vowels are substituted by a /ə/ or /ɨ/[2] sound (central sounds).

The aim of this study was to perform speech analysis of Polish bilingual SNHL individuals, whose Second Language (L2) was English. The authors were interested in the difference between L2 performance and L1 performance of speakers with hearing impairment. Based on the previous studies, as well as the predictions made on the basis of the theoretical implications of NP and PHB, it was hypothesised that (1) speech impairment would be more salient in L2 and more processes would

[2] The vowel /ɨ/ is classified as a high front sound, however, it is located very close to the mid central region, thus it is a neutral sound requiring just a subtle raising movement of the tongue.

be applied there. L2 is a more difficult linguistic context and to facilitate articulation, speakers are bound to compromise the communicative value of their utterances more than in the case of L1; (2) sibilant imprecision and vowel centralisation would be expected to be frequently applied in both languages; (3) more processes would be applied in more complex tasks (e.g. more processes in spontaneous speech than in read speech).

Method

Three hard-of-hearing individuals agreed to take part in the experiment. They were all native speakers of Polish who had learnt English at some point in their life and were able to communicate in this language. They all had a bilateral SNHL and wore hearing aids. All of them received treatment in the Polish Deaf Association's Rehabilitation Clinic in Toruń, and prior to the experiment, they underwent the Pure Tone Audiometry (PTA) in this clinic. During the PTA, the subjects were examined without their hearing aids. The audiologist established their hearing threshold for eight pure tones (250 Hz, 500 Hz, 1000 Hz, 2000 Hz, 3000 Hz, 4000 Hz, 5000 Hz and 8000 Hz), for both ears. The results of the PTA are presented in table 1.

The first participant (P1) was a 26-year-old female who acquired her Hearing Loss (HL) in the first months of life, after being given an ototoxic drug. She attended a normal school and is a university graduate. Her HL was assessed as moderate (35dB for lower frequencies, 55dB for higher frequencies). The second participant (P2) was a 20-year-old male, a university student with a congenital profound HL (hearing threshold below 90 dB for both ears). His speech therapist suspected that the participant might have been suffering from a minor organic speech disorder (muscle paresis) in addition to SNHL, however he has never been officially diagnosed with such a disorder. The third participant (P3) was a 28-year-old female with a profound congenital HL (75-85 dB for the right ear, 95-105 dB for the left ear for lower frequencies, no residual hearing for higher frequencies). She was the only participant who used to attend a special school for deaf children (the remaining two participants had attended normal schools) and the only one able to communicate in Polish Sign Language in addition to oral Polish. Thus, P3 should be in fact considered trilingual: a simultaneous bilingual in oral Polish and Polish Sign Language, with English as an additional, foreign language (L2 in terms of oral languages, L3 in terms of natural languages). All the relevant information pertaining to the subjects are collated in table 2.

The participants were interviewed about their experience in learning English and were asked to perform *The Clinical Test of Proficiency in English as the Second Language* (CTP ESL) (Połczyńska-Fiszer 2008, Połczyńska-Fiszer and Mazaux 2008).

P1 was fairly communicative in her L2, even though she exhibited some grammar problems. Her proficiency level was pre-intermediate, according to the test results. She divulged that she had been learning English both at school (she started at the age of 10-11) and at the university, but it was not very regular and, at the time of the interview, she did not have contact with this language. P2's L2 proficiency level was assessed as intermediate, however, this result might have stemmed from general comprehension problems that he displayed, also during an interview in Polish (he did not seem to be as proficient in lip reading as the remaining two participants). The participant spoke good, communicative English during the test and at times he used more advanced vocabulary items. The participant had been learning English for 10 years, both at school and during private classes. He told the interviewer that listening and grammatical exercises are problematic for him and this was reflected in the results of the test. P3's proficiency in her oral L2 (English) was poor – the lowest of all the participants. She had attended a language course for two years, two years prior to the interview. She did not feel herself to be a competent English speaker and she claimed that writing was her preferred modality of communication in this language. This was also visible during the test. During spontaneous speech tasks she often pronounced words as if she had only seen them in writing before (for instance, she pronounced the word "duck" as /dus̱k/).

Each of the participants was examined individually. They were recorded on Acer Aspire 3630 computer with an Audacity programme. Then, the speech samples were analysed with PRAAT and transcribed by the authors. On the basis of this transcription, phonological processes were identified in the speech of the participants. Next, the number of processes was counted in the following way:

1. For all the participants (together):
(a) in both languages overall
(b) separately for L1 and L2
(c) in both languages in word initial, medial and final position
(d) separately for L1 and L2 in word initial, medial and final position

2. For every participant individually:
(a) in both languages overall
(b) separately for L1 and L2
(c) in both languages in word initial, medial and final position
(d) separately for L1 and L2 in word initial, medial and final position

Typical pronunciation errors made by Polish speakers of English (such as obstruent final devoicing) were not counted as phonological processes when they occurred in the speech of the participants. Also errors that appeared to result from pronouncing English words through L1 grapheme-to-phoneme correspondence were not counted as processes. For instance, if the participant produced the word "duck" as /du͡tsk/, we assumed that the person relied solely on the L1 orthography. Hence, we did not treat this form as containing phonological processes because this is how a typical Polish person with low L2 proficiency would read this word.

To enable a comparison between speech samples of different length, we counted the number of phonemes in the target forms of the participants' utterances and introduced the measure of the number of phonological processes per 100 phonemes (pp/100 phon). We assumed that this measure would be more reliable than one based on the length of utterances, as every person has their own pace of speaking. We also decided not to base our analysis on the number of words and syllables uttered. This is because words and syllables can differ in length (compare two Polish one-syllable words: "pstrzyć" /pstʃɨ͡tɕ/ – "to splatter, to fleck" – containing six phonemes, vs. "i" /i/ – "and" – containing just one).

Another measure that was taken into consideration was the number of types of phonological processes (e.g. sibilant imprecision, vowel centralisation, consonant deletion, etc.) applied by the participants in their speech. We also calculated how frequent a given process was (x%) in relation to all the processes applied by a given participant (100%).

The judgement concerning alternations of phonemes by the participants was based upon the spectrographic analysis of a given sound in the PRAAT software and upon the perceptual analysis performed by the authors. For instance, we assumed that a vowel was centralised by the speaker if we perceived it aurally as centralised (the vowel was played several times in isolation and in the context of the whole word) and if the F1 and F2 values of a given vowel, as indicated on the spectrogram, were deviating from the typical F1 and F2 values for this vowel (as uttered normally by this particular speaker) and were approaching the average F1 and F2 values for the sounds /ə/ or /ɨ/. Similarly, we assumed that a sibilant was imprecise, if we perceived it aurally as altered and if the frequency values of the noise indicated on the spectrogram and spectral slices deviated from the standard values of frequency expected for a given sibilant. Usually the differences between /ʂ̻/, /s/ and /ç/ in the utterances of Polish speakers are indicated by the peaks of amplitude of the fricative noise that fall within different frequency ranges for different places of articulation. /s/ is the sound of the highest frequency and here the peak of amplitude can be observed between 5000 and 10000 Hz. /ʂ̻/ is a lower frequency sound, and its peak of amplitude is located between 1000 and 7000 Hz. /ç/ is characterized by two peaks of amplitude: a lower one (2000-3000 Hz) and a higher one (5500-8000 Hz). Of course, these values are more of a general tendency than accurate measures and they vary from speaker to speaker, but combined with perceptual analysis they can be useful in establishing the articulation accuracy of a sibilant.

The tasks performed by the participants were taken from the *Polish Dysarthria Test for TBI Patients* (Połczyńska-Fiszer and Pufal 2006) and the *ESL Test in Dysarthria* (Połczyńska-Fiszer 2009).

The tasks used for the assessment of speakers' L1 were as follows:

1) Producing six Polish vowels in isolation (/a/, /ɛ/, /i/, /ɨ/, /o/, /u/). The aim of the task was to establish the participants' mean vowel formants for each Polish vowel.
2) Picture naming. The participants were to name twelve items shown in the pictures. Our aim was to examine the quality of speech sounds in a relatively easy task.
3) Spontaneous speech task. The participants were to retell a story by Piątkowska and Talko (2002, 74-77) about a married couple shopping for a suit. Our aim here was to examine the quality of speech sounds in a more challenging task.

The tasks used for the assessment of L2 speech were as follows:

1. Producing twelve British vowels in isolation (iː, ɪ, e, æ, ə, ɜː, ʌ, aː, ɒ, ɔː, ʊ, uː). The aim of the task was to establish the participants' mean vowel formants for British vowels.
2. Performing the Goldman Fristoe Test of Articulation 2. The participants were to read a list of words. Our aim was to establish the quality of speech sounds in a less demanding task with a limited phoneme environment.
3. Reading task. The participants were to read a short text (modified

from *Sounds English*, O'Connor and Fletcher 1989). Our aim was to establish the quality of speech sounds in a more challenging task.

4. Spontaneous speech task. The participants were to talk about a series of absurd cards that were shown to them. Our aim was to examine the quality of speech sounds in the most challenging task, that is, creating one's own output in a foreign language.

Results

The general results of the study are presented in table 3. The overall length of speech samples analysed in the study was 4360 phonemes: 1419 phonemes for L1 and 2841 phonemes for L2. In these samples, phonological processes were applied 1373 times: 422 times in Polish and 951 in English. This gives a measure of 31.5 pp/100 phon for the two languages together, 30 pp/100 phon for Polish and 32pp/100 phon for English. As can be seen, the difference in the number of pp/100 phon between English and Polish is not very significant. It is only in the individual participants' results that the difference between L1 and L2 becomes more salient.

Additionally we counted the number of types of phonological processes applied by the participants in the two languages. In general, in all of the speech samples, there were 45 types of phonological processes applied. Thirty types of processes were applied in Polish speech samples and 43 types of processes – in English samples. On average, the participants applied 17.6 types of processes in L1 and 27 types of processes in L2. This implies that some processes were prevalent in both languages and some processes were applied only in one of the languages (i.e., they were idiosyncratic in the speakers' L1 or L2).

As predicted, the most frequently applied processes were sibilant imprecision and vowel centralisation. Sibilant imprecision was applied 400 times in all of the speech samples, which constitutes 29% of all the processes applied and 9pp/100 phon. In Polish samples sibilant imprecision was applied 124 times (29% of processes applied in Polish, 9pp/100 phon) and in English speech samples – 276 (also 29% of processes applied in English, 9pp/100 phon). Vowel centralisation was applied 367 times in both languages (27% of processes, 8pp/100 phon): 121 times in Polish (29%, 9pp/100 phon) and 246 times in English (26%, 8pp/100 phon). Other frequent processes included voicing (6% for L1, 6% for L2, 6% for both) and devoicing (8% for L1, 4% for L2, 5.5% for both), however, these were not applied consistently by all of the participants. These results are represented in table 4.

Another measure that was taken into consideration was the number of deletions (consonant, vowel and syllable deletions), as these are the most radical processes, pointing to the greatest degree of difficulty in disordered speakers. Deletions in the participants' speech constituted 4% of all the processes in L1 and 7% of processes in L2 (6% of processes in all L1 and L2 speech samples). In the speech of the participants, most processes were applied in word medial position (55% for L1, 46% for L2, 49% in total). The percentage of processes applied in word initial position was 23% for L1, 21% for L2, 21% in total, while the percentage of processes applied in word final position was 22% for L1, 33% for L2, 30% in total. The results were reiterated in the individual results of the participants.

When it comes to the results in specific tasks, the expected correlation between the difficulty of the task and the frequency of phonological processes did not occur, i.e., the differences were not substantive. However, generally, the more demanding the task, the more types of processes the participants applied. In L1, participants applied 12 types of processes on the whole (5.7 on average) in the less demanding picture naming task and 27 types of processes (16.3 on average) in the spontaneous speech task. In L2, the participants applied on the whole 24 types of processes (14.3 on average) in the word list reading task and 31 (19 on average) and 30 (15.3 on average) in the reading task and spontaneous speech task respectively.

Due to the differences in L2 proficiency and HL severity of the participants, the results show a considerable degree of variation. On the whole, the participants with a more severe HL had a higher number of phonological processes than the subject with a less severe HL. P1, the participant with a moderate HL applied 15pp/100 phon in L1, 20 pp/100 in total. In P2 and P3, who both had profound HL, these numbers were considerably higher (P2: 47pp/100 phon in L1, 39pp/100 phon in total, P3: 27pp/100 phon in L1, 35pp/100 phon in total). The results of all the participants are compared in table 4 and represented graphically in figure 1. The difference between the participants was also reflected in the number of types of processes applied by them, as can be seen in figure 2. P1 applied 12 types of processes in L1, 22 for L2 and 25 in total. Those numbers were significantly higher in the case of P2 and P3. P2 applied 20 types of processes in L1, 26 in L2, 30 in total, while P3 applied 21 types in L1, 33 in L2 and 35 in total.

As for the two participants with lower L2 proficiency, there were more processes applied in L2 than in L1. This tendency was reversed in P2, who was an experienced learner (he had learned L2 for over 10 years) and whose L2 proficiency was significantly higher than that of the remaining two participants.

Individual results of the SNHL participants show that P1, the participant with a moderate HL and pre-intermediate L2 proficiency, applied 15pp/100 phon in L1 (processes were applied 74 times in a sample of 481 phonemes) and 22pp/100 phon in L2 (processes were applied 226 times in a sample of 1036 phonemes). Moreover, the participant applied 12 types of processes in L1, while in L2, 22 types of processes were applied.

The processes that were the most frequent ones in the speech of the participant, regardless of the language used or the type of a task, were vowel centralisation and sibilant imprecision. Vowel centralisation constituted as much as 39% of all the processes applied in the L1 tasks (they occurred 29 times) and 40% of all the processes applied in the L2 tasks (occurred 90 times). Sibilant imprecision constituted 34% of all the processes applied in L1 (occurred 25 times) and 35% of all the processes applied in L2 (occurred 79 times). Another process frequently used by the participant was affrication of stops (4% of all processes in L1, 9% in L2), which was an idiosyncratic process of this very speaker.

Most of P1's processes were applied in word medial position (50% for L1, 52% for L2, 52% for both), and 16% of processes in word initial position (the result is the same for L1, L2 and both languages in total). P1 applied 34% of all her L1 processes in word final position, while in L2 the processes in final position constituted 32%. For both languages in total the percentage of processes applied by P1 in word final position also equalled 32%.

When it comes to the speaker's results with regard to task difficulty, there was a significant difference between the number of processes applied in easier tasks and the more difficult ones. We are speaking here of the difference between the picture naming task (9pp/100 phon) and spontaneous speech task (16pp/100 phon) in L1 and the difference between the list reading (16.5pp/100 phon) and dialogue reading (24pp/100 phon) and spontaneous speech task (23pp/100 phon) in L2. The participant also applied more types of processes in more difficult tasks than in the easier ones (L1 picture naming – 2, L1 spontaneous speech – 12, L2 list reading – 7, L2 dialogue reading – 15, L2 spontaneous speech – 11).

P2 (profound SNHL, intermediate level of L2 proficiency) applied more processes in L1 than L2. The amount of phonological processes per 100 phonemes equalled 47 for L1 (219 occurrences in a sample of 464 phonemes) and 36 for L2 (406 occurrences in a sample of 1123). However, the participant applied a few types of processes more in L2 (26) than in L1 (20).

The most frequently applied processes were, just as in case of P1, vowel centralisation and sibilant imprecision. Vowel centralisation constituted 29% of all the processes applied by P2 in his L1 (it occurred 63 times in this language). In L2, the percentage of vowel centralisation equalled 31.5% (applied 128 times). Sibilant imprecision constituted 26% of L1 processes (it was applied 57 times) and 31% of L2 processes (occurred 125 times). Other frequent processes were devoicing (10% in L1, 3% in L2) and voicing (9% in L1, 10% in L2).

The percentage of processes with regard to the position of the word was the following: in L1 20% of processes were applied word initially, 63.5% word medially and 15.5% word finally; in L2 20% of processes were applied in word initial position, 49% in word medial position and 31% in word final position. In total 20% of processes occurred word initially, 54% word medially and 36% word medially.

The results of P2 concerning the expected difference in the number of phonological processes between more and less difficult tasks were rather inconclusive. He applied 49 pp/100 phon (10 types of processes) in the L1 picture naming task, 47 pp/100 phon (16 types) in the L1 spontaneous speech task, 43 pp/100 phon (16 types) in the L2 list reading, 31 pp/100 phon (17 types) in the L2 dialogue reading and 37 pp/100 phon (16 types) in L2 spontaneous speech.

P3, the participant with a profound HL and L2 at an elementary level, had a significantly larger number of phonological processes in L2 than in L1, thus confirming our hypothesis. The frequency of occurrence of these processes in L1 was 27pp/100 phon (129 processes in a sample of 474 phonemes) and in L2 – 40pp/100 phon (319 processes in a sample of 789 phonemes). What is more, the participant applied 21 types of processes in L1 and 33 in L2.

The most frequently applied process in L1 was sibilant imprecision, constituting 32.5% of all the processes applied in this language (the participant applied it 42 times) and vowel centralisation (it occurred 29 times). In L2 sibilant imprecision was the most frequent process (22%, 71 occurrences), but the second most frequent process was consonant deletion (11%, 35 occurrences). Overall deletions (vowel, consonant and syllable deletions) constituted 18.5% of all the processes in L2. Vowel centralisation was the third most frequent L2 process (9%, 28 occurrences). The speaker also applied a relatively high number of devoicing (8.5% for L1, 5% for L2) and voicing (3% for L1, 6% for L2).

It is noteworthy that in P3's speech there was a very high percentage (51%) of processes other than sibilant imprecision, vowel centralisation, voicing and devoicing. In contrast, in P2 the remaining processes constituted 25% of all the processes applied (in both languages) and in P1 this percentage was even lower.

The processes applied by P3 word medially constituted 45% of all her L1 processes, 38.25% of L2 processes, 40% of all the processes. Thirty two per cent of L1 processes, 24.5% of L2 processes and 26.5% of all processes in total occurred word initially. Twenty three per cent of L1 processes, 36% of L2 processes and 32.5% of all the processes in total were applied in word final position[3].

In the results of P3, there was no clear-cut correlation between the task difficulty and the frequency of occurrence of processes, but in some of the more difficult tasks (spontaneous speech for L1, dialogue reading in L2), the participant applied more types of phonological processes than in the easier tasks (picture naming in L1 and list reading in L2). The L2 spontaneous speech task results did not follow the pattern, however, in this task the speech of the patient was barely intelligible and thus the analysis might have been distorted. The results are as follows: in the L1 picture naming task five types of processes were applied (27 pp/100 phon); in the L1 spontaneous speech 21 types of processes were applied (27 pp/100 phon); in the L2 list reading task P3 applied 20 types of processes (46 pp/100 phon); in the L2 dialogue reading task the number of types equalled 25 (38 pp/100 phon) and in the L2 spontaneous speech task – 19 (38 pp/100 phon).

Discussion

The results have partially confirmed our hypothesis. In general, L2 required the application of more processes, more types of processes and more radical processes, especially in the less proficient speakers. The results also show that the participants applied more deletions in L2 than in L1. These results are in line with NP and PHB which predict that the more difficulties the speaker experiences while articulating a sound, the more radical processes are applied. Because deletions are the most radical processes and have no communicative value, their presence in L2 would testify to more problems with L2 articulatory patterns.

Moreover, the participants applied more processes in L2 but only if their L2 proficiency was low. For P1, the pre-intermediate L2 speaker, and especially for P3, whose L2 performance was very poor, there were significantly more processes in L2. This might be explained by the fact

[3] In the L2 reading task P3 also omitted whole function words such as *a* or *the*. This process could not be classified as word initial, medial or final so it formed a different category. This category constituted 1.25% of all the L2 processes and 1% of all the processes applied by the speaker.

that the articulatory patterns of L2 were less exercised and, thus, they were more difficult for the speakers (Połczyńska 2009). Both participants did not use the foreign language on a regular basis at the time when the experiment was conducted. What is more, in the case of P3, the speaking modality was resisted in L2. As a result, the speakers encountered several articulatory difficulties that they tried to overcome with phonological processes. The articulatory problems in L2 were particularly severe in the case of P3, which was mirrored in her frequent use of deletions. Deletions constituted 18.5% of all L2 processes applied by the participant, which is an unusually high number. Deletions are the most radical process, in which the communicative value is sacrificed for the ease of articulation (Połczyńska-Fiszer 2009, Tobin 2009). Therefore, they are applied by the speakers when they encounter severe difficulties. In the case of P3, deletions were frequent in both languages due to the severity of her hearing loss, as well as her background. Since she attended the school for the deaf and had a connection with the community of deaf people using sign language, her desire to master the oral language might have been less motivated than in the case of the participants using oral languages only. Still, the difference between the levels of deletions in L1 and L2 is far greater than in the case of the remaining participants, indicating a significant difficulty during L2 articulation. P1 and P3 also applied more types of phonological processes in L2 than in L1. This difference is again especially noticeable in the case of P3. This result implies that, due to differences between the languages, the participants had to employ new and different compensatory strategies. It is noteworthy that some processes were idiosyncratic only for L1 or only for L2 tasks.

The pattern predicted in our hypothesis was reversed in the results of P2 who applied more processes in L1 than in L2 (47 vs. 36 pp/100 phon). The data, however, can be explained by the fact that the participant had learnt L2 for a long time and used it very frequently. Despite the relatively poor CTP ESL results, most likely stemming from the speaker's overall comprehension problems, he was, in fact, quite proficient in L2. He was able to talk about a wide range of subjects and to use fairly advanced vocabulary items in his utterances (including phrases such as “shooting rifle” or “approach”). It can be speculated that through the frequent use of the L2 articulatory patterns, L2 phonemes and phoneme sequences became less difficult for the participant, thus, resulting in a smaller number of phonological processes in L2. Another explanation might be that the participant had received a significant amount of formal instruction concerning L2 (being taught the language both at home and at school) and, therefore, was more conscious about the possible mistakes he might make.

This, in turn, might have led to a conscious avoidance of certain errors. Another noteworthy fact about P2's performance was that despite the higher frequency of occurrence of phonological processes in L1, he applied six types of processes more in L2 than in L1. This might point to the fact that even though the participant managed to limit the number of errors in his speech, he still needed to apply extra coping strategies in his L2, due to differences in the articulatory patterns between his native tongue and the foreign language.

As predicted, the most frequent processes in the participants' speech were vowel centralisation and sibilant imprecision. Together, they constituted 58% of all the processes applied in L1 and 55% in L2. It is important to notice that sibilant sounds and vowels were problematic even for P1, the SNHL individual, whose speech impairment was not very severe (in fact, the participant's utterances were completely intelligible and sounded quite natural). It is also noteworthy that the two processes were prevalent in both languages and in all the tasks performed by the speakers. This result is consistent with previous studies (Richardson 1993, Mathies et al. 1994, Huttenen 2001, Kosky and Boothroyd 2001, McGarr et al. 2004) and it might imply that the two processes are universal for SNHL individuals.

The high occurrence of idiosyncratic sibilant imprecision can be easily explained by the characteristics of SNHL. Sibilants are high frequency sounds, which are usually not perceptible to SNHL speakers (Bystrzanowska 1963, Jürgens, Brand and Kollmeier 2009). The high frequencies are problematic even for those individuals whose HL is only moderate, which explains the results of P1. Moreover, it is difficult to perceive the differences in frequencies, especially for speakers with SNHL, who exhibit a poorer resolution of frequencies (Boothroyd 1984, Moore 1995, Halpern and Tobin 2008). Hence, it is not surprising that the minor differences in frequency that occur between sibilants might be blurred for these individuals. This has an effect on production of these sounds. It has been shown by several studies (Svirsky et al. 1998, Higgins et al. 2001, Goffman et al. 2002) that poor auditory input influences the articulatory coordination of the speaker. Even when the lack of auditory input is temporary (as in the case of deaf speakers with cochlear implants who have their implants turned off for just one hour) the articulatory patterns of the individual change significantly (Svirsky et al. 1998, Higgins et al. 2001). Therefore, it is by no means surprising that the constant lack of auditory input regarding sibilants leads to an inaccurate rendition of these sounds. We further hypothesise that the participants might have an underdeveloped phonological inventory of sibilants, which results in a general articulatory merger of these segments.

The high number of vowel centralisation in Polish SNHL speakers might seem unusual, as in Polish this process does not occur in the speech of normally hearing individuals, i.e., Polish does not reduce vowels in unstressed positions. However, it is likely that vowels undergo centralisation in the speech of hard-of-hearing individuals because these segments lack tactile cues that would enable the control of vocal performance. It has been suggested by Nasir and Ostry (2008) that in the cases where auditory feedback is removed, tactile feedback takes its place. In vowels, where articulators do not come into close contact, this tactile feedback is weakened and, hence, the speaker cannot fully control their production, which might result in centralisation.

When it comes to the remaining processes, the relatively high percentage of voicing and devoicing in speakers with profound SNHL is worth mentioning. This tendency conforms to the findings of Halpern and Tobin (2008), who also found a large number of these processes in the speech of individuals with severe-profound HL. In SNHL individuals, the perception of features, such as voice, is often disabled. Moreover, the voice-voiceless contrast is not indicated very well by tactile cues. Finally, this contrast is not communicative for hard-of-hearing individuals because it cannot be read from the lips of the speakers. If this feature is not heard, it is practically useless for the language user. Thus, in accordance with the PHB principle of acquiring maximal communication with minimal effort (Tobin 1997, Tobin 2009), the feature of little communicative value undergoes assimilation.

Apart from the aforementioned tendencies, there was a lot of variability in the results of the participants. Interestingly, while P1 and P2 seemed to consistently apply just a few processes and only occasionally some other strategies were necessary for them, P3 had a high ratio of processes other than the commonly applied processes, such as sibilant imprecision, vowel centralisation, voicing and devoicing. The fact that she applied such a wide range of coping strategies might be indicative of her problems in many areas, not just the sibilants and vowels. This might be a result of a high degree of hearing loss, the social background and the educational history of P3.

When it comes to the expected correlation between the number of processes and task difficulty, there were generally more types of processes applied in the more difficult tasks. For P1, also the frequency of occurrence of processes was significantly higher for the more challenging tasks. However, most of the results were not very transparent and thus a follow-up study with larger samples would be beneficial.

In this study, about a half of all the processes were applied in word medial position. This result is very salient and it has very important implications. NP and PHB assume that the communicative value of the utterances is one of the major factors that influence the use (and distribution) of phonological processes (Dziubalska-Kołaczyk 2004, Tobin 2009). Therefore, if a part of a phrase carries a significant communicative load and is crucial for understanding this phrase, this part is less likely to undergo phonological processes, especially radical ones (Halpern and Tobin 2008). This is why, for instance, stressed syllables are very rarely deleted. According to Diver (1979) and Tobin (1997), most processes should occur in word final position, because this position is the least communicative one. This tendency was observed, for instance, in the study by Połczyńska-Fiszer and Mazeaux (2006), Połczyńska (2009) and Połczyńska, Tobin and Sapir (2009). The results of the present study can perhaps be explained on statistical grounds. Given that there are more sounds in the middle of words than in marginal positions, it is logical to assume that most of the processes should occur in word medial position, on condition that the processes are randomly distributed. Thus, if one supports the claim by Tobin (1997), our result suggests that the distribution of processes was to a large extent context-free in the SNHL participants. This, in turn, would imply that these speakers have an underdeveloped inventory of speech sounds and, thus, they simply alter them in any position. An alternative explanation is that, contrary to the aforementioned assumptions, it is the frame of the word – the beginning and the end – that is most important for comprehension. Following this reasoning, we can expect fewer processes in the word-marginal positions and more processes in the middle of the word.

Conclusion

The presented study investigated the speech of Polish SNHL speakers whose L2 was English. We examined three SNHL individuals, one male and two females. One of the speakers had a moderate SNHL, while the other two had a profound SNHL. The participants performed the tasks from the *Polish Dysarthria Test for TBI Patients* (Połczyńska-Fiszer and Pufal 2006) and the *ESL Test in Dysarthria* (Połczyńska-Fiszer 2006) and their performance was recorded, acoustically analysed and transcribed phonetically and phonemically by the authors. The results indicate that bilingual SNHL speakers apply more phonological processes in their L2, unless their L2 proficiency level is high. As predicted by the authors, the most frequent processes applied by the participants were sibilant imprecision and vowel centralisation. This result is very robust, as the two processes constituted more than 50% of all the processes applied and they occurred frequently in all the tasks, in both languages. This conforms to the predictions made by NP and PHB that idiosyncratic phonological processes mirror individual speakers' difficulties. The high occurrence of sibilant imprecision stems from the fact that sibilants are high frequency sounds, while SNHL disrupts the perception of high frequencies. Moreover, differences in frequency between sibilants are difficult to perceive for the SNHL speakers, who have a poor resolution of frequencies. The occurrence of vowel centralisation might be explained by the fact that in the production of vowels the articulators do not come into close contact, so speakers have weaker tactile feedback when uttering these sounds. This leads to a poorer control of vocal performance and consequently to the centralisation of vowels. In the speakers with profound SNHL, voicing and devoicing occurred relatively often, due to the fact that for these individuals the voice-voiceless contrast has little communicative value. In this study, most processes were applied in word-medial position. This result might stem from the fact that in this position there are more sounds and, thus, it is statistically more probable that processes may occur there. This in turn might imply that SNHL speakers apply some of the processes at random and that they have an underdeveloped phonological inventory, due to their distorted input.

Table 1: The results of the PTA for the three participants (the numbers in brackets refer to the bone conduction)

	P1		P2		P3	
Pure tones	Right ear	Left ear	Right ear	Left ear	Right ear	Left ear
250 Hz	35 dB (10 dB)	40 dB (10 dB)	90 dB	95 dB	70 dB (35 dB)	80 dB (35 dB)
500 Hz	35 dB (15 dB)	35 dB (15 dB)	90 dB	95 dB	75 dB (55 dB)	80 dB (60 dB)
1000 Hz	50 dB (35 dB)	40 dB (30 dB)	100 dB	100 dB	85 dB	90 dB
2000 Hz	50 dB (45 dB)	50 dB (40 dB)	95 dB	95 dB	85 dB	no res. hearing
3000 Hz	50 dB (40 dB)	50 dB (45 dB)	90 dB	90 dB	85 dB	no res. hearing
4000 Hz	45 dB	50 dB	90 dB	105 dB	80 dB	no res. hearing
5000 Hz	55 dB	55 dB	90 dB	90 dB	85 dB	105 dB
8000 Hz	50 dB	55 dB	85 dB	80 dB	80 dB	no res. hearing

Table 2: Background information about the participants

	P1	P2	P3
SEX	female	male	female
AGE	26	20	28
LOSS	Moderate (35-60 dB)	Profound (>90)	Profound (>90)
ONSET	7 months	Congenial	Congenital
AETIOLOGY	Ototoxic medicine	Not known (genetic?)	Genetic
COMMUNICATION	Speech	Speech	Speech and sign language
HEARING AID	Frequently	Yes	Yes
COMMENTS	Intralingual loss, benefits a lot from hearing aids	Additional minor muscle paresis possible	Trilingual (oral Polish, Polish Sign Language, oral English), used to attend a school for the deaf

Table 3: Overall results of the participants (their length of utterances, number of processes and types of processes applied, along with the number of processes per 100 phonemes)

	P1			P2			P3			All participants		
	L1	L2	In total	L1	L2	In total	L1	L2	In total	L1	L2	In total
Length of utterances in phonemes	481	1036	1517	464	1123	1587	474	789	1263	1419	2941	4360
Number of processes	74	226	300	219	406	625	129	319	448	422	951	1373
Pp/100 phon	15	22	20	47	36	39	27	40	35	30	32	31,5
Number of types of processes applied	12	22	25	20	26	30	21	22	25	30	40	45

Table 4: The most frequent processes applied by the participants in L1, L2 and in total

		L1	L2	IN TOTAL
sibilant centralisation	Number of processes	124	276	400
	Processes/100 phonemes	9	9	9
	% of all processes	29,00%	29,00%	29,00%
vowel centralisation	Number of processes	121	246	367
	Processes/100 phonemes	9	8	8
	% of all processes	29,00%	26,00%	27,00%
voicing	Number of processes	25	60	85
	Processes/100 phonemes	2	2	2
	% of all processes	6,00%	6,00%	6,00%
devoicing	Number of processes	34	42	76
	Processes/100 phonemes	2	1,4	2
	% of all processes	8,00%	4,00%	5,50%
deletions	Number of processes	16	63	79
	Processes/100 phonemes	1	2	2
	% of all processes	4,00%	7,00%	6,00%

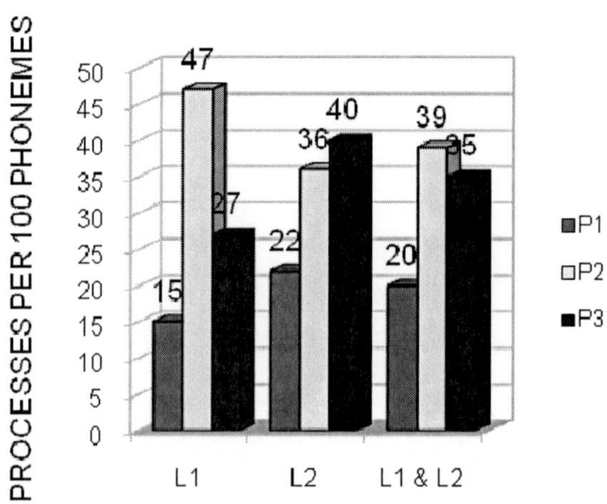

Figure 1. The number of processes per 100 phonemes as applied by the participants (P1, P2 and P3) in the L1 tasks, in the L2 tasks and in all of the tasks

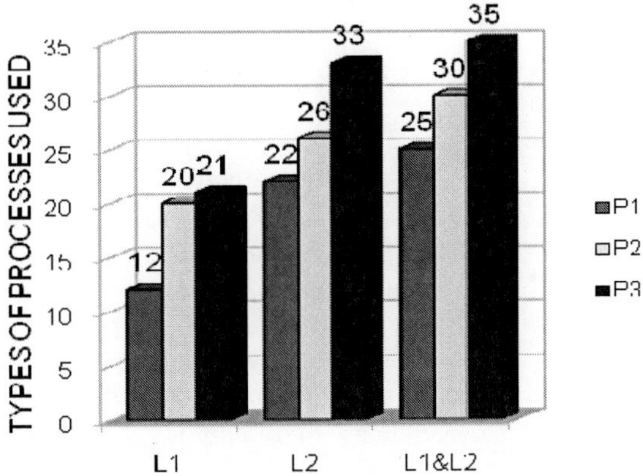

Figure 2. The number of types of processes applied by the participants (P1, P2 and P3) in the L1 tasks, in the L2 tasks and in all of the tasks

References

Boothroyd, A. 1984. "Auditory perception of speech contrasts by subjects with sensorineural hearing loss." *Journal of Speech, Language, and Hearing Research* 27: 133-144.

Boothroyd, A. and L. Medwetsky. 1992. "Spectral Distribution of /s/ and the Frequency Response of Hearing Aids." *Ear and Hearing* 13 (3): 150-157.

Bystrzanowska, T. 1963. *Audiologia kliniczna.* Warszawa: Państwowy Zakład Wydawnictw Lekarskich.

Diver, W. 1979. "Phonology as human behavior." In *Psycholinguistic research: Implications and applications,* edited by D. R. Aaronson and R. W. Reiber, 161-188. Hillsdale: Lawrence Erlbaum Associates.

Donegan, P. and D. Stampe. 1979. "The study of Natural Phonology." In *Current Approaches to Phonological Theory,* edited by D. A. Dinnsen, 126-173. Bloomington: IUP.

Dressler, W. U. and K. Dziubalska-Kołaczyk. 1995. "Syllable and morpheme in aphasia." In *Crossdisciplinary approaches to morphology,* edited by W. Dressler and C. Burani, 115-130. Wien: Verlag der Österreichischen Akedemie der Wissenschaften.

Dziubalska-Kołaczyk, K. 2002. *Beats-and-binding phonology*. Frankfurt am Main: Peter Lang.

Dziubalska-Kołaczyk, K. 2004. Modern Natural Phonology: the theory for the future. http://ifa.amu.edu.pl/~dkasia/?Courses:Natural_Phonology (date of access: 8 Feb. 2009).

Goffman, L., Ertmer, D.J., and Erdle, C. 2002. "Changes in speech production in a child with a cochlear implant: Acoustic and Kinematic Evidence." *Journal of Speech, Language, and Hearing Research*, 45: 891-901.

Gussmann, E. 2007. *The phonology of Polish*. Oxford: Oxford University Press.

Halpern, O. and Y. Tobin. 2008. "'Non-Vocalisation'–A phonological error process in the speech of severely and profoundly hearing impaired adults according to the theory of phonology as human behaviour." *International Journal of Clinical Phonetics and Linguistics*. 22 (10-11): 824-834."

Higgins, M.B., McCleary, E.A., and Schulte, L. 2001. "Articulatory changes with short-term deactivation of the cochlear implants of two prelingually deafened children." *Ear and Hearing*, 22: 29-45.

Huttenen, K. H. 2001. "Phonological development in 4–6-year-old moderately hearing impaired children." *Scandinavian Audiology* 30 (53): 79-82.

Jürgens, T., T. Brand and B. Kollmeier. 2009. "Predicting consonant recognition in quiet for listeners with normal hearing and hearing impairment using an auditory model." *The Journal of the Acoustical Society of America*. 125 (4): 2533.

Kosky, C. and A. Boothroyd. 2001. "Perception and Production of Sibilants by Children with Hearing Loss: A Training Study." *Volta Review* 103 (2): 71-98.

Lane, H. and J. Webster. 1991. "Speech deterioration in postlingually deafened adults." *The Journal of the Acoustical Society of America* 89: 859-866.

Lane, H., M. Matthies, F. H. Guenther, M. Denny, J. S. Perkell, E. Stockmann, M. Tiede, J. Vick and M. Zandipour. 2007. "Effects of short- and long-term changes in auditory feedback on vowel and sibilant contrasts." *Journal of Speech, Language, and Hearing Research* 50: 913-927.

Marecka, M. and M. Połczyńska. 2009. "Phonological processes in Polish speakers with sensorineural hearing loss." In *Proceedings of the II International Conference on Clinical Linguistics,* edited by V. Marrero and I. Pineda, 54-62. Madrid: Euphonia Ediciones.

Matthies, M. L; M. A Svirsky, H. L Lane and J. S. Perkell. 1994. "A preliminary study of the effects of cochlear implants on the production of sibilants." *The Journal of the Acoustical Society of America* 96: 1367-1373.

McGarr, N.S, L. J. Raphel, B. Kolia, H. K. Vorperian and K.Harris 2004. "Sibilant production in speakers who have hearing loss: Electropalatographic and Perceptual Evidence." *The Volta Review* 104 (3): 119-140.

Ménard, L., M. Polak, M. Denny, E. Burton, H. Lane, M. L. Matthies, N. Marrone, J. S. Perkell, M. Tiede and J. Vick. 2007. "Interactions of speaking condition and auditory feedback on vowel production in postlingually deaf adults with cochlear implants." *Journal of the Acoustical Society of America* 121 (6): 3790-3801.

Moore, B. C. J. 1995. *Perceptual consequences of cochlear damage.* Oxford: Oxford Medical Publications.

Nasir, S. M. and D. J. Ostry. 2008. "Speech motor learning in profoundly deaf adults." *Nature Neuroscience* 11: 1217 – 1222.

O'Connor, J. D. and C. Fletcher. 1989. *Sounds English.* Harlow: Longman.

Piątkowska, M. and L. Talko. 2002. *Talki w wielkim mieście.* Warszawa: WAB.

Pittman, A. and P. Stelmachowicz. 2000. "Perception of voiceless fricatives by normal-hearing and hearing impaired children and adults." *Journal of Speech, Language,and Hearing Research* 43: 1389–1401.

Połczyńska, M. 2009. "Dysarthric processes in first and second language used by patients with traumatic brain injury." *The Asia Pacific Journal of Speech, Language and Hearing* 12 (2): 137-156.

Połczynska, M., Y. Tobin and S. Sapir. 2009. "Correlation between vowel centralisation and incomplete stop articulation in patients with traumatic brain injury." *Poznań Studies in Contemporary Linguistics* 45 (2): 281-299.

Połczyńska-Fiszer, M. 2008. "Acoustic analysis of first and second language speech in patients with traumatic brain injury." In *NorClinLing 2008. Proceedings from the 1st Nordic Conference in Clinical Linguistics. Studies in Languages 44,* edited by J. Niemi and S. Werner, 102-112. Joensuu: University of Joensuu.

Połczyńska-Fiszer, M. and A. Pufal. 2006. "Classification of dysarthria in Polish TBI patients using acoustic analysis." *Acta Neuropsychologica* 4 (4): 257-285.

Połczyńska-Fiszer, M. and J. M. Mazeaux. 2008. "Second language acquisition after traumatic brain injury: A case study." *Disability and Rehabilitation* 30: 1397-1407.

Pruszewicz, A, ed. 2003. *Audiologia kliniczna – zarys*. Poznan: AM Poznan.

Richardson, L. M., P. A. Busby, P. J. Blamey, R.C. Dowell and G.M Clark. 1993. "The effects of auditory feedback from the Nucleus cochlear implant on the vowel formant frequencies produced by children and adults." *Ear and Hearing* 14: 339-349.

Stampe, D. 1969. "The acquisition of phonetic representation." *CLS* 5: 443- 453. [Reprinted in: Barbara Lust and Claire Foley, eds. 2004. *First Language Acquisition*. Oxford: Blackwell Publishing Ltd., 307-316.]

Steffens, M. L., R. E. Eilers, L. Fishman, D. K. Oller and R. C. Urbano. 1994. "Early Vocal Development in Tactually Aided Children With Severe-Profound Hearing Loss." *Journal of Speech and Hearing Research* 37: 700-711.

Svirsky, M.A., Jones, D., Osberger, M.J. and Miyamoto, R.T. (1998). "The effect of auditory feedback on the control of oral-nasal balance by pediatric cochlear implant users." *Ear and Hearing*, 19: 385-393.

Tobin, Y. 1997. *Phonology as human behaviuor: Theoretical implications and clinical applications.* Durham: Duke University Press.

Tobin, Y. 2009. "Phonology as Human Behaviour: Clinical Phonetics, Phonology and Prosody." *Poznań Studies in Contemporary Linguistics* 45 (2): 327-352.

Vick, J., H. Lane, J. Perkell, M. Matthies, J. Gould and M. Zandipour. 2001. "Covariation of cochlear implant users' perception and production of vowel contrasts and their identification by listeners with normal hearing." *Journal of Speech, Language, and Hearing Research* 44: 257–1267.

LANGUAGE USED BY POLISH AMERICANS: YET ANOTHER VARIANT OF ENGLISH SPOKEN BY POLES

ŁUKASZ FURTAK
JOHN PAUL II CATHOLIC UNIVERSITY OF LUBLIN

Abstract

Ponglish (Szumer 2007) is a term used to describe Polish spoken by Polish communities in English speaking countries. Its characteristic feature is the significant number of forms, which first are borrowed from English and then phonetically adapted to the Polish phonological system. Such forms have been frequently mentioned in the literature (Mańczak-Wohlfeld 1995, Dubisz 1997, Bloomfield 1933). The type of Ponglish specifically referred to in this paper is the language used by the Polish communities of New York, Long Island and Chicago, also known as *Polamer*. Consequently, the terms which the author has decided to use interchangeably in reference to the lexical items characteristic of this type of speech are *Polamer words, Polamer items*, and *Polamer forms* because they accurately denote the dialectal forms under discussion and do not make reference to any linguistic processes which might have contributed to their creation. A brief selection of Polamer words is included underneath.

water ['wɔra]

daugther ['dɔra]

thirty ['tɔrɨ]

I don't know ['arɔ̃nɔw]

sample ['sɛ̃mpɔw]

title ['tajlɔ]

cable ['kɛjbɔ]

truck ['trɔk]

junk ['d͡ʑɔ̃ŋk]

job ['d͡ʑap]

The above examples suggest that the process of the phonetic adaptation of Polamer words might be perception-based, which makes it different from the spelling-supported adaptation taking place during any English lesson in Poland.

The aim of the study: to test the validity of the above conclusion, i.e. whether Polamer words have come into existence as a result of perception-based phonological interference without the support of orthography.

The experiment: to examine Polish native speakers' perception of the American intervocalic flap and dark /l/ in a number of lexical gaps read by a native speaker of American English and to determine whether the results of the statistical analysis correspond to the phonetic form of the Polamer words presented above. The participants of the experiments are inhabitants of the town of Tarnobrzeg, aged 20-60, lacking or having very little prior exposure to the English language, which refers to the level of English competence of Polish immigrants in the USA. None of the participants have been paid for taking part in the experiment.

The results of the experiment: A significant number of participants indicated that, in the majority of cases, their perceptions of the intervocalic flap and dark /l/ were [r] and /u/,/o/ or /w/, respectively.

The interpretation of the results: A statistical analysis seems to confirm the conclusion drawn from the analysis of Polamer words that the creation of such forms must have been predominantly perception-based. Additionally, the paper contains some acoustical and historical facts which seem to further corroborate the above reasoning.

Introduction

A number of classical introductions to the study of Polish dialects (Nitsch 1960; Dejna 1973; Dejna 1981; Urbańczyk 1962) traditionally describe the varieties of Polish spoken in Poland, but there has also been some interest in the Polish spoken abroad. One of such variety is a dialect which has developed in the U.S.A. In this paper, it will be referred to as "Polamer", which is a term used e.g. in Chicago.[1] It is most commonly

[1] This type of speech has been variously termed in the literature: Dubisz (1981) Strybel (1990) – "dialekt polonijny" (the Polish community dialect, transl. mine) ;

used by Polish Americans living in the cities of New York and Chicago, as these two cities are the home of millions of Polish immigrants.

It is difficult to track precisely the date of the creation of the first Polamer forms but it is certain that some of them were in use as early as in the second half of the 19th century. In his "Listy z podróży z Ameryki"[2], Henryk Sienkiewicz wrote (quoted after Gruchmanowa 2003, 223)

> Rzekłbym, pod wpływem angielszczyzny wytwarza się
> Osobny, polsko-amerykański język, którego wyrazy
> potoczne są polskie, wszystkie zaś inne angielskie
> I would say that, under the influence of English,
> a new separate dialect whose common words are
> Polish and all the remaining ones English is being
> created (...)
>
> (transl.mine).

Two such forms can be found in the letter which was written by Józef Cybulski in 1891[3], and sent to his wife, Józefina Cybulska. The forms are ['tʲikʲet] (i.e. ticket) (the original spelling was "tiket") and [kasɛl'gada] (i.e. CastleGarden) (the original spelling was "Kaselgada").

The most characteristic and striking feature of Polamer is the fact that, in its very beginnings, it used to be the consequence of phonetic interference in the speech of Polish migrant workers, the majority of whom did not speak English[4]. What is more, most of them were peasants (Pilch 1984, 159, 196; Kołodziej 1998, 12) or members of the working class (Dubisz 1997, 238) who could not even read or write in their mother

---

Gruchmanowa (1997, 193) – "polszczyzna mówiona w Stanach Zjednoczonych Ameryki Północnej" (the spoken variety of Polish used in the U.S.A, transl. mine), Gruchmanowa (1997, 193) – "słownictwo środowisk polonijnych w U.S.A" (the lexicon of the Polish communities residing in the U.S.A), Morawski (1981, 131) – "język polskoamerykański" (the Polish-American language, transl. mine), Szlifierstajn, S. (1951, title) – "język polskich środowisk emigracyjnych" (the language of the Polish emigrant communities, transl.mine), to name just a few.

[2] H.Sienkiewicz resided in the U.S.A. from 1876-1878.

[3] Retrieved from www.emigrantletters.com in August 2009.

[4] Gruchmanowa (2003, 215) writes that one of the reasons for the form of the words used by the Polonia is "the phonetic nature of the borrowings so characteristic of the monolingual community of working-class emigrants (...)" (transl. mine). The author continues to say that "the phonic reception of americanisms is conducted via the native phonetic and phonological system (...)" (transl.mine).

tongue[5, 6]. They tried to speak English in work places such as workshops, shipyards, butcheries or construction sites where Poles and Americans worked side by side. Poles tried to imitate the English spoken around them in an attempt to give names to different objects in the new reality which surrounded them. Nowadays, the manner of acquiring Polamer forms by the newcomers on the American soil is different. Those forms are heard from the Polish Americans already living in the Polish communities of New York and Chicago[7]. Very quickly, they become an important element of the emigrants' new spoken Polish[8,9]. That way, the pronunciation of these forms is not, and cannot, be English, but Polish. Hence, in the 19th century, the forms were instances of Polish phonetic adaptations from English; nowadays, however, they are instances of simply Polish words which a newcomer accepts and uses as Polish[10].

Examples of Polamer forms have been provided in table 1[11].

---

[5] Żak-Pławska (1981, 70) states that the majority of her informants had no education at all, and very few of them graduated from elementary school.

[6] According to Pilch (1984, 255), in 1900, 67.7% of the residents of the Austrian partition were illiterate.

[7] "Contemporary emigrants (…) acquire ready and common linguistic habits of the community they live in. For them, it may be the first, preliminary and transitional phase of assimilation." (Gruchmanowa 2003, 224) (transl.mine)

[8] According to Dubisz (1997, 252), the speech of the Polish community living in the U.S.A. "is used in local, restricted and private linguistic contexts(...)"

[9] Żak-Pławska (1981, 93) notices that, even though her informants did not live in the U.S.A. for a long period of time, the number of Polamer items in their speech was suprisingly high.

[10] Strybel (1990, 97) comments that, in the new words which were borrowed into Bay City Polamer, the English sounds were frequently substituted by Polish sounds. That process of replacement, however, was not operative in his informants' speech. He concludes that "the pronunciation of the borrowed English items had its current form due to the fact that, presumably, they had first been used by the generation of immigrants."

[11] The items in table 1 seem to exemplify the third phase of linguistic influence i.e. the result of interference: borrowing, as described in Dubisz (1997, 327); Haugen (1950,216) refers to it as "a pre-bilingual period(...)".

Table 1. Exemplary Polamer items.

Number	English spelling	Pronunciation in Polamer
1	saws-all	['sɔzɔ]
2	water	['wɔra]
3	daughter	['dɔra]
4	thirty	['tɔrɨ]
5	I don't know	['arɔ̃nɔw]
6	sample	['sɛ̃mpɔw]
7	title	['tajlɔ]
8	cable	['kejbɔ] / ['kejbɔl]
9	label	['lɛjbɔ]
10	level	['lɛvɔ]
11	drywall	['drajwɔ]
12	schedule	['skeʥ͡ɔ]
13	party	['parɨ] (Dubisz 1997, 246)
14	dirty	['dɔrɨ]
15	cottage	['karɨdẑ̦] (Dubisz 1981,62)
16	daddy	['dɛrɨ] (Dubisz 1981, 63)
17	butter	['barɛ] (Strybel 1990, 79)

All the words have bearing to the analysis presented in this paper. The above list is not in any respect exhaustive since there are many hundreds of words like the above used by Polamer speakers. This is a mere sampling of words most of which contain one of two types of phonetic interference. One type refers to the dark [ɫ] and the way it is realised in Polamer forms[12]. The other type contains instances of the American tap[13] and its realisation in the dialect of the Polish communities[14, 15].

The aim of the paper is, in analysing the two processes mentioned above, to find evidence that Polamer forms were originally created predominantly on the basis of perception, without the support or intervention of thc spelling. In order to do that, articulatory, acoustic and statistical analyses of a perception experiment conducted as a part of research in preparation for this paper will be presented.

The experimental set-up

The participants of the experiment were 32 native speakers of Polish residing in Podkarpacie. They were divided into four groups depending on their level of English.

Group 1 – E_0 (i.e. no command in English) (n=10)
Group 2 – E_1 (i.e. communicative English) (n=10)
Group 3 – E_2 (i.e. intermediate English (n=6)
Group 4 – E_3 (i.e. advanced English (n=6)

The stimuli were a set of 83 words (see the Appendix) and phrases containing instances of AE dark [ɫ] and AE taps or flaps in a variety of phonetic contexts. The stimuli were divided into two sets. Set 1 (1-17) contained actual Polamer forms, i.e. words used by Polamer speakers, whereas set 2 (18-83) contained mostly lexical gaps. That division allows one to see the difference (if there is any) between the perception of the two sets. The stimuli were recorded and digitised at a recording studio. The speaker whose voice was used for the recording was a native speaker of American English permanently living in Chicago, temporarily residing in Poland.

---

[12] The change: the dark [ɫ] → [w][u][l] is reported in Dubisz (1997, 246)

[13] The terminology adopted in this paper follows that used in both Ladefoged (1975, 147) and Kreidler (1989, 109). The term "tap" is used for the intervocalic realisation of the phonemes /t/ and /d/ in North American English e.g. in "latter" or "water", whereas the notion of "a flap" is reserved for cases in which the sequence of letters -rt- is sounded as "a forward flap of the tongue-tip against the alveolar ridge." (Kreidler 1989, 109)

[14] The change: tap → [r] is reported in Dubisz (1997, 244)

[15] The forms may also be referred to as "second-hand English" (Gonet, W., pers.comm)

The rationale behind the choice of the dark [ɫ] and a tap for the experiment is that those two segments have no direct equivalents in contemporary Polish. A tap is similar to the Polish /r/ phoneme, whereas the dark [ɫ] is close to an allophone of the Polish phoneme /l/ used in the past but not used very often nowadays (Jassem 1976, 94). The assumption is that if there is any correlation between the listener's competence in a foreign language and his/her perception of a foreign segment then his/her knowledge of that foreign language - and especially its spelling - should have influence on the perception of its sounds.[16] In that case, the participants' perception of the stimuli should depend on both their command of English and on whether the words listened to are actual Polamer forms or lexical gaps. Hence, knowing that taps are spelled either with a "t" or a "d" should shift their perception towards that of [d]. In order for that to happen, a person's level of English should be high enough for him/her to know the spelling of words used in the recording. A similar reasoning applies to the dark [ɫ]. For a person of sufficient knowledge of the English spelling, its perception should, statistically speaking, shift towards [l], whereas for somebody who has never studied English it should alternate between [w], [u] and [ɔ].

Each word was played twice with an interval of about 3 seconds between playings. The cassette-player used was Sony CFD-G30L. The participants listened to the recording in small groups in quiet classrooms without any sound reverberation. Before the actual experiment, the listeners were played five trial forms to make them acquainted with the timbre of the speaker's voice on the one hand, and establish a comfortable listening volume on the other.

Before the experiment, the listeners were handed out questionnaires and asked to complete them. The questionnaires consisted of two parts. Part 1 contained questions about the participants' age, command of English, sex and whether they had ever been to the USA. Part 2 contained questions referring to the perception of the stimuli. After two or three minutes, the experiment proper started and the listeners were asked to write down in special boxes what they could hear. Since the persons taking part in the experiment did not know phonetic transcription, they wrote everything using Polish letters, which was sufficient to decide whether the percept was spelling-supported (i.e. "t" / "d" for taps and "l" for the dark

[16] Haugen (1950, 223) states that "Spelling pronunciations may be suspected wherever the reproduction varies from normal in the direction of a pronunciation traditionally given to a letter in the borrowing language (...)."

[ɫ]) or purely perception-based (i.e "r" for taps, "ł" / "u" / "o" for the dark [ɫ]). Completing both parts of the questionnaires lasted about 20 minutes.

Acoustic and articulatory analysis

The analysis of the questionnaires reveals that the participants perceived the dark [ɫ] in several different ways. Those ways can be classified into two groups – consonantal and non-consonantal. The consonantal set refers to the consonant [l] whereas the non-consonantal one contains three elements: [ɔ], [u] and [w].

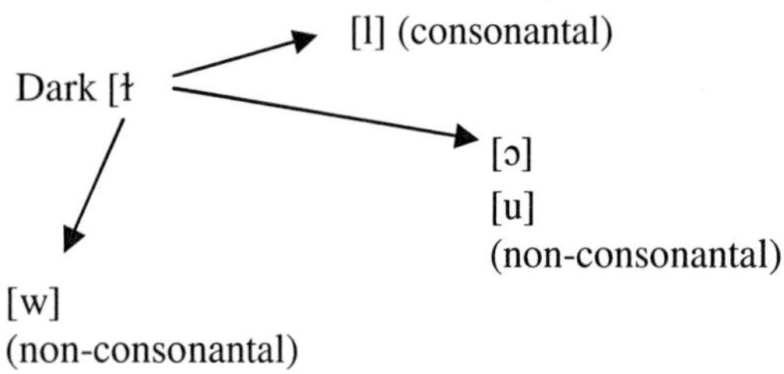

From the perspective of articulation, the English dark [ɫ] is similar to a sound used by the older generations or actors – the difference lies in the place of articulation the Polish sound being dental and the English sound alveolar (Jassem 1976; 94 translation mine). The basic difference between the clear and dark [ɫ], is that, in the velarized variant, there is an additional place of articulation at the back of the oral cavity formed by the dorsum of the tongue rising towards the velum (Davenport and Hannahs 1998, 32). That movement of the back of the tongue "can be considered as the addition of an [u]-like tongue position, but without the addition of the lip rounding (...)" (Ladefoged 1975, 208).

Fig.5 contains spectrograms of three words: zill [ˈz ɪ ɫ] (English), zył [ˈz ɨ w] (Polish), and zyl [ˈz ɨ l] (Polish). A number of acoustic similarities between [w] and [ɫ], on the one hand, and differences between [w]/[ɫ] and [l], on the other hand, can be observed. Firstly, F2 goes down in [ɫ] and [w], whilst it is steady in [l]. For clear [l], the value of F2 ranges from 1200 to 1800Hz, whereas for the dark [ɫ] it is about 700 Hz (Jassem 1983, 225). Secondly, F3 has a pronounced movement up in [ɫ] and a gentle one in [w]; for [l], however, it is level. A very important similarity amongst the three segments is located in F1 – for all three of them, it is steady at about

400Hz (Jassem 1973, 218). Additionally, in laterals there is an anti-formant located in the region of 3500Hz-4500Hz (Jassem 1973, 218).

Figure 5. The spectrograms of the words [ˈzɪł][ˈzɨw][ˈzɨl]

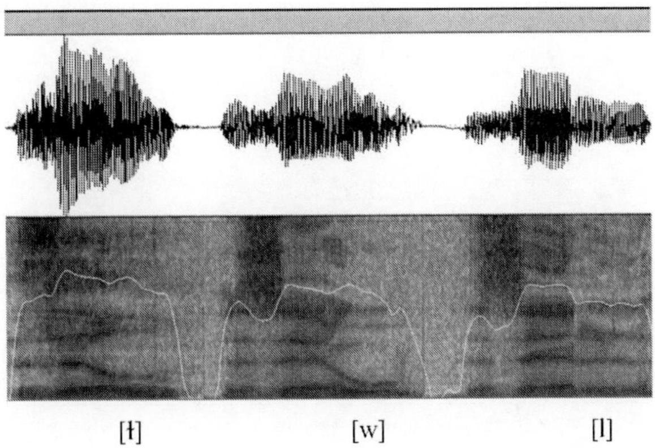

The listeners identified their perceptions of a tap as either [r] or [d].

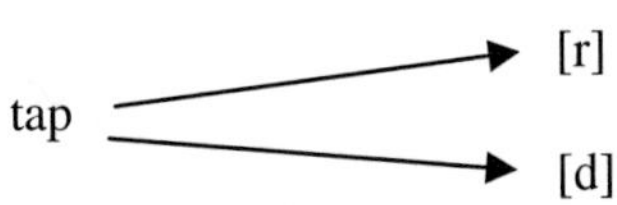

From the point of view of articulation, in a tap, "the tongue-tip brushes quickly against the alveolar ridge rather than being held there long enough for air pressure to build up behind the tongue as in the usual articulation of a stop" (Kreidler 1989, 109). Similarly, Ladefoged (1975, 147) defines a tap as a segment which "is caused by a single contraction of the muscles so that one articulator is thrown against another. It is simply a very rapid articulation of a stop closure". In Polish, the alveolar /r/ can be realized as a trill consisting of a number of vocalic and consonantal elements (Jassem 1974, 117, transl. mine) However, in careless articulation, the Polish phoneme /r/ may be realized as a tap, e.g. kara, pora, as in British English (very, hurry) (Jassem 1971, 260, transl. mine).

Fig. 6 shows spectrograms of three words – maddy [ˈmæɾi](English), medi [ˈmɛdi](Polish), meri [ˈmɛɾi] (Polish). Acoustically speaking, there are both differences and similarities between the sounds. Let us discuss the differences first.

Figure 6. The spectrograms of the words [ˈmæɾi][ˈmɛdi][ˈmɛri]

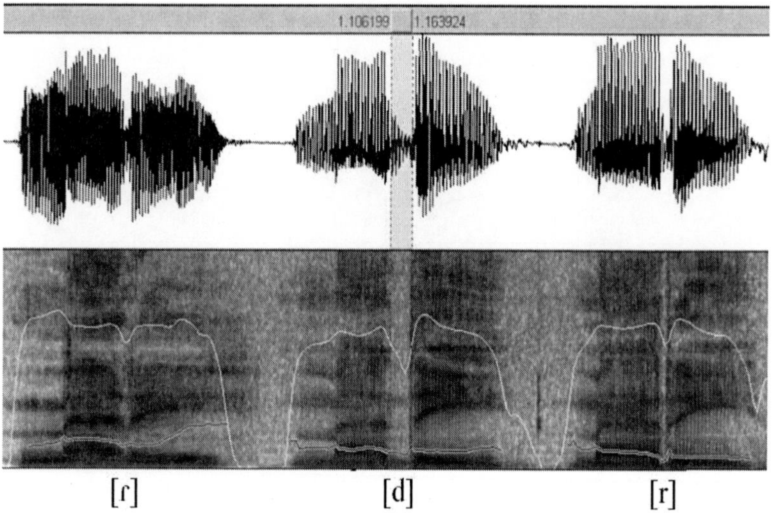

Firstly, the duration of the sounds varies – the Polish [d] (approximately 60ms in this case) is much longer than a tap or the Polish [r] (approximately 20ms). Secondly, a drop in intensity is much greater for the Polish [d] than for either a tap or the Polish [r][17]. Thirdly, the formants end before the Polish [d] and resume after it; there is continuity of formants for both a tap and [r], however. The most important similarities between the three sounds refer to F1 and F2. Whereas F1 is steady in all the cases, F2 goes down before the segment and goes up after the segment.

Statistical analysis

The statistical analysis of the data collected from the questionnaires can be divided into a number of stages. Firstly a normality-of-distribution test will be run to decide whether a parametric or non-parametric technique should be used. Secondly, certainty must be made that the differences between the sets of the listeners' results are not random, i.e. come from factors other than pure chance. Thirdly, an analysis of correlation using correlation coeffcients will be conducted. Fourthly, an

---

[17] The common feature of all variants of the Polish phoneme /r/ is a momentary weakening of the spectrum which lasts about 20-30 ms (Jassem 1974, 117)

interpretation of the results of the analysis will be provided taking into consideration a number of psychological factors.

In order to analyse the data gathered from the study, the dataset has been divided into sixteen subsets. The number sixteen comes from two variables (the level of English-four levels, the set of words-4 levels). There are four levels in the second variable because each dataset contains both the list of actual words used in Polamer and lexical gaps recorded especially for the experiment. One must not forget, however, that there are two datasets due to the fact that the perception of two sounds (1. the dark [ɫ], 2. a tap) was investigated in the study. The total calculation gives us 4x4, hence, sixteen subsets of data.

An examination using the Wilkinson-Shapiro test revealed that about half the subsets do not meet the criterion of the normal distribution which is a necessary condition for the application of any parametric method. As a result, the analysis will be based on non-parametric techniques.

A method selected to make sure whether the observed values are the result of participants' varying command of English or merely chance is the Mann-Whitney test. Its results show that, at the level of $p \leq 0.005$, all the subsets can be stated to come from different populations. Hence, the differences between the sets are not random.

The analysis of the data in order to specify whether the differences in values as a function of the type of the set (lexical gaps vs actual Polamer words) cannot be conducted using the Mann-Whitney test because the test should not be used for correlated pairs[18], and this would be the situation in this case. We need to see whether the pairs of values from each and every listener for both types of sets are the result of random factors or not. In order to achieve that goal, a method which analyses the differences between correlated sets has to be used. The technique chosen here is the Wilcoxon test. Its results reveal that, at the level of $p \leq 0.005$, it can be stated that the subsets come from different populations. Hence, the differences between them are not random.

Since the requirement of the normality of distribution is not met, the analysis has to rely on the non-parametric methods of testing correlation. The two most popular ones are the Spearman's 'r' and Kendall's tau.[19] [20] Table 2 provides the values of both the coeffcients for the four sets of data.

---

[18] Clegg (1994, 89)

[19] Both the coeffcients are provided due to the fact that, Spearman's r, although quite popular, is theoretically incorrect (Zimny 2007, 171)

[20] Both the coeffcients refer to a monotonic relation between the data sets

Table 2. The values of Kendall's Tau and Spearman's R.

SET	KENDALL'S TAU	SPEARMAN'S R
DARK [ɫ] - 1	- 0.81 p<.05	- 0.87 p<.05
DARK [ɫ] - 2	- 0.65 p<.05	- 0.69 p<.05
TAP - 1	- 0.64 p<.05	- 0.76 p<.05
TAP - 2	- 0.50 p<.05	- 0.64 p<.05

DARK [ɫ] - 1 – a set of the actual Polamer words containing the dark [ɫ]
DARK [ɫ] - 2 – a set of the lexical gaps containing the dark [ɫ]
TAP – 1 - a set of the actual Polamer words containing a tap
TAP – 2 - a set of the lexical gaps containing a tap

As can be seen from table 2, all the coefficients are negative. This indicates that the higher the level of English, the lower the number of non-consonantal perceptions of the dark [ɫ] on the one hand, and of [r] perceptions of a tap on the other. It results from the fact that knowledge of English increases the learner's awareness of English spelling, and that awareness influences his or her perception. In other words, if a listener's level of English is advanced, his or her knowledge of the English spelling will, statistically speaking, have influence on him/her so that, listening to American taps, what he or she is actually perceiving is not anything similar to the Polish [r], but rather something close to the segment [d] because the letter "d" is one of the ways that a tap is symbolised in the spelling. A similar conclusion can be drawn from the results referring to the dark [ɫ]. The most common spelling of that segment is the letter "l"; hence, a Polish person whose English is very good will be more prone to perceive it as a [l] segment, whereas a participant who has no command of English whatsoever will, statistically speaking, perceive it as [w], [ɔ] or [u]. Another regularity which can be inferred from table 2 is that, in all the cases, the correlation for Polamer words is stronger than the correlation for lexical gaps. A possible interpretation of that observation is that Polamer words and lexical gaps are differently processed by the participants. The former seem to exert considerable influence on the perception of the groups above a no-English level, whereas the latter appear to be indicating 'pure' perception with an insignificant effect of spelling-based distortion. Hence, the relation between the level of English and the number of non-consonantal perceptions for the dark [ɫ] and [r]-perceptions for a tap is much stronger for Polamer words than for lexical gaps. The explanation above seems to be confirmed by an examination of the diagrams in Figures 1-4, which illustrate the mean numbers of non-consonantal perceptions of the dark [ɫ] and [r]-perceptions of a tap, expressed in percentage terms.

Figure 1.The non-consonantal perception of [ɫ] in Polamer words as a function of the level of English.

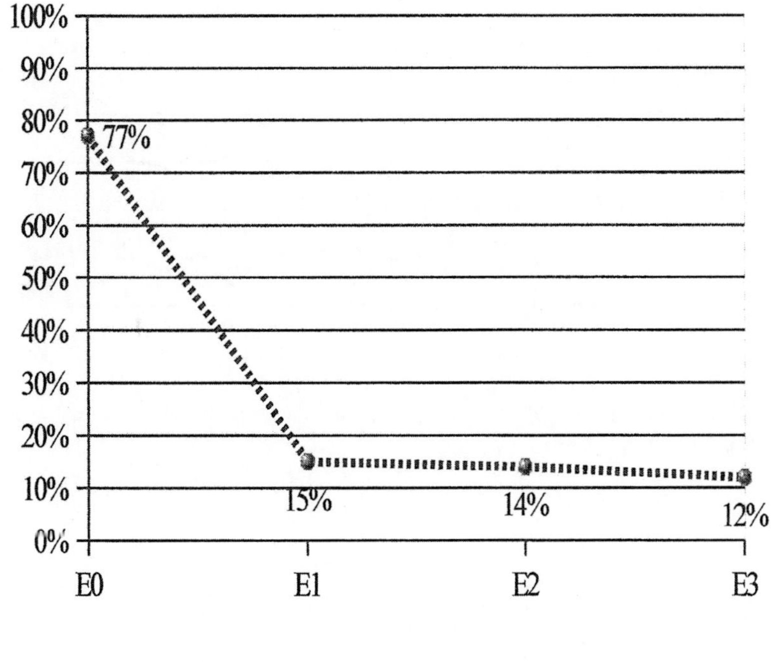

Figure 2. The non-consonantal perception of [ɫ] in lexical gaps as a function of the level of English.

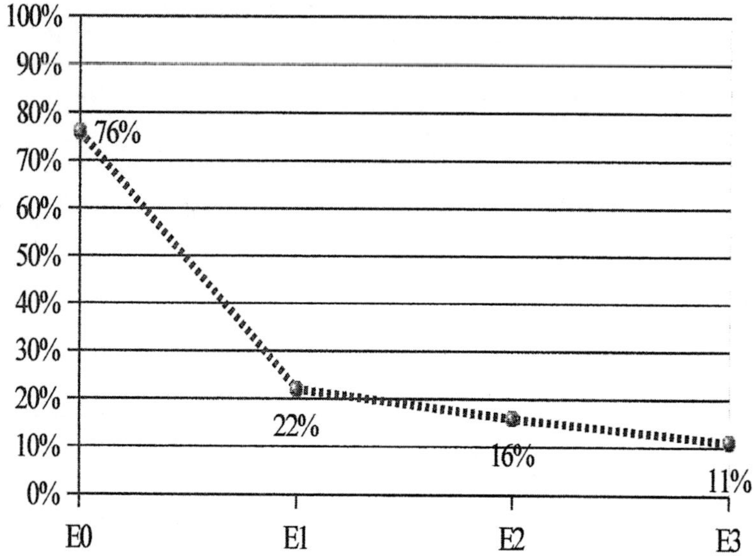

Figure 3. [r]-perception of the American tap in Polamer words as a function of the level of English.

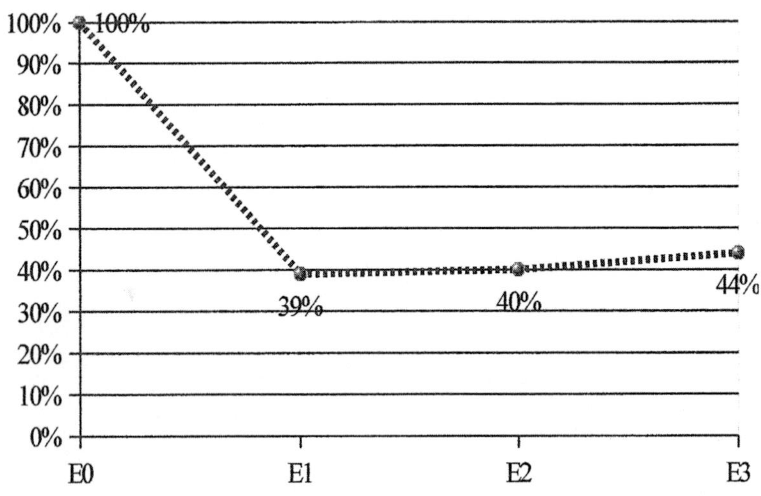

Figure 4.[r]-perception of the American tap in lexical gaps as a function of the level of English.

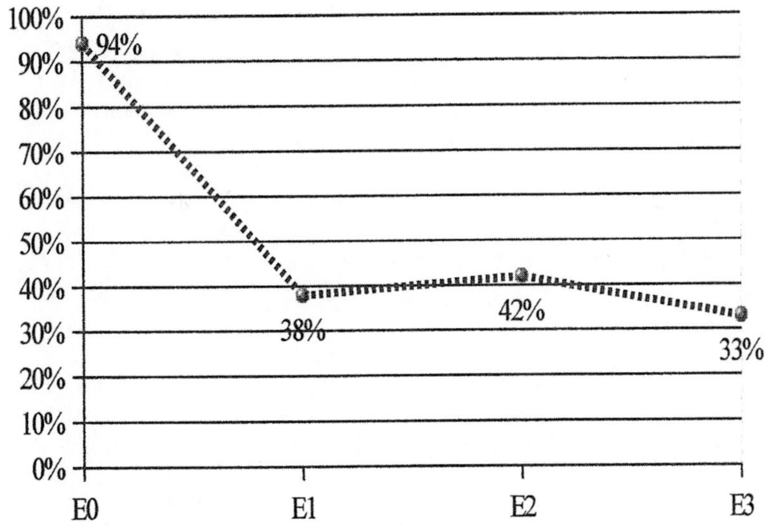

As can be seen, the part of the diagram between E_0 and E_1 on the absissa falls much more steeply in the case of Polamer words than for the lexical gaps for both the dark [ɫ] set (77% →15% vs 76%→22%) and the words containing a tap (100%→39% vs 94%→38%).

In a perception study like the one described here, psychology may play, if not a crucial, then a significant role. It may, for example, affect the very classification of participants in groups. It is not very common for an experimenter to know each listener's level of English precisely. An ideal situation is when one has enough information about the people taking part in the experiment beforehand, and there is no need for additional classificatory questions. Unfortunately, it is not always so. In consequence, a researcher has to rely on the answers from the questionnaires. Very often the subjective nature of the terms used in the questionnaire may be a bit confusing. If a participant of a study states that his or her level of English is intermediate, we assume that he/she knows the difference between elementary, intermediate and advanced, and consciously qualifies his/her knowledge as intermediate. But then, an ambitious person whose English is elementary might overrate it and say it is intermediate. A person whose English is intermediate, but who believes it qualifies as advanced, may state it so. In view of this, the very classification of participants into groups on the basis of their own assessment should be treated with caution and considered ordinal, not numerical. Hence, the assumption which has been introduced into the statistical analysis that the no-English level is numerically equal to zero, the elementary level is equal to one, the intermediate level is equal to two, and the advanced level to four is a useful shortcut which is appropriate for an ordinal analysis only. The coefficients in the table may only be compared with one another, but their actual numerical values are of secondary importance.

Another instance of the human factor in the study may be observed in the answers proper and refers to the advanced group. Some of its members have some knowledge of phonetics and know, or at least feel, what element is being studied. A question referring to a tap which the author has been asked by the members of that group on several occasions is the following: "I can clearly hear a [d], but I know that this sound is articulated in American English as something close to [r], so is this what you're expecting me to put down?" Consequently, some of the listeners would write down 'r', in spite of the fact that they could clearly hear a [d]. Paradoxically then, both the no-English and advanced groups would provide similar answers but for completely different reasons.

General discussion and conclusions

The above articulatory and acoustic facts clearly show that the dark [ɫ] and a tap have, acoustically speaking, a lot in common with /w/, /ɔ/, /u/ and the Polish /r/, respectively. The conclusion which can be drawn from the statistical analysis is that the better a person's command in the foreign language, the more his or her perception of a foreign segment is likely to be drawn in the direction of the letter used to symbolise the segment in the spelling, and away from the actual percept relying on the signal only[21]. Historical sources state that a significant number of Polish immigrants crossing the Atlantic at the presumed period of the creation of the first Polamer forms not only did not speak English but were often illiterate in their own mother tongue. Hence, it seems logical to claim that Polamer forms must have been created on the basis of pure perception, without any intervention of the spelling. The examples of Polamer forms cited at the beginning of the paper, in which /w/, /ɔ/, /u/ are substituted for the dark [ɫ]

---

[21] Vendelin and Peperkamp (2006, 1004-1005) observe that "loanword adaptations are influenced by orthography". The authors go on to say that "(...) the data on which most phonological and phonetic analyses of adaptation patterns are based can be contaminated by the influence of orthography".

and /r/ for a tap, seem to confirm that conclusion. Moreover, the above analysis can be corroborated by quoting instances of similar processes happening in the speech of the Polish communities living in Canada (examples 1-3, see table 3) and Australia (example 4, see table 3)

Table 3. Illustrations of the dark [l] changed into [w] in the English used by the Polish communities in Canada and Australia.

English spelling	Phonetic transcription	Original spelling in the source	source
1.summerfal	['sãmɛrfaw]	sommerfał	Członkowska 1981, 158
2.principal	[pr̃ɨn'cɨpaw]	principał	Członkowska 1981, 160
3.baseball	['bɛzbɔw]	bezboł	Członkowska 1981: 161
4. Angle?(unclear)	['ãŋgɔw]	angoł	Dolański 1981, 115

An additional consequence of the processes indicated above is the existence of variants in standard Polish, on the one hand, and Polamer, on the other hand. Three such variants are included in table 4.

Table 4. Variants of words in standard Polish and Polamer.

English spelling	Standard Polish	Polamer
saloon	Salon [ʻsalɔ̃n]	Salun [ʻsalũn]
sample	sample [ʻsãmplɛ]	Sample[ʻsɛ̃mpɔw]
party	party ['partɨ]	pary ['parɨ]

APPENDIX

1. SAMPLE ['sæmpɫ]

2. LABEL ['leɪbɫ]

3. LEVEL ['levɫ]

4. SAW-ZALL ['sɑ:zɑ:ɫ]

5. DRYWALL ['dɹaɪwɫ]

6. CABLE ['keɪbɫ]

7. SCHEDULE ['skeʤɫ]

8. TITLE ['taɪɾɫ]

9.DAUGHTER ['dɑ:ɾɚ]

10.THIRTY ['θɝ:ɾi]

11.WATER ['wɑ:ɾɚ]

12.DIRTY ['dɝ:ɾi]

13.PARTY ['pɑ:ɾi]

14.I DON'T KNOW [aɾɔ'noʊ]

15.GET OUT OF HERE [ge'ɾaʊdəfhɪɹ]

16.WHATEVER [wɑ:'ɾevɚ]

17.SHUT UP [ʃʌ'ɾʌp]

18.BEEDER ['bi:ɾɚ]

19.SITTER ['sɪɾɚ]

20.METTER ['meɾɚ]

21.GATTER ['gæɾɚ]

22.DURTER ['dɝ:ɾɚ]

23.BUDDER ['bʌɾɚ]

24.ODDER ['ɑ:ɾɚ]

25.PORDER ['pɔ:ɾɚ]

26.FOODER ['fu:ɾɚ]

27.FOOTER 'fʊɾɚ]

28.FEETY ['fi:ɾi]

29.DITTY ['dɪɾi]

30.HETTY ['heɾi]

31.MATTY ['mæɾi]

32.LURTY ['lɝ:ɾi]

33.GUDDY ['gʌɾi]

34.CODDY ['kɑ:ɾi]

35.PORDY ['pɔ:ɾi]

36.BOOTY ['bu:ɾi]

37.FOOTY ['fʊɾi]

38.BEAL ['bi:ɫ]

39.ZILL ['zɪ ɫ]

40.JELL ['ʤ eɫ]

41.FAL ['fæɫ]

42.RULL ['ɹʌɫ]

43.NOLL ['nɑ:ɫ]

44.TOOL ['tu :ɫ]

45.PULL ['pʊɫ]

46.CHITTLE ['ʧɪ ɾɫ]

47.BADDLE ['bæɾɫ]

48.BAMPLE ['bæmpɫ]

49.RABBLE ['ɹæbɫ]

50.SEEGIL ['si:gɫ]

51.RACKLE ['ɹækɫ]

52.RENCIL ['ɹensɫ]

53.ROOZIL ['ɹu :zɫ]

54.MAFLE ['mæfɫ]

55.FIVIL ['fɪvɫ]

56.ROTHLE ['ɹɑ:θɫ]

57.BATHLE ['beɪðɫ]

58.BASHEL ['bæʃɫ]

59.BEISUAL ['beɪʒɫ]

60.ROCHILL ['ɹ:ʧɫ]

61.MAJILL ['meɪʤɫ]

62.RENNEL ['ɹenɫ]

63.SIMMLE ['sɪmɫ]

64.SOYAL ['sɔɪəɫ]

65.MEURAL ['mju:ɹɫ]

66.FOOWIL ['fu :wəɫ]

67.MOONGIL ['mu:ŋgɫ]

68.FELP ['fe ɫp]
69.GULB ['gʌɫb]
70.SELT ['se ɫt]
71.ZOOLD ['zu:ɫd]
72.CHILK ['ʧɪ ɫk]
73.LILG ['lɪɫg]
74.KILS ['kɪ ɫs]
75.RELZ ['ɹe ɫz]
76.KELF ['keɫf]
77.MELV ['meɫv]
78.SOOLTH ['su :ɫθ]
79.MELTHE ['m eɫð]
80.MELCH ['m eɫʧ]
81.GULJ ['gʌɫʤ]
82.BILN ['bɪ ɫn]
83.SEALM ['seɫm]

Bibliography

Baugh, A., and T. Cable. 1994. *A History of the English Language*. London: Routledge.

Blalock, H. 1977. *Statystyka dla Socjologów*. Warszawa: Państwowe Wydawnictwo Naukowe.

Członkowska, H. 1981. "Elementy angielskie w języku „Pamiętników emigrantów w Kanadzie." In *Z Badań Nad Językiem Polskim Środowisk Emigranckich,* edited by S. Szliferszteјn,149-173. Wrocław: Zakład Narodowy Imienia Ossolińskich.

Clegg, F. 1994. *Po Prostu Statystyka*. Warszawa: Wydawnictwa Szkolne i Pedagogiczne.

Dejna, K. 1973. *Dialekty Polskie*. Wrocław: Zakład Narodowy Imienia Ossolińskich.

—. 1981. *Atlas Innowacji Dialektalnych*. Warszawa: Państwowe Wydawnictwo Naukowe.

Dolański, B. 1981. *Trzy epoki z życia mego czyli wyjazd do Australii, tamże mój pobyt i powrót do Europy*. Kraków: Wydawnictwo Literackie.

Dubisz, S. 1981. "Formy i typy funkcjonalnej adaptacji leksemów w dialekcie polonijnym Nowej Anglii (USA)." In *Z Badań Nad Językiem Polskim Środowisk Emigranckich,* edited by S. Szliferszteјn, 51-68. Wrocław: Zakład Narodowy Imienia Ossolińskich.

—. 1997. "Język Polski Poza Granicami Kraju-Próba Charakterystyki Kontrastowej." In *Najnowsze dzieje polszczyzny. Język Polski poza granicami Kraju*, edited by S. Dubisz, 324-376. Wrocław: Zakład Narodowy im. Ossolińskich.

—. 1997. Polonia i Jej Język w Stanach Zjednoczonych Ameryki Północnej. In *Najnowsze dzieje polszczyzny. Język Polski poza granicami kraju.*, edited by S. Dubisz, 237-262. Wrocław: Zakład Narodowy im. Ossolińskich.

Fry, D. 2001. *The Physics of Speech*. Cambridge: CUP.

Gruchmanowa, M. 2003. *Gwary w Ojczyźnie i na Obczyźnie*. Poznań: Wydawnictwo Poznańskich Studiów Polonistycznych.

Haugen, E. 1950. "The analysis of Linguistic Borrowing." *Language* 26: 210-231.

Jasscm, W. 1971. *Podręcznik Wymowy Angielskiej*. Warszawa: Państwowe Wydawnictwa Naukowe.

—. 1973. *Podstawy Fonetyki Akustycznej*. Warszawa: Państwowe Wydawnictwa Naukowe.

—. 1974. *Mowa a nauka o łączności*. Warszawa: Państwowe Wydawnictwa Naukowe.

—. 1976. *Fonetyka języka angielskiego*. Warszawa: Państwowe Wydawnictwa Naukowe.

—. 1983. *The Phonology of Modern English*. Warszawa: Państwowe Wydawnictwa Naukowe.

Kołodziej, E. 1998. Emigracja z ziem polskich od końca XIX w. do zasów współczesnych i tworzenie się skupisk polonijnych. In *Emigracja z Ziem Polskich w XX Wieku,*edited by A. Koseski 1998, 11-24. Pułtusk: Wyższa Szkoła Humanistyczna w Pułtusku.

Kreidler, C. 1989. *The Pronunciation of English. A Course Book in Phonology*. Oxford: Basil Blackwell.

Ladefoged, P. 1975. *A Course in Phonetics*. New York: Harcourt Brace Jovanovich, Inc.

Laver, J. 1994. *Principles of Phonetics*. Cambridge: CUP.

Nitsch, K. 1960. *Wybór Polskich Tekstów Gwarowych*. Warszawa: Państwowe Wydawnictwo Naukowe.

Pilch, A. 1984. *Emigracja z ziem polskich w czasach nowożytnych i Najnowszych (XVIII-XXw).*Warszawa: Państwowe Wydawnictwa Naukowe.

Strybel, M. 1990. Teksty Polonijne Z Bay City. In *Wybór Tekstów Polonijnych.*, edited by S. Dubisz 1990, 77-107. Wrocław: ZakładNarodowy im. Ossolińskich.

Urbańczyk, S. 1962. *Zarys dialektologii polskiej*. Warszawa: Państwowe Wydawnictwo Naukowe.

Vendelin, I., and S. Peperkamp. 2006. "The influence of orthography on loanword adaptations." *Lingua* 116 (2006): 996-1007.

van Gelderen, E. 2006. *A History of the English Language*. Amsterdam: John Benjamins Publishing Company.

Wierzchowska, B. 1980. *Fonetyka I Fonologia Języka Polskiego*. Wrocław: Zakład Narodowy Imienia Ossolińskich.

Żak-Pławska, B. 1981. O dzisiejszym języku polskim w USA(na

podstawie korespondencji nadesłanej do Polskiego Radia). In *Z Badań Nad Językiem Polskim Środowisk Emigranckich,* edited by S. Szlifersztejn, 69-130. Wrocław: Zakład Narodowy Imienia Ossolińskich.
http://www.emigrantletters.com

INTERNAL VOWEL ALTERNATION AS CLASSIFICATION IN NOMINAL AND VERBAL SYSTEMS IN ENGLISH ACCORDING TO THE THEORY OF PHONOLOGY AS HUMAN BEHAVIOUR

ELENA EVEN-SIMKIN AND YISHAI TOBIN
BEN-GURION UNIVERSITY OF THE NEGEV

> Irregular verbs are a historical vestige, but so are the regular verbs (so is everything in language). That does not stop the irregular verbs from being rule-governed and meaningful synchronically, if we can only find the rule(s) and the meaning(s).
>
> —Beedham (2005, 112)

> …my own view is that the irregularity of the irregular verbs is an artefact of an incorrect analysis, and that they are in reality regular if we could only find the rule or rules by which they are formed… .
>
> —Beedham (2002, 346)

Abstract

Internal Vowel Alternation (IVA) is a morphophonemic process found in many Indo-European, Semitic and other language families. In Modern English, however, IVA appears in a very limited number of forms which are, therefore, commonly referred to as being "irregular" Noun Plurals (e.g. '*goose-geese*', '*mouse-mice*') and "irregular" Past Tense verb forms (e.g. '*sing-sang*', '*take-took*'). Historically, however, as in other Germanic languages, IVA was a prevalent and productive process in Old English in both nominal and verbal systems. Furthermore, it was possible to distinguish nominal versus verbal forms by the opposed phonological processes they displayed in their IVA: nominal forms underwent a kind of *fronting process* while, conversely, verbal forms underwent a kind of *backing process*. We will present both the so-called irregular nouns and verbs with

IVA that survived in Modern English as well as their original Old English forms. The data indicate that IVA still maintains its systematic nature in Modern English despite the historical phonological changes that have occurred in the language. This means that today we can still distinguish phonologically between nominal and verbal forms with IVA by the same historically opposed phonological processes of *fronting* versus *backing*. We will show further that some of the additional so-called irregular IVA verb forms today that originally were "weak—ed" verbs, i.e., were not derived from the IVA verbs in Old English (that historically were referred to as "strong" verbs), nevertheless, still conform to the phonological process of *backing* that characterizes the IVA verb system in English. This provides further evidence for the systematic backing of IVA verbs in English over time. Therefore, this paper supports a sign-oriented analysis which defines language as a "system of systems composed of various sub-systems … which are organized internally and systematically related to each other and used by human beings to communicate" (Tobin 1990, 47).

1. Introduction

Internal Vowel Alternation (IVA) is a morphophonemic process prevalent in many Indo-European, Semitic and other language families. In Modern English, however, it appears in a very limited number of forms which are, therefore, commonly referred to as being “irregular” Noun Plurals (e.g. '*goose-geese*', '*mouse-mice*') and “irregular” Past Tense verb forms (e.g. '*sing-sang*', '*take-took*'). In this paper we analyse the IVA in both "irregular" nominal and verbal forms in English. However, in Old English, like in other Germanic languages, IVA was a prevalent and productive process in both the nominal and the verbal systems and we claim that all the IVA forms were part of a larger system.

Furthermore, it was possible to distinguish nominal versus verbal forms by the opposed phonological processes they displayed in their IVA: nominal forms underwent a kind of *fronting process* of different degrees, while, conversely, verbal forms underwent a kind of *backing process* of varied degrees as well. We will present both the so-called irregular nouns and verbs with IVA that survived in Modern English as well as their original Old English forms. The data indicate that IVA still maintains its systematic nature in Modern English despite the historical phonological changes that have occurred in the language. This means that today we can still distinguish phonologically between nominal and verbal forms with IVA by the same historical polar phonological processes of *fronting* versus *backing*. We will show further that there are some additional so-called irregular IVA verb forms today that originally were "weak—ed" (also called consonantal verbs): i.e., that were not derived from the IVA verbs in Old English (historically referred to as "strong"[1] (*ablaut-vocalic* verbs). For example, verbs like '*ring*', '*stick*', '*wear*', etc., though in Modern English are part of the IVA system, following Emerson's (1910) historical study of the English language, originally belonged to the "weak" class of verbs, i.e. to the *consonantal* verbs. Nevertheless, these particular historically "weak" verbs that are now IVA verbs still conform to the phonological process of *backing* that characterizes the IVA verb system in English. This provides further evidence for the systematic *backing* of IVA verbs in English over time.

In this paper we will examine the phonological aspects of the IVA system in English according to the Sign-Oriented linguistic theory in general (e.g. Saussure [1916] 1959, 1983) and the Columbia School (CS) in particular (e.g. Contini-Morava and Sussman-Goldberg 1995; Contini-Morava et al. 2004; Contini-Morava and Tobin 2000; Davis et al. 2006; Diver 1975, 1995; Klein-Andreu 1983; Reid et al. 2002; Tobin 1990, 1993a,b, 1994) and the phonological component of CS theory *Phonology As Human Behaviour* (PHB) (e.g. Diver 1979, 1993; Davis 1987[1984]; Tobin 1997, 2009).

PHB was developed within the larger framework of the CS by William Diver (1979) in his study of initial consonant clusters in English expanded to Italian (Davis 1987[1984]) and then to almost fifty languages from seven different language families (Tobin 2002). Diver (1993, 1995) and Davis (1987[1984]) expanded their analyses of initial consonant clusters in English and Italian to the entire combinatory phonological systems of these languages as well. PHB then has been further applied to diverse aspects of the combinatory phonological systems of other languages (e.g. Hebrew, Arabic, Latin, Urdu, Hungarian, Japanese, Old Church Slavonic, Old and Modern Russian, Byelorussian, Portuguese, Ladino, Spanish and French). In addition, PHB has been extended to a wide range of clinical and developmental phonological and prosodic phenomena in several languages (e.g. Hebrew, Spanish, Japanese, Polish and English). In all of the above studies the common denominator underlying the theory of PHB is to analyse the sound systems of language and the non-random distribution of sounds in language from the synergetic point of view of achieving *maximum communication with minimal effort,* taking into account the different roles of encoders and decoders needed to produce

[1] The terms "weak" versus "strong" for the so-called regular versus irregular verbs in Modern English, respectively, was introduced by Jacob Grimm (Prokosch 1938, 159-60, Smith 2009, 122).

efficient communication. Indeed, the most important contribution of CS-PHB theory is in providing "an explanation for the distribution within the speech signal: i.e., it tells us why the distribution of phonemes within a language is not random but motivated"(Tobin 2006, 64).

The goal of this paper is to uncover the underlying phonological system of the nominal and verbal forms containing IVA in a diachronic analysis comparing these opposed IVA systems from the point of view of their forms (*signifiants)* in Old and Modern English. We would like to add that in our research we have also uncovered common semantic denominators (semantic fields sharing similar *signifiés*) for each sub-system of IVA for both the nominal and the verbal forms (Even-Simkin and Tobin 2011, Even-Simkin 2011). However, in this paper, we will primarily focus on the phonological aspects of the IVA sign system in English.

The CS-PHB sign-oriented or semiotic approach to language originally defined language as:

> A system of systems composed of various sub-systems (revolving around the notion of the linguistic sign) which are organized internally and systematically related to each other and used by human beings to communicate. (Tobin 1990, 47)

The above definition is inspired by Ferdinand de Saussure (1959/[1916]), who is generally considered to be the father of modern semiotics and linguistics. According to Tobin (1990, 37-38), Saussure wanted to replace the traditional grammatical and sentence-oriented categories by the linguistic sign which he placed in the forefront of language research because, for him, language was:

> …intrinsically linked to the concept of the linguistic sign which does not separate form from meaning and which functions as part of systematic structure. (Tobin 1990, 35)
>
> Not unsurprisingly, de Saussure's concept of the linguistic sign directly reflects his view of language: a unit where the sound (or signal) in the form of concrete morphological forms or more abstract zero morphology or word order (the *signifiant* or 'signifier') is inseparably united with a concept in the form of an invariant meaning (the *signifié* or 'signified'). (Tobin 1990, 39-40)

Thus, following sign-oriented CS-PHB theory, we view the phenomenon of IVA in English as a system of linguistic signs which reflects the revised CS definition that language may be viewed as a symbolic tool whose structure is shaped both by its communicative function (the *communication factor*) and by the characteristics of its users (the *human factor*) (Tobin 2009).

We claim that the IVA nominal and verbal systems reflect this semiotic and functional point of view because they are neither "irregular" nor random, but perform specific communicative functions that we contend were semantically motivated (the communication factor) and are systematically expressed by the individual forms found in the IVA phonological processes which can be efficiently identified, classified and remembered (the human factor). CS-PHB theory is based on the synergetic principle that language represents a constant struggle between the *communication* and the *human* factors: i.e., human beings striving to achieve maximum communication through the use of minimal effort by a trade-off or compromise between the opposed forces of both of these factors in language (Tobin 1997).

We will now reiterate the basic principles of the communication and human factors attributed to CS-PHB theory that are relevant to explain the IVA system (adapted from Tobin 1997, 19-20). By the communication factor we mean the creation of systematic, meaningful and distinct perceivable oppositions in the language system as they appear in the phonological processes of the IVA system. By the human factor we mean:

1. *Human intelligence*. Human beings can draw far-reaching abstract conclusions from minimally salient concrete cues through the cognitive process of inference: we infer (i.e., we can perceive the opposed *fronting* and *backing* processes and associate them with the nominal and verbal IVA systems respectively).
2. *Human efficiency*. Human beings invest minimal effort for maximal results in the semiotic communication process: by inferring the different invariant meanings associated with the common semantic denominators postulated for the different fronting nominal and backing verbal IVA forms.
3. *Memory limitations*. Human beings have large but limited memories that can be directly related to human intelligence and human efficiency. The IVA nominal and verbal systems can be easily perceived and distinguished phonologically and can be directly associated with and categorized by the specific communicative functions they perform, thus making them easier to remember within our limitations of memory.

The above principles of the CS-PHB theories underlie the analysis of the IVA nominal and verbal systems. In other words, we claim that it is the struggle to reach a compromise between the opposed forces of the communication and human factors that provides us with efficient communication. We maintain that both the non-random distribution of sounds in language as well as the non-random distribution of the linguistic signs in language are motivated and can be explained in terms of the axiom that: language represents the striving *to achieve maximum communication (the communication factor) with minimal effort (the human factor)* (Tobin 1997).

In this study we show and explain in terms of CS-PHB theory: why some Noun Plural forms and Past Tense forms are favoured over others and are, therefore, called "regular" or "irregular" in Modern English. Following this sign-oriented approach we postulate that it is possible to distinguish between IVA for nouns and verbs by their different phonological processes and further classify them by their common semantic denominators. These divergent phonological processes that are semantically motivated serve to distinguish between nominal versus verbal vowel alternation systems, thus making them easier to identify, acquire and retain: i.e., they are systematic.

2. "Irregular" versus "Regular" Nominal and Verbal Forms in English

The IVA nominal and verbal forms today are considered "irregular" because the rules of the IVA system are neither obvious nor transparent in Modern English contrary to the way they may have been in Old English. Thus, all of the so-called IVA-based irregular nouns and verbs are acquired today as random and individual lexical items (Kuczaj 1977, Pinker 1999, Pinker and Ullman 2002) despite the fact that they were part of a productive and prevalent paradigmatic system in Old English, the verbs of which have been clearly divided into seven subclasses of "strong" verbs (e.g. Quirk and Wrenn 1955, Baugh 1957, Hulbert 1963, Smith 2009, Lass and Anderson 2010[1975]). This transformation from a systematic grammatical system to an idiosyncratic lexical one has been the subject of much research. For example, in their research on first language acquisition, Plunkett and Marchman (1993) indicate the *multi-lateral pattern of errors*: i.e., the 'irregularization' of some "regular" known and novel forms and the overgeneralization or "regularization" of some "irregular" lexical and novel forms. Similarly, Marchman's (1997, 300) findings, in her study of school-aged children's productivity in the "irregular" versus "regular" Past Tense in English, "are consistent with the conclusion that the mechanisms underlying the productive use of regular and irregular patters are actually more similar than they are different". Moreover, Kuczaj's (1977) study of the "irregular" Past Tense forms, where he examines the spontaneous speech of pre-school-aged children, indicates the absence of incorrect IVA forms. Following Bybee and Slobin (1982, 266), such results "would be predicted if the child were formulating vowel-change rules, rather than learning rote forms". Plunkett and Joula's (1999) single-process model/network that handles the regular and irregular Past Tense inflection of verbs and Plural inflection of nouns in English, also indicates the absence of error in the initial performance of irregular forms including IVA. Moreover, Plunkett and Joula (1999, 486) also note that the "onset of over-regularization errors on nouns tends to occur earlier than overgeneralization errors on verbs in the network", which is most probably because the number of irregular nouns versus verbs is smaller and they are used more frequently (Marcus 1995). These studies imply that there may be some covert mechanism underlying the so-called irregular verbal Past Tense forms in addition to the overt mechanisms of the so-called regular formations composed of lexical item plus suffix, i.e. verb + past "ed". Moreover, the etymology of the so-called regular and irregular Past Tense formations, i.e. the fact that both "strong and weak verbs follow regular patterns or paradigms, called conjugations" (Smith 2009, 109) strengthens our prediction that the IVA forms in Past Tense inflection are not irregular patterns but rather grammatically structured forms. Furthermore, additional support for the systematic character of the so-called irregular Past Tense formation comes from Bybee's (2001, 110) study. Her findings of "the model developed in Bybee (1985, 1988a, 1995), along with the connectionist models (Rumelhart and McClelland 1986) and the analogical model (Skousen 1989, 1992), would claim that both regulars and irregulars are handled by the same storage and processing mechanisms."

In addition to Plunkett and Marchman's (1993) and Marchman's (1997) studies, it is important to point out the overwhelming *rule-like generalization* (lexical item + *-d/-s*) in Past Tense and Noun Plural formations with nonsense words proposed by Berko (1958) in her study of the acquisition of "irregular" and "regular" morphology by children. The further evidence for the remarkable tendency of the 'regularization' process in Past Tense formation in English is provided in Rumelhart and McClelland (1986), who suggest that children predominantly extend the suffixation system of the "regular" forms to the "irregular" ones. In sum, the results of Berko (1958) and Rumelhart and McClelland (1986) as well as of Marcus et al. (1992) and of the more recent studies by e.g. Albright and Hayes (2002) point out a preference by children to "regularize" "irregular" lexical and nonsense items rather than the reverse process. Indeed, this tendency of overwhelming *rule-like generalization* by children will be explained in terms of the principles of CS-PHB theory in Figures 1 and 2.

There have been other studies questioning the "irregularity" of the IVA verb forms. Hoard and Sloat (1973, 107) claim that "irregular … [verbs] are much more regular than they seem". They have proposed a small number of very abstract rules that partially define some vowel variations in the "strong" conjugation of verbs. However, in the opinion of most researchers, the precise phonological characteristics that exhaustively define the so-called irregular Past Tense class of verbs have not yet been proposed (e.g., Pinker and Prince (1988); Plunkett and Marchman (1993)). In the present analysis we provide the phonological characterization that distinguishes between the nominal and verbal IVA systems and introduce the notion of their semantic motivation as full-fledged linguistic sign systems. Our analysis supports Beedham's (2005, 114) claim that: "[s]tructuralism does not allow for some forms to exist outside the system, meaningless and not part of the rules of the game". Thus, the purpose of this study is to find the system that underlies the diverse forms of the IVA in both the nominal and the verbal systems of Old and Modern English.

3. Overview of Noun Plural and Verbal Past Tense Formations in English

3.1 Parallel Systems Following CS-PHB Theory: Noun Plural versus Verbal Past Tense Inflection

In Modern English there are the remnants of at least five different parallel systems for Plural Formation in nouns and Past Tense formation in verbs (including the IVA systems) which are presented in Figures 1 and 2. These systems can be labelled for their morphological processes such as: *Suppletion*, *Syncretism*, *IVA* and *Consonant Suffixation*. It is worth noting the fact that the same historical morphological processes appear in both systems, i.e., the Nominal Plural and Past Tense formations, which lends further support to the definition of language as a system of systems creating communicative oppositions (the communication factor) on the one hand and makes these parallel systems easier to acquire and remember on the other (the human factor).

Figure 1. Five Systems of Plural Formation of Nouns in English:

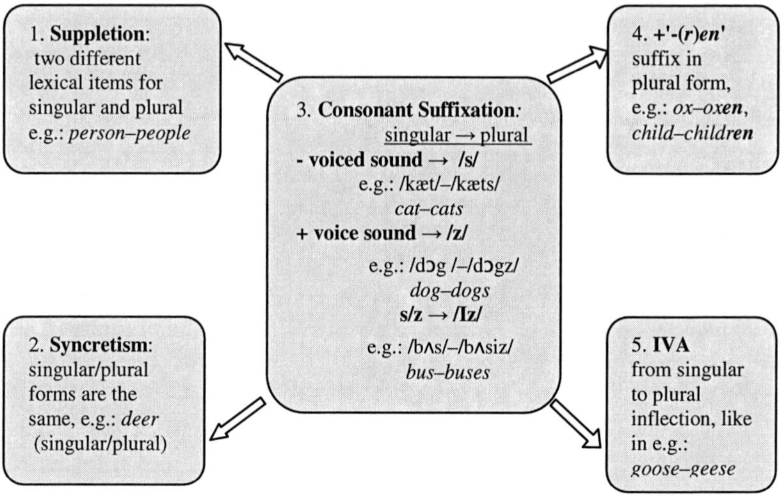

Figure 2. Five Systems of Past Tense Formation of Verbs in English:

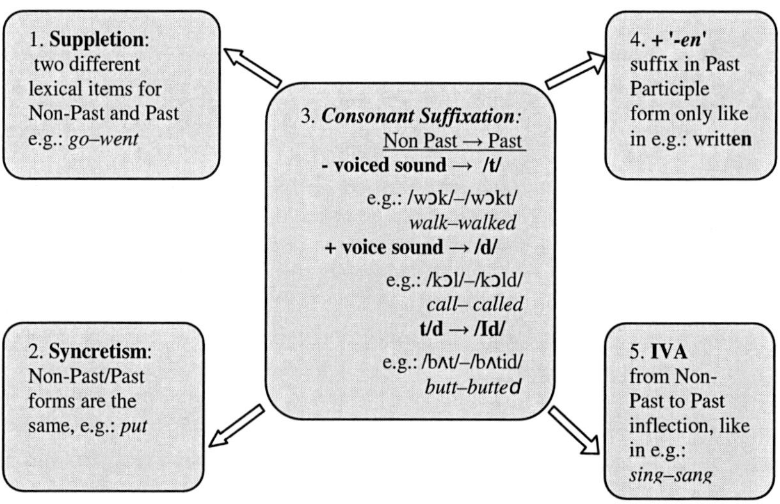

The parallel historical morphological systems found in Figures 1 and 2 include:

1. Suppletion: There are two separate and distinct lexical items for singular and plural forms in nouns, like in *'person'* (sg.) → *'people'* (pl.) (OALD 1995, 863) (Fig. 1), and in past and non-past forms of the verbs like *'go'*(non-past) → *'went'*(past). Following the mini-max axiom of CS-PHB theory: the communication factor is "the best" for *Suppletion* because we obtain optimally distinct oppositions that cannot be confused. However, the human factor is "the worst", because of *memory limitations*: i.e., two distinct lexical items have to be learned for the same concept.

It is also worth noting that in Modern English the *Suppletion* system has merged with the so-called regular system (*Lexical Item + Inflectional Apical Suffix*): i.e., there is the new plural form of *'person'*(sg.), which is *'persons'* (pl.), but in this case it refers to the separate individuals (such as VIPs) and not to the group itself like in *'person'* (sg.) → *'people'* (pl.). By the same token, there is a new plural *'peoples'*: as in *'the peoples of Africa'* which refers to a plurality of groups of people. These examples illustrate both the desire to achieve maximum communication as well as human efficiency by converging both a remnant of the *Suppletion* system with the most commonly used system number three (*Lexical Item + Inflectional Apical Suffix*), commonly known in Modern English as the "regular" Plural formation of nouns, in order to communicate a new subtle semantic distinction within the plural.

The present analysis views this semantic distinction as being motivated by the semiotic feature *Semantic Integrality*, i.e., "the perception of potentially discontinuous entities in continuous space" (Tobin 1993a, 147, inspired by the sign-oriented linguist Hirtle 1982), rather than presenting these kinds of additional novel Singular and/or Plural formations as being idiosyncratic deviations from the so-called regular Singular/Plural Noun formations found in prescriptive and descriptive grammars. Therefore, our analysis supports an alternative view of the opposition between the concepts of singularity versus plurality in English. This different perspective first appeared in an analysis of the dual number in Hebrew (Tobin 1990, 91-125) and then was further elaborated for "irregular" plurals and mass/count nouns and number agreement in English (Tobin 1995 [1994], 76-79). This new sign-oriented analysis was based on the postulation of a marked distinctive semantic feature called *Semantic Integrality*, which describes two alternative ways of perceiving entities in space, time, or existence either as discrete entities viewed in discontinuous or separate space: (a + b = a + b) or as potentially discrete entities perceived in continuous space as part of a larger set: (a + b = ab) (Tobin 1995 [1994], 71). Tobin (1993a, 148) states that:

> The semantic domain of the system of number is: alternative perceptions of entities in continuous (singularity) or discontinuous (plurality) space. There is a whole set of entities which may be viewed either in continuous space or in discontinuous space depending on whether we view them alternatively as a group or as individuals. The choice of how we view them in space (singular vs. plural) will also give a consistent difference in message and is therefore not chosen arbitrarily or by an absolute rule. The choice of one form or the other is therefore motivated by the difference in meaning each sign will provide.

Similar to Diver's (1984, 1987) and Tobin's (1990, 1993a, b) studies of singularity versus plurality, Reid (1991, 45) treats the *-s* suffix:

> as a fully-fledged linguistic sign, a unit composed of a *signal* paired with a *meaning*. This places the *-s* on a par with a lexical stem: an expressive unit that directly contributes to the communication of messages through its intrinsic semantic content. The analytical possibility then arises of treating the interpretation of a noun in context as a semantic synthesis of two meaning-bearing units. [Then, for example,] [i]n the case of *people* we will maintain a single semantic value for the stem, while attributing its shifted interpretation in the plural to a user-mediated interaction between it and the meaning of the *-s*.

Reid (1991, 46) then returns to the *Entity Number System* in English by stating that it:

> consists of two linguistic signs, an *-s* signalling the meaning MORE THAT ONE, and the absence of an *-s*, a zero signal, signalling the meaning ONE. Together, they form a system in the Saussurean sense of a set of relationally defined units. On the morphological side the *-Ø* is defined in terms of *-s*. On the conceptual side the meaning MORE THAN ONE is defined in terms of the meaning ONE.

Or, following Tobin (1995 [1994], 48), "[e]very lexical stem can be attached either to a singular or a plural suffix at any one time thus giving us a clear-cut paradigmatic grammatical system". It is also worth mentioning that the remnants of the *Suppletion* and the other systems (the so-called irregular forms) are all commonly used lexical items directly related to human beings, animals and other entities that are commonly used or important to our sustenance, thus they are worth retaining and remembering (the human factor).

Besides, we may also see this kind of *Suppletion* merging effect with the "regular" system in the Past Tense verbal formation of the verb *'go'*, which, sometimes, is *overgeneralized* by children to *'goed'* (instead of the so-called irregular form *'went'*) (Pinker 1999, Beedham 2002); however, such errors of the "strong" verbs are very rare, i.e., "the average error rate [of children's incorrect use of "strong" verbs] is only 4%" (Beedham 2002, 354) and unlike *'persons/peoples'* have not as yet developed into new and distinct lexical items and oppositions. It is even more interesting that these kinds of errors occur despite the fact that: "children really do know irregular past tense forms like *went* and *read*; their errors must be slip-ups in which they cannot slot an irregular form into a sentence in real time" (Pinker 1999, 200).

2. Syncretism: The singular and plural forms are identical *'lexical item'* + */Ø/ (zero)*, as in Noun Plural formation like: *'money'*(sg.) = *'money'*(pl.), *'water'*(sg.) = *'water'*(pl.), as well as in Past Tense formation of verbs like in *'put'* (non-past) = *'put'* (past), *'fit'* (non-past) = *'fit'* (past). Following the mini-max axiom of CS-PHB theory: the human factor is "the best" in *Syncretism* because of the lack of any change /+Ø/ (zero) which requires no effort whatsoever. However, the communication factor is "the worst" since there is no perceptible communicative opposition between these identical forms. Thus, from the point of view of the communication factor a formal distinction does not exist, neither in the singular versus plural, nor in the past versus non-past forms.

It is also worth noting that in Modern English the system of *Syncretism* (like the *Suppletion* system) has merged with the so-called regular system. For Plural Formation we have examples such as: *'There are different fish/fishes here'*–in the sense of different groups vs. kinds/species of fish. This view of the alternative readings of the common or mass nouns like e.g., *'fish, antelope, money, possum, water, deer, sheep, sand'*, etc., are discussed in Tobin (1993b, 149) as presenting diverse semantic readings: either viewing these items as sets/groups perceived in continuous space or individual groups perceived in discrete or discontinuous space:

> [D]ifferent ways of viewing sets or groups (traditionally called common or mass nouns) … [and when] the individual groups are compared and contrasted with each other, they then become 'pluralized common nouns' indicating that each one of them is perceived as occupying a discrete space.
> …
> [For example, when] the hunters refer to the species of game which they are in pursuit of, they use the marked integral form indicating continuous space. On the other hand, when they are concentrating on individual kills they use the plural form indicating distinct individuals perceived in discontinuous space.
> … [Like in the example:] I short three elephant/elephants today. (species vs. individuals)

A further support for the non-random exploitation of *Syncretism* versus the system of *Lexical Item + Inflectional Apical Suffix*, is presented by Reid (1991, 164, 166-7) in a questionnaire testing the *Entity Number System* on thirteen mass/common nouns, like *'deer, sheep, antelope, giraffe'*, etc. In this questionnaire (presented to five hundred high school students) Reid's aim was to show that speakers:

> ... exploit the opposition between its two meanings ONE and MORE THAN ONE according to the precision strategy to distinguish between different levels of contextually-implied individuality.
> But since the gradations of individuality can be greater than the number of linguistic contrasts available, different speakers will exploit the opposition in different places ... . Only the *direction* of the exploitation is fixed: MORE THAN ONE indicates greater individuality [like in e.g., *deers*] than ONE [e.g., *deer*] (when applied to a referential plurality).
> ...
> In sign-based terms, the questionnaire data show speakers choosing different linguistic signs according to their contrasting systemic values for subtly different messages.

This questionnaire presented well-established commonly taught mass/count nouns belonging to the *'lexical item' + /Ø/ (zero)* system in alternative contexts. Each context presents the noun in question with more or less detail in its description representing different degrees of individuality for each nominal form. At the end of the description, the subject of the questionnaire was asked to fill in the missing nominal form in two contrasting sentences representing different degrees of individuation for each lexical item to see whether the subject used the *'lexical item' + /Ø/ (zero)* system versus the *'lexical item' +Inflectional Apical Suffix*. For example, for the lexical item *'deer'*, Reid (1991, 140) provided the following context of presenting a family of deer: the buck-father, the doe-mother and the fawn (baby) in great individual detail where the first sentence to fill in was: (1) "*Close by, from behind the tree, I watched the doe nurse the new-born fawn while the buck stood watch nearby. Suddenly their ears pricked up and the __________ were off in a flash in different directions*". The response for this sentence was overwhelmingly *'deers'* perceived as individuals rather than *'deer'*. The form *'deer'*, however, was predominantly chosen by the subjects in another context, i.e., in the second sentence where the deer were not described with a high degree of individual detail that focussed on their individuality in the sentence: (2) "*Hunters can track _______ most easily in the spring snow.*"(Reid 1991, 141). Here the reference is to a group or family of deer as opposed to another species, thus, supporting the fact that the exploitation of one system over the other is both consistent and semantically motivated. In fact, the results for this lexical item in the questionnaire, revealed that eighty five per cent of the subjects responded with the hybrid form *'deers'* for the first sentence presenting the lexical item in great detail in a high degree of individuation. However, at the same time, the traditional form *'deer'* was preferred in the second sentence presenting a less detailed description and a lower degree of individuation for the lexical item.

By the same token, we can observe a parallel phenomenon in the verb system where there are two alternative Past Tense forms for the verb with the convergence of the *Syncretism* and the *Inflectional Apical Suffixation* systems: like in *'fit'*: *e.g., 'My clothes fit today/yesterday, but the tailor fitted my clothes today/yesterday'*, distinguishing between the transitive and intransitive use of the verb without distinguishing between the time of the action. This further supports our definition of language as a system of systems and exemplifies the mini-max principle by providing additional (albeit subtle) communicative distinctions efficiently by combining these two systems for commonly used lexical items.

3. The "regular", i.e., the most frequently used system in Plural and in Past Tense formation in English is the third group called Lexical Item + Inflectional Apical Consonant Suffix. Tobin (2006), in a diachronic study of the inflectional morphology of English, postulates that this subsystem was shown to be (for English at least) the most efficient system following the tenets of CS-PHB theory which may explain why it became the dominant or "regular" system over time. Indeed, this system appears to provide "the best" or the optimal compromise in the struggle between the communication and the human factors for the following reasons:

a. The order of presentation: the lexical item remains intact and appears first. To it is added a purely grammatical inflectional suffix, thus rendering this system to be the most transparent and iconic.

b. The suffix appears as a consonant rather than a vowel which is conducive to clearer communication: the communicative oppositions made by consonants are more clear-cut and salient than those made by vowels. Indeed, the alternative historical systems of *Lexical Item + Inflectional Vowel Suffix* (which we have not included in Figures 1 and 2, above) have disappeared from the language for various reasons. One such reason is that the unstressed vowel suffixes in these systems were reduced to *schwa* in spoken English, thus having them lose their clear and distinct perceptual opposition and rendering them inefficient for this communicative opposition.

c. Furthermore, it is not by chance that the consonants chosen for these inflectional suffixes are all apical: according to PHB the apex is the most flexible, sensitive and the easiest to control active articulator, thus making it ideal to be exploited as a frequently used inflectional suffix. It is, therefore, not surprising that the *International Phonetic Association's* (IPA) chart of consonants reveals the apex (labelled by the passive receptors the apex can join with) as: *'dental/alveolar/post-alveolar'*) and as having the largest number of consonants across languages (Diver 1979, Tobin 1997).

d. Moreover, the choice of the allomorphic or allo-morpho-phonemic inflectional suffixes of the */-s/* versus */-z/* (for Plural formation) and */-t/* versus */-d/* (the phonetic realization of *-ed* in Past Tense formation) is determined by the voicing value of the consonant preceding the suffix: e.g., *'cat'* + */s/* (voiceless); *'dog'* + */z/* (voiced); *'walk'* + */t/* (voiceless); *'jog'* + */d/* (voiced). It is not by chance that the voicing values are maintained and there is a matching co-articulation of the voicing values between the final consonant of the lexical item and the allomorph of the inflectional apical consonant suffix. From the point of view of CS-PHB, there is a natural flow of speech which does not require any additional laryngeal gestures to alter the voicing values, thus maintaining the axiom of *maximum communication with minimal effort.* (Tobin 2006, 73)

e. Not unsurprisingly, there is the alternative syllable (*-VC#*), i.e., the inflectional allomorph */ -Iz/-Id /* consisting of: the lax vowel */ I /* plus the voiced inflectional apical consonant */ z/d /,* for both systems when the lexical item ends with the same consonant (or an acoustically very similar consonant) as the *inflectional vowel + Apical Consonant Suffix* (e.g., *'bus-buses, wait-waited'*). This final apical consonant in the lexical item which is identical to the inflectional apical consonant suffix could lead to a confusion of whether the lexical item is singular or plural or even to a slight breakdown in communication (Tobin 2006, 74). In fact, there are instances of back formation in English that point to the disfavouring of the collocation of acoustically similar consonants. For example, according to the *Oxford English Dictionary* (OED), the new singular form *'pea'* was derived by back formation from the historical singular form *'pease'*, which was originally opposed to the plural form *'peasen'*. We maintain that the potential confusion between the final */s/* in the lexical item and the now dominant *-s* plural suffix most probably led to a confusion between the forms resulting in the creation of the new singular/plural opposition *'pea/peas'*. The other possibility (requiring more effort) would be the now non-existent opposition of *'pease/peases'*.

Furthermore, it has been established by several phonological theories that the production or repetition of the same consonant (or a consonant very similar to it in its acoustic features) in an adjacent phonetic environment is disfavoured. This phonotactic generalization has been presented in the basic principles (2, 3, 11) of PHB in Tobin (1997, 41-44, 120-121):

> 2. co-articulation by near articulators is disfavoured;
> 3. co-articulation by the same articulators/phoneme is even more highly disfavoured (particularly in the roots of Semitic languages);
> ...
> 11. sequences of phonemes with the same articulators are disfavoured unless their juxtaposition is, by virtue of some other factor, mutually beneficial; … .

This disfavouring appears in other phonological theories as well, for example, the *Obligatory Contour Principle* (OCP) in Optimality Theory that prohibits phonetic similarity, i.e., the co-occurrence of the consonants with the same place of articulation (e.g., Boersma 1998, Bakovic 2003, Katamber 2006). It is worth the effort of producing the inflectional syllable (*-VC#*) rather than a suffix composed of a single consonant (*-C#*) in order to produce a more distinct communicative opposition with a relatively small degree of effort.

f. One can also find that there are additional instances of verb alternations employing both the voiceless and the voiced apical suffix to the same lexical verb regardless of the voicing value of the final consonant of that lexical verb + Past Tense suffix, i.e., the adding of either the voiceless apical suffix */-t/* or its voiced counterpart */-d/* in certain English Past Tense forms regardless of the voiced value of the final consonant of the lexical verb like *'spoil'* →. *'spoiled'* vs. *'spoilt'*; *'smell'* → *'smelled'* vs. *'smelt'*; *'burn'* → *'burned'* vs. *'burnt'*; *'learn'* → *'learned'* vs. *'learnt'*; which may include even IVA verbs such as: *'dream'* → *'dreamed'* vs. *'dreamt'*; *'kneel'*→ *'kneeled'* vs. *'knelt'; 'leap'* → *'leaped'* vs. *'leapt'*. For example, the results of the study of both preterit alternative suffixes by Quirk (1970, 306) "show a convincing tendency to distinguish between the –t and –ed variant preterits on an aspectual basis". That is, the synchronic evidence of the 'forced-choice' selection tests presented in Quirk's study (1970, 308) shows that:

> ... the aggregates [in British English] point unambiguously to the existence of a general contrast between preterit –t and –ed such that –t corresponds significantly to effective and –ed to durative aspect; ... although the aspectual association seems unquestionably less strong in American English, it nevertheless unambiguously presents in some verbs with identical potentiality in form and meaning.

The above observations indicate that the particular choice of one form over another, i.e., either voiced or voiceless apical Past Tense inflection is not random but is semantically motivated. This is yet another example showing that once the *Lexical Item + Inflectional Apical Suffix* became the dominant system, it has been exploited to create new subtle semantic distinctions either by itself and/or has converged and functions simultaneously with the other historical systems to create new subtly distinctive alternative Plural and Past Tense forms similar to *'person(s)'* versus *'people(s)'* and *'fit(ted)'*, mentioned above.

To summarize: we first maintain that the forces of linguistic or grammatical economy favour the use of this *Inflectional Apical Suffixation* system and support its high degree of efficiency because:

> [p]honemes produced by the apex of the tongue – the most flexible, sensitive, and easiest to control active articulator – are the most numerous and frequent; have the highest functional load; are acquired early; and the process of fronting or apicalization, (i.e., non-apical sounds are replaced by apical ones), are among the easiest and most common in first language acquisition and in the clinic. (Tobin 2002, 196)

The word-final apical sound (which is an *obstruent* that is easier to hear clearly)(Davis 1987[1984], Tobin 1997) makes this system of *Lexical Item + Inflectional Apical Consonant Suffix* the favoured system over the others, such as group number four: *Lexical Item + Nasal Consonant Suffix*, i.e., *-(r)en* system, because following CS-PHB principles "[s]tops ... are favoured over nasals"(Tobin 2006, 72) and this points to the human factor, which is optimal for this group, due to *human efficiency* reflected by the use of the easiest and most communicatively salient consonants. Moreover, the non-random phonetic environment of the *Inflectional Apical Consonant Suffix* also points to the human factor in favouring the allomorph consisting of an unstressed syllable with the *Vowel + (voiced) Apical Consonant* (*-VC#*) where the apical consonant is voiced as a co-articulatory device to avoid additional laryngeal gestures in order to enhance communication.

Besides, the efficiency of the *Lexical Item + Inflectional Apical Consonant Suffix* group–the most productive system in Modern English–is even further strengthened by both communication and human factors by providing the singular lexical item intact initially and then adding the easiest inflectional apical suffix (or syllable) as a bound morpheme in word final position, where according to CS-PHB the least effort is required in the search for a compromise to achieve *maximum communication with minimal effort* (Diver 1979, Tobin 1997). Thus, it is not by chance that the subsystem became the main or dominant system in Modern English from Old English and has been labelled as being regular today. We will discuss the etymology of the *-ed* Past Tense formation in section (3.2).

4. The additional system – lexical item + suffix: *-(r)en* – was a full-fledged subsystem but it is now used much less frequently in the language possibly because the communicative distinctions created by nasals–like vowels–are less clear-cut than those of consonants (Tobin 1997, 42, 317-318; Tobin 2006, 72). This system should be a subject of further study exploring among other things the possible semantic and other motivations for having these alternative systems: *Lexical Item + Inflectional Apical Consonantal (/-s/-z/-t/-d/-Iz/-Id/)* or *syllable /-(r)en/* inflectional systems.

5. The IVA system composed of the nominal Plural forms (e.g., *'goose'* (sg.) → *'geese'*(pl.), *'foot'*(sg.) → *'feet'*(pl.)) and verbal Past Tense forms (e.g., *'sing'*(non-past) → *'sang'*(past), *'take'*(non-past) → *'took'*(past)). This IVA system is less efficient than the *Lexical Item + Inflectional Apical Consonant Suffix* system for the following reasons:

a. the forms are less transparent and iconic and, therefore, produce less optimal communicative distinction via the IVA process;
b. the change is vocalic rather than consonantal, therefore, making it less clear-cut, salient and distinctive–albeit easier to produce;
c. the IVA appears in the less optimal word medial position.
d. However, it appears predominantly in monosyllabic words, thus, making the IVA in medial position easier to perceive and relatively more salient.

In short, in this IVA subsystem, the compromise between the human and communication factors is achieved but not in the most efficacious way: i.e., the less salient internal vowel change in the same lexical item appears in the less optimal word medial position albeit of predominantly monosyllabic stems. There is empirical support for the fact that medial position is less optimal than initial and final positions. In cognitive psychological experiments the *Serial Position Effect* has been found: namely, people remember the first and the last items presented to them in a list and fail to recall items that appear in the middle position (first discussed by the German physiologist Hermann Ebbinghaus in his experimental studies of memory in 1885, and presented in other research in the 19th century, for more recent studies: Luchins (1957), Murdock (1962), Glanzer and Cunitz (1966), Atkinson and Shiffrin (1968), Crano (1977), Frensch (1994), Healy et al. (2000), etc.). Moreover, the system of IVA contains a vocalic rather than a consonantal change, thus providing a less clear-cut opposition:

> Although phonemes of constriction are more difficult to produce than phonemes of aperture, the communication distinctions they create are clearer. Therefore there are more consonants than vowels in all languages. (Tobin 2002, 196)

In other words, vowels provide less clear-cut distinctions than consonants (the communication factor), but they are easier to produce (the human factor). Furthermore, it is worth pointing out that as with the *Suppletion* and *Syncretism* systems, there are also certain IVA forms that have converged with the "regular" forms (*Lexical Item + Inflection Apical Suffix*) to create new subtle communicative distinctions. Some examples of these include: *'mouse'*(sg.) → *'mice'*(pl.) or *'mouses'*(pl.), where the new alternative plural form of *'mouses'* refers to the computer mouse or to a cowardly man: *'Are you a man or a mouse'/'Are you men or mouses?'* (taken from a Warner Brothers' cartoon). These distinctions point to the obvious semantic and pragmatic motivation that underlies the particular choice of one system over the other. There is also a pejorative metaphoric anthropomorphic use of the new additional alternative forms: e.g., *'goose'(sg.)–'geese'*(pl.) (animals) versus *'stupid goose'(sg.)–'stupid gooses'* (pl.)' (metaphorically referring to unintelligent people) or *'louse'*(sg.)–*'lice'*(pl.) (parasitic insect) versus *'dirty louse'*(sg.)–*'dirty louses'*(pl.) (metaphoric use for (possibly parasitic?) people); as well as for the */-(r)en/* system *'ox'* (sg.)–*'oxen'*(pl.) (animals) versus *'stupid ox'*(sg.)–*'stupid oxes'*(pl.) (metaphorically referring to unintelligent people) This same phenomenon may also be observed in IVA verbs where we are witness to the merging effect with the system of *Lexical Item + Inflection Apical Suffix*, as found in the verb: *'shine'*(non-past) → *'shone'*(past) or *'shined'*(past) i.e., alternative systematic verb formation to distinguish between transitive versus intransitive verbs, e.g., *'The sun **shined/shone** yesterday.'* but only *'He <u>shined</u> his shoes.'*; or *'dive'* (non-past) → *'dove'*(past) or *'dived'*(past), where though both of the forms appear in Modern English, in the metaphoric sense only the new form is used, e.g., *'He **skydived/nosedived'***, etc. These examples further illustrate the non-random use and preference of one system over another, hence emphasizing the semantic and pragmatic motivation that underlies these diverse processes today.

Applying the mini-max axiom of CS-PHB theory to Figures (1 and 2), we claim that the most efficient system for Plural and Past Tense formation in English is system number three: *Lexical Item + Inflectional Apical Consonant Suffix.* This contention is even strengthened by the results of the predominate rule-like generalization (adding suffix *-s/-es* to nouns and *-d/-ed* to verbs) in Plural nominal and/or Past Tense verbal formations of lexical and nonsense items by children presented in the research by e.g., Berko (1958) and Rumelhart and McClelland's (1986) which we discussed in section (2). Therefore, accepting that it is the most efficient system, explains why many neologisms and lexical formations that historically belonged to the other systems, as in the examples presented above, today, predominantly follow the so-called regular *consonant suffixation* system. Indeed, the IVA system has been reduced over time from a larger and productive system in Old English to only seven IVA nouns and only seventy six predominantly monosyllabic IVA verbs that were originally "strong".

As a result, in contemporary English, the IVA morphological process "represent[s] limited historical remnants of former grammatical inflectional systems which were probably semantically based and are now acquired lexically for frequently used lexical [nominal and verbal] items rather than as grammatical systems" (Tobin 2006, 73). In the following section we will discuss the historical background to the IVA process and mention some additional processes in English and other languages.

3.2. Historical Background of the Regular and IVA Systems of Noun Plural and Verbal Past Tense Inflections

Historically, English had various alternative ways to indicate Past Tense. English verb morphology was originally based on the "strong" verbs, “those which form the Principal Parts with a variation of the radical vowel” (Hulbert 1963,1vi), i.e. (verbs with the *vowel-gradation,* which, was first termed *Ablaut* by Jacob Grimm (Quirk and Wrenn 1955), for example: *'see-saw'*, *'give-gave'*. The other major conjugations include "weak" verbs (that are associated with the Past Tense formation like *verb + ed*) like in: *'play-played', 'claim-claimed'*, which following Smith (2009, 23) is equivalent to the suffix *–ode* that indicates the *Preterit* (Past) Tense. According to Hulbert's (1963) and Baugh's (1957, 70) studies, we may also add two other suffixes: *-ede* and *-de* which formed an important and a large inflectional group of the Past Tense verb forms in Old English. However, it is worth noting that the "origin of the dental suffixes by which weak verbs form their past tense … is not known. [Though] [E.E-S. and Y.T.] It was formerly customary to explain these as part of the verb *do*, as though *I worked* was originally *I work-did* (i.e., *I did work*)"(Baugh 1957, 70). In addition, the "strong" verbs appeared long before the "weak" verbs in English and they are, indeed, "the original verbs of Indo-European"(Beedham 2005, 111). Similar to Beedham, Quirk and Wrenn (1955, 130) note that "root-gradation was in IE [Indo European] as one of the means of conjugating verbs, and it is as a development of this practice that the Gmc [Germanic] (and therefore the OE) vocalic verbs are differentiated in their tenses to a large extent by variation of their root-vowel in accordance with regular series [of seven classes]".

The Indo-European language family dates back to the period somewhere between 3500 and 2000 BC (Smith 2009, Beedham 2005; Gamkrelidze and Ivanov 1995; Pinker 1994, 251-255, Baugh 1957, Emerson 1910), i.e., the "strong" verbs of contemporary English are over 4000 years old. This leads to the plausible prediction that these strong verbs, which "Old English had just over 300 reduced now to about 170" (Beedham 2005, 112; Baugh and Cable 2002, 60; Pinker 1999, 80) could not survive for four millennia if they were just learned by rote, but rather we would have expected them to become analogous with the so-called regular system. In the previous section, we gave the number of only those IVA verbs that have remained and have not been "regularized". The reason for the reduction in number presented by Beedham above is because Beedham included all classes of the so-called irregular verbs that have not been "regularized" and not just the IVA forms. At any rate, the general agreement is that there has been a strong tendency over time to reduce the number of verbs in the other irregular systems and transform them into the so-called regular system of *Lexical Item + Inflectional Apical Suffix*.

It is well-known that the morphology of Old English (a synthetic language) was levelled or minimized in Middle English, resulting in Modern English (an analytic language). This is the reason that the IVA or "strong" verbs are believed to be irregular. In addition to the "strong" verbs "there was a large number of weak or regular verbs in Old English, which continued to expand; for almost every new verb was inflected weak"(Lehmann 1962, 182). That is, the number of "weak" verbs versus "strong" verbs has expanded because of the efficiency of the former system (as attributed to the mini-max axiom of CS-PHB that was discussed in the previous section), thus making it the most predominant and productive system. From the point of view of language acquisition and learning: the "regular" verbs are perceived as the only grammatical system today while the "irregular" verbs are acquired as separate lexical items and have to be "memorized". Indeed, as we have previously mentioned, "strong" verbs date back to Indo-European, and appear in English and other Germanic and non-Germanic and non-Indo-European languages. For example, as Beedham (2005, 112, 182) notes, Modern German has about 200 strong verbs, and Modern Russian has 400 (and Russian speakers do not make mistakes with these verbs). However, as in English, the number of "strong" verbs both in German and Russian has generally been reduced over time. If we compare the thousands of "regular" verbs to the reduced number of the "irregular" ones in English, it becomes evident that the number of "irregular" verbs, which have to be learned by the speakers, amounts to a very small percentage of lexical verbs in the lexicon. Following Beedham's (2005, 113) study of monosyllabic "strong" verbs:

> 170 English irregular verbs set against 1,768 regular [monosyllabic] verbs [and that] gives a percentage of nearly 7% irregular. The analogous comparison and calculation made for German delivers a percentage of 10% irregular (Beedham 1995-1996, 143-4). To claim that speakers can learn off by heart the irregular preterits and 2nd participles of 0.1% of all verbs is one thing. But to claim that they learn those forms off by heart for 7% or 10% of the relevant verbs is not plausible, and stretches the bounds of credibility. It is too big a proportion of the relevant verbs.

Therefore, even though a relatively small number of "strong" verbs in English have remained, they still represent a large number of verbs that have to be learned as separate lexical items and remembered by the speakers. The goal of our study (as well as Beedham's approach to the so-called irregular forms) is to understand and uncover the system that underlies these "irregular" variations in the formation of the verb from Non-Past to Past as well as of the nouns from Singular to Plural, because: "[a]ll linguistic forms must fit into the system somehow" Beedham (2005, 114). It is worth noting that Old English, as a representative of the Teutonic branch, distinguished not only between a "weak" versus a "strong" conjugation of verbs, but also between the two major classes of nouns, i.e. the "weak" versus a "strong" declension (as well as the other minor classes in both the nominal and verbal systems). In the two major classes of nouns, there was a vowel (strong) and a consonant (weak) declension with different subdivisions based on case, grammatical number and person within each of these types (Baugh 1957, 64-5, Smith 2009). Nouns that had the following stem-thematic vowels: *a, o, i*, or *u*, belonged to the "strong" declension, while noun stems that originally ended in *-an/n*, or *-t* (that almost vanished from the language by the time of Proto-Germanic) belonged to the "weak" declension (Emerson 1910, Baugh 1957, Hulbert 1963, Smith 2009, 60). Moreover, it should be remembered that Old English had three grammatical genders and four or five cases, which also affected the multiple varied forms of the "strong" and "weak" declension that underwent radical simplification in Modern English that reduced the more varied historical forms to *-es.* However, beside the "strong" and "weak" declension of nouns, there "remain a few nouns of certain minor classes in Old English. The most important of these are the plurals with mutation, as *man–men, foot–feet* … and a few other words which have lost the mutated forms "(Emerson 1910, 300). These are the IVA nominal forms, which are related to the most common phenomena known in German as *umlaut*, the term that was introduced by Jacob Grimm and implies "the change from one vowel to another through the influence (by attraction, assimilation, or anticipation) of a vowel in an immediately following syllable."(Quirk and Wrenn 1955, 150). But, although this term is most commonly used in referring to German, English as a Germanic language also shares this process. Emerson (1910, 224) describes this phenomenon in the following way:

> In Old English, several vowels, and even the palatal consonants, could produce mutation, but the only one of these changes preserved in its effects to Modern English is the *i*-mutation, as it is called. Considering for the time only the Mercian dialect, from which our modern [English] speech has sprung, the phenomena of *i*-mutation may be stated in this way. Whenever in the earliest English an accented *a, o, u* long or short was followed by an *i* or the semi-vowel *y* in the succeeding syllable, they changed according to this scheme:
>
> a became e. ā became ē (open) WS ǣ
> o became y (e) ō became ē (close)
> u became y. ū became y [long]
>
> The cause of this change, which is a wide reaching one, is often obscured by the fact that after mutation the *i* or *y* was frequently weakened to *e* or lost altogether, so that many cases of the change can only be determined by a comparison with the cognate languages, especially Gothic, which does not show mutation.

As Emerson (1910, 229) further elaborates "*i*-mutation probably began to be in force as early as the beginning of the seventh century (600 A.D.), and … it had spent itself about the close of that century (700 A.D.)." Moreover, "[a]bout 650 A.D. *i*-mutation may be said to have been most active, all words capable of the change being affected at that time." But, not many plural nominal forms with *i*-mutation have been retained in Old English. Indeed, in Modern English there is a very small number of IVA Plural forms. These will be discussed and shown to be systematic in the next section.

4. Analysis

We decided to test both IVA phonological systems separately in order to verify our prediction regarding the distinctive phonological processes of *fronting* for Noun Plural formation versus *backing* for Past Tense formation.

4.1 The Nominal IVA System in Old and Modern English

We first examined the so-called irregular Plural formations of nouns in English. In Table 1, we present the remnants of the Plural formation of the nominal system in Old English (O.E.): i.e., the seven nouns that have been carried over into Modern English (Mod.E.) which undergo IVA from the singular to plural declension. We show how they all reflect the phonological process of *fronting*.

Table 1. The *Fronting Process* in Nouns from Singular to Plural Formation in Modern English

Singular Form of Mod.E. Nouns with the Following Phonological Representation of the Vowels: [ʊu, au, æ]	*Plural Form of Mod.E. Nouns with the Following Phonological Representation of the Vowels:* [e, Ii, aI]	*Fronting Process* (+)
man (mann)	men(menn)	[æ] → [e] = (+)[2]
woman (wīfmann)	women (wīfmenn)	[æ] → [e] = (+)
foot (fōt)	feet (fēt)	[ʊu] → [Ii] = (+)
tooth (tōð)	teeth (tēð)	[ʊu] → [Ii] = (+)
goose (gōs)	geese (gēs)	[ʊu] → [Ii] = (+)
mouse (mūs)	mice (mys)	[au] → [aI] = (+)
louse(lūs)	lice (lys)	[au] → [aI] = (+)

From Table 1, it is evident that the so-called irregular Plural formations of nouns in Modern English systematically follow different degrees of the *fronting process* of IVA that are also found in other Germanic and non-Germanic languages (Emerson 1910, Crystal 1995). Such a regularity of the phonological *fronting process* of IVA in the nominal forms cannot be accidental. It is worth noting that there are various degrees of the *fronting process*: some of the examples go from historical long back vowels to

[2] Although both [æ] and [e] share the phonetic feature [+front], [æ] is both lower and "less front" than [e]. In our discussion of phonological IVA variations we will include all degrees of fronting as part of the fronting process, not limiting ourselves only to back vowels becoming front vowels.

front vowels (*'foot, goose, tooth'*). Others go from historical long back vowels that were changed to central-back diphthongs to central-front diphthongs (*'mouse, louse'*), while others go from the historical low back vowel /a/ to the medium-low front vowel /æ/ for the singular, to the medium or medium-high front lax vowels /ɛ, I/ for the plural (*'man, woman'*). Regardless of the degree (from back vowel or diphthongs to different front vowels and diphthongs) each of these Plural formations still displays a variation or a degree of the *fronting process*. Indeed, this process originates in Germanic *i-mutation*, which we have discussed in the previous section. For example, Crystal (1995, 19) describes this process as a natural and thus widely spread process in Germanic and other languages as well:

> … in Germanic there were many words where a vowel in a stressed syllable was immediately followed by a high front vowel ([i]) or vowel-like … ([j]) in the next syllable. The plural of **fōt* is thought to have been **fōtiz*, with the stress on *fō*. For some reason …, the quality of this high front sound caused the preceding vowel to change (mutate). In the case of **fōt*, the ō became ē, which ultimately came to be pronounced [i:], as in modern *feet*. The *–iz* ending dropped away, for once the plural was being shown by the e vowel, it was unnecessary to have an ending as well. … [T]his is what happened in 7th-century Old English. All back vowels in the context described above were changed into front vowels–and all short front vowels and diphthongs were affected, too, being articulated even further forward and higher (with the exception of [i], of course, which is already as far forward and as high in the mouth as any vowel can be).

Crystal's (1995) historical overview of the origin of the plural *i-mutated* form such as *feet* further strengthens our claim that the IVA Plural Nouns are not arbitrary or "irregular", but are the remnants of an earlier phonological system, i.e. the fronting process still found in IVA. In other words, despite all of the simplifications and changes from earlier Germanic to Old English to Modern English, we still observe a consistency in the fronting process of the IVA in singular to plural nominal declension.

Moreover, it is also worth pointing out that there are several Modern nominal plurals that now follow the "regular" rules for adding the suffix (*-s/-es*) in Plural formation that originally were part of the IVA system. These nouns also followed the same phonological *fronting process* of IVA in Old English. In Table 2, we repeat the present-day IVA nouns and add the additional now "regularized" nouns that have followed the IVA in Old English from the Singular to Plural declension. The reader will note that in all of the forms presented in Table 2, as in Table 1, regardless of the degree (from back vowel or diphthongs to different front vowels or diphthongs), each plural formation still displays a variation of the *fronting process*.

Table 2. *Fronting Process* in Nominal Forms from Singular to Plural Formation in Old English

Singular O.E. Forms of Nouns with the Vowels: /ō, ā, a, ū, ēō/	Plural O.E. Forms of Nouns with the Vowels: / ē, e, ǣ, y, īē/	Mod.E. forms of these Nouns	*Fronting Process* in O.E. Forms of Nouns (+)
mann	menn	man	/a/ → /e/ = (+)
wīfmann	wīfmenn	woman	/a/ → /e/ = (+)
fōt	fēt	foot	/ō/ → /ē/ = (+)
tōð	tēð	tooth	/ō/ → /ē/ = (+)
gōs	gēs	goose	/ō/ → /ē/ = (+)
brōc	brēc(OE)/brēche(ME)	breeches, trousers, pants	/ō/ → /ē/ = (+)
bōc	bēc	book	/ō/ → /ē/ = (+)
fēōnd	fīēnd/fynd	foe	/ēō/ → /īē/ or /y/ = (+)
frēōnd	frīēnd/frynd	friend	/ēō/ → /īē/ or /y/ = (+)
hōnd	hēnd	hand	/ō/ → /ē/ = (+)
gōte	gēt	goat	/ō/ → /ē/ = (+)
hnute	hnyte	nut	/u/ → /y/ = (+)

burg	byrg	fortress	/u/ → /y/ = (+)
āc	ǣc	oak	/ā/ → /ǣ/ = (+)
mūs	mys	mouse	/ū/ → /y/ = (+)
lūs	lys	louse	/ū/ → /y/ = (+)
cū	cy	cow	/ū/ → /y/ = (+)

From Tables 1 and 2 above, we observe a fixed phonological process of vowel and diphthong fronting of different degrees in the Singular to Plural declensions of not only historical IVA forms of nouns that have remained IVA in Modern English, but also in IVA nouns that have become "regularized". In other words we may trace this phonological regularity in Old English (as well as in other Germanic and other language families), which clearly points to a phonological systematization in nominal forms with IVA.

We also believe that the IVA (as well as all the other systems) is semantically motivated. Our claim is that there is a semantic similarity among the so-called irregular IVA nouns in English. There are others who have maintained that there is a similar connection as part of an "interaction of form and meaning in the grammar of English"(Baayen and Martin 2005, 668). This common semantic connection is cited in the work of Baayen and Martin (2005) and Quirk, Greenbaum, Leech and Svartvik (1985) among others. However, they have not postulated a single distinctive semantic feature for the so-called irregular IVA Noun Plurals (which we have introduced as *Semantic Integrality* in the Syncretism part of section 3.1). We claim that all of the IVA nouns share the same distinctive semantic feature, i.e., *Semantic Integrality,* which is based on the alternative viewing of entities in either continuous or discontinuous space (as seen in the mass versus non-count opposition in nouns, (e.g., *'money', 'water', 'antelope'* (Tobin 1997)), presented in the second group of Figure 1). We maintain that the IVA nouns in English like *'foot', 'tooth', 'man'*, etc., (similarly to the dual number in Hebrew), are marked for the same semantic feature of *Semantic Integrality*, i.e. "'plural' entities potentially perceived in discontinuous space viewed as 'a unity' perceived in continuous space"(Tobin 1990, 121). These IVA nouns generally describe two or more units or sets which may: (a) be either paired (e.g. *'foot/feet'*, *'hōnd/hēnd'* (hand), etc.) or (b) viewed as being complementary polarized pairs (e.g. *'man/men–woman/women'*, *'frēōnd/frīēnd'*(friend)–*'fēōnd/fīēnd'* (foe), etc.). Thus, these examples represent an entity or entities that can be perceived as being part of an integral set in continuous space, the notion which was originally discussed in Tobin (1990, 1993a,b, 1994) and in section 2.

As previously discussed, the common semantic denominator expressed by the distinctive feature of *Semantic Integrality*, postulated for the IVA noun system, is similar to that of mass/common nouns in the *Syncretism* system. But, whereas the *Syncrety* system, may include monosyllabic as well as polysyllabic nouns, the IVA nouns are predominantly monosyllabic, e.g., *'foot', 'tooth', 'goose'*, thus making the IVA in word medial position more salient and easier to perceive. Such apparent regularity and consistency in the IVA system clearly points to the non-arbitrariness of the IVA process. Moreover, this phonological *fronting process* in the Singular to Plural declension of IVA may be iconic because it points to the metaphoric fronting as a representation for the addition of plural (i.e., 'moving forward' (p.c. Roni Henkin)) just as the *backing process* is iconic for Past Tense formation ('moving backward in time'). These additional iconic elements provide further support for viewing the IVA system in both nouns and verbs in English as being systematic and not "irregular".

4.2 The IVA Past Tense Formation in Old and Modern English

As previously mentioned, Teutonic and consequently Old English verbs had two main groups of verbs (e.g. Emerson (1910, 344), Hulbert (1963)): "the strong and the weak, or as we call their descendants respectively the irregular and the regular". Following Quirk and Wrenn (1955, 40), Old English comprises about one-quarter of the "strong" verbs. They originally were divided into Seven Classes in which the Past Tense form was distinguished by variable stem-vowel from Non-Past Tense form and each class represented a qualitative *ablaut (Abtönung)* system (Quirk and Wrenn 1955, Lass and Anderson 2010[1975]) that traces back to the Teutonic language (Emerson 1910, Quirk and Wrenn 1955, Hulbert 1963, Mitchell and Robinson 1982) and, which is "derived from Proto-Indo-European Ablaut variation"(Smith 2009, 114).

Table 3. Seven Classes of Strong Verbs in Old English following e.g., Emerson (1910), Quirk and Wrenn (1955), Lass and Anderson (2010[1975])

CLASS	PRESENT	(PRET1 /PRET2) = PAST	
I	ii	aa	i
II	eo	æa	u
III	1). i	a	u
	2). e	ea	u
	3). eo	ea	u
IV	e	æ	ææ
V	e (i, ie)	æ	ææ
VI	a	oo	oo
VII	ea	eo	eo

Table 3, presents the vowel-gradation of the seven classes in Old English, where VV (Vowel + Vowel) implies a long vowel. Therefore, Old English had seven classes of "strong" verbs with a large variety of stem-vowel grading and phonemic vowel length: long and short. There was also a differentiation between a singular and a plural form of the "strong" verbs in the Past Tense in Old English. However, in all of these seven classes of Old English "strong" verbs in which the Past Tense form was distinguished by variable stem-vowel from Non-Past Tense form (following e.g. Quirk and Wrenn's 1955 as well as Lass and Anderson's 2010[1975] account of the phonological system of Old English), all of the classes of IVA in the verb forms represent varying degrees of the *backing process* either in the singular or the plural Past Tense forms or in both. For example, in the first class of Table 3, the IVA process is from a long high front /i/ to a low back /a/ in the singular and to a high front /i/ in the plural form. Following Emerson (1910, 346), "[o]f the two preterit stems in Old English, sometimes one, sometimes the other, has been retained in modern speech, but more commonly the singular has outlasted the plural". The second class contains the IVA process from the medium-front back diphthong /eo/ to the medium-low-front back diphthong /æa/ in the singular and high back /u/ in the plural. In the third class, there are more kinds of IVA variations; however, all of them display different degrees of *backing*: from front /i/ or medium-front /e/ or the medium-front back diphthong /eo/ to low back /a/ or the medium-front low-back diphthong /ea/ in the singular and to high back /u/ in the plural. In classes four and five, there is another degree of *backing* from medium-front /e/ to a medium-low front /æ/ in the singular and a long medium-low front /ææ/ in the plural, which according to spectrographic analysis (e.g. Ladefoged (1993, 197) is "less front" or further back than [e]. In class six, there is a transition from a low back /a/ to a long back /oo/ in both singular and plural forms, where [o] is higher and further back than [*a*] (Ladefoged 1993,197); and in the seventh class or, the *reduplicating verbs*, following Quirk and Wrenn (1955, 46) "[t]he changes of vowel in Cl. VII are of obscure origin, … [not like] in Cl. I-VI [that] have arisen by **gradation**", however we still observe a slight variation of the backing process similar to the previous class: from a medium-front back diphthong /ea/ to medium-front-back diphthong /eo/ in both singular and plural forms.

In Table 4, we present the fourteen groups of Modern English IVA verbs arranged in form classes. The vast majority of the Modern English IVA verbs display *backing*, however, there are seven Modern English IVA verbs that did not preserve *backing* in Modern English*: 'run, fall, bite, slide, come, lie, hold'*. In Table 4, we also include the Old English *backing process* for these verbs.

Table 4. ***Backing Process*** **of IVA in Non-Past to Past Tense Conjugation of Originally "Strong" Verbs in English**

Group No.	Stem-Vowel in Non-Past Tense Form in O.E. or Mod.E.	Stem-Vowel in Past Tense Form in O.E. or Mod.E.	No.of Verbs	Backing Process in Mod. E or O.E. (+)	The Verbs
1	Mod.E.:[I],[aI],[æ]	Mod.E.: [ʌ]	10	+	slink, wring, swing, sting, strike, sling, cling, fling, win, hang

2	Mod.E.:[I],[aI], [ɛ]	Mod.E.: [ɔ:] [ɔ]/[ɒ][3]	4	+	fight, see, get, tread
3	Mod.E.: [aI]	Mod.E.: [aʊ]	4	+	find, grind, bind, wind
4	Mod.E.: [I] O.E.: /i/ Mod.E.: [ʌ]	Mod.E.: [æ] O.E.: /o/ or /u/ Mod.E.: [æ]	4 1	+ +	drink, begin, sit, swim, run
4 or 1	Mod.E.: [I]	Mod.E.: [æ] or [ʌ]	6	+	sink, spin, stink, sing, shrink, spring
5	Mod.E.: [Ii] O.E.: /ea/ Mod.E.: [ɔ]	Mod.E.: [ɛ] O.E.: /ēo/ Mod.E.: [ɛ]	1 1	+ +	eat fall

[3] It is worth noting the dialectal variation of these IVAs of the verbs: *tread* and *get* in transcribing the different vowels of American and British English. Thus, there is some difference in the transcription of vowels (cf. Ladefoged 1993, 70). In the chart of English vowels, Ladefoged compares and presents the IPA symbols that are used by different authors. For example, [ɒ] used by J. C. Wells(1990) in the *Longman Pronunciation Dictionary* in the transcribtion of the internal vowel sound of the word "bother" corresponds to the [ɔ] used by Jones (1977) in the *Everyman's English Pronounciation Dictionary* (14th ed.). Also, [ɔ:] used by Jones (1977) in this dictionary in transcribing the internal vowel sound of the verb "brought" differs from the transcription of this sound: [ɔ] given in the other dictionaries: e.g. J. S. Kenyon and T. A. Knott (1953), C. Prator and B. Robinett (1985). Moreover, the *New Collins Concise Dictionary of the English Language* (1982, xix), by McLeod and Hanks, also has the following remark concerning the merging of both sounds [ɔ:] and [ɒ], i.e. "[t]he old-fashioned /ɔ:/ in words like *off, cloth, cross* is abandoned in favour of /ɒ/".

	O.E.: /ea/ Mod. E.:[əʊ]	O.E.: /ēo/ Mod.E.:[ɛ]	1	+	hold
6	Mod.E.:[ɔ:], [əʊ], [aI]	Mod.E.: [ʊu]	6	+	draw, grow, know, blow, throw, fly
7	Mod.E: [eI], [æ]	Mod.E.: [ʊu]	5	+	take, shake, stand, forsake, slay
8	Mod.E: [aI]	Mod.E: [əʊ]	8	+	(a)bide, rise, shine, drive, strive, dive, stride
9	Mod.E.: [eə]	Mod.E: [ɔə]	4	+	swear, tear, shear, bear
10	Mod.E.: [Ii]	Mod.E: [əʊ]	6	+	speak, weave, steal, heave, freeze, yield
11	Mod.E: [eI]	Mod.E.: [əʊ]	3	+	awake, break, wake
12	O.E.: /ī/ Mod.E.: [aI]	O.E.: /ā/ or /i/ Mod.E.: [I]	2	+	bite, slide
12 or 8	O.E.: /ī/ Mod.E.: [aI]	O.E.: /ā/ or /i/ Mod.E.: [I] or [əʊ]	3	+	ride, write, smite

13	O.E.: /ē̆o/ Mod.E.: [ʊu]	O.E.: /ē̆a/ or /u/ Mod.E.:([ɒ/ɔ]/[əʊ])	2	+	choose, shoot
14	O.E.: /i/, /ie/, /ē̆o/ Mod.E.: [I]	O.E. : /æ/ or /ǣ/, /ea/, /ē̆a/, /u/ Mod.E.:[eI]	3	+	bid, give, cleave
	O.E.: /e/ Mod.E.: [ʌ]	O.E.: /ō/ Mod.E.:[eI]	1	+	come
	O.E.: /i/ Mod.E.: [aI]	O.E.:/æ/ or /ǣ/(/ā/) Mod.E.:[eI]	1	+	lie

Table 4 also indicates that the Modern English IVA verbs are fundamentally phonologically systematic and not "irregular". The Modern English like Old English IVA forms display various degrees of *backing,* such as: from mid-high front lax [I] or low front [æ] or the low-central mid-high-front diphthong [aI] → to mid-low-central [ʌ]; from mid-high front lax [I] or mid-low-front [ɛ] or low-central mid-high-front diphthong [aI] → to long mid-low back [ɔ:]; from low-central mid-high-front diphthong [aI] → to low-central mid-high-back diphthong [aʊ]; from mid-high lax front [I] → to low front [æ], which spectrographically (cf. Ladefoged (1993,197) appears as a lower and further back vowel than [I] or mid-low-central [ʌ]; from high-front diphthong [Ii] → to mid-low-front [ɛ], which is marked by a slight backing from [Ii] (cf. Ladefoged's spectrographic analysis); from long mid-low back [ɔ:] or mid-central high-back diphthong [əʊ] or low-central mid-high-front diphthong [aI] → to high-back diphthong [ʊu]; from mid-front mid-high-front diphthong [eI] or low-front [æ] → to high-back diphthong [ʊu]; from low-central mid-high-front diphthong [aI] → to mid-central high-back diphthong [əʊ]; from mid-front mid-central diphthong [eə] → to mid-low-back mid-central [ɔə]; from high-front diphthong [Ii] → to mid-central high-back diphthong [əʊ]; from mid-front mid-high-front diphthong [eI] → to mid-central high-back diphthong [əʊ].

As previously mentioned, there are seven Modern English forms — *'run, fall, bite, slide, come, lie, hold'* — which have not retained the original *backing process* found in Old English: from medium-high front /i/ to medium-low back /o/ in the singular form or to medium-high back /u/ in the plural; from medium-front low-back diphthong /ea/ to high-medium-front-long back diphthong /ēo/, where [o] is further back than [*a*] (Ladefoged 1993,197); from high front long /ī/ to long low back /ā/ in singular and medium-high front lax /i/ in plural; from medium-front /e/ to long medium-back /ō/; from medium-high front lax /i/ to medium-low front /æ/ or long low back /ā/. Regardless of the individual degree (e.g from front or central vowel or diphthong to different further central or back vowels and diphthongs) each Past Tense formation still displays a variation of the *backing process*.

Moreover, in Modern English, following Emerson's (1910) historical study of the English language, there are some additional IVA verbs like: *'ring'-'rang/rung', 'dig'-'dug', 'stick'-'stuck', 'string'-'strung', 'spit'-'spat', 'wear'-'wore', 'reeve'-'rove', 'stave'-'stove', 'chide'-'chode'*, that originally were "weak—ed", i.e. historically were not derived from the "strong" *vowel-gradation* verbs. These newly transformed IVA verbs, however, still follow the *backing process* in the Non-Past to Past Tense conjugation of verbs: from mid-high lax front [I] → to low front [æ], which is articulated further back in the mouth (cf. Ladefoged 1993, 197) or mid-low-central [ʌ]; or from mid-front mid-central diphthong [eə] → to mid-low back mid-central [ɔə]; from high-front diphthong [Ii] or from mid-front high-front diphthong /eI/ or from low-central high-front diphthong [aI] → to mid-central high-back diphthong [əʊ]. Thus, these transformed weak to strong IVA verbs still conform to the phonological process of *backing*. This instance of *backing*, which characterizes the IVA verb system in English, further provides evidence not only for the systematic *backing* of IVA verbs in English over time, but also for the productivity of this IVA process that was addressed in Keuleers and Sandra (2003).

As well as in these originally "weak" verbs that became "strong", in the historical "strong" IVA verbs which became "weak", we witness the same phonological process, i.e. various degrees of the *backing* process: e.g. *'rive'-'rove' [rived], 'climb'-'clomb' [climbed], 'shave'-'shove' [shaved], 'heave'-'hove' [heaved], '(a)bide'-'(a)bode' [(a)bided], 'crow'-'crew' [crowed], 'sow'-'sew' [sowed], 'shear'-'shore' [sheared], 'shrive'-'shrove' [shrived], 'weave'-'wove' [weaved], 'yield'-'yold' [yielded], 'wake'-'woke' [waked], 'awake'-'awoke' [awaked], etc.,* with the IVA from low-central high-lax-front diphthong [aI] → mid-central high-lax-back diphthong [əʊ]; from high-front diphthong [Ii] or from mid-front high-lax-front diphthong [eI] → to mid-central high-lax-back diphthong [əʊ]; from mid-front mid-central diphthong [eə] → to low back mid-central [ɔə]; from mid-central high-lax-back diphthong [əʊ] → to high-back diphthong [ʊu]. In the above examples, we consistently observe different degrees of the phonological process of *backing* in the conjugation of IVA verbs from Non-Past to Past Tense, thus further supporting the systematic nature of the IVA process.

We also maintain that the IVA verbs, like the IVA nouns, are semantically motivated (Even-Simkin and Tobin 2011, Even-Simkin 2011). It is worth noting that this common semantic aspect for the so-called irregular verbs was demonstrated in psycholinguistic studies by Plunkett and Juola (1999), and in neuroimaging studies by Paterson, Lambon Ralph, Hodges, and McClelland (2001), where they report on selective problems of patients with semantic dementia in the formation of the so-called irregular Past Tense. Moreover, there is additional experimental evidence to suggest that "irregular verbs can be semantic attractors" (Baayen and Martin 2005, 670) that also appears in other studies e.g., by Bybee and Slobin (1982), Bybee (1985), Ramscar (2002). In our preliminary studies of the semantic aspect of the so-called irregular IVA verbs we also have found a semantic motivation for the IVA verbs that matches their systematic phonological IVA patterns. For example, for the second group of IVA verbs: from Non-Past [I], [aI] to Past Tense [ɔ:] and from Non-Past [ɛ] to Past Tense [ɔ]/[ɒ], in verbs like: *'fight, see, get, tread'*, we have postulated the following common semantic denominator: *'to perceive/ to get'*. Historically, *'to perceive/ to get'*, appears in the complex diachronic *OED* definitions for each one of these verbs. In the third group of IVA verbs: *'bind', 'grind', 'wind', 'find'* from Non-Past [aI] to Past Tense [aʊ], there is also a common semantic denominator (literal or metaphoric) based on all of their diachronic *OED* definitions: '*some turning movement round something or to and fro against*'. We have also postulated a common semantic denominator for all the other groups of IVA verbs marked by the distinctive semantic feature +RESULT (Even-Simkin and Tobin 2011, Even-Simkin 2011). This indicates that there may be a direct connection between form and meaning for the entire IVA verb system. A more detailed analysis of the semantic motivation of the IVA nominal and verbal forms will be discussed in further research. As we have previously noted about the *fronting* process for the IVA nominal forms (going forward in number), the phonological *backing process* in the

Past Tense formation ('moving backward in time') is also metaphorically iconic. This additional iconic element provides further support for our claim that the IVA nominal and verbal forms are systematic and not "irregular".

5. Conclusions

This study discusses two different phonological processes: the *fronting process* in the so-called irregular nominal forms in their Singular to Plural declensions and the *backing process* for the so-called irregular verbal forms in the Non-Past to Past Tense conjugation. The goal of this paper was to show that the IVA in nouns and verbs represents a consistent and motivated classification system. In particular we have described and explained the different phonological processes of the IVA forms which can be used to demarcate, classify and differentiate between the nominal and verbal IVA systems. We have viewed IVA as a classification system for the following reasons: first, we have shown that the internal vowel variations are consistent. Even though the IVA system has changed over time, the opposed phonological processes of *fronting* versus *backing* still distinguish between the IVA forms for nouns and verbs, respectively. We have also introduced the idea that each of these IVA systems shares a common semantic denominator. Thus, we have suggested that these morpho-syntactic systems are not only distinguished phonologically but are also motivated semantically within the grammar of English. For example, Stemberger (2001, 19) has shown that "phonology affects syntax, both in grammar (e.g., Rice and Svenonius 1998; Broadwell 2000) and in language acquisition (Stemberger and Bernhardt 1997)". In other words, in Modern English as well as in Old English, IVA preserved its phonological features as part of a full-fledged morpho-syntactic classification system in both nominal and verbal systems. Moreover, the cross-linguistic study of apophonic alternations, i.e. the IVA forms by Ségéral and Scheer (1998, 57), in languages like Classical Arabic, Somali, Berber and New High German, in which they have found the apophonic regularity of Ablaut in the verbs: Ø→ I→ A→ U→ U, further supports the systematic and universal character of the IVA in Old English as well as in Modern English. We have also maintained that in addition to the phonological characteristics, the IVA systems are not only semantically motivated but are polar and iconic. The semantic motivations and the iconic values for the IVA system are being further developed in our research.

References

Albright, Adam and Bruce Hayes. 2002. "Modeling English Past Tense Intuitions with Minimal Generalization." In *Proceedings of the 6th Meeting of the ACLSspecial Interest Group in Computational Phonology,* edited by M. Maxwell, New Brubswick, NJ; Association for Computational Linguistics.

Atkinson, Richard. C., and Richard M. Shiffrin. 1968. "Human Memory: A Proposed System and Its Control Processes." In. *The Psychology of Learning and Motivation (Volume 2)*, edited by K.W. Spence and J.T Spence, 89–195. New York: Academic Press.

Baayen, Harald R., and Fermín Moscoso del Prado Martín. 2005. "Semantic Density and Past-Tense Formation in Three Germanic Languages." *Language* 81(3): 666-698.

Baković, Eric. 2003. "Counterfactual Considerations (in Phonology)." Southwest Optimality Theory Workshop (SWOT) 8. University of Arizona, Tucson, AZ. Apr. 2003.

Baugh, Albert C. 1957. *A History of the English Language*. Second Edition. New York: Meredith Corporation.

Baugh, Albert C. and Thomas Cable. 2002[1951]. *A History of the English Language*. Fifth Edition. London: Routledge.

Beedham, Christopher. 2002. "Irregularity in Language: Saussure versus Chomsky versus Pinker. A review of Words and Rules, by Steven Pincker." *Word* 53: 341-367.

—. 2005. *Language and Meaning*. Amsterdam/Philadelphia: Benjamins.

Berko, Jean. 1958. "The Child's Learning of English Morphology." *Word* 14: 150-177.

Bloch, Bernard. 1947. "English Verb Inflection." *Language* 23: 399-418.

Boersma, Paul. 1998. "The OCP in Functional Phonology." *Proceedings of the Amsterdam Institute of Phonetic Sciences* 22: 21-45.

Broadwell, George Aaron. 2000. *On the Phonological Conditioning of Clitic Placement in Zapotec*. ROA-422.

Bybee, Joan L. 1985. *Morphology: a Study of the Relation Between Meaning and Form*. Philadelphia: Benjamins.

—. 1988a. "Morphology as Lexical Organization." In *Theoretical Morphology*, edited by M. Hammond and M. Noonan, 119-41. San Diego, CA: Academic Press.

—. 1988b. "The Diachronic Dimension in Explanation." In *Explaining Language Universals*, edited By J. Hawkins, 350-79. New York: Blackwell.

—. 1995. "Regular Morphology and the Lexicon." *Language and Cognitive Processes* 10. 425-55.
—. 2001. *Phonology and Language Use.* Cambridge and New York: Cambridge University Press.
Bybee, Joan L., and Dan I. Slobin. 1982. "Rules and Schemas in the Development and Use of the English Past Tense." *Language* 58: 265-289.
Contini-Morava, Ellen, Kirsner, Robert S., and Betsy Rodríguez-Bachiller, eds. 2004. *Cognitive and Communicative Approaches to Linguistic Analysis*. Amsterdam/Philadelphia: John Benjamins.
Contini-Morava, Ellen, and Barbara Sussman Goldberg. 1995. *Meaning as Explanation: Advances in Linguistic Sign Theory.* Berlin: Mouton de Gruyter.
Contini-Morava, Ellen, and Yishai Tobin. 2000. *Between Grammar and Lexicon*. Amsterdam/Philadelphia: John Benjamins.
Crano, William, D. 1977. "Primacy versus Recency in Retention of Information and Opinion Change." *Journal of Social Psychology* 101: 87-96.
Crark, John Williams. 1964. *Early English: A Study of Old and Middle English*. New York: W. W. Norton and Company, Inc.
Crystal, David. 1995. *The Cambridge Encyclopedia of the English Language.* Cambridge: Cambridge University Press.
Crowder, Robert G. 1969. "Behavioral Strategies in Immediate Memory." *Journal of Verbal Learning and Verbal Behavior* 8: 524-528.
Davis, Joseph. 1987[1984]. "A Combinatory Phonology of Italian." *Columbia University Working Papers in Linguistics* 8: 1-99.
Davis, Joseph, Gorup, Radmila J., and Nancy Stern, eds. 2006. *Advances in Functional Linguistics: Columbia School Beyond Its Origins.* Amsterdam/Philadelphia: John Benjamins.
Diver, William. 1975. "Introduction." *Columbia University Working Papers in Linguistics* 2: 1-20.
—. 1979. "Phonology as Human Behavior." In *Psycholinguistic Research: Implications and Applications*, edited by Dorothy Aaronson and Robert W. Reiber, 161-186. Hillside, N.J.: Lawrence Erlbaum.
—. 1984. "The Grammar of English." Unpublished manuscript.
—. 1987. "The Dual." *Columbia University Working Papers in Linguistics* 8: 100-114
—. 1993. "The Phonology of the Extremes: The Correlation of Initials and Finals." Paper given at the Third International Columbia School Conference on Linguistics. Rutgers University, New Brunswick, N.J., October 11, 1993.

—. 1995. "The Theory." In *Meaning as Explanation: Advances in Linguistic Sign Theory,* edited by Ellen Contini-Morava and Barbara Sussman Goldberg, 43-114. Berlin: Mouton de Gruyter.

Ebbinghaus, Hermann. 1885. *Über das Gedchtnis.Untersuchungen zur Experimentellen Psychologie*. Leipzig: Duncker and Humblot; translated from German by Henry A. Ruger and Clara E. Bussenius. (1913). *Memory. A Contribution to Experimental Psychology*. New York: Teachers College, Columbia University.

Emerson, Oliver Farrar. 1910. *The History of the English Language*. New York and London: Macmillan and CO., Ltd.

Even-Simkin, Elena. 2011. "Internal Vowel Alternations in Nominal and Verbal Forms According to Sign-Oriented Theory and the Theory of Phonology as Human Behavior." Ph.D. dissertation. Ben-Gurion University of the Negev, Israel.

Even-Simkin, Elena and Yishai Tobin. 2011. "Semantic Regularities in the So-Called Irregular Internal Vowel Alternation (IVA) Nominal (*umlaut*) and Verbal (*ablaut*) Forms in Old and Modern English." In *Linguistic Theory and Empirical Evidence*, edited by Bob de Jonge and Yishai Tobin, 45-81. Amsterdam: John Benjamins.

Frensch, Peter A. 1994. "Composition During Serial Learning: A Serial Position Effect." *Journal of Experimental Psychology: Learning, Memory, and Cognition* 20(2): 423-442.

Gamkrelidze, T. V., and V.V. Ivanov. 1995 [1984, in Russian]. *Indo-European and the Indo-Eurpeans: A Reconstruction and Historical Analysis of a Proto-Language and a Proto-Culture.* Vols. I and II. Translated from the Russian by J. Nichols. Berlin: Mouton de Gruyter.

Glanzer, Murray, and Anita R. Cunitz. 1966. "Two storage mechanisms in free recall." *Journal of Verbal Learning and Verbal Behaviour* 5: 351-60.

Griggs, Silas and Curt M. Rulon. 1974. *English Verb Inflection: A Generative View*. The Hague, Mouton.

Guillaume, Gustave. 1984. *Foundations for a Science of Language*. Amsterdam/Philadelphia: John Benjamins.

Healy, Alice F., Havas, David A., and James T. Parker. 2000. "Comparing Serial Position Effects in Semantic and Episodic Memory Using Reconstruction of Order Tasks." *Journal of Memory and Language* 42(2): 147-167.

Hoard, James E. and Clarence Sloat. 1973. "English Irregular Verbs." *Language* 49(1): 107-120.

Hirtle, Walter. 1982. *Number and Inner Space: A Study of Grammatical Number in English*. Quebec: Presse de l'Université Laval.

Hulbert, James R. 1963. *Bright's Anglo-Saxon Reader*. Unites States: Holt, Rinehart and Winston, Inc.

Jember, Gregory K. 1975. *English-Old English, Old English-English Dictionary*. United States: Westview Press, Inc.

Jones, Daniel. 1977. *Everyman's English Pronouncing Dictionary*, 14th. ed. London: Dent.

Juilland, Alphonse and James Macris. 1962. *The English Verb System*. Netherlands: Mouton and Co., Printers, The Hague.

Katamba, Francis. 2006. "Phonetically Motivated Word-Formation". *The Encyclopaedia of Language and Linguistics.(2nd ed.)*. Oxford: Elsevier, 411-414.

Keuleers, Emmanuel and Dominiek Sandra. 2003. "Similarity and Productivity in the English Past Tense." *Computational Linguistics* 234: 1-49.

Kenyon, J.S. and T.A. Knott. 1953. *A Pronouncing Dictionary of American English*. Springfield, Mass.: G. and C. Merriam.

Klein-Andreu, Flora. 1983. *Discourse Perspectives on Syntax*. New York: Academic.

Kuczaj, Stan A. 1977. "The Acquisition of Regular and Irregular Past Tense Forms." *Journal of Verbal Learning and Verbal Behavior* 16: 589-600.

Ladefoged, Peter. 1993. *A Course in Phonetics*. (3rd ed.) Fort Worth: Harcourt Brace Jovanovich College Publishers.

Lass, Roger and John M. Anderson. 2010[1975]. *Old English Phonology*. New York and Cambridge: Cambridge University Press.

Lehmann, Winfred P. 1962. *Linguistics: an Introduction*. Unites States: New York: Holt, Rinehart and Winston, Inc.

Luchins, Abraham S. 1957. "Primacy-Recency in Impression Formation." Hovland C (ed.). *The Order of Presentation in Persuasion*. New Haven, CN: Yale University Press.

Marchman, Virginia A. 1997. "Children's Productivity in the English Past Tense: The Role of Frequency, Phonology, and Neighborhood Structure." *Cognitive Science* 21(3): 283-304.

Marcus, G. F. 1995. "Children's Over-regularization of English Plurals: A Quantitative Analysis." *Journal of Child Language* 22(2): 440-460.

Marcus, G., Pinker, S., Ullman, M., Hollander, J., Rosen, T., and Xu, F. 1992. "Over-regularization in Language Acquisition." *Monographs of the Society for Research in Child Development 57 (4): Serial No. 228.*

McLeod, William and Patrick Hanks. 1982. *The New Collins Concise Dictionary of the English Language*. London and Glasgow: William Collins Sons and Co Ltd.

Mitchell, Bruce and Fred C. Robinson. 1982. *A Guide to Old English.* Oxford: Basil Blackwell

Murdock, Bennet. B. Jr. 1962. "The Serial Position Effect of Free Recall." *Journal of Experimental Psychology* 64: 482-488.

Oxford English Dictionary. Available online *http://oed.com* [cited in the text as OED].

Oxford Advanced Learner's Dictionary. 1995. UK: Oxford University Press [cited in the text as OALD].

Patterson, K., Lambon Ralph, M., Hodges, J., McClelland, J. 2001. "Deficits in Irregular Past-Tense Verb Morphology Associated with Degraded Semantic Knowledge." *Neuropsychologia* 39: 709-724.

Partridge, Eric. 2006. *Origins: A Short Etymological Dictionary of Modern English.* London/ New York: Routledge Ltd.

Pinker, Steven. 1994. *The Language Instinct: The New Science of Language and Mind.* London: Penguin.

—. 1999. *Words and Rules: The Ingredients of Language.* London: Weidenfeld and Nicolson.

Pinker, Steven, and Alan Prince. 1988. "On Language and Connectionism: Analyses of a Parallel Distributed Model of Language Acquisition." *Cognition* 28: 59-108.

Pinker, Steven, and Ullman, MT. 2002. "The Past and Future of the Past Tense." *Trends in cognitive Sciences* 6: 456-463.

Plunkett, Kim and Virginia A. Marchman. 1993. "From Rote Learning to System Building: Acquiring Verb Morphology in Children and Connectionist Nets." *Cognition* 48: 21-69.

Plunkett, Kim and Juola Patrick. 1999. "A Connectionist Model of English Past Tense and Plural Morphology." *Cognitive Science* 23(4): 463-490.

Pollington, Stephen. 2003. *Wordcraft: Concise New English to Old English Dictionary and Thesaurus.* Norfolk: Anglo-Saxon Books.

Prator, C. H., and B. W. Robinett. 1985. *Manual of American English Pronunciation*, 4th. ed. New York: Holt, Rinehart and Winston.

Prokosch, E. 1938. *A Comparative Germanic Grammar.* Chicago: Linguistic Association of America.

Quirk, Randolph. 1970. "Aspect and Variant Inflection in English Verbs." *Language* 46: 300-311.

Quirk, Randolph, and Charles L. Wrenn. 1955. *An Old English Grammar.* Great Britain: Methuen and Co., Ltd., London.

Quirk, Randolph, Greenbaum, Sidney, Leech, Geoffrey, and Jan Svartvik. 1985. *A] Comprehensive Grammar of the English Language.* London: Longman.

Quirk, Randolph and Sidney Greenbaum. 1993. *A University Grammar of English*. England: Longman Group UK Limited.

Ramskar, M. 2002. “The Role of Meaning in Inflection: Why the Past Tense Doesn't Require a Rule.” *Cognitive Psychology* 45: 45-94.

Reid, Wallis. 1991. *Verb and Noun Number in English: A Functional Explanation*. London/New York: Longman Publishers.

Reid, Wallis, Ricardo Otheguy, and Nancy Stern. (eds.). 2002. *Signal, Meaning and Message: Perspectives on Sign-Based Linguistics*. Amsterdam/Philadelphia: John Benjamins.

Rice, Curt, and Peter Svenonius. 1998. “Prosodic V2 in Northern Norwegian.” Paper presented at the 17th West Coast Conference on Formal Linguistics, Vancouver, BC, February 1998.

Rumelhart, David. E., and James L. McClelland. 1986. “On Learning the Past Tense of English Verbs.” In J. L. McClelland, D. E. Rumelhart, and the PDP Research Group (Eds.), *Parallel distributed processing: Explorations in the Microstructure of cognition, Vol. 2: Psychological and Biological Models* (pp. 216-271). Cambridge, MA: MIT Press.

Saussure, Ferdinand de. 1959 [1916]. *A Course in General Linguistics/Cours de Linguistique Général*. Paris: Payot, New York: Philosophical Library.

—. 1983. *Course in General Linguistics* [1916]. Edited by C. Bally and A. Sechehaye, in collaboration with A. Riedlinger. Translated and annotated by Roy Harris. London: Duckworth.

Ségéral, Philippe and Tobias Scheer. 1998. A Generalized Theory of Ablaut: the Case of Modern German Strong Verbs. *Models of Inflection*, edited by Albert Ortmann, Ray Fabri and Teresa Parodi, 28-59. Tübingen: Niemever.

Skeat, Walter W. 1879. *An English–Anglo-Saxon Vocabulary.* Cambridge: University of Cambridge Press.

Skousen, Royal. 1989. *Analogical Modelling of Language*. Dordrecht: Kluwer.

—. 1992. *Analogy and Structure.* Dordrecht: Kluwer.

Stemberger, Joseph Paul, and Barbara H. Bernhardt. 1997. “Syntactic Development Limited by Phonological Development.” Paper presented at the 38th meeting of the Psychonomic Society, Philadelphia, November 1997.

—. 2001. *Overtensing within Optimality Theory.* [ROA nº 477,] http://ruccs.rutgers.edu/roa.html

Sturtevant, Edgar. 1917 [1961]. *Linguistic Change: An Introduction to the Historical Study of Language.* Chicago: The University of Chicago Press.

Smith, Jeremy J. 2009. *Old English: a linguistic introduction*. United Kingdom: Cambridge University Press.

Tobin, Yishai. 1989. *From Sign to Text: A Semiotic View of Communication*. Amsterdam/Philadelphia: John Benjamins.

—. 1990. *Semiotics and Linguistics*. London and New-York: Longman.

—. 1993a. *Aspect in the English Verb: Process and Result in Language*. London and New York: Longman.

—. 1993b. "Showing Native Speakers What and Why They Say What They Do Say: Awareness Raising From a Semiotic Point of View." *Language Awareness* 2(3): 143-158.

—. 1995[1994]. *Invariance, Markedness and Distinctive Feature Analysis: A Contrastive Study of Sign Systems in English and Hebrew*. Amsterdam /Philadelphia: John Benjamins [hardcover] [1994], Be'er-Sheva: Ben-Gurion University Press (paperback) (1995)

—. 1997. *Phonology as Human Behavior: Theoretical Implications and Clinical Applications*. Durham, NC/London: Duke University Press.

—. 2002. "Phonology as Human Behavior: Initial Consonant Clusters Across Languages." In *Signal, Meaning and Message: Perspectives on Sign-Based Linguistics*, edited by Wallis Reid, Ricardo Otheguy, and Nancy Stern, 191-255. Amsterdam /Philadelphia: John Benjamins.

—. 2006. "Phonology as Human Behaviour: Inflectional Systems in English." In *Advances in Functional Linguistics: Columbia School Beyond Its Origin,* edited by Joseph Davis, Radmila J. Gorup and Nancy Stern. 63-86. Amsterdam/Philadelphia: John Benjamins.

—. 2009. "Phonology as Human Behavior: Applying Theory to the Clinic." *Asia-Pacific Journal of Speech, Language and Hearing* 12(2): 81-100.

Well, J. C. 1990. *Longman Pronunciation Dictionary*. Harlow, U.K.: Longman.

Wright, Joseph and Elizabeth Mary Wright. 1908. *Old English Grammar*. London: Oxford University Press.

SOUND CHANGES AND VARIATION IN THE VOWEL SYSTEM OF THE VIENNESE DIALECT[1]

SYLVIA MOOSMÜLLER
AUSTRIAN ACADEMY OF SCIENCES, VIENNA, AUSTRIA

Abstract

In the present study, the effects of two sound changes are discussed. The Viennese Monophthongization and the confusion of the vowels /e/ and /ɛ/. The Viennese Monophthongization was first observed around 1900 and added two long vowels to the existing vowel system of the Viennese dialect. This sound change was completed around 1940. The second sound change started around 1920. In a first stage, a merger of the vowels /e/ and /ɛ/ in favour of the vowel /ɛ/ was observed. However, this change never reached a stage of completion. Around 1970, an opposite ongoing change could be observed: /ɛ/ tended to be merged with /e/. Again, this change never reached the stage of completion. To complicate matters further, the interaction with Standard Austrian German, which has a well-defined distribution of the vowels /e/ and /ɛ/, put an additional challenge on the realization of this vowel pair. As a consequence, the situation with respect to the realization of the vowels /e/ and /ɛ/ has still not stabilized; the distribution of the two vowels is completely arbitrary.

[1] This investigation was partly funded by the WWTF (http://www.ftw.at/ftw/research/projects/ProjekteFolder/U5). I am grateful to two anonymous reviewers and to Hannes Scheutz for their helpful comments on an earlier version of this paper.

1. Introduction

1.1 A brief overview of the socio-linguistic situation in Vienna

One characteristic of urban varieties is that they are predominantly social varieties. Nonetheless, some folk-linguistic beliefs circulate that the varieties spoken in Vienna are regionally distributed, i.e., that each district of Vienna shows specific linguistic traits. This belief might well be rooted in the fact that the diverse social classes of Vienna reside in specific districts. It is known that the 10th, 11th, 12th, 16th, and 17th districts are among those traditionally populated by the lower social classes, whereas the 1st, 13th, 18th, and 19th districts are the traditional living environments of the upper social classes. Additionally, this belief about district specific linguistic traits may stem from the fact that at around 1900, 25% of the population of the 10th district consisted of Czech immigrants (Glettler 1972). Although after World War I, around two-thirds of the Czech population moved to the newly founded Czechoslovakian Republic, the belief that a pervasive Czech influence on the Viennese varieties existed, especially on the Viennese dialect, held its ground until the 1970s. It then diminished as a consequence of the new groups of immigrants, of which today people from the former Yugoslavia and from Turkey form the most populous groups. In Vienna, the number of people with a migrant background doubled between 1999 and 2009 (Biffl 2009).

Except for the newly emerged contact varieties, the varieties of Viennese can be conceptualized as lying on a line between two extreme varieties, the Viennese dialect (VD) and the Viennese Standard Austrian German (VSAG) variety. In many ways, these two extreme varieties developed independently from each other, and their relationship can therefore be best grasped by a two-competence-model (Dressler/Wodak 1982). In this model, the forms which show a diverging development from Middle High German (MHG) for the VD and VSAG are considered as input-switch rules, since no intermediate steps can be found between the two opposing forms (e.g. /u:/ ↔ /uɐ/ < MHG. *uo*). Both from the production and from the perception point of view, these forms are very salient and therefore the dialectal forms are avoided in VSAG and in varieties striving for VSAG. The same holds for processes restricted to the VD, e.g. the Viennese monophthongization or the vocalization of the lateral[2]. The vast majority of processes hold both for the VD and for VSAG, e.g. r-vocalization, assimilation and reduction processes. These processes are phonetically motivated and gradual, and consequently contain many intermediate steps (e.g. /ha:bɛn/ → [ha:bm̩] → [ha: m̩] → [ham] "haben" (to have)). In most of these cases, the difference between the VD and VSAG is a statistical one, the forms nearer to the underlying form being found to a higher degree within VSAG and varieties striving for VSAG, whereas the forms on the other end of the line are more often used within dialect-near varieties[3].

The VD is attributed to the lower social classes of Vienna. However, it has to be noted that during the 1970s, as a consequence of the social and socio-political movements of the 1960s, a new variety emerged. It seems that one of the effects of this movement was a higher awareness of the social implications of the use of specific language varieties. Especially in the big cities, above all in Vienna, many speakers of the dialects started to abandon the negatively associated dialect[4] and started to use the prestigious standard variety. In striving for the standard variety, speakers concentrated mainly on the phonology, especially on the very salient input-switch rules, which were abandoned first. The prosody, syntax, and morphology of the dialect were preserved. For speakers of the upper social classes, this variety was even more negatively evaluated than the dialects. Speakers of the lower social classes did not, however, give up, and raised their children in this new variety, so that today, a second and third generation of speakers of this new standard variety exists. Depending on the education of these second and third generation standard speakers, morphology and syntax were adapted more or less successfully to the true standard variety. Less educated speakers retained the syntax and morphology of the dialect, so that today the lower social classes of Vienna speak two varieties, the original VD and the new VD-based standard, the former being spoken by the older generation (> 50), the latter mainly by the younger generation (< 30). This paper focuses on some salient sound changes and variations in the VD.

---

[2] Many of the alternations or processes described hold for the Middle-Bavarian varieties – both dialectal and standard – in general, therefore, the model can be extended to the description of other varieties in Austria as well (see e.g., Soukup 2009)

[3] See Moosmüller 1987, 1991, for a list and analysis of the interaction between dialect and standard forms.

[4] The Viennese dialect is the most negatively evaluated variety in Austria, see Moosmüller (1991).

1.2 The Viennese Monophthongization

Around 1900, a process of monophthongization was observed among the speakers of the lower social classes of Vienna (Gartner 1900, Luick 1904)[5]. In this process, the diphthongs /aɛ/ and /ɑɔ/[6], which have evolved from MHG *î* and *û*, were monophthongized to /æ:/ and /ɒ:/, respectively. E.g.:

/vaɛt/ → /væ:d̥/ “weit” (wide)
/hɑɔs/ → /hɒ:s/ “Haus” (house)

It has to be noted that this process does not hold for the Standard (Austrian) German diphthong /aɛ/ which evolved from MHG *ei*, because MHG *ei* developed into /ɔɐ/ in the Middle-Bavarian dialects[7] and, in a later step, into /ɑ:/ in the Viennese dialect and in the dialect of southern Carinthia. Therefore, the Middle-Bavarian dialects have preserved a distinction which has been lost in Standard (Austrian) German (see Table 1).

Table 1: Development of MHG *ei* and *î* in Standard (Austrian) German and in the dialects.

	“weiß” < MHG *ei* (to know)	“weiß” < MHG *î* (white)
Standard (Austrian) German	/vaɛs/	/vaɛs/
Middle-Bavarian dialects	/vɔɐs/	/vaɛs/
Viennese dialect	/vɑ:s/	/væ:s/

The Viennese monophthongization is an assimilation process, whereby one part of the diphthong is assimilated to the other. From an articulatory

5 Around 1900, the number of Czech immigrants had reached its climax. According to Kranzmayer (1953), Czech might be a leading force in the process of monophthongization.

6 The diphthong /ɔɛ/ collapses into /aɛ/ in the Austrian dialects.

7 The development of MHG *ei* to /ɔɐ/ holds for the Bavarian dialects in general, but to avoid extending beyond the scope of this paper, the further developments in other Bavarian dialects are not dealt with.(see Kranzmayer 1956).

point of view, different manoeuvres take place for the two diphthongs. As concerns the monophthongization of the diphthong /aɛ/, the tongue is raised, and the constriction location, which is pharyngeal for both /a/ and /ɑ/, is fronted towards the palatal region. The position of the jaw does not change. For the diphthong /ɑɔ/, the constriction location of /ɔ/ changes from uvular to pharyngeal, the jaw lowers at the /ɔ/-part, and possibly the tongue lowers too[8]. Lip protrusion remains. Therefore, both monophthongs share elements of either part of the original diphthong.

In the case of the monophthongization of /aɛ/, it is the degree of openness which reminds of the former /a/-part. Consequently, F1 is relatively high. The constriction location and constriction degree are, however, assimilated to the /ɛ/-part of the former diphthong, resulting, as compared to /a/, in a higher F2 and F3.

In the case of the monophthongization of /ɑɔ/, the protruded lips remind of the former /ɔ/-part, the remaining articulatory manoeuvres are assimilated to the /ɑ/-part. Acoustically, these movements result, as compared to /ɔ/, in a higher F1 and in a higher F2, the values of the latter are – due to lip-protrusion – in-between /ɑ/ and /ɔ/.

The inherent long duration of the diphthongs is preserved by compensatory lengthening. As a result of the process of monophthongization, the vowel inventory of the Viennese dialect is enriched by two new long vowels: /æ:/ and /ɒ:/, leading to the following minimal pairs (see Table 2):

Table 2: Minimal pairs for the front vowels /æ:/ – /ɛ:/ and for the back vowels /ɒ:/ – /ɔ:/.

Item	Gloss	Item	Gloss
/hæ:d̥/	today	/hɛ:d̥/	would have
/hɒ:s/	house	/hɔ:s/	rabbit

This sound change was completed by the 1940s (Kranzmayer 1953). It then spread from the lower to the upper social classes. In VSAG, spoken by the upper social classes, the process of monophthongization was first applied in unstressed positions. There is an important difference in process application between the VD and VSAG: Since monophthongization started in unstressed positions in VSAG, it is the result of a reduction process. Consequently, compensatory lengthening is missing. Even if applied in

[8] As articulatory studies have shown, the tongue might even be higher for /ɑ/ than for /ɔ/ (see Bohn et al. 1992).

more prominent positions, monophthongized diphthongs of VSAG are still approximantely one third shorter than the respective monophthongized diphthongs of the VD. To a large extent, these durational differences draw a clear line between the VD and VSAG.

Therefore, being a salient feature of the VD, monophthongization did not win through completely in VSAG. From Vienna, the process also spread to other parts of Austria. So far, no consequences for the phonological systems of the other dialects have been observed. Therefore, the Viennese monophthongization is a prevailing Viennese dialect characteristic, associated with the speech behavior of the lower social classes and, consequently, negatively evaluated.

1.3 The vowel system of the Viennese Dialect

The Viennese monophthongization had quite some effects on the vowel system of the VD. Two vowels were added to the existing front (palatal) /i, e, ɛ/, velar /u/, uvular /o, ɔ/, and pharyngeal /a, ɑ/: palatal /æ:/ and pharyngeal /ɒ:/. As concerns the status of duration, Wodak-Leodolter / Dressler (1978) argue that singular and plural are discerned by duration, e.g., /fi: ʃ/ (fish: SG) vs. /fiʃ/ (fish: PL). In the data analyzed for the current investigation, no such distinction is made any more. Vowel duration is, however, strongly linked to timing relations specific for the Middle-Bavarian dialects (see Moosmüller 2007b). According to these timing relations, the duration of the vowel is determined by the status of the subsequent obstruent (lenis vs. fortis). Due to neutralization of the front obstruents[9], vowels preceding front obstruents are long, vowels preceding fortis velar or palatal obstruents are short. Vowels in CVC words are usually long, even when followed by a fortis obstruent, e.g., [lɔ:x] (to laugh: IMP), as opposed to [lɔxŋ̍] (to laugh: INF).Therefore, except for the new monophthongs /æ:/ and /ɒ:/, the vowels of the Viennese dialect are not specified for length.

Generally, vowels are articulated on four constriction locations: palatal, velar, uvular, and lower pharyngeal (Wood 1979, 1982). Therefore, the back vowels have more constriction locations at their disposal than the front vowels. For small vowel inventories, this causes no problem, since palatal /i, e, ɛ/ can be discerned by constriction degree (=height) and jaw

[9] Old High German geminates constitute an exception to this rule. They became fortis obstruents, e.g. OHG bittar > [b̥itɐ] (bitter).

opening[10]. However, languages which have to discern more than three palatal vowels[11] might make use of a further, pre-palatal constriction location. This pre-palatal constriction location has been demonstrated for Egypt (Wood 1979), for Swedish and Russian (Fant 2001), for Estonian (Eek / Meister 1994), for French (Tabain / Perrier 2005), and for Standard Austrian German (Moosmüller 2007a).

With the introduction of the monophthongized /æ:/, four palatal vowels had to be discerned by constriction degree. In order to solve this undesirable situation, several options arise:

/ɛ/ and /e/ might merge,
/i/ might be shifted to the pre-palatal constriction location,
/æ:/ and /ɛ:/ might merge.

However, another change, known as the Middle-Bavarian "e-confusion", further complicated matters.

1.4 The confusion of the vowels /e/ and /ɛ/ in Vienna

The linear historical development of the vowels /e/ and /ɛ/ was disturbed by mainly five factors in the Middle-Bavarian dialects. This disturbance came to be known as the Middle-Bavarian "e-confusion". By and large, this confusion of the vowels /e/ and /ɛ/ is transparent (Scheuringer 1990).

In the VD, around 1920, and clearly as a response to the Viennese monophthongization, the vowels /e/ and /ɛ/ started to be neutralized to /ɛ/ (Kranzmayer 1953). However, the former nasalized vowels, which resulted from the deletion of the subsequent nasal consonant, e.g., /g̥ẽ:/ "gehen" (to go), were not affected by this neutralization, and, therefore,

---

[10] It is worth noting that jaw opening can be combined with constriction degree in such a way that four distinct vowels can be produced: /i, ɪ/ [-open], /e, ɛ/ [+open], /i, e/ [+constricted], /ɪ, ɛ/: [-constricted] (Wood 1982).

[11] It has to be noted that the constriction location of both /a/ and /ɑ/ is in the pharynx, therefore, they are back vowels. This can easily be exemplified by the complementary distribution of the velar and palatal fricative in German, including the Middle-Bavarian dialects: the front vowels require the palatal fricative, the back vowels, including /a/, the velar fricative (e.g. [b̥ax] ("Bach" (brook)). Further evidence comes from vowel harmony (e. g. Turkish and Hungarian).

the subsequent process of denasalization reintroduced /e/ (Seidelmann 1971).

In the 1970s, Seidelmann (1971) reported a high variability and interchangeability of the vowels /e/ and /ɛ/, with a tendency towards a neutralization in the direction of /e/. For this reason, Seidelmann (1971) assumed only one /e/-vowel, namely /e/, with high variability.

However, in addition, the new instability with regard to the realization of /e/ and /ɛ/ might as well be caused by an ever increasing interaction with Standard Austrian German, which has a well-defined distribution of the vowels/e/ and /ɛ/. In combination with the Middle-Bavarian "e-confusion", a confusion with respect to the "right" application of this vowel pair is obvious.

2. Method

Interviews were conducted with nine speakers of the Viennese dialect. The interviews were comprised of spontaneous speech, reading of sentences and of texts, sentences to be repeated, and pictures to be named in the Viennese dialect. For the current contribution, the picture naming task was analyzed.

All /i/-, /e/-, and /ɛ/- vowels in stressed position (646 in total) of the picture naming task were segmented manually. F1, F2, and F3 were extracted by means of LPC. A 46 ms long gliding Hanning window was applied with an overlap of 95%. Depending on the length of the vowel, the measurement procedure described rendered 20 to 150 measurements per vowel, i.e., the formant movements over time enter the analysis. This method was chosen, because vowels, especially when short, often expose no steady state portion. Duration was measured as well.

For the statistical analysis, one-tailed t-tests, a cluster analysis and the DIP-test (Hartigan/Hartigan 1985) were performed. The DIP-test examines, whether, for each speaker, a uni-modal or a bi-modal distribution of the vowels /e/ and /ɛ/ exists. In the case of a uni-modal distribution, the speaker distinguishes only one quality of the vowel /e/, in the case of a bi-modal distribution, the speaker distinguishes /e/ and /ɛ/. Figure 1 gives an example of a uni-modal and a bi-modal distribution of the /e/-vowels.

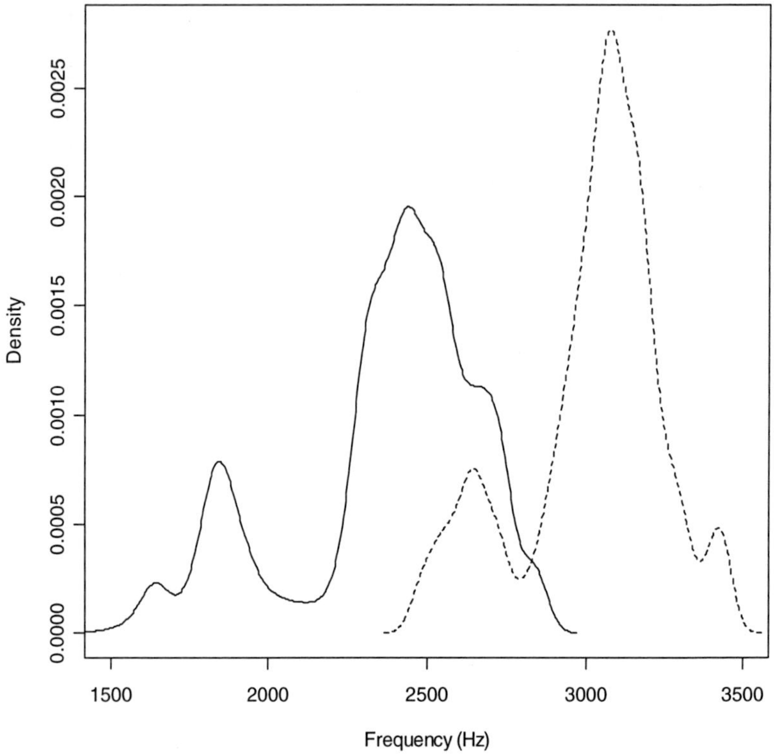

Figure 1: Examples of a uni-modal (top) and a bi-modal (bottom) distribution of the vowel /e/. Solid line: F2, dashed line: F3.

The density distributions of F2 (solid line) and F3 (dashed line) expose only one peak for each formant in the left figure of Figure 1, whereas in the right figure, two peaks for both F2 and F3 are apparent. From these results it is concluded that the speaker represented in the left figure distinguishes one vowel /e/, whereas the speaker represented in the right figure distinguishes both /e/ and /ɛ/.

Acoustically, the pre-palatal articulation of the vowel /i/ is manifested by a high value of F3, which approaches F4 (Stevens 1999). F2, however, hardly moves or even lowers as compared to the palatal constriction location. Consequently, without fail a pre-palatal constriction location can be assumed when F3/F2 > 1.35 (see Moosmüller 2008). If the vowel /i/ of a given speaker never displays a F3/F2 ratio > 1.35, a palatal constriction location is assumed for this speaker.

3. Results

3.1 The vowel /i/.

As becomes apparent from Table 3, all speakers expose an F2/F3 ratio > 1.35 for the vowel /i/. This means that all speakers make use of the pre-palatal constriction location. For two female speakers (Sp 191 and Sp211), however, the percentage of vowels with an F3/F2 ratio > 1.35 is rather small; this might indicate that the pre-palatal constriction location might be shifted to the palatal constriction location. For all other speakers, more than 50% of all /i/-vowels expose an F3/F2 ratio > 1.35; i.e., these speakers articulate the vowel /i/ at the pre-palatal constriction location.

Table 3: Percentage of incidences of /i/-vowels with F3/F2 > 1.35.

Speaker	Year of birth	F3/F2 > 1.35 (in %)
Sp198 ♂	1937	65.63
Sp 191 ♀	1947	13.33
Sp 194 ♂	1947	62.5
Sp 211 ♀	1950	18.75
Sp 207 ♀	1950	70.59
Sp 224 ♂	1950	64.29
Sp 209 ♀	1955	52.00
Sp 195 ♂	1956	66.00
Sp 210 ♂	1963	97.14

The F3/F2 ratio is rather sensitive to constriction degree, i.e., a slight increase in constriction degree might cause a shift in cavity affiliation of F2 and F3, and, consequently lower F3. Therefore, duration might affect this relation in the sense that a shortening increases the degree of constriction. However, no correlation between duration and the obtained F3/F2 ratios occurred.

The results for the vowel /i/ are consistent with the results obtained for Standard Austrian German (Moosmüller 2007a, 2008).

3.2 The vowels /e/ and /ɛ/

To test whether the speakers distinguish one or two qualities for the vowel /e/, the DIP-test was performed for each speaker[12]. In Table 4, the results are listed for each speaker and for F1, F2, and F3 separately.

Table 4: Type of distribution for F1, F2, and F3, according to speaker.

Speaker	Year of birth	F1	F2	F3
Sp198 ♂	1937	uni-modal	uni-modal	uni-modal
Sp 191 ♀	1947	uni-modal	uni-modal	uni-modal
Spr 194 ♂	1947	uni-modal	bi-modal	bi-modal
Sp 211 ♀	1950	bi-modal	uni-modal	uni-modal
Sp 207 ♀	1950	bi-modal	bi-modal	bi-modal
Sp 224 ♂	1950	bi-modal	uni-modal	uni-modal
Sp 209 ♀	1955	bi-modal	bi-modal	bi-modal
Sp 195 ♂	1956	uni-modal	uni-modal	uni-modal
Sp 210 ♂	1963	bi-modal	uni-modal	uni-modal

Three speakers (Sp 198, the oldest speaker, Sp 191 and Sp 195) distinguish only one quality of the vowel /e/; they show a uni-modal distribution for all three formants. Three speakers (Sp 209, Sp 211, Sp 224) show a bi-modal distribution for F1 only; i.e., they distinguish the vowels mainly by the degree of jaw opening. One speaker (Sp 194) distinguishes the vowels by means of F2 and F3; i.e., mainly by the degree of constriction. And, finally, two speakers (Sp 207 and Sp209) show a bi-modal distribution of all three formants.

Cluster analysis confirms the results obtained by the DIP-test. Figure 2 shows the results of the cluster analysis for speaker 209 who distinguishes two vowel qualities:

[12] I want to thank my colleague Ewald Enzinger for having performed the statistical tests.

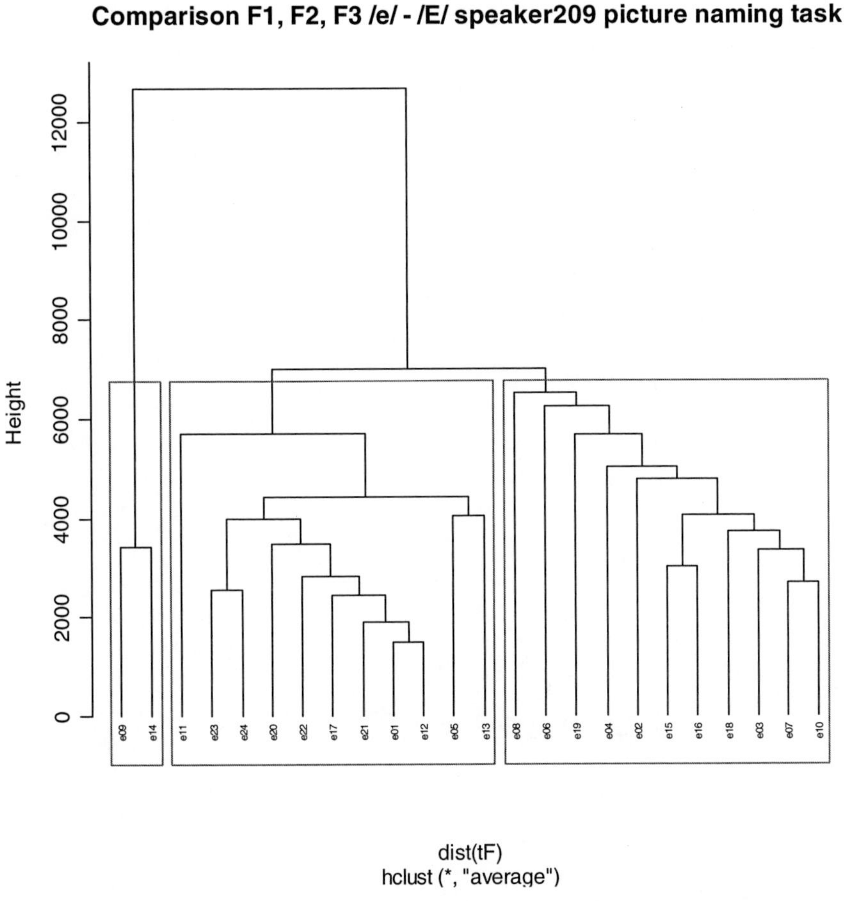

Figure 2: Cluster analysis of all /e/-vowels with respect to F1, F2, and F3. Speaker 209.

Three clusters were defined in order to capture outliers. Two outliers were found in the present case. Figure 3 shows the movement of F1, F2, and F3 for the same speaker. Items are grouped according to the results of the cluster analysis. It can be seen from the formant frequency contour in Figure 3 that the main differences between the two qualities of the vowel /e/ are to be found in the movement of F2, mainly in the onset. There is some tendency of lower absolute F2 values for the vowels grouped in cluster 1 (gray), but the most obvious difference can be attributed to the onset.

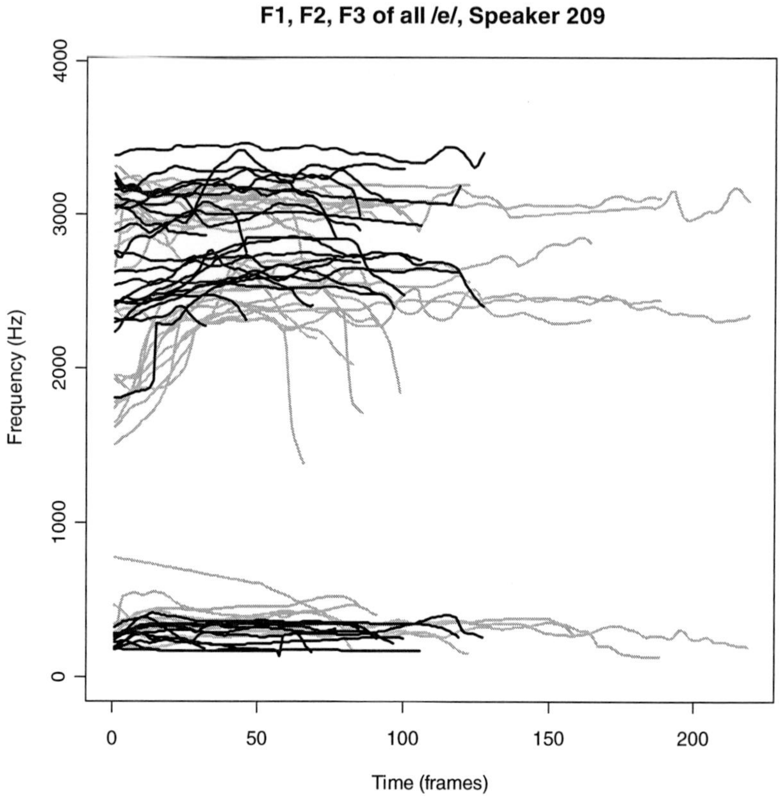

Figure 3: Movement of F1, F2, and F3 over time. Speaker 209, black = cluster 1, gray = cluster 2.

It has to be emphasized, however, that the clusters brought to light reveal no meaningful distribution of the two vowel qualities. The two qualities of the vowel /e/ are neither distributed according to historical and dialectal principles, nor according to the distribution of Standard Austrian German. For example, the vowel /e/ of the word "Häferl" (cup: DIM), realized four times by this speaker, was assigned twice to cluster 1 and twice to cluster 2. From this follows that the situation has not stabilized since the late 1960s: The vowels /e/ and /ɛ/ are either interchangeable in an arbitrary manner or they tend to be neutralized in the direction of the vowel /e/.

4. Discussion

The Viennese monophtongization is a phonetically well motivated assimilation process which affected the vowel system of the VD. From a socio-linguistic point of view, the Viennese monophthongization started as a change from below, carried through to completion, and spread to other social groups and regions. However, women did not lead this sound change. This contradicts Labov's (2001, 293) gender paradox.

However, the effects of the Viennese monophthongization on the vowels /e/ and /ɛ/ did not result in a sound change. The first attempt to neutralize the vowels /e/ and /ɛ/ to /ɛ/ did not reach a stage of completion or stability. From a phonological point of view, the withdrawal of this change is quite reasonable because /ɛ/ and /æ/ differ only slightly by constriction degree and jaw opening. /e/ and /æ/, on the other hand, show a much greater difference in constriction degree and jaw opening. Finally, /e/ and /i/ differ by either constriction location or constriction degree and by the degree of jaw opening. Therefore, neutralization of /e/ and /ɛ/ to /e/ is definitely the more reasonably solution.

This raises the question why a neutralization of the vowels /e/ and /ɛ/ to /ɛ/ ever took place. Kranzmayer (1953) offers some sociolinguistic explanations with reference to World War I and II. In addition, an alleged Czech influence persistently holds its ground. Unfortunately, none of these explanations have ever been subjected to empirical investigation.

Since no reasonable explanation is documented for the preference of the vowel /ɛ/ in the 1920s, it can only be noted that, since the late 1960s, a high variability and interchangeability of the vowels /e/ and /ɛ/, with a preference for the vowel /e/, can be observed. Berg (1998) elaborates that a period of indecision might take some time; however, today, 40 years later, the tendency described by Seidelmann (1971) should have stabilized. Yet, no such stabilization can be observed in the data at hand.

Therefore, a further disturbance has to be considered: In the 1960s, VD speakers started to use the more prestigious VSAG, at first in specific situations or as a discursive marker. However, the distribution of VSAG vowel qualities, though well defined, is not fully transparent to VD speakers. In VSAG, duration is, if at all, a secondary feature, and interdependency of vowel quality and consonant quality does not hold in the same way as it holds for the Middle-Bavarian dialects (Moosmüller 2007b).

As a consequence, three stages can be observed in the course of time, and none of these stages ever reached a stable state:

Stage 1: Neutralization of /e/ and /ɛ/ to /ɛ/.
Stage 2: Neutralization of /e/ and /ɛ/ to /e/.
Stage 3: Adoption of the VSAG vowel system by an increasing number of VD speakers starts.

Given these three stages, it is also worth noting that the first stage is motivated phonologically and sociolinguistically; the second stage has purely phonological reasons; and the third stage is triggered by sociolinguistic factors only.

The succession of these stages provides evidence for the fact that a sound change does not necessarily need a state of stability in order to start. An unsatisfying situation, as it is caused by stage 1, might seek for a remedy. External factors, such as the adoption of another variety, might disturb an ongoing sound change and lead to further variation. Competing forms, resulting in variation, are pre-requisites for a change (Berg 1998, Blevins 2004). However, what makes the present situation special is the fact that in the VD two ongoing and contradictory sound changes, namely the neutralization of the vowels /e/ and /ɛ/ and the adoption of the VSAG vowel system, run parallel. Considering this situation, the insecurity of VD speakers with respect to the "right" realization of the vowels /e/ and /ɛ/ is not surprising.

References

Berg, Thomas. 1998. *Linguistic Structure and Change. An Explanation from Language Processing*. Oxford: Clarendon Press.

Blevins, Juliette. 2004. *Evolutionary Phonology. The Emergence of Sound Patterns.* Cambridge: Cambridge University Press.

Bohn, Ocke-Schwen, James E. Flege, Paul A. Dagenais and Samuel G. Fletcher. 1992. "Differenzierung und Variabilität der Zungenpositionen bei der Artikulation deutscher Vokale." In *Beiträge zur angewandten und experimentellen Phonetik*, edited by Wolfgang Hess and Walter F. Sendlmeier, 1-26. Stuttgart: Steiner, (=Zeitschrift für Dialektologie und Linguistik, Beiheft 72)

Biffl, Gudrun. 2009. Universitäre Weiterbildung und die Rolle der Sprachkenntnisse. Talk given at the Österreichische Linguistiktagung, Salzburg, December 5-7, 2009.

Dressler, Wolfgang U. / Ruth Wodak. 1982. "Sociophonological methods in the study of sociolinguistic variation in Viennese German." *Language in Society* 11: 339-370.

Eek, Arvo / Meister, Einar. 1994. "Acoustics and perception of Estonian vowel types." *PERILUS XVIII*, 55-90.

Fant, Gunnar. 2001. "Swedish vowels and a new three-parameter model." *TMH-Quarterly Progress and Status Report* 1/2001: 43-49.

Gartner, Theodor. 1900. Lautbestand der Wiener Mundart. *Zeitschrift für hochdeutsche Mundarten Bd.* 1: 141-147.

Glettler, Monika. 1972. *Die Wiener Tschechen um 1900*. München, Wien: Oldenbourg Verlag.

Hartigan, John A. / Hartigan, P. M. 1985. The Dip Test of Unimodality. In: Annals of Statistics 13/1, 70-84.

Kranzmayer, Eberhard. 1953. "Lautwandlungen und Lautverschiebungen im gegenwärtigen Wienerischen (Eine phonetisch-phonologische Studie auf soziologischer Grundlage)." *Zeitschrift für Mundartforschung* 21: 197-239.

Kranzmayer, Eberhard. 1956. *Historische Lautgeographie des gesamtbairischen Dialekt raumes*. Graz, Köln: Hermann Böhlaus Nachf.

Labov, William. 2001. *Principles of linguistic change: Vol. 2: Social factors.* Malden, Oxford: Blackwell Publishers.

Luick, Karl. 1904. *Deutsche Lautlehre. Mit besonderer Berücksichtigung der Sprechweise Wiens und der österreichischen Alpenländer.* Leipzig und Wien: Franz Deuticke.

Moosmüller, Sylvia. 1987. "Soziophonologische Variation im gegenwärtigen Wiener Deutsch. Eine empirische Untersuchung." *Zeitschrift für Dialektologie und Linguistik. 56.*

—. 1991. *Hochsprache und Dialekt in Österreich*. Wien: Böhlau.

—. 2007a. *Vowels in Standard Austrian German*. Habilitationsschrift, Universität Wien.

—. 2007b. "On some timing aspects of the Viennese dialect." *The Phonetician* 95, 19-27.

—. 2008. "Interaction of phonetics, phonology, and sociophonology – illustrated by the vowels of Standard Austrian German." In *Proceedings of ISCA Tutorial and Research Workshop on Experimental Linguistics, 25-27 August 2008, Athens, Greece* , edited by Botinis Antonis, 173-176.

Scheuringer, Hermann. 1990. "Sprachentwicklung in Bayern und Österreich." *Eine Analyse des Substandardverhaltens der Städte Braunau am Inn (Österreich) und Simbach am Inn (Bayern) und ihres Umlandes.* Hamburg: Helmut Buske Verlag.

Seidelmann, Erich. 1971. "Lautwandel und Systemwandel in der Wiener Stadtmundart. Ein strukturgeschichtlicher Abriss." *Zeitschrift für Dialektologie und Linguistik* 38: 145-166.

Soukup, Barbara. 2009. *Dialect use as interaction strategy. A sociolinguistic study of contextualization, speech perception, and language attitudes in Austria.* Wien: Braumüller.

Stevens, Kenneth N. 1999. *Acoustic Phonetics.* Cambridge Mass.: The MIT Press.

Tabain, Marija / Pascal Perrier. 2005. "Articulation and acoustics of /i/ in preboundary position in French." *Journal of Phonetics* 33, 77-100.

Wodak-Leodolter, Ruth / Wolfgang. U. Dressler. 1978. "Phonological Variation in colloquial Viennese." *Michigan Germanic Studies* 4.1, 30-66.

Wood, Sidney. 1979. "A radiographic analysis of constriction location for vowels." *Journal of Phonetics* 7, 25-43.

—. 1982. "X-Ray and Model Studies of Vowel Articulation." *Lund Working Papers* 23.

N-WORDS: PREDICATES OR QUANTIFIERS?*

MOJMÍR DOČEKAL
MASARYK UNIVERSITY, CZECH REPUBLIC

Abstract

The present analysis of n-words shows that Czech n-words are of the set type ($\langle e,t \rangle$). N-words in argument position are interpreted as other indefinites through choice functions; in predicate position their type remains the same. Negative morphology of n-words is the only agreement feature which signals propositional negation. N-words can be interpreted in opaque contexts selecting for properties; they can appear in predicative nominal constructions; they can be mapped to the atomic element representing the relevant group of objects, and as such they can be arguments of collective predicates; and they can form summation of their arguments in coordination, which is then interpreted as a generalized quantifier ranging over collective predicates.

1. Introduction

The goal of this article is to argue that in contrast to n-words in English, Czech n-words are not quantifiers, but they should be analyzed as indefinites in the scope of sentential negation. One of the most reliable diagnostics for determination of quantifier status of a natural language expression is an ability to appear in so called predicative position. In contrast to APs and PPs, only some nominals may appear in the predicative position; quantifiers are generally banned from this position

* I would like to thank Ivona Kučerová and audience at the PLM 2009 conference for helpful comments and suggestions. Many thanks also to two anonymous reviewers. Unfortunately, some of their suggestions have not been incorporated into this paper for space limitations. All remaining mistakes are of course entirely mine. The work on this article is supported by the grant no 405/07/P252 GAČR.

(for one of the early formulations of this constraint, see Doron (1983)) as is exemplified in (1) and (2):

(1) John is [$_{AP}$ tall]/[$_{PP}$ in the room]/[$_{NP}$ a teacher]
(2) a. *John is every member of the club.
b. *John is each man.
c. *John and Mary are most students.
d. *John is exactly one teacher.

This ban on quantifiers in predicative positions can be explained quite easily if we assume classical Montague's typing of quantifiers and proper names: quantifiers are of the $\langle\langle e,t\rangle,t\rangle$ type and proper names are also of the same type (proper names denote principal ultrafilters, set of properties which a given individual has). We cannot combine these two types $\langle\langle e,t\rangle,t\rangle X \langle\langle e,t\rangle,t\rangle$ by functional application as none of them can be a function or an argument of the other type. (For an introductory discussion of type compatibility see Heim and Kratzer (1998).) The treatment of proper nouns as generalized quantifiers stems from the formidable tradition of Montague's treatment of all NPs as generalized quantifiers (see Montague (1973)) as is reflected in the framework of generalized quantification in Barwise and Cooper (1981).

What is crucial for my argumentation is that we can use the predicative position as a test for whether something is a quantifier. Interestingly, there are exceptions to this generalization. Notably, *no*-NP ('n-words') may be predicative as in (3).

(3) John is no friend of mine.

According to Partee (1987) quantifiers can appear in predicative position if reanalyzed as involving lowering of the standard generalized quantifier (e.g. *no friend of mine* $\rightarrow$ set of entities disjoint from the set of my friends). The type-lowering operation is realized by type-shifting operator BE: $\langle\langle e,t\rangle,t\rangle \rightarrow \langle e,t\rangle$.

(4) BE = $\lambda Q \lambda x.Q(\{x\})$

Consequently, the shifted quantifier can appear as a predicative NP. The meaning of (3) in Partee's system is that John doesn't have property be_friend_of_mine among the set of his properties, which seems to fit.

(5) John is no friend of mine.

a. $(BE(no(friend')))(j')$

$(BE(\lambda P.P \cap friend' = \varnothing))(j')$

$(\lambda x.\{x\} \cap friend' = \varnothing)(j')$

$\{j'\} \cap friend' = \varnothing$

$\neg friend'(j')$

What I want to show is that this type shifting solution gives wrong predictions and we will get better results if we assume that (at least Czech and probably generally Slavic) n-words are not quantifiers but their semantic type is predicative ($\langle e,t \rangle$ type).

This paper is organized as follows. Sections 2 and 3 outline the basic assumptions concerning type shifting mechanisms, choice functions and the syntactic structures corresponding to the different semantic types. Sections 4, 5 and 6 discuss predictions made by the introduced assumptions for the analysis of different phenomena, including n-words in the predicative and argument positions, the collective interpretation of n-words and their semantics in the scope of intensional predicates. In section 7 I show some open questions. Finally, section 8 offers a review of the arguments presented in the paper.

2. The puzzle

As it stands, Partee's proposal makes some incorrect predictions. Mainly, as it is clear from the data, only some quantifiers can appear in the predicative position, but the proposal predicts that BE could apply to *any* quantifier. Partee herself acknowledges this problem and proposes a remedy in terms of pragmatic restrictions on type-shifting. For general criticism of her account, see Winter (2001) and the next section. As we will see, however, this solution cannot account for data from negative-concord languages. Crucially, the original type shifting strategy overlooks the fact that quantifiers banned from the predicate position cannot have collective interpretation and opaque reading under intensional predicates (besides other things). Czech n-words (as well as English negative quantifiers as in (3)) are grammatical as predicate nominals:

(6) Petr není žádný můj student.
'Petr is no student of mine.'

But (at least in Czech and at least not in English, although the distinction probably holds between Slavonic and Germanic languages generally) they can have collective interpretation:

(7) a. Žádní mí studenti nejsou dobrá parta.
‘#No students of mine are good team.’
b. *No students are a good team.

A de dicto reading in the scope of an intensional verb is grammatical for them, a fact which holds for both Germanic - (8-b) from Landman (2004) - and Slavonic - (8-a) and (9) from Błaszczak (2001, 224) - languages.

(8) a. Petr nehledá žádné jednorožce.
‘Petr is seeking no unicorn.’
b. Dafna zoekt geen griffioens.
Dafna seeks no griffins.
‘Dafna doesn’t seek any griffins.’
(9) Janek nie szuka żadnego jednorożca.
Janek NEG seek-3.SG.PRES no-GEN unicorn-GEN
‘Janek does not seek any unicorns.’

Moreover Slavic n-words in the scope of intensional verbs allow only de dicto reading but Germanic languages allow both de dicto and de re reading. I will show more about this prediction in the next sections. Besides that, uncontroversial quantifiers like *ani jeden student* `not a single student', despite having the same truth-conditional import, contrast with n-words in the way they behave in the mentioned contexts (no collective reading, ungrammatical in predicative position and only de re reading in intensional contexts).

(10) *Petr není ani jeden můj student.
‘*Petr is not a single student of mine.’
(11) Petr nehledá ani jednoho jednorožce.
‘Petr is seeking not a single unicorn.’

This shows that there are systematic differences between n-words and quantifiers in Slavonic languages (more differences than in Germanic languages) and, moreover, that the difference between n-words and quantifiers cannot stem from semantics only, as it's clear from the minimal contrast between quantifier *ani jeden student* and the negative noun phrase *žádný student*.

2.1 Partee's pragmatic restriction on type shifting

In this section I will only briefly repeat Partee's pragmatic argumentation which should restrict the application of the BE operator. Her argument is aimed at the inability of *every* quantifier to appear in predicative position. I think that Winter (2001) quite conclusively shows that this cannot work but let's repeat Partee's proposal first.

Partee (1987) claims that applying the BE operator to generalized quantifier semantics of DP like *every student* would produce a trivial interpretation (empty set) unless the interpretation of the noun *student* is a singleton set. Partee argues that this clashes with the presupposition of universal quantifiers in natural language. According to her, DPs of the form *every* NP presuppose that their NP complements denote non-singleton sets. This looks like a plausible interpretation of the ungrammaticality of sentences like (12) where the BE operator cannot be used to lower the generalized quantifier to set an interpretation, given the following reasons. DP *every student of mine* presupposes a non-singleton interpretation of the set denoted by NP *student of mine*, so applying BE to the DP *every student of mine* would lead to presupposition failure (if we cancel the presupposition) or to trivial interpretation (if the presupposition is accepted and the BE operator is applied anyhow). The generalized quantifier is of the incorrect type to combine with a proper name, so not applying BE operator leads to semantic incompatibility in a third imagined scenario.

(12) *Petr is every student of mine.

The trouble with this account, as Winter (2001) shows, is that it isn't able to explain argument/predicate asymmetry of the presupposition defeasibility. As the following example (13) shows, in argument position the non singleton presupposition of the *every* NP phrase is defeasible but in predicate position the same presupposition cancellation doesn't work. The example shows the singleton interpretation of *every* NP is available (even if pragmatically strange) when the DP is in subject position. Moreover both sentences denote the same situation but the acceptability of (13-a) is based solely on the argument syntactic position of the quantifier. That means that the non singleton meaning constraint for the big quantifier is probably only conversational implicature, not the presupposition, as presuppositions aren't generally suspensible in the way as in (13-a).

(13) a. If John and Mary failed entry exams, and Petr didn't, then every student of mine is Petr.
b.*If John and Mary failed entry exams, and Petr didn't, then Petr is every student of mine.

The grammaticality of (13-a) is predicted if we assume that in predicative position the proper noun can be type lifted to set type ($\langle e,t \rangle$ - set of all things called 'Petr') which is then fetched as argument to generalized quantifier in the subject position. This strategy isn't available when the proper noun is in subject position.

I will show in next section how the ungrammaticality of *every* NP in predicative positions can be explained without the type shifting operator BE. The solution will also explain the puzzles mentioned at the beginning of section 2.

3. The proposal

3.1 Framework

My general framework will be Flexible Boolean semantics of Winter (2001), Winter (2005), a.o., which uses ideas about semantic layers within DP that distinguish between predicate denoting layer and quantifier denoting layer. My assumptions are as follows: there are three syntactic layers in DP for English (Winter 2005, Figure 1), see (14). The symbols φ_{cf} and φ_{min} in the tree refer to two type shifting operations, a choice function and a minimum sort respectively. Their formalizations can be found in Section 3.2.

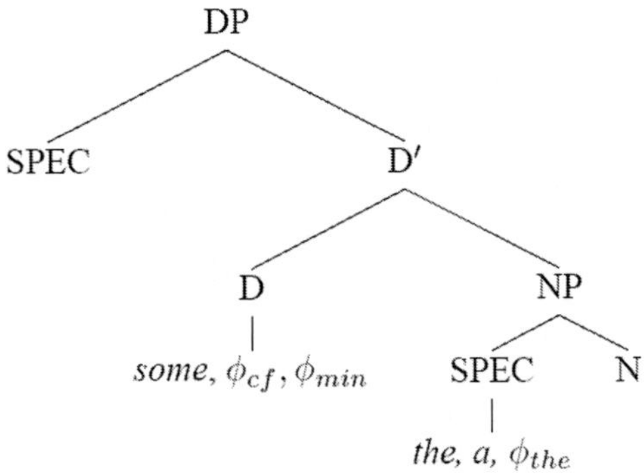

(14)

Nominals are classified into three types according to the portion of the NP/DP structure they fill:

4) Nominals that contain a full spec-DP position. These nominals can only be analyzed as DPs. They appear only in *argument* positions.
5) Nominals that contain an empty spec-DP and a full D position. These nominals can be analyzed as either DPs or D's. They can only appear in predicate positions with overt copula.
6) Nominals where both spec-DP and D are empty. These nominals can be analyzed as DPs, D's or NPs. They can appear only in predicate positions.

There is syntax-semantics matching for these layers:

5. Under their NP analysis, nominals unambiguously denote predicates (type $\langle e,t \rangle$).
6. Under their DP analysis, nominals unambiguously denote generalized quantifiers (type $\langle\langle e,t\rangle,\langle\langle e.t\rangle.t\rangle\rangle$ before adding a NP argument to a determiner and $\langle\langle e,t\rangle,t\rangle$ after applying the determiner to the NP argument).
7. Under their D' analysis, the interpretation of nominals is free to move back and forth between predicates and quantifiers. The example (16), table *Indefinites*, represents an instance of such a D'-level predicate (a good example from English is e.g. NP headed by an unstressed determiner *some*).

Some illustrations of the system are as follows:

(15)

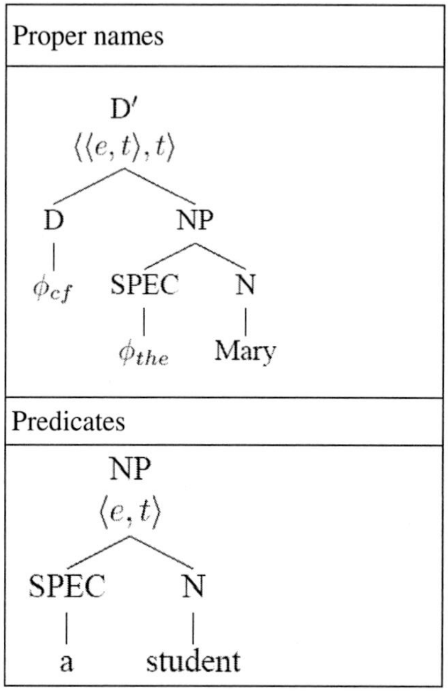

(16)

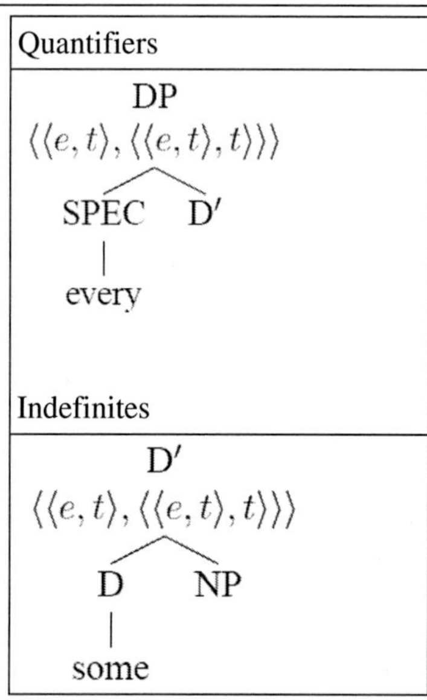

For English n-words Winter (2001) assumes that in argument positions they are negative quantifiers (generalized quantifiers) and that they are syntactically rigid nouns. Their syntax and semantics is then as follows:

(17)

English n-words

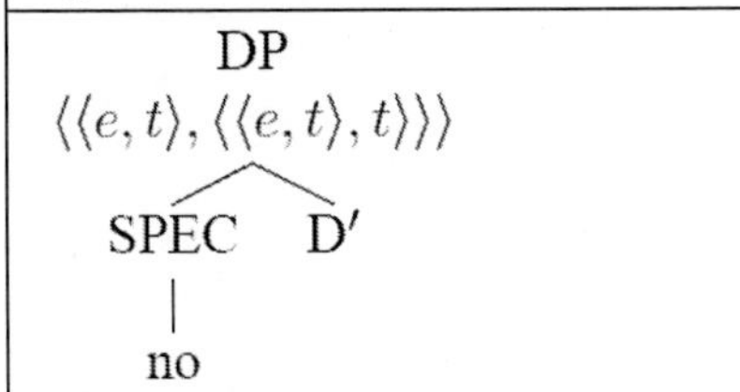

no'(X)(Y) iff
$X \cap Y = \varnothing = \neg\exists x[X(x) \wedge Y(x)]$

Discussing English negative noun phrases would take us too far afield, so I will simply assume that it's right to assume that English negative noun phrases are quantifiers but see Penka (2007) for a careful discussion pointing to another solution or Landman (2004) for arguments that at least the negation part cannot be interpreted in the same place where the existential part of the quantifier is interpreted.

3.2 Choice functions

The flexible interpretation of the D' level is by virtue of phonologically covert operators that apply at this level and map predicates to quantifiers and vice versa. These operators are called category shifting principles.

Winter (2001) proposes two such principles: *a choice function* (CF) operation that maps predicates to quantifiers, and a *minimum* operator that maps quantifiers to predicates. Let's assume the following common definition of CFs, where they are used as category shifting principles from predicates to entities. Winter (2001) proposes a more general framework where CFs are operators from predicates to generalized quantifiers, but for simplicity I adopt a more intuitive definition from Winter (2005, def. 1)):

(18) For any set E, a *choice function* over E is a function that maps every non-empty subset A of E to a member of A.

The opposite of choice function is the Minimum operator, which maps quantifiers to predicates (it produces e.g. a minimal set from the conjunction of two principal ultrafilters : $min(M \sqcap J) = \{\{m', j'\}\}$

(19) Minimum sort
$$min_{(\tau t)(\tau t)} = \lambda Q_{\tau t}.\lambda A_{\tau}.Q(A) \wedge \forall B \in Q\ [\mathrm{B} \sqsubseteq \mathrm{A} \rightarrow \mathrm{B{=}A}]$$

The main motivation for using CFs is for a systematic treatment of the wide scope behavior of indefinites.

(20) If some relative of mine dies, I will inherit a house.

a. $$[\exists f[CH(f) \wedge dies'(f(relative\_of\_mine'))]] \rightarrow inherit'(I', house')$$

b. $$\exists f\left[CH(f) \wedge \begin{bmatrix} dies'(f(realitve\_of\_mine')) \rightarrow \\ inherit'(I', house') \end{bmatrix}\right]$$

As is well known, indefinites give the appearance of scoping out of syntactic islands, as in the example (20), cited in Reinhart (1997) with two readings: in (20-a) existential closure takes place within the antecedent of the conditional; we get the "narrow scope" reading but in (20-b) existential closure takes scope over the conditional and this results in a "wide scope" reading.

Existential closure is a mechanism for interpreting indefinites in argument positions. The logic behind it is a second order quantification over choice functions. According to Reinhart (1997) and Winter (2001) this closure can take place on any level of syntactic structure. This leads to apparent wide scope effects with indefinites.

3.3 Czech n-words

For Czech (and I assume generally for Slavic but that would need, of course, careful research) I assume a basically indefinite structure for n-words, corresponding to that of indefinite semantics. In the flexible Boolean semantics of Winter there's a question if Czech n-words are more like English *some* indefinites (D') or like (NP) *a/the* (in)definites.

Winter (2005) proposes a criterion to distinguish between D' and NP level: conjunctions of singular D' are plural, whereas conjunctions of singular NPs inherit their number features. That is parallel to conjunctions of other predicative categories such as VP/TP, PP and AP. In (21) we see that Czech negative noun phrases can be conjoined in argument position with singular agreement on verb and that they both can be interpreted as attributes of one individual (unlike *jeden* indefinites in (21-b) which are parallel to *some* indefinites in English). We can interpret (21-a) as (22) which shows that Czech n-words are NP indefinites.[1]

(21) a. Žádný velký básník a žádný národní hrdina dnes nepronesl řeč.
'#No big poet and no big national hero gave a speech today.'
b. Jeden velký básník a jeden národní hrdina dnes *pronesl/pronesli řeč.
'Some big poet and some national hero gave a speech today today.'

(22) $$\neg\exists f\begin{bmatrix} CH(f)\wedge give\_speech\_today' \\ (f(big\_poet'\wedge national\_hero')) \end{bmatrix}$$

Let's start with the hypothesis that Czech n-words have an indefinite NP syntax and that the indefinite semantics of the determiner is simply zero. In that case the only semantics is set denotation contributed by NP. Let's see how far this can lead us. There is, of course, need of Czech n-words to be licensed by verbal negation, and I assume that some version of syntactic agreement theory of n-words in the style of Penka (2007) is on the right track.

Under Winter's approach indefinites are flexible nominals (predicates) and as such can be type-shifted into quantifiers in some syntactic constructions. This shifting is obligatory every time when n-words are in argument positions as their set $\langle e,t\rangle$ type would lead to type incompatibility in any argument position. We will see that in argument

[1] As one anonymous reviewer correctly points out, the singular agreement with conjoined NPs is at best a suggestive evidence but not a sufficient argument for the NP nature of n-words. One of the tests which would offer insight into the DP/NP status of n-words is opaqueness for extraction: DPs are usually taken as opaque for left branch extraction but NP's are transparent in this respect; see Boškovic (2005) for Slavonic languages. But as Abels (2003) convincingly shows, the left branch extraction data can be still explained by remnant movement analysis, which means alas that locality effects cannot be used as a test for the DP/NP status of n-words. And as I'm not aware of any other syntactic tests which can prove or refute the NP status of n-words, I will stick to the assumption that n-words are NPs even if we are still missing conclusive evidence for this claim.

positions choice function builds the next level of structure above indefinites.

As predicates we would expect n-words to appear in predicate positions. In contrast, quantifiers of the 'not a single one' type are rigid nominals though and cannot be shifted into predicates. The distinction between n-words and 'not a single one' quantifiers is at least partially syntactic, as n-words belong to the flexible nominals type and quantifiers to the rigid nominals type in Winter's system. I think that this is the right hypothesis as there's no semantic distinction between both types in Generalized quantifiers theory. From the point of view of truth conditions, both n-words and negative quantifiers of the 'not a single one' type can be correctly represented as an operation of a noninteresction on any two sets. But if we look more carefully at the syntactic and semantic behavior of n-words in the different environments, we will see that predicate semantics and NP syntax, as depicted in (23), predict their properties much more correctly. And that is exactly what I will show in sections 4, 5 and 6.

(23)

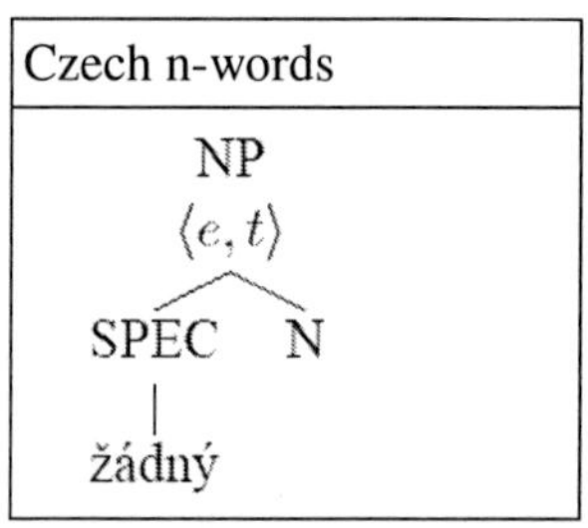

4. Prediction I: predicative positions

Let's repeat my main assumption: n-words in the negative concord languages are restriction predicates ($\langle e,t \rangle$ type) and their type does not change in predicate position. From that it follows that their appearance in predicative position is expected as their type is similar to other predicates like syntactic APs, PPs, ... If n-words were to be generalized quantifiers (sets of sets), it would be predicted that they shouldn't appear in predicative positions.

N-words in argument position are interpreted through choice functions (this will be needed for collective interpretation of them). So n-words are indefinites of a special sort (for a closely related proposal, see Penka (2007); Zeijlstra (2004); Baszczak (2001)).

N-words can appear in predicative nominal constructions (they are not quantifiers there) but the question is why quantifiers of the *every* type cannot occur in this position as well if the flexible Boolean semantics has a minimum operator as (19). In Winter's system this follows from the syntactic ban on type shifting rigid DPs. The min operator can shift quantifiers to predicates (e.g. principal ultrafilter) if they are flexible. This is needed e.g. for derivation of sentences like (24).

E is an existential raising operator which turns predicates into quantifiers, and choice function is a generalization of this operator, see (25), cited from Winter (2001, 147).

(24) This woman is Sue.

$$\left(E\left(min\left(\|this\_woman\|\right)\right)\right)\left(min(S)\right)$$

On the assumption that $\|this\_woman\| = \lambda P.P(a_c)$,

where $a_c \in woman'$ is determined by the context of the utterance:

$$\left(E\left(min\left(\lambda P.P(a_c)\right)\right)\right)\left(min(S)\right)$$

(25)
$$E = \lambda A.\lambda B.\exists x\left[A(x) \wedge B(x)\right]$$
$$= \lambda A.\lambda B.\exists f\left[CH(f) \wedge \langle f \rangle(A)(B)\right]$$

For Czech n-words we don't need a min operator for n-words in the predicative position because they are basically predicates there. On the other hand, quantifiers of the 'not a single one' type are rigid nominals, so in predicative position they would need a min operator to turn them into a set type; but this type shifting is forbidden as they are rigid nominals. They are DPs and their logical type cannot be shifted.

Czech n-words are grammatical in predicative positions and moreover they permit distributive reading there as in the example below. As they are interpreted as predicates, they can be conjoined by a boolean conjunction, and the proper name *Petr* in the subject is interpreted as a set of sets and is applied to them. The result then is logically equivalent to the conjunction of two predicates applied to a term denoting the atomic individual Petr. If the n-words in (26) would be quantifiers, then the boolean conjunction of them would assemble the set of properties common to both quantifiers and this set would be applied to the subject. This would lead to the same type problems discussed in Section 2 for simple quantifiers in predicative position.

(26) Petr není žádný můj kamarád ani žádný můj soused.
'Petr is no friend of mine and no neighbor of mine.'
a. $\neg P(friend\_of\_mine \cap my\_neighbour')$
$\Leftrightarrow \neg friend\_of\_mine'(p') \wedge \neg my\_neighbour'(p')$

5. Prediction II: collectivity

My basic hypothesis is that n-words in negative concord languages like Czech are simply indefinites which must syntactically agree with verbal negation, and this negation is the locus of logical negation interpretation.

As indefinites, n-words denote set(s) of objects (depending on their morphological number) and we should expect them to be grammatical with collective predicates which demand plural arguments. On the other hand if n-words would be generalized quantifiers (at least in classical Montague's typing) we wouldn't expect them to be grammatical with genuine collective predicates.

In this section I will look at the behavior of n-words with collective predicates. There are two sentence types which are important in this respect. The first one (example (27)) will be dealt with in the first part of this section and the second one (example (28)) in the subsection 5.2. (27) is an interesting sentence because predicates like *be a good team* are good testing ground for the quantifier/set type of their arguments. Basically all quantifiers are banned as their arguments, as (29-b) shows, which is behavior not shared by all collective predicates (e.g. collective predicate *meet* allows as its arguments quantifiers if they are in the plural - see (29-a)).

(27) Žádní mí studenti nejsou dobrá parta.
'#No students of mine are good team.'
(28) Žádný můj student a žádný můj učitel se v Praze nesešli.
'No student of mine and no teacher of mine met in Prague.'
(29) a. All the students are meeting in the hall.
b.*All the /exactly four/between four and ten/at least ten/many/no/most of the students are a good team.

5.1 Impure atoms

Landman (2000) proposes that nouns referring to sets can be shifted to sets of plural atoms, so they can be mapped to the atomic element representing the relevant group of objects, and as such they can be arguments of collective predicates, as in (7-a). Their denotation then is similar to singular noun phrases like *the group of students* or *the committee*.

Basic assumptions about collective predicates like *be a good team* in Winter's flexible Boolean semantics is that they are atom predicates where each atom denotes a plural entity. And according to him, these predicates are genuine collective predicates. The distinction between collective predicates like *be a good team* and distributive predicates like *laugh* is that distributive predicates are atom predicates as well but in their uninflected denotations they range only over regular individuals.

Winter's typology of semantic number classifies predicates according to their behavior in sentences like the following.

(30) a. all the/no/at least/many students/committees PRED
b. every/no/more than one/many a student/committee PRED

PRED is a predicate (verb, noun or adjective) like *be a good team* or *laugh*. If the sentences in (30-a) and (30-b) are equally acceptable and, if acceptable, are furthermore semantically equivalent, then PRED is called an *atom predicate*. If the sentences differ in either acceptability or truth-conditions then PRED is called a *set predicate*.

According to this criterion, a collective predicate like *meet* is a set predicate but a collective predicate like *be a good team* is an atom predicate, compare (31-a) and (31-b) with different acceptability and (32-a) and (32-b) with similar (un)acceptability. All distributive predicates (like *laugh*, *smile*, *sleep*) are of course atom predicates.

(31) a. All the/no/at least two/many students met.
b. *Every/*no/*more then one/*many a student met.
(32) a. *All the/*no/*at least two/*many students are a good team.
b. *Every/*no/*more then one/*many a student is a good team.

Winter's system builds on the distinction between the semantic number of a predicate (the atom/set distinction) and the morphological number of the predicate (sg./pl. distinction); see (33) and (34). In (35) are presented lexical entries for illustration.

(33) Principle 1
When uninflected for number, atom predicates denote sets of ***atomic*** *entities. Uninflected set predicates denote sets of* <u>*sets*</u> *of atomic entities.*

(34) Principle 2

Number features change the semantic number of predicates so that all ***singular*** *predicates denote sets of atoms whereas all* ***plural*** *predicates denote sets of sets.*

(35) a. student'={j',m',p'}
b. students = {{j'},{m'},{p'},{j',m'}...,{j',m',p'}}
c. committee'={c'_A,c'_B}
d. is_a_good_team={c'_A,c'_B}
e. meet'={{j',m'},{c'_B}}

If we accept Montague's classical treatment of quantifiers then there's a type problem because there is no semantic difference between the singular and plural determiner quantifiers (*all, every,* no_{sg}, no_{pl}, ...). All of them are of the type $\langle\langle e,t\rangle,\langle\langle e,t\rangle,t\rangle\rangle$ but in Winter's system (following Bennett) singular predicates are of the $\langle e,t\rangle$ type although plural predicates are of the $\langle\langle e,t\rangle,t\rangle$ type. Given these assumptions, plural marked arguments of a quantificational determiner yield a type mismatch and should yield prima facie uninterpretability.

The situation is rescued via a special interpretation rule called "determiner-fitting" triggered by the presence of morphological plurality. The working of dfit is a bit complicated but let's say that it can explain the distinction between (37-a) and (37-b).

An important prediction of the system is that quantifiers are incompatible with genuine collective predicates like *be a good team* (even if the quantifiers are in the plural). They are compatible with set predicates like *meet* via dfit strategy but this strategy is unavailable to rescue grammaticality for collective atom predicates.

(36) Determiner fitting

$$dfit = \lambda D_{(et)(ett)}.\lambda A_{ett}.\lambda B_{ett}.D(\cup A)(\cup(A\cap B))$$

(37) a. All students met in the hallway.
b.*All students are a good team.

Nevertheless some apparent quantifiers can be subjects of these atom collective predicates like *be a good team*, see (38). They are quantifiers of the flexible type (their syntactic projection is only D', not full DP), so they can be type shifted into set type and then be arguments of the quantifier which ranges over $\langle e,t\rangle$ type both in its restrictor and nuclear scope.

Winter (2001) generalizes that for rigid nominals this mapping is not available but for flexible ones it is.

(38) a. The students are a good team.
b. Some students I know are a good team.
c. Five students I know are a good team.

If we return to example (27), repeated below as (39), we can say that the system predicts that it can be grammatical only if the n-word isn't a generalized quantifier and rigid nominal. So this is another piece of puzzle which points to the predicate nature of n-words.

(39) says that any plural atom which can be chosen from the set of "my students" doesn't have the property of being a good team. This is close to the intuitive meaning of (27).

(39) Žádní mí studenti nejsou dobrá parta.
'#No students of mine are good team.'

(40) $\neg\exists f\left[CH(f) \wedge f(\downarrow(my\_students'))(good\_team')\right]$
$\neg\exists x \in (\downarrow \{A \subseteq my\_student'\})[good\_team'(x)]$

The corresponding English sentence in (41) is ungrammatical. That shows that English n-words are at least syntactically rigid nominals – read DPs – and because of that, unlike Czech n-words, they cannot be mapped to impure atoms.

(41) *No students are a good team.

5.2 Coordination of n-words

The next important piece of data is exemplified by sentence (42) which shows that with set predicates n-words can assemble a plural entity with property assigned to them by the set predicate. This property is then negated because of the propositional negation (signalized by negative concord both on n-words and on the verb).

The generalized quantifiers approach cannot explain this sentence interpretation because the basic denotation of the negative quantifier in GQ theory is a disjoint operation on sets (*no student of mine* would denote a set of sets disjoint from my students) and the only meaning which GQ theory can assign to (42) would be that some intersection of a set of entities disjoint from my students and teachers met in Prague. That is, of course, a very implausible reading for (42).

In Partee's type shifting system the truth conditions would be similar to GQ treatment. (42) would mean that some non-student of mine and some non-teacher of mine met in Prague, again wrong meaning of sentence (42). This also supports the syntactic theory of negative concord phenomena, as proposed in Penka (2007), because the scope of negation is interpreted at the propositional level and the scope of n-words is interpreted under the collective predicate *meet* (first there is summation of the two indefinites which is type shifted with *E* operator, then taking the collective predicate as argument).

But if we follow the main line of argumentation here and treat n-words as indefinites, the intuitive meaning of (42) is that for any chosen pair consisting of my student and my teacher, this pair doesn't have a property "met_in_Prague", which is exactly what (43) formalizes. As the grammatical judgment in English translation shows, this sentence is either ungrammatical in English or it has the peculiar meaning discussed in the last paragraph which probably leads to its unacceptability.

(42) Žádný můj student a žádný můj učitel se v Praze nesešli..
'#No student of mine and no teacher of mine met in Prague.'

$$(43)\ \neg\exists f\exists g\begin{bmatrix}CH(f)\wedge CH(g)\wedge \\ E(min(f(my\_student')\cap(my\_teacher')))(meet')\end{bmatrix}$$

$$\Leftrightarrow \neg\exists x\exists y\begin{bmatrix}my\_student'(x)\wedge my\_teacher'(y) \\ \wedge\, meet'(\{x,y\})\end{bmatrix}$$

6. Prediction III: intensional predicates

Let's repeat: n-words are indefinites and without additional structure they denote sets. From that it follows that they should be grammatical in environments selecting for sets or properties. Intensional predicates were argued to be property selecting, and we will see that this works well with the indefinite status of Czech n-words.

Indefinites in scope of intensional verbs are generally able to have two readings, de dicto and de re, as (44) illustrates, which can mean either that there are two criminals such that the inspector must arrest them or that there is a norm for the inspector to arrest two criminals per week, irrespective of their identity.[2]

[2] The problem of de dicto/de re interpretation in the scope of modal verbs is one of the big topics of formal semantics going back at least to Montague (1973). For the

(44) The inspector must arrest two criminals this week. .
a. de dicto: norm for the inspector per week is two criminals
b. de re: there are two criminals such that the inspector must arrest them

N-words in negative concord languages like Czech can be interpreted only de dicto in these constructions as I want to show in this section. Let's look at (45) and first it's de dicto reading.

(45) Petr nehledá žádného jednorožce.
'Petr doesn't seek any unicorn.'

In Montague's classical analysis, the de dicto reading would be analyzed as a relation SEEK between Petr and the intension of a generalized quantifier as in (46-a); in other words, intensional verbs denote relations between individuals and quantifier intension, i.e. they are of the type $\langle s,\langle\langle e,t\rangle,t\rangle,\langle e,t\rangle\rangle$. This reading is very weak. It expresses that Petr stands in the SEEK relation to the function which assigns to every possible world the set of properties that no unicorn has.

It's because, on Montague's analysis of the de dicto reading, the negation is sitting in the wrong place. For Montague, the only alternative is to scope it out. But that gives the de re reading, which is also wrong.

Zimmermann (1993) argues against Montague's analysis of quantifiers in the scope of intensional verbs, and in favor of an analysis where the complement of SEEK is an intensional property, rather than the intension of a generalized quantifier.

This is exactly in accordance with the analysis which postulates an indefinite analysis for n-words and is also one of the main arguments for separating negative and the indefinite part of n-words (irrespective of the negative concord status of the examined language), as Landman (2004) and Penka (2007) show, because otherwise we would end up with the same problems as in (46-a). This is because, at the level of properties, the only plausible analysis of negation is as complementation as in (46-b).That would mean that Petr is seeking non-unicorns and not that Peter is not searching for unicorns. The most plausible meaning of (46) is (46-c) where negation takes scope over the whole formula

---

discussion of Germanic n-words and their semantics in the scope of intensional verbs see Penka (2007, chap. 3).

(46) Petr nehledá žádného jednorožce.

a. $seek'\left({}^{\wedge}\lambda P.\neg\exists x[unicorn'(x) \wedge P(x)]\right)(p')$

b. $seek'\left({}^{\wedge}(ATOM-unicorn)(p')\right)$

c. $\neg seek'\left({}^{\wedge}unicorn'\right)(p')$

Let's return to the de re reading of Czech sentences with n-words. It's easier to test them when embedding the n-word under the modal verb than under an intensional verb like *seek*. Sentence (47), under the de dicto reading, means that there's no obligation for the inspector to arrest two criminals this week.

But what would be the de re reading? The de re reading would be true in situations in which the de dicto reading is false. If the norm of work for inspectors says that there are no criminals, say murderer and burglar, who have to be arrested this week, but only that two criminals must be arrested per week, then (47) under the de dicto reading is false but under the de re reading is true.

This is so because in the de re reading an indefinite (choice function) would scope over the modal verb but under negation. This reading is unavailable for sentence (47), so I conclude that n-words in Czech don't have the de re readings. This follows from the predicate semantic type of Czech n-words. On the other hand, in Germanic languages negative noun phrases as quantifiers can quantifier raise over the modal verb, which is the reason for their ability to have the de re reading also.

(47) Inspektor nemusí tento týden zavřít žádné dva zločince.
'The inspector need not arrest two criminals this week.'

a. $\neg$ must $> \exists$

b. $* \neg > \exists >$ must

7. Open questions

As is well known, the choice function approach to indefinites is mainly motivated by their peculiar wide scope behavior (see e.g. Fodor and Sag (1982), Kratzer (1998), ...). Let's remind ourselves about the contrast between the universal quantifier in (48) and the indefinite one in (49).

(48) Jestliže Petr koupí každou knihu v tomhle knihkupectví, tak přijde na buben.
'If Petr buys every book in this book shop, then he will be broke.'

a. $[\forall x[book'(x) \rightarrow buy'(p',x)]] \rightarrow broke'(p')$
b. $* [\forall x[book'(x) \rightarrow buy'(p',x)] \rightarrow broke'(p')]$

(49) Jestliže Petr koupí jednu knihu v tomhle knihkupectví, tak přijde na buben.
'If Petr buys some book in this book shop, then he will be broke.'
a. $[\exists x[book'(x) \wedge buy'(p',x)]] \rightarrow broke'(p')$
b. $\exists x[book'(x) \wedge [buy'(p',x) \rightarrow broke'(p')]]$

If we used a choice function treatment of n-words, then it would be appropriate to check if their behavior shows something similar in this respect. At first sight this is not true as we see from (50): the only grammatical reading is in (50-a) and a very weak ungrammatical reading is in (50-b).

(50-b) can be paraphrased as: there is a choice function such that if Petr will not buy the book which this function chooses then he will remain rich. This would be true in a situation where one very expensive book in the bookshop would make Peter poor; buying other books, however, would be harmless to his wallet. By contrast, sentence (50) is much stronger - it says that any book in this bookshop would ruin Petr.

(50) Jestli si Petr nekoupí žádnou knížku v tomhle knihkupectví, tak zůstane bohatý.
'If Petr will buy no book in this book shop, then he will remain rich.'
a. $\neg[\exists f[CH(f) \wedge buy'(f(book'))(p')]] \rightarrow remain\_rich'(p')$
b. $\exists f\left[CH(f) \wedge \neg\left[\begin{array}{l} buy'(f(book'))(p') \\ \rightarrow remain\_rich'(p') \end{array}\right]\right]$

Let's follow an established practice and describe the fact by a stipulatively named rule and because it's just the opposite of the specificity marking of *certain*, let's call it an unspecificity marking rule.

(51) Unspecificity marking rule
The n-words in Czech denote a CF variable that must be existentially closed under the scope of verbal negation and also under the scope of any other logical operator.

Following this tenet is in accordance with Geist (2008), who treats various classes of Russian indefinite pronouns as Skolemized functions. Hence, (51) can be just special instance of general rule restricting the scope of Skolemized Choice functions. A Skolemization operation adds an argument to a CF; thus a choice from the set denoted by the argument of our CF is relativized: the function can pick different individuals from the set for different values of the additional argument.

And, e.g., Czech *-koli(v)* indefinites have peculiar property: they generally must take scope under some logical operator in their sentence (see Geist (2008) for a similar observation about Russian *-nibuď* pronouns). This can be nicely predicted if we assume that the free argument of Skolemized choice functions must be bound by some (not necessarily) nearest logical operator.[3]

(52) Petr si chtěl vzít jakoukoliv řeznici.
 'Petr wanted to marry any woman butcher.'
 a. want > ∃ woman butcher
 b. * ∃ woman butcher > want

(53) Každý řezník zabil jakéhokoliv vola.
 'Every butcher killed any ox.'
 a. ∀ butcher > ∃ ox
 b.* ∃ ox > ∀ butcher

(54) Petr často jedl jakýkoliv řízek.
 'Petr frequently ate any schnitzel.'
 a. frequently > ∃ schnitzel
 b. * ∃ schnitzel > frequently

The same holds also for n-words, but their scope possibilities are even more restricted: they must be interpreted within the scope of negation and moreover within the scope of any other logical expression in their sentence.

---

[3] As an anonymous reviewer correctly points out, a sentence like *Karel popřel, že si mohl koupit jakoukoliv knihu* is ambiguous and reports either that Karel couldn't buy any book he wanted (modal > ∃) or that no book was such that Karel could buy it (∃ > modal). That means that *-koli(v)* pronouns must take scope under some logical operator but it doesn't need to be the closest one. That also means that the unspecificity marking rule is correct only for n-words. For the *-koli(v)* words we would need to substitute their end "...under the scope of any other logical operator" with "...under the scope of some other logical operator".

(55) Petr si nechtěl vzít žádnou řeznici.
'Petr wanted to marry no woman butcher.'
a. $\neg$ > want > $\exists$ woman butcher
b.* $\exists$ woman butcher > $\neg$ > want
c. * $\neg$ > $\exists$ > want

(56) Dva řezníci nezabili žádného vola.
'Two butchers killed no ox.'
a. 2 butchers > $\neg$ > $\exists$ ox
b.* $\exists$ ox > 2 butchers > $\neg$

(57) Petr často nejedl žádný řízek.
'Petr frequently ate no schnitzel.'
a. frequently > $\neg$ > $\exists$ schnitzel
b.* $\exists$ schnitzel > frequently > $\neg$

A closing remark: The reason why n-words are incompatible with modifiers of the *certain* type is maybe semantic: *certain* wants to have the widest existential closure of choice function, but *no* goes in the opposite direction. From that it follows that no closure is available and ungrammaticality arises.

(58) *Petr si nechce vzít žádnou jistou studentku.
'Petr wants to marry no certain student.'

8. Summary

The present analysis of n-words has shown that Czech n-words are of the set type ($\langle e,t \rangle$) and that their type does not change in predicate position. N-words in argument position are interpreted, like other indefinites, through choice functions. Negative morphology of n-words is only agreement feature which signals propositional negation (negative n-words in Slavonic languages must be accompanied by a negated verb where negation is high enough to have scope over event variable). So n-words are indefinites of a special sort.

As predicates of the set type, n-words can be interpreted in opaque contexts selecting for properties; they can appear in the predicative nominal constructions (they are not quantifiers there); they can be mapped to the atomic element representing the relevant group of objects, and as such they can be arguments of collective predicates; and they can form summation of their arguments in coordination, which is then interpreted as a generalized quantifier ranging over collective predicates.

The choice function treatment of n-words predicts scope possibilities which are not attested in Czech but this can be solved by treating n-words as skolemized choice functions where negative morphology (besides signaling negative concord) forces the scope of n-words to be within scope of any other logical operator in the sentence.

References

Abels, K. 2003. *Successive cyclicity, anti-locality, and adposition stranding*. PhD thesis, University of Connecticut.

Barwise, J. and Cooper, R. 1981. "Generalized quantifiers and natural language." *Linguistics and Philosophy*, 4:159-219.

Błaszczak, J. 2001. *Investigation into the interaction between the indefinites and negation. vol. 51: Studia Grammatica*. Akademie Verlag, Berlin.

Boškovic, v. 2005. "Left branching extraction, structure of NP, and scrambling." In *The free word order phenomenon: Its syntactic sources and diversity*, edited by J Sabel. and M. Saito. Mouton de Gruyter, Berlin.

Doron, E. 1983. "Verbless Predicates in Hebrew." PhD thesis, University of Texas, Austin.

Fodor, J. and Sag, I. 1982. "Referential and quantification indefinites." *Linguistics and Philosophy*, 5:355-398.

Geist, L. 2008. "Specificity as referential anchoring: evidence from russian. In *Proceedings of SuB12*, Oslo. ILOS 2008, edited by A. Grønn.

Heim, I. and Kratzer, A. 1998. *Semantics in Generative Grammar*. Blackwell, Oxford.

Kratzer, A. 1998. "Scope or pseudo-scope? Are there wide-scope indefinites?" In *Events in grammar*, edited by S. Rothstein, 163-196. Kluwer, Dordrecht.

Landman,F. 2000. *Events and Plurality*. Dordrecht: Kluwer.

—. 2004. *Indefinites and the Type of Sets*. Blackwell Publishing, Oxford.

Montague, R. 1973. "The proper treatment of quantification in ordinary English." In *Approaches to Natural Language,* edited by Jaakko Hintikka and Julius Moravcsik, 221–242. Dordrecht.

Partee, B. H. 1987. "Noun phrase interpretation and type shifting principles." In *Studies in Discourse Representation Theories and the Theory of Generalized Quantifiers*, edited by J. D. Groenendijk and M. S de Jong. Dordrecht. Foris.

Penka, D. 2007. "Negative Indefinites." PhD thesis, Universität Tübingen.

Reinhart, T. 1997. "Quantifier scope: How labor is divided between QR and choice functions." *Linguistics and philosophy* 20:335-397.

Winter, Y. 2001. *Flexibility Principles in Boolean Semantics: coordination, plurality and scope in natural language*. MIT Press, Cambridge, Mass.

—. 2005. "On some problem of (in)definiteness within flexible semantics. *Lingua* 115:767-786.

Zeijlstra, H. 2004. "Sentential Negation and Negative Concord." PhD thesis, University of Amsterdam.

Zimmermann, E. 1993. "On the proper treatment of opacity in certain verbs." *Natural Language Semantics*, 1.

NOUN CLASS ASSIGNMENT IN SWAHILI VIA BAYESIAN PROBABILITY

JOHN OLSTAD
UNIVERSITY OF NEWCASTLE

Abstract

Noun class systems are grammaticalized agreement systems that some languages use to categorize nouns. As noted in Contini-Morava (1994), analyses of Bantu noun class systems have resulted in the thought that assignment is only somewhat generalizable and otherwise arbitrary. Contini-Morava seeks to show that there is more systematicity than received wisdom has led us to believe. Specifically, she considers all nouns of Johnson's (1939) Standard Swahili-English Dictionary (Johnson, 1939) and subcategorizes them according to a set of semantic and morphological criteria. I hypothesize that these features (or some feature set like them) are predictive of noun class in the presence of semantic productivity. I implement a supervised machine learning algorithm to test the predictiveness of Contini-Morava's analysis. Swahili noun class is not fully predictable by the model, but the model is particularly strong in predicting the 'human' class 1/2, consistent with data from child language acquisition in other Bantu languages.

1. Introduction

Noun classes (or grammatical gender) are "grammaticalized agreement systems which correlate—at least in part—with certain semantic characteristics" (Aikhenvald, 2000:19). In many languages such as English, any notion of gender in language refers to sex gender, not grammatical gender; in many others, such as the romance languages, 'masculine' and 'feminine' genders are largely independent of sex gender for inanimate objects where gender is specified on a word-by-word basis. As noted by Dixon (1968:105), when linguists began to really study languages outside the Indo-European family, categories were discovered that looked like grammatical gender but lacked the possibility of semantic correlation with only the notions masculinity, femininity and neuter. The term 'noun class' has been adopted to an extent with 'gender' being a particular instance of 'noun class'. Noun class is now usually defined as follows (reproduced from Contini-Morava, 1994; originally Dixon, 1968:106):

> (a) all nouns in the language are divided into a small and closed set of classes signaled by inflectional morphology;
> (b) the class of a noun is obligatorily co-referenced on other elements in the sentence via grammatical agreement

An example of a language family for which 'gender' in its original sense was perhaps unsuitable, the Bantu language family is well known for its rich noun class system. However, still not very well understood are the circumstances under which nouns have been assigned historically—or are assigned in real-time—to respective noun classes. Contini-Morava (1994) attempts to further that understanding by examining Swahili, a member of the Sabaki subgroup of Northeast Coast Bantu, which has a noun class system that is typical of Bantu languages. While most earlier treatments of Swahili have concluded that noun class is somewhat generalizable by semantic principles, but that much of class assignment is arbitrary, Contini-Morava argues that it is systematic given her analysis. Having manually tagged in the neighborhood of 5000 nouns from the Standard Swahili-English Dictionary with a feature set of semantic and morphological values, she attempts to discover more of the previously undiscovered systematicity of the Swahili noun class system.

In this study, I assume that if that systematicity exists, a proper set of features and corresponding values ought to be predictive of noun class. I hypothesize that Contini-Morava's analysis will be predictive of the nouns in her database. A semantic analysis should be more predictive of noun classes that are semantically productive. It may be the case that noun class is predictable based on a semantic feature set completely, somewhat, or not at all. I test this using a probabilistic supervised machine learning algorithm; a probabilistic classifier model known as naïve Bayes. I hypothesize that the model can do three interesting things:

1. Evaluate the systematicity of a noun class assignment system.
2. Detect prototypical exemplars of each noun class.
3. Predict which classes are apt to be semantically productive.

The whole process rests on the assumption that the tagger knows the meaning of each word and that the tagger should therefore be able to make accurate judgments on the semantic features inherent in each word. Accurate machine classification does not imply that the semantic representation has any sort of psychological reality, although it would warrant further investigation into that claim. And, as I will show later on, the results of the classifier model support data from child language acquisition that suggests that animate and certain other classes in Bantu languages are semantically active (see, for example, Demuth, 2000).

2. A semantic analysis of Swahili noun classes

Swahili has a system of eleven different noun classes reflected in a complex agreement system[1]. It is typical of Bantu languages to have several genders that are realized in this way. Below is a typical example of gender agreement in Swahili:

1) ki-kapu ki-kubwa ki-moja ki-languka
   CL7-basket CL7-large CL7-one CL7-fell
   'One large basket fell.'
   (Corbett 1991:43)

The adjective, numeral and verb are all targets of the controller noun *kikapu* 'basket'; all agree in noun class and thus take the prefix *ki-*. If the controller noun belonged to a different noun class, the prefixes on each of the targets would instead take on the prefix from that class. Below is a list of all the different noun classes and the prefixes they assign (taken from Contini-Morava, 1994):

[1] The number of classes is counted by morphology in Bantuist literature, effectively doubling the count where a morpholgical distinction exists between singular and plural affixes. A semantic analysis should be based on semantic classes, which then reduces the number to six. I ran the model I describe in this paper with both six and eleven classes and found similar results since number is specified in the database and thus contributes significantly to output probabilities.

Table 1: The classes and their prefixes

Class	nominal/adjectival	pronominal
1	*m-*	*a-/m-; yu-; w-;ye-* (depends on stem)
2	*wa-*	*wa-*
3	*m-*	*u-*
4	*mi-*	*i-*
5	zero or *ji-*	*li-*
6	*ma-*	*ya-*
7	*ki-*	*ki-*
8	*vi-*	*vi-*
9	zero or *n-*	*i-*
10	zero or *n-*	*zi-*
11/14	*u-/m-(nominal form)*	*u-*

In certain cases, such as class 1, 3 and 4, the nominal and adjectival prefixal reflection of class is of a different form than the pronominal reflection. With so many possible noun classes employed in Swahili and other such languages, the question becomes: How do nouns get assigned to their respective classes?

According to Corbett (1991:33-49), Swahili and other Bantu languages are considered to be systems of both 'semantic assignment' and 'formal assignment'. That is, some of the rules that can be formulated can be said to be semantic assignment rules; others, formal assignment rules, are morphological or phonological. Of note on the semantic side: it can be shown that Swahili assigns augmentatives to gender 5/6, e.g. *j-oka* 'giant snake', and diminutives to 7/8, e.g. *ki-j-oka* 'tiny snake'. Unfortunately, such rules only cover a very small subsection of the lexicon. He notes that "it is often stated that the distribution of nouns over genders is largely arbitrary"(1991:49), but that there are some interesting subregularities. For example, plants are often found in gender 3/4, fruits in 5/6, animals in 9/10, etc. However, there are numerous exceptions. Nouns denoting any of the general categories above can fall into other classes and by no means are any of the classes restricted to such general categories. The assignment of such general meaning to genders results in a group that isn't much bigger than the number of exceptions. This is problematic for analyses that attempt to determine noun classification by assigning a single invariant to each class such as '5/6=fruits' above or '5/6=non extended (rounded, protruded, bunched)' as in Denny and Creider (1986:232; for a review of several such treatments see Zawawi, 1979). However, as George Lakoff and others have pointed out, membership in a given linguistic category (in this case, noun class) may be based on multiple criteria—metaphor, metonymy, family resemblance (Lakoff, 1987:12-57), for example—and some members may be more and less prototypical than others. As I will show later on, this prototypicality can be modeled probabilistically.

In Contini-Morava's database, she has manually tagged approximately 5000 Swahili nouns with values for a series of features. Her proposed features are HUMAN, ANIMAL, PLANT, INANIMATE, SHAPE, SIZE, NUMBER, AFFECT, DERIVED, NATURAL FORCE and LOAN. Underneath any given feature is a list of possible values for that feature. For example, under the human feature are values such as OCCUPATION, RELIGIOUS, CHARACTER, AGENTIVE, etc. In her analysis, none of the subcategories are meant to be mutually exclusive; more than one value may apply to any given feature of any given noun. For example, *kumba*, 'a plaited coconut leaf used for fencing', would have the feature values shown in Table 2:

Table 2: One example from the semantic feature database

CLASS	HUMAN	ANIMAL	PLANT	NANIM.	SHAPE	SIZE	NUMBER	AFFECT	DERIVED	NATUR. FORCE	LOAN
5	n	n	Part and material	ool	long	large	sg	neut	?	n	n

The value under the feature plant has both PART and MATERIAL as well as a semantic value of TOOL for feature INANIMATE. The other feature values are either not applicable or are morphological characteristics. She also tags values for an etymological feature signifying loan source. Etymological features are unlikely to be useful in real-time noun class assignment (if such a process even exists) but they could possibly be useful in assigning class via a probabilistic model.

3. Hypotheses

The motivation for my hypotheses (i, ii and iii below) is the following question: What is the nature of the native speaker's actual noun class system enabling it to produce intended results time and again? There seem to be three logical possibilities:

1. Noun class is lexically specified (each form is memorized).
2. Noun class assignment is generalizable on some set of principles.
3. Noun class is best described as a hybrid of 1 and 2.

If 1 is true, we would expect little, if any, semantic productivity in class assignment. That is, noun class would have to be memorized. If 2 is true, we would expect noun class assignment to be entirely productive. Since every noun class assignment could be arrived at via some generalization, that same generalization could extend to novel forms. That is, loan words would be distributed amongst class based on semantic content rather than being almost entirely cast into class 9 (Zawawi, 1979) as is actually the case for Swahili. What I assume is that 3 is the best choice; the noun class system of Swahili is a hybrid of learned (memorized) class assignments and graded predictability based on semantic knowledge of prototypical exemplars. This assumption allows me to test the hypotheses below and as I will explain later on, the output predictions of the model lend support to the idea. The hypotheses to be tested are as follows:

i. Noun distribution over noun class is predictable by semantic features.
ii. Output predictions of the model will identify prototypical and non-prototypical exemplars.
iii. Accuracy of predictability will have rank assignability for individual classes.

The first hypothesis holds if the model is able to predict noun class for a simple majority of the dataset. Unfortunately, however, the hypothesis is not neatly falsifiable for my data because the model could fail if the semantic feature analysis is inadequate. This would call for rethinking of the feature set. On the other hand, if the model shows that the semantic features are indeed predictive of class, the hypothesis holds and the semantic analysis can be deemed viable. So, in a sense, this method can be used to evaluate semantic analyses in general.

The second hypothesis holds true if the model outputs a group of examples for each class whose output probabilities of class membership are extremely high (close to 1.000) and others that are correctly predicted by the model but are of much lower probability (say, less than .500). Unfortunately for this hypothesis, the only available scale to test whether outputted prototypical exemplars of the dataset are in any sense prototypical of that class in actual human conceptualization is that of human intuition. To put it another way, below I list some of the predicted prototypical exemplars for each class, but there is no real quantitative way to test if they are in fact prototypical for Swahili speakers. They are only unequivocally prototypes of the dataset itself.

The third hypothesis holds true simply if there are classes which are more predictable than others. Ideally, there should be some independent experimental evidence that the ranking predicts. For example, it is widely accepted that the class which contains human terms is the only major semantically assigned class in Bantu languages, and there is experimental child language acquisition evidence that supports this as well (presented in Demuth, 2000). At the very least, the model should predict this by more accurately classifying class 1/2 than the other classes. A highly predictable class should be representative of a class that is apt to be semantically productive. Further psycholinguistic studies could confirm whether there is any merit to the ranking assigned to the other classes. Below I explain the model I used and show that its output predictions support the above hypotheses.

4. Probabilistic classifier models

Probabilistic classifier models take a set of feature values and compute the probability that each value should occur given a particular class. Such a model needs exactly three things:

- A list of classes.
- A list of feature values.
- A list of examples with given classes and feature values.

The semantic analysis proposed by Contini-Morava (1994) therefore lends itself perfectly to this task. The list of classes is given; in this case the class names given by Corbett (1991:47) are used. The list of feature values comes from the analysis proposed by Contini-Morava as described in section 2 of this paper. The list of examples and tags for class values and feature values comes again from the effort of Contini-Morava. She compiles a database of nouns and corresponding noun class assignments based on Johnson's (1939) Standard Swahili English Dictionary and manually tags each of over 5000 examples for her proposed semantic feature values[1]. On the other hand, a major weakness of computing probability of class, given features, in this case is that the analysis *is* done manually. Without supplied tags for class and features this would be impossible, so any attempt to use this approach in the future for other languages or for machine translation purposes would require the same type of effort that went in to compiling the Swahili database. In addition, the chance of predictions being applicable to the human Swahili conceptualization system is at the whim of the educated opinion—but opinion nonetheless—of the tagger. So in a sense, if noun class is indeed predictable by a given set of features, the whole endeavor will reflect how accurately Contini-Morava's tagged feature set depicts the inherent set of feature values for the set of nouns in the Swahili database. If the depiction is accurate and noun distribution over noun class is systematic, a probabilistic classifier will be able to predict noun class.

4.1 Methodology

The database of approximately 5000 Swahili nouns with given class and feature values were preprocessed in the following way: Features that were tagged for multiple values were expanded out to allow independent values to be assigned to each feature value. In other words, for example, if PLANT can contain the values MATERIAL and PART, then the feature PLANT needed to be extended so that its value could contain the product of the probabilities associated with those values. The calculations that build the probabilistic model will be explained in more detail in the next section. Single-value features were not problematic. After the database was preprocessed, it was imported into the software package Weka (Witten and Frank, 2005), which allowed me to view the predictions central to my hypotheses even with such a large dataset.

---

[1] A profuse thank you to Professor Contini-Morava for this hard work and especially for sharing the database with me.

4.2 Naïve Bayes classification

Naïve Bayes is a supervised machine learning algorithm based on Bayesian statistics. In Bayesian statistics, unlike the more popular frequentist statistics, probability is conceived of as the way in which an idealized rational thinker responds to all the evidence given. Probability as a number between 0.00 and 1.00, represents the degree of belief of the ideally rational thinker. Naïve Bayes classifiers have been traditionally used in document classification assigning articles to classes based on the probability of certain keywords being present in the article (e.g. Maron, 1961), but also for many other data mining applications including SPAM e-mail filtering. There are a host of other more powerful supervised machine learning classifiers in existence, but I chose to implement naïve Bayes due to its–perhaps relative—simplicity. The probability model for naïve Bayes classification is:

$$p(C|F_1,\ldots,F_n)$$

or the probability of a class *C,* given the features F_1 through F_n, where *n* equals the total number of features. The naïve Bayes assumption is that features of a class are a conditionally independent given class. That is to say, even though features of an entity depend on the existence of the other features of that entity, a naïve Bayes classifier considers that all of the features independently contribute to the probability that it is what it is. For example, if something barks, is furry, and has a wet nose, it may be considered to have high likelihood of being a dog, even though other entities may share these properties.

What we are looking for in a naïve Bayes classification problem is the joint probability that a noun belongs to a certain noun class given the probability of the value for feature 1, feature 2 … feature n. The assumption of conditional independence allows us to simplify the calculation:

$$p(C|F_1,\ldots,F_n) = p(C)\,p(F_1|C)\,p(F_2|C)\,p(F_3|C)\ldots$$

Now the probability that a noun belongs to a particular noun class is simply the product of the prior probability (or the frequency of nouns assigned to each noun class) and the probability of each feature value tagged for each noun to occur with that same class.

What this all amounts to in terms of the Swahili data is that for each value of each feature tagged in the database, there is a probability that it is likely to occur given each class. The class with the highest of these probabilities is chosen for each noun as part of the classification algorithm. The accuracy of this speaks to hypothesis (i). In addition, the more prototypical examples of each class will have probabilities nearest to one (1.000) (hypothesis ii). The model also outputs accuracies for classification attempts on each class (hypothesis iii).

4.3 Results and discussion

Training the model on a randomly selected third of the database and attempting to generalize to the remaining two-thirds of the database resulted in 59.59% accuracy. That is to say, 59.59% of the time the model was able to predict the correct class of 11 possible choices. This is considerably higher than chance given that there are 11 possible choices, as opposed to only 2, for example. Kappa scores were between 42 and 60 for all runs of the algorithm. However, around 60% accuracy is much lower than what would presumably be a native speaker's score; that is, somewhere in the neighborhood of 100% for familiar nouns. In general, we can conclude that noun class distribution is partially predictable by the semantic feature set. This supports hypothesis (i).

The model outputs the probabilities that derive the predictions for each noun in the database. Below are a few examples of prototypical and non-prototypical examples of each class. Subregularities from Corbett (1991) are given mainly as a point of reference. It should be noted that in this study I assume that these kind of all-inclusive categories do not exist as such.

The output predictions of the model support hypothesis (ii). For each class there are a number of examples of very high probability and a number of examples of very low probability. This reflects a general pattern of graded criteria for class membership. A noun in any class can share certain features with a noun in any other class. Class assignment is determined by the highest joint probability of these features, in this case simplified to conditional independence. In some cases, this probability is very high, approaching 1 (a prototypical exemplar, perhaps). In other cases this probability is not so high (a non-prototypical exemplar, perhaps).

Table 3: Possible prototypical and non-prototypical examples by class

Class	Subregularities (Corbett, 1991)	Prototypical examples (> .900) Non-prototypical examples (<.500)
Class 1/2	animates	*mtu*, 'person' 1.000 *muminina*, 'true believer' *0.511[2]
Class 3/4	plants	*mbambakofi*, 'good timber tree', 0.99 *mbibi*, 'cashew apple tree', 0.99
Class 5/6	fruits	*kombe*, 'rope sling', 0.99 *limau*, 'lemon', 0.99 *kope*, 'eyelid, eyelashes', 0.49 *koti*, 'coat, jacket', 0.305
Class 7/8	small objects	*kitani*, 'flax', 0.99 *kipato*, 'earnings', 0.99
Class 9/10	animals	*mbuzi*, 'goat', 0.92 *namba*, 'number', 0.9 *mudir*, 'village chief', 0.2
Class 11/10	long objects	*ushungi*, 'cloth worn on body', 0.9 *usimeme*, 'firmness', .35

A consequence of this ends up being explanatory of examples such as 'rope sling' being a prototypical member of class 5/6, which fruits tend to belong to. For the present study, this means that members of class 5/6 may include fruits, but also include anything whose features contain a higher joint probability of that class than any other class. The same is true with 'flax' and 'earnings' being highly probable members of class 7/8. While it does not take much imagination to see how both notions fit into the same category—individual flax seeds are small objects as are coins, and although most people would consider their earnings to be small, the

[2] As an anonymous reviewer points out, *muminina* is ambiguous between class 1/2 and class 9/10. However, that ambiguity does not figure into the assignment because naïve Bayes classification assumes that features *given* class are independent of class. This means that 0.511 is the probability that *muminina* belongs to class 1/2 even if it belonged to a different class. This also means that the probability that *muminina* belongs to class 9/10 is less than 0.511 given the semantic feature set.

abstract idea of 'earnings' does not fit—the fact is that the model cannot consider these things; it only outputs probabilities.

The model also provides accuracy of predictions for each class individually. Based on the output of the model, the classes can be ranked for predictability as shown in the table below:

Table 4: Class predictability ranking

Evaluation	Class	ROC area
Excellent	Class 1/2	0.99
Fair to good	Class 3/4 Class 5/6 Class 9/10	0.830 0.826 0.800
Fair	Class 7/8 Class 11/10	0.760 0.780

ROC area refers to the area under a curve which plots true positive rate on the y-axis and false positive rate on the x-axis; it is a common measure in evaluating accuracy in machine learning. In this case, true positive rate refers to the rate at which a class that is predicted for each noun is the correct class from the dataset. The ROC areas are all considered at least fair on the grade scale shown below:

- .90-1 = excellent (A)
- .80-.90 = good (B)
- .70-.80 = fair (C)
- .60-.70 = poor (D)
- .50-.60 = fail (F)

Given this scale, only class 1/2 is in the (A) 'excellent' range, in line with the child language acquisition data. Classes 3/4, 5/6 and 9/10 are in the (B) 'good' range. 7/8 and 11/10 are in the (C) 'fair' range. This provides the rankability required for hypothesis (iii). However, the position of class 9/10 in this ranking conflicts with Contini-Morava's observation that 9/10 is the least semantically coherent of all the classes. Although not perfectly objective like a mathematical model, this observation has the potential to be problematic for my analysis in the explanatory sense. The reason the model should have a tendency to predict 9/10 in the absence of good systematicity is because at 0.190, the prior probability for a given example to be 9/10 is greater than for any other class and prior probabilities are equal in weight to the probabilities of features given class. However, if we assume that speakers are aware of loanwords, the story once again adds up. Then, due to the influx of loans into class 9/10, we can say that class 9/10 is reasonably predictable, however not owing to semantic coherence. Further studies in acquisition of Bantu languages are required to support the model's predictions in actual human systems.

5. Conclusion

Although Swahili noun class was not completely predictable by the semantic feature set, the model did fairly well overall. It was especially effective in predicting classes 1/2, 3/4, 5/6 and 9/10, though the success of 9/10 may not be due to semantic factors[3]. If a noun class system is semantically non-productive, it should be expected that noun class in said system cannot be predicted by a set of semantic features; however, noun class was nearly perfectly predictable for class 1 as predicted by the child acquisition data and elsewhere. The model outputs the probability that each noun would belong to each class. Examples that have very high probabilities represent the prototypical feature values for the predicted class. Interestingly, nouns in differing noun classes can share feature values. This reflects the situation predicted by prototype theorists (cf. Rosch, 1973). The model is able to proceed in the face of uncertainty, it does not require that rules and class properties are Aristotelian. Instead, the model is '*x*% certain' that each noun belongs to each noun class and simply proceeds with the most highly probable noun class assignment. Givón (1986:98) argues that this ability to "proceed well with high-but-not-perfect predictability" is both akin and advantageous to biological organisms. And not all classes were shown to be highly predictable. For example, class 7 was given the grade of 'C'. Since a native speaker of Swahili presumably achieves near perfect noun class assignment, it is likely that class 7 is the beneficiary of human beings' ability to store a huge amount of forms in the lexicon. The model still shows evidence of systematicity in class 7, despite claims that assignment outside class 1/2 is all but arbitrary.

So it seems that within each noun class, for each noun, there is a continuum of arbitrary-approaching-fuzzy-approaching-certain as to which class the noun belongs to—with perhaps neither of the far poles ever being reached. Assuming that this claim is entirely true, a simple probabilistic

[3] Thank you to an anonymous reviewer for helping me come to this conclusion.

classifier is able to proceed, predicting noun class without any fear of being unable to generate the conditions of class membership *prima facie*.

References

Aikhenvald, A.Y. 2000. *Classifiers: A typology of Noun Categorization Devices*. Oxford: Oxford University Press.

Contini-Morava, E. 1994. Noun Classification in Swahili. Publications of the Institute for Advanced Technology in the Humanities, University of Virginia. Research Reports, Second Series.

Corbett, Greville. 1991. *Gender*. Cambridge University Press.

Craig, Colette (ed.) 1986. *Noun classes and categorization*. Amsterdam: John Benjamins.

Denny, J. Peter and Chet Creider. 1976. "The semantics of noun classes in Proto-Bantu." *Studies in African linguistics* 7.1: 1-30. Reprinted in Craig (ed.), 217-239.

Demuth, K. 2000. "Bantu noun class systems: Loan word and acquisition evidence of semantic productivity. " In *Classification Systems*, edited by G. Senft, 270-292. Cambridge: Cambridge University Press.

Dixon, R.M.W. 1968. "Noun Classes". *Lingua*. 21, 104-125.

Givón, Talmy. 1986. "Prototypes: Between Plato and Wittgenstein". In *Noun classes and categorization*, edited by C. Craig. 77-102. Amsterdam: John Benjamins.

Johnson, Frederick. 1939. *A standard Swahili-English dictionary*. Oxford: Oxford University Press.

Lakoff, G. 1987. *Women, fire and dangerous things: What categories reveal about the mind*. Chicago and London: University of Chicago Press.

Maron, M. E. 1961. "Automatic Indexing: An Experimental Inquiry." *Journal of the ACM (JACM)* 8(3): 404–417.

Rosch, E.H. 1973. "Natural categories." *Cognitive Psychology* 4, 328-350.

Witten, I. and Eibe Frank. 2005. *Data Mining: Practical machine learning tools and techniques, 2nd Edition*. San Fransisco: Morgan Kaufman.

Zawawi, Sharifa. 1979. *Loan words and their effect on the classification of Swahili nominals*. Leiden: E.J. Brill.

ARCHITECTURE OF GRAMMAR AND PHI-FEATURE VALUING IN CLAUSE-INITIAL DISCOURSE ELLIPSES

MARI NYGÅRD

NORWEGIAN UNIVERSITY OF SCIENCE AND TECHNOLOGY (NTNU)

Abstract

In spoken Norwegian, subjects in a topicalized position are frequently omitted. One issue to be addressed is whether it is plausible to assume a full sentence structure for these cases, and if so, what this structure contains? I propose an analysis where syntactic structure is present independently of lexical insertion, and where the structure contains abstract formal features. Focussing on agreement, I argue that phi-features are present in syntax also when no lexical item is inserted. Support for this is found in ellipses where anaphors, verbs and predicatives show agreement with null subjects.

I discuss data displaying so called semantic agreement, and I argue that in a manner parallel to the ellipses, these examples point to a separation between visible morphology and abstract grammatical features. I therefore propose a unified analysis for the two groups of data, where phi-features are not directly tied to lexical items. Instead, there are unvalued phi-feature matrixes linked to syntactic positions. These matrixes are valued from inserted lexical items, yet depending on how these items are semantically conceived of. The unvalued phi-features in the subject position are valued from information in the inserted lexical subject. Further, Agree holds between the probe in [T] and the goal in [spec,vP]. Crucially though, contextual or semantic information can influence the features of the subject, as is the case for the semantic agreement data. This triggers a different value on the phi-features, and consequently also a different feature specification on T. Importantly, the suggested analysis also accounts for agreement in subject ellipses. If phi-features are present independently of lexical insertion, they can be valued by information from the C-I interface. Consequently, if the contextual information is sufficiently prominent, there's no need to insert a concrete lexical item.

1. Introduction

A characteristic feature of discourse ellipses in spontaneous spoken Norwegian is that elements of different categories can be left out, primarily sentence initially. In particular, subjects in the front position are frequently omitted, as illustrated in example 1-5:[1]

1. Ø gikk rett i gulvet.
   Ø went right to floor-the.
   '(He) fell right down.'
2. Ø tar ting som det kommer.
   Ø take things as it comes.
   '(He) takes things as they come.'
3. Ø føler deg litt viktig.
   Ø feel you (reflexive) a little important.
   '(You) feel a little bit important.'
4. Ø gifter oss her.
   Ø marry us (reflexive) here.
   '(We) are getting married here.'
5. Ø hadde blitt kaos her da.
   Ø had become chaos here then.
   '(It) had become chaotic here then.'

It is worth mentioning that elements of other categories can occasionally also undergo such clause-initial discourse ellipsis. Hence, both omitted initial objects, complements of prepositions and verbs are attested. Nevertheless, such examples will not be included in the present article. The main focus will be on the subject. [2]

Norwegian is not a pro drop language. On the contrary, the presence of a subject is usually obligatory in all finite clauses. Still, despite

[1] For each of the examples, I have given an English translation with a phonetically realized subject (in parenthesis). However, note that in many of these elliptical sentences, the underlying subject cannot be unambiguously stated. Still, in order to facilitate the understanding, I have chosen to insert the contextually most probable subject.

[2] The phenomenon of clause-initial ellipses, so-called topic drop, is known also from other Germanic varieties, such as German and Dutch. However, a comparison of the similar and different characteristics of discourse ellipses in these languages lies beyond the scope of this article, which concentrates primarily on Norwegian data.

representing a violation of the standard norm for Norwegian, examples like the ones in 1-5 are very frequent in informal registers. Yet, in traditional grammars, they are often presented as marginal exceptions, or just not treated at all. This is quite unfortunate, considering that discourse ellipses constitute an essential characteristic of spoken language.

In this paper, I will first discuss whether it is plausible to assume an underlying syntactic structure for these cases, and if so, what this structure contains. Secondly, I look at agreement and phi-features in discourse ellipses, as well as examples displaying so called semantic agreement, and I present a unified analysis of agreement and phi-feature valuing for the two groups of data.

2. An underlying syntactic structure?

Ellipses give rise to two important questions which, I believe, deserve separate answers. Firstly, how are ellipses derived, and secondly, which types of ellipsis are possible, which ones are not, and why? Thus, we crucially do not want to mix up the *mechanisms* involved in the derivation, with the *restrictions* or *licensing conditions* imposed on discourse ellipses in general. The discussion in this article will limit itself to the first one of these questions. Hence, it will not seek to answer questions such as 'Why is ellipsis restricted to main clauses?', 'Why is the elided material string initial', and 'Why does the elision of the finite verb depend on the elision of the topic in preverbal position?'.[3] For an up-to-date overview and analysis of licensing conditions for argument drop cross-linguistically, see Sigurðsson (2010) and Sigurðsson and Maling (2010).

Concerning the elliptical data, an interesting question is the following: Given that certain elements are not expressed, what does the underlying structure contain? Is the ellipsis site completely empty, or does it consist of syntactic features despite the lack of phonological material? The point is this – should the data be treated as syntactic ellipses, where whole syntactic nodes are deleted, or does the omission only concern phonological content, so that the syntactic features in the nodes stay intact? I will sketch three alternative answers to these questions.

The first alternative is to claim that the syntactic position is non-existent, and that the syntactic structure is truncated. Interestingly, Haegeman and Guéron (1999) suggest an analysis along these lines for abbreviated registers of English. They propose a missing C-projection for

[3] It is of course beyond any doubt that questions of this kind are both interesting and relevant, and in my future work I will most certainly seek for answers to them.

sentences with initial subject drop, pointing to the fact that in these abbreviated registers, null subjects can only occur in a restricted set of environments. Null subjects are not permitted in embedded clauses, root interrogatives, embedded interrogatives, in sentences with topicalized arguments or with topicalized predicates (Haegeman and Guéron 1999, 622). From this fact, the authors conclude that non-overt subjects must be the leftmost elements in the structure. Crucially, they are excluded if the CP layer is filled by an overt element.

However, I will reject this truncation analysis, mainly because of examples such as 6-8 (Nygård 2004, Nygård, Eide and Åfarli 2008).

6. Ø fikk ikke demonstrere.
   Ø could not demonstrate.
   '(They) were not allowed to demonstrate.'
7. … at hun ikke fikk demonstrere.
   … that she not could demonstrate.
   '… that she could not demonstrate.'
8. * Ø ikke fikk demonstrere.
   **Ø not could demonstrate.*
   '(They) were not allowed to demonstrate.'

In Norwegian, being a V2 language, the finite verb moves to C in main clauses. Hence, it moves across the sentence adverbial, as seen in (6), contrary to what happens in subordinate clauses (7). If we were to adopt the truncated structure analysis, with no CP layer, we would have no way of explaining why (8) as a main clause is unacceptable, and why the word order must be as in (6). However, if we assume a full sentence structure with a CP layer also for ellipses, this follows naturally given that the finite verb moves to C like in the corresponding non-elliptical sentence.

A second alternative is to assume that the underlying structure is present, but that it has no content. If all feature information is incorporated into lexical items, then this information will disappear when a lexical item is omitted. The structure will be rendered empty. However, assuming the commonly accepted idea of endocentricity, a projection cannot project from nothing. Consequently, a completely bare structure should not be possible. Furthermore, in the Minimalist Program, every structure is built by means of the operation Merge, which takes two syntactic objects and unifies them. Merge can only apply if a local asymmetric relation can arise between two merged elements. Obviously, such a relation is only possible if the objects have some kind of content. If the nodes are empty, no grammatical relation is possible between them. The operation Merge would then be free and without purpose. This is of course theoretically unsatisfactory. Hence, I conclude that also this analytical option must be dismissed.

I therefore propose a third alternative, namely that syntactic structure contains certain formal grammatical features independently of the insertion of lexical items with their semantic and phonetic features. In other words, grammatical features are present despite the lack of lexical insertion. In arguing for this view, I will limit myself to the treatment of phi-features (gender, number, person), because it is not the main goal in the present article to give an exhaustive account for all kinds of features, but rather to outline a possible line of thought.

3. Feature content in the ellipsis site

The hypothesis that lexically empty nodes contain grammatical phi-features is supported by so called connectivity effects, which are defined as grammatical dependencies similar to the dependencies manifest in non-elliptical sentences (Merchant 2004). As will be illustrated, it is symptomatic that the elided items are syntactically active. This indicates that the data involve an omission only of phonological content, rather than a syntactic deletion. Several of the cases displaying connectivity effects are outlined below.

3.1 Anaphor agreement

Firstly, subject ellipses can contain anaphors which need to be bound and thereby c-commanded by antecedents with specific phi-features, triggering agreement on the anaphors. This is illustrated in 9 and 10:

9. Ø har valgt å ikke trene meg i hjel.
   Ø have decided to not exercise myself to death.
   '(I) have decided not to work out so hard that it will kill me.'
10. Ø har meldt seg.
   Ø has turned himself in.
   '(He) has turned himself in.'

In 9, the anaphor "meg" is 1st person singular, despite there being no visible subject to bind it. 10 is a parallel case. Here, the anaphor is 3rd person singular or plural.[4] Thus, even when the subject is apparently missing, the number and person feature must still be present and specified, in order to assure the right agreement morphology on the anaphor. These data clearly indicate that it is not necessarily the morphologically visible features of the lexical item which determine agreement.

3.2Question tags

Secondly, in subject ellipses with tag questions, such as 11 and 12, a matrix subject which is coreferential with the subject in the tag, must be present at some point in the derivation. Similar arguments have been made for silent subjects in imperatives (Jacobsen 1986, McCawley 1998, Akmajian and Heny 1975), which are fully transferable to the subject ellipses investigated here.

11. Ø fikk ikke demonstrere, fikk du?
    Ø could not demonstrate, could you?
    '(You) could not demonstrate, could you?'
12. Ø kan ikke lese enda, kan han?
    Ø can not read yet, can he?
    '(He) cannot read yet, can he?'

3.3 Subject-verb agreement

Another group of data supporting the same hypothesis is found in languages with subject/verb agreement. The relevant data are examples where finite verbs seem to agree in person and number with invisible subjects. 13-15 show examples of diary drop from the French translation of Bridget Jones Diary (Stroumza 1998) – from Haegeman and Ihsane (2001):

---

[4] There is of course a possibility that the underlying subjects of 9 and 10 are not 1st person. Then, 'meg' and 'seg' would probably not be reflexive anaphors, but rather objects. However, in this case, the context of the sentences in 9 and 10 strongly favours a first person interpretation of the subjects, and if so, 'meg' and 'seg' are unambiguously reflexives.

13. Ø me rappelle tout à coup que Ø portais jupe noire Lycra dernière fois.
    me remember suddenly that wore skirt black Lycra last time
    'I suddenly remember that I was wearing the Lycra skirt the last time.'
14. En cherchant le lait Ø me suis aperçue qu' Ø ai laissé filet.
    while looking (for) the milk myself am become-aware that have left basket.
    'While look the milk I realize that I have left the basket behind.'
15. Ø suis tellement énervée que Ø me suis assise sur la télécommande.
    am so nervous that me am seated on remote control.
    'I am so nervous that I have just sat down on the remote control.'

The verbs in these examples "rappelle", "suis" and "ai", as well as the reflexive pronoun, are 1st person singular, despite there being no instantiated 1st person singular subject. This reveals the presence of an underlying, fully inflected, but non-realized subject. Examples of traditional pro drop underline the same point, here illustrated by the Italian examples in 16-17:

16. Ø ha parlato.
    Ø has (3sg) spoken.
17. Ø ho telefonato.
    Ø have (1sg) telephoned.

The assumption that these data demonstrate the existence of an underlying, syntactically active subject rests of course on the traditional, widespread theoretical assumption that it is the verb which agrees with the subject and not the other way around. More specifically, it is commonly assumed that agreement morphology on arguments is inherent, while agreement morphology on verbs is not. As will also be discussed in what follows, this assumption is fundamental also for the minimalist approach to subject/verb agreement.

3.4 Predicative agreement

Examples of subject-verb agreement are not very relevant for Norwegian, for the simple reason that Norwegian lacks this type of agreement.

However, in fragment headlines, we find predicative adjectives agreeing in number with omitted subjects, as illustrated in 18-20:

18. Ø Ø slitne etter ferien.
Ø Ø tired (3 pl) after the holiday.
'(They are) tired after the holiday.'
19. Ø Ø sultne på Sultan-madrass.
Ø Ø hungry (3 pl) for Sultan matress.
' (They are) eager to get a Sultan mattress.'
20. Ø Ø fornøyde etter sommerjobb i Sjøfartsdirektoratet.
Ø Ø content (3pl) after summer job in Sjøfartsdirektoratet.
' (They are) content after summer job at Sjøfartsdirektoratet.'

Obviously, headlines represent a different register than spontaneous discourse. Nevertheless, I will assume that the same derivational mechanisms are at work, despite the fact that the restrictions for licensing might be different for the two groups. As mentioned earlier, it is crucial to maintain a clear distinction between these two aspects. Moreover, even though 18-20 are headlines, they would also be perfectly acceptable as discourse ellipses in spontaneous speech; hence I believe their relevance to be unquestionable.

These different groups of data strengthen the hypothesis that the syntactic nodes in discourse ellipses hide underlying phi-features which can trigger agreement on other elements in the sentence. I therefore conclude that the ellipsis sites are not vacuous, but rather that they contain a collection of active syntactic features which can trigger agreement on other elements in the sentence, be it the finite verb, a predicative element or an anaphor. Adopting such a view will of course entail certain consequences for the assumed overall model of agreement and phi-feature valuing. An issue which requires discussion is then of course how the values of these phi-features are fixed. This will be the topic of the next section.

4. Agreement and phi-feature valuing

As a point of departure, consider the traditional view in linguistic theory, where it is assumed that the form of anaphors and agreeing verbs are defined by the form of the subject. This idea can also be traced in recent versions of the Minimalist Program, where agreement is analyzed by the operation Agree, through which a probe searches for a relevant goal to agree with (Chomsky 2001, Adger 2003, Hornstein et al. 2005). Adger (2003) formalizes the operation Agree as follows:

Agree (… = c-command, and uF = unvalued feature):

X (F:val) … Y (uF:) → X (F:val) … Y (~~uF~~: val)

An implication of the Agree relation is that items enter the syntax with some of their features already valued and others as yet unvalued. In the course of the derivation, unvalued features must be valued from a matching valued feature through Agree, to be legible to PF and LF. This stands in contrast to earlier versions of the theory, such as the Move F approach, where all lexical items enter the derivation fully inflected, and the features are checked in a specifier-head relationship during the derivation (Hornstein et al. 2005). According to Chomsky (1998), the difference between valued and unvalued grammatical features correlates with a distinction between interpretable and uninterpretable features. Under this view, only interpretable features are fully valued in the lexicon. Uninterpretable features, on the other hand, enter the derivation unvalued, and must acquire their value in the course of the derivation to ensure that the derivation doesn't crash.

Because the subject-verb relation will be relevant for my purposes, I present briefly how subject-verb agreement is analysed in the Agree system, based on Adger's (2003) implementation of the operation. Finite T bears unvalued phi-features, which need to be valued. The subject DP on the other hand, bears inherently valued phi-features. In the Agree relation, finite T serves as a probe, whereas the subject DP serves as a goal. Agree then holds between the valued phi-features of the subject DP and the unvalued phi-features of T. Hence, the phi-features of the subject DP are transmitted to T, such that the features of T are valued.

Let's consider how this analysis would proceed in a simple sentence like "Peter carries a suitcase". The subject DP "Peter" bears the inherent phi-features 3rd person, masculine, singular. Finite T bears unvalued phi-features. Through Agree the features of the subject DP values the features of T, as illustrated below. The first structure displays the situation before Agree, and the other one after it is fulfilled. In these representations, *u* means unvalued, *Ø* stands for a non-instantiated item. G is gender, N is number, P is person. ~~uN~~: sgN signifies that the unvalued number feature has been valued to singular, following the model in Adger (2003).

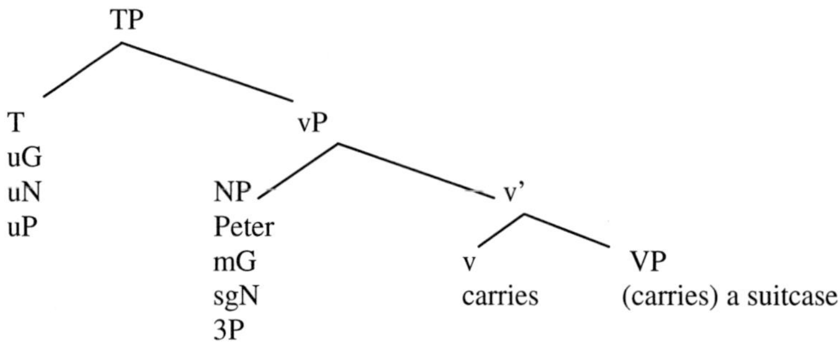

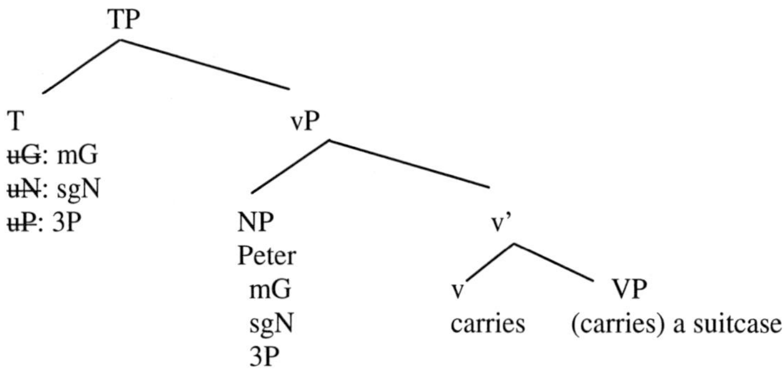

Crucially then, the phi-features of DPs are assumed to be inherently valued when a DP enters the derivation. As seen, this is contrary to those of verbs, which are valued by the inherent features of the subject. The same goes for anaphors and predicative adjectives. Consequently, when a subject is left out, the need immediately arises for a mechanism to account for the morphological form of anaphors, verbs and predicatives, all of which are normally dependent on the subject for this form. As the data has shown us, these items display agreement with null subjects, which entails that on some level the subjects are still needed for syntactic relations. Hence, the discourse ellipses demonstrate a separation between realised morphology on lexical items on the one hand, and abstract syntactic features on the other.

What is often postulated for ellipses is a deletion of lexical items or syntactic nodes (Chomsky 1965, Haegeman and Guéron 1999). For subject drop, this means that the subject is assumed to be merged into the structure, and then deleted, after having fulfilled its syntactic assignments, such as Agree. Nevertheless, this kind of approach doesn't seem very economical. Why should one insert an item into syntax only to remove it? Intuitively, it seems more plausible not to insert it in the first place.

I therefore propose a change of perspective, where syntax is not merged from lexical items with inherent grammatical features. Rather, lexical elements are inserted at a late point of the derivation. In this respect, the proposal bears certain similarities to the theory of Distributed Morphology (Harley and Noyer 1999, Josefsson 2006), of which a core idea is exactly that syntax does not handle phonological material, but rather generates structures by combining abstract morpho-syntactic features. Following the same line of thought, I suggest that feature matrixes are not directly tied to lexical elements. Instead, there are undefined feature matrixes linked to syntactic positions. The setting of these values happens in principle independently of lexical insertion.

In the subject position, there are unvalued phi-features waiting and demanding to be valued in order for the derivation not to crash. In non-elliptical cases, a subject DP is inserted into this position. The DP bears its own set of phi-features, with fixed values. In the majority of cases, the features of this DP are adopted into the subject position. Once they are fixed, they can undergo Agree and value the phi-features of different probes, such as anaphors and agreeing verbs. This is shown in figure 1:

Figure 1 – non-elliptical sentence

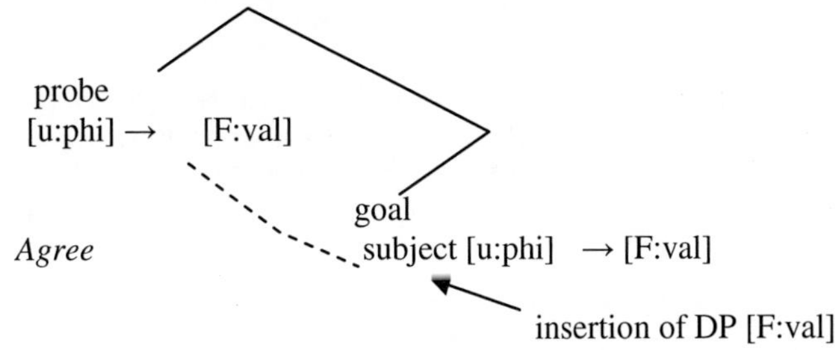

However, what the subject ellipses so neatly illustrate is that this valuing can very well happen despite the lack of an inserted subject DP. In such cases, the bare conceptualisation of the subject is enough to fix the value of the phi-features in the subject position, as shown in figure 2:

Figure 2 – subject drop

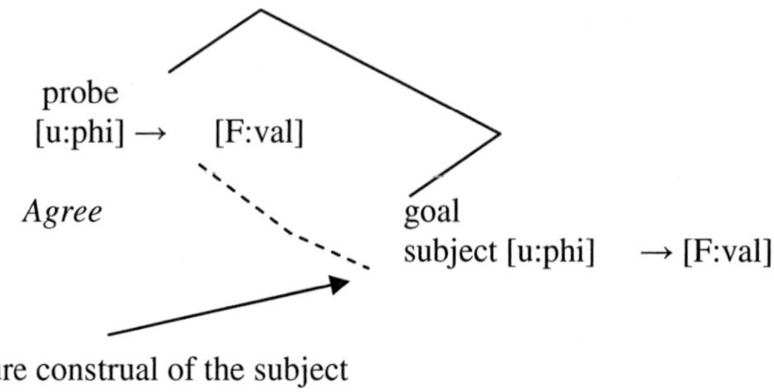

In other words, the choice of adopting a late insertion analysis, where grammatical and phonological features are in principle torn apart from their lexical concepts, provides a straightforward solution to the issues concerning anaphors, verbs and predicatives agreeing with omitted subjects. Phi-features are then assumed to be present independently of lexical items, and they are valued from insertion or from prominent information from the conceptual-intentional interface.

5. Semantic agreement

Additional support for the analysis that I have proposed comes from data displaying so called semantic agreement (Corbett 2000, Bosque 2006), which are characterized by an apparent mismatch of the phi-features of the subject and those of the verb:

21. Peter and Mary travel in Royal circles.
22. Politiet er snille.
    The police (sg) are(pl) nice (pl).
23. Russen er snille.
    The graduates (sg) are (pl) nice (pl).
24. The real reasons why the police are failing.
25. The police are a bunch of monkeys.

As seen, in the minimalist analysis finite T is assumed to exhibit unvalued phi-features which receive their values from the inherently valued features of the subject. However, the examples in 21-25 represent a challenge to this analysis. Let's consider how. In 21 the subject "Peter and Mary" consists of two DPs, each of them specified with the feature singular. The verb, on the other hand, has plural morphology. This clearly looks like a mismatch. The problem is thus how two singular DPs can value a plural feature on the verb in T? It appears as if the Agree operation has to include some kind of mathematical adding mechanism. Perhaps even more striking are the sentences in 22 and 23, where the subjects are singular ("politiet" + "russen"), while the predicative elements ("snille") are plural. The problem is the same, namely how a singular subject can value a plural predicative? The English examples in 24 and 25 illustrate the same point. The subject "the police" is singular, while the verb is plural.

The issue is that such data seem to open up for the possibility of a mismatch between visible morphology and underlying abstract features triggering agreement. It looks as if it is not the morphologically visible features of the lexical words which trigger agreement and value the unvalued phi-features. The examples thus point to a division or cleft between visible morphology and agreement valuing. In other words, they point in the same direction as the elliptical examples. Both groups of data demonstrate a separation between visible morphology on lexical items, on the one hand, and abstract grammatical features on the other. The ellipses display agreement despite the lack of a lexically instantiated subject. In these examples (21-25), the verb seems to agree with something else, maybe more abstract, than the visibly instantiated subject. But if the unvalued phi-features are not valued by visible features on the instantiated lexical words, how should we then assume that they are valued?

Examples like the ones in 21-25 have occasionally been given the label "semantic agreement" (Corbett 2000, among others), a problem which has not received much attention within generative theory (Sauerland and Elbourne 2002). I will briefly present two different accounts of the phenomena. Den Dikken (2001) notes that it is a curious fact about British English verbal agreement that collective noun phrases headed by a formally singular noun, can trigger plural agreement with the finite verb. He gives the following examples:

26. The committee has decided.
27. The committee have decided.

Den Dikken labels these noun phrases "pluringulars", which emphasizes precisely the point that these nouns seem to be both singular and plural at the same time. Furthermore, he points to a general distinction between the singular- and plural-agreeing types of DPs, namely that they are characterized either by collectivity or by individuality. When a DP is conceived of as several people or things, a plural verb is used. When it denotes a unit, a singular verb is chosen. This insight is equally noted in

Quirk et al. (1985, 758): "The choice between singular and plural verbs depends in BrE on whether the group is being considered as a single undivided body, or as a collection of individuals." Also Sauerland and Elbourne (2002) treat the issue that DPs denoting groups can take either singular or plural verbal agreement. The authors give a list of nouns which behave this way:

> They are morphologically singular in terms of overt morphology: *committee*, not *committees*, and so on. They are semantically singular in that it is still clear, in sentences like (...), that only one committee, battalion, or set is being referred to. (Sauerland and Elbourne 2002, 289)

These authors further claim that the fact that these singular nouns behave as if they were plural can be observed by several diagnostics. The nouns can be used with the determiner "each" (28), they can license plural anaphors (29-30), they can bind plural pronouns (31) and they can, as seen, be used with plural verb agreement (32), all these facts being indications of plurality:

28. *The committee each* received a pay-rise.
29. I want *the battalion* to get *themselves* under cover.
30. *The Labour Party* scare *each other.*
31. *The rugby team* like *their* coach and the football team do too.
32. {3,5,7,9} *This set are* all odd.

A curious fact is also that these nouns, as well as being able to bind plural pronouns, can actually bind singular pronouns when used with plural verb agreement:

33. All the rugby team are carrying its mascots and all the football team are too.

The analysis proposed by Sauerland and Elbourne (2002) is that British English DPs have, instead of one single number feature, two distinct feature categories with the values [singular] and [plural]. One of them is the traditional Number feature, which for any nominal indicates how many things are being referred to. The other feature is labelled Mereology, and indicates "whether or not the entity under discussion is being conceived of as consisting of more than one member" (Sauerland and Elbourne 2002, 291). The proposal is thus that processes like verbal agreement and the licensing of singular and plural anaphors and pronouns, can refer either to the Number feature or to the Mereology feature. For subject-verb agreement in the cases demonstrated above, Sauerland and Elbourne (2002, 291) propose that:

> (…) there are uninterpretable Person, Number, and Mereology features on T that are checked by the φ-features of the subject. The morphological operation that copies φ-features from T and manifests them in overt verb endings copies the Person feature and one of the Number and Mereology features.

These two different proposals are attempts to analyze examples of semantic agreement within the frames of the minimalist program. Whereas den Dikken (2001) points to a distinction between collectivity and individuality in the plurilinguals, Sauerland and Elbourne (2002) propose an additional Mereology feature to indicate roughly the same distinction. In the next section, I present a different analysis, which can give a unified account of agreement in discourse ellipses as well as semantic agreement data.

6. An alternative analysis

Despite the differences of the two analyses presented, the underlying insight remains the same, namely that the agreement process appears to be sensitive to semantic information about plurality or collectivity of the subject DP. More generally, information from the conceptual-intentional interface seems to influence the feature specification of the subject, or maybe rather the agreement process. The analysis I will suggest builds explicitly on this insight. I propose that the valuing of phi-features is dependent upon how the items in question are conceived of mentally. More specifically, in certain cases information from the conceptual-intentional interface can influence narrow syntactic operations and can overrule the morphologically visible inflection and lead to an alternative feature construal of the agreement features. Hence, the semantic agreement data can be straightforwardly accounted for within the analysis suggested for discourse ellipses. This is illustrated in figure 3:

Figure 3 – semantic agreement

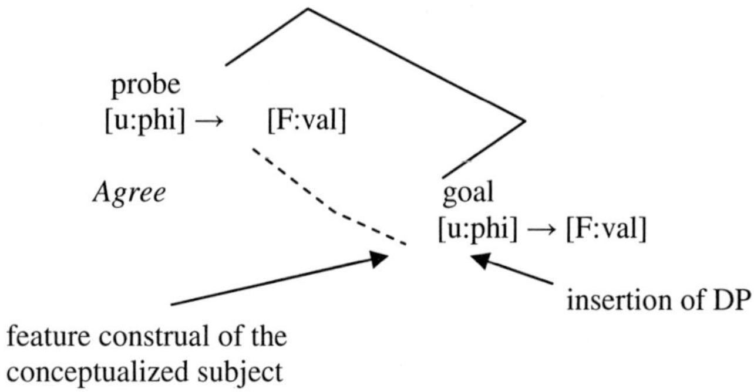

As before, the subject position contains unvalued phi-features. However, at the point of lexical insertion, instead of adopting the features of the DP subject, the phi-features in the subject position are valued by the features of the concept that the DP denotes. This is then parallel to what happens in the elliptical examples. For instance, the DP "the police" is conceived of as plural, despite being morphologically singular, and consequently, it triggers plural morphology on the verb.

It must be specified, though, that this conceptual valuing influences the valuing process rather than the lexical DP itself. All the cited examples clearly show that the subject DP itself retains its phi-features. Even if it is conceptualized as a collective plural, the subject cannot appear as "the polices", "the governments" or "the peoples". The DP is therefore assumed to be merged separately in a proper subtree, stored in the derivational work memory, which is subsequently inserted as a whole into the subject slot. It appears that the semantic plural meaning affects the subject DP at the point of insertion, triggering plural agreement. Hence, what is observed is that an apparently singular subject can trigger plural agreement on the verb in cases where the subject is conceived of as a collective plural. This is obvious in the examples above, where "the police" can be conceived of as several policemen, despite the fact that the DP is morphologically singular. Consequently, it values a plural feature on the predicative and the verb (in English), which then receive a plural form. Example 21 can be treated in like fashion. The subject is conceived of as two persons; therefore the verb is in the plural.

The main steps in the analysis proposed are then first the merging of the syntactic structure with unvalued feature matrixes. Secondly, the valuing of phi-features happens from lexical insertion or from an alternative feature construal by taking into account the conceptual content of the DP in question. Then, in order to make the abstract syntax possible to process for the recipient, a certain level of phonological realisation is mandatory. Even though it would be conceptually conceivable, a fully derived syntactic structure with no audible or visible words is not desirable. Realisation is a PF phenomenon, which has no effects on the abstract narrow syntax. The realisation can happen either directly, by an insertion of a phonologically instantiated lexical item, or it can be indirect, via for instance Agree. This is the case for agreeing anaphors and verbs. As a third alternative, there can be no phonological realisation at all. In general, the process of realisation is governed by recoverability conditions as well as other licensing conditions, but, as already mentioned, the exact nature of these principles lies beyond the scope of this paper.

An important characteristic of discourse ellipsis which is straightforwardly explained by the suggested analysis, is optionality with respect to phonetic realisation. This is exemplified in 34-38.

34. **Ø / Han** gikk rett i gulvet.
__Ø / he__ went right to the floor.
__'He__ fell right down.'
35. **Ø/Det** hadde blitt kaos her da.
***Ø/It** had become chaos here then.*
'It would have become chaotic here then.'
36. Har du gjort leksene dine? **Ø / De_** gjorde jeg i går.
Have you done your homework? __Ø / They__ did I yesterday.
'Have you done your homework? I did them yesterday.'
37. **Ø Ø/Har du** vært på kino i det siste?
***Ø Ø/Have you** been to the movies lately?*
'Have you been to the movies lately?'
38. **Ø Ø/Er du_** klar til å dra?
***Ø Ø/Are you** ready to go?*
'Are you ready to go?'

If grammatical features are incorporated inseparably in lexical items, it is difficult to explain why these subjects are sometimes realised, sometimes not, even if the same agreement patterns occur independently of instantiation. On the other hand, if phi-features are present and valued independently of instantiated lexical items, it follows naturally that lexical insertion is not so restrictive.

Assuming a late insertion hypothesis, I propose that the conceptual valuing of lexical items takes place at the point of insertion. More specifically, in an example like "The police are nice", the subject DP is first merged independently, and the morphological phi-features are valued.

Hence, the visible DP results as singular, not plural (*The polices). Then, when the DP is to be inserted into its suitable slot in the sentence structure, there are unvalued feature matrixes in the node, waiting to be valued by the features of the DP. Most often, the morphological phi-features of a DP correspond directly to the conceived features, and then the valuing process is completely straightforward. However, in examples such as the ones I have discussed, conceptual information can overrule the morphological features in this insertion process. Furthermore, it's crucial to point out that since conceptual valuing is assumed to operate at the point of insertion, the Agree relation can remain a purely structural relation between phi-features of the probe and the goal. Hence, as a part of Narrow Syntax the Agree relation is not affected by information from the conceptual-intentional interface, contrary to processes at the point of insertion.

In modern generative syntax, it seems to be a tacit assumption that feature specification is inherent in the lexical word, or at least that this is to be considered a one-to-one relationship. However, this should not be seen as a relation of direct identity. Rather, it is the case that the visible morphology manifests the abstract features. In a purely lexicalist minimalist model, where all features enter the derivation specified, the analytical solution to agreement mismatches that I have proposed, would be impossible. In such a model, one would have to postulate that the phi-features of a lexical element could undergo change under the course of the derivation. In an example like "The police are nice", it would be necessary to assume that the phi-feature matrix itself was changed in order to be able to include examples with semantic agreement. Of course, this doesn't sound plausible. Another solution would be to introduce a completely new feature to the derivation, as proposed by Sauerland and Elbourne (2002).

Still, it's worth mentioning that the insight of this analysis is not very surprising if we consider what is really intended by the notion of features. Crucially, a feature is not identical to the actual morphological realisation of the same feature. It lies on another level of abstraction. A feature is an abstract entity, but can yield concrete morphological consequences on lexical items (Adger 2003). For instance, the feature plural on a noun can yield many different concrete representations. In this perspective, the idea of tearing features apart from the morphological form is not revolutionary. Rather, it's a matter of taking seriously the abstractness of features.

As already mentioned, the analysis proposed in this article bears certain similarities to the theory of Distributed Morphology (Harley and Noyer 1999, 7). In particular, their thesis of separationism is adopted:

> Separationism characterizes theories of morphology in which the mechanisms for producing the form of syntactico-semantically complex expressions are

> separated from, and not necessarily in a simple correspondence with, the mechanisms which produce the form ("spelling") of the corresponding phonological expressions.

That is, the syntax does not manipulate lexical items, but rather it generates structures by combining abstract morpho-syntactic features. I further endorse Distributed Morphology's view on Late Insertion of lexical elements, which says that the phonologically expressed Vocabulary Items are inserted into syntax at a late point.

It is important, though, to point out that this analysis does not open up an anarchistic system where feature specification becomes random and without any connection to formal categories. This kind of exceptional valuing can only be assumed to be active in cases where it is natural that a notion is conceived differently from what morphology indicates. Also Sauerland and Elbourne (2002, 292n) underline the point that their Mereology feature must be optional.

This point deserves some further discussion. We have seen that agreement can be either formal or semantic, and consequently that 'police' can occur either with singular or plural agreement. Still, this choice is obviously not possible for all subjects, as the following examples clearly illustrate:

39. The binoculars are working.
40. *The binoculars is working.
41. A man and a woman were/*was in the garden.
42. There were/was a man and a woman in the garden.

In 39 and 42 semantic agreement is clearly ungrammatical. Hence, it appears that semantic agreement is not always optional after all. This failure of free optionality would seem to be at odds with the analysis presented in this article. Two possible types of accounts could be envisioned; either the restrictions are purely conventional, or they could be based on fine-grained conceptual distinctions. In any case, the answer lies beyond the scope of this article. It has not been my goal to develop a full-fledged analysis of both semantic agreement and discourse ellipses. Rather, the crucial point has been to point out how examples displaying semantic agreement illustrate that there exists a possibility that agreement is not always defined exclusively by formal elements of the derivation. Hence, agree is not always a simple function of formal features on the subject and the verb. As seen, there exists exceptional cases. The point is that by tearing, *in principle,* the specification of features apart from the morphological form of the single word, it becomes possible to account for such slightly peripheral data.

Crucially, this alternative agreement process is useful for the account of the elliptical data. If the unvalued phi-features in the syntactic node can be valued from features in the morphologically inserted element or by the construed features of a conceptualized inserted element, it's plausible that the features can also be valued from a purely conceptual, non-instantiated element or discourse marker. Still, note that agreement in the ellipses is not necessarily semantic. In a parallel manner as for non-elliptical data, we find both options also in the subject ellipses. Hence, we could imagine a sentence where the subject 'police' was elided. In that case, the verb could have either singular or plural morphology, just as in examples where the subject is phonetically realised.

Additional striking evidence for the argument outlined is English loan words in Norwegian. Despite there being no gender specification in English, these loan nouns require a grammatical gender when used in Norwegian:

43. a manager – en/*et manager (masculine/*neuter)
44. a party – *en/et party (*masculine/neuter)
45. a shopping bag – en/*et shopping bag (masculine/*neuter)

These data can easily be accounted for within the frames of the late insertion analysis proposed here. It is a parametric difference between English and Norwegian that all Norwegian nouns must be specified for gender. In English, there is no such gender specification. Hence, in an English sentence structure, there is no slot for a gender feature in DP positions. However, in Norwegian, all DP slots have an unvalued gender feature, waiting to be specified by lexical insertion. Consequently, when an English noun without gender specifications is inserted into a Norwegian sentence, it is required that this noun is assigned a gender. More specifically, the gender feature in the relevant slot in the sentence must be valued. Hence, a gender specification is assigned to the English noun incorporated into the Norwegian language by being inserted into a Norwegian sentence.

7. Conclusion

The proposed analysis suggests that conceptual properties can influence the formal process of agreement, entailing an interaction between the conceptual-intentional interface and the computational system of narrow syntax. This may appear to be at odds with the widespread assumption within generative theory that narrow syntax does not have access to information in the interfaces, as it is previous to it. In other words, the analysis challenges the autonomy of syntax. This issue is very wide-ranging, and it would be hazardous to even attempt to propose a solution for it.[5]

Still, what I hope to have shown in this article is that it is fruitful to assume a late insertion approach where syntactic structure, containing unvalued feature matrixes, is present independently of lexical insertion. As we have seen, in most cases phi-features appear to be valued by inserted lexical items, whereas in cases of semantic agreement, subjects can be conceptually valued at the point of insertion. This shows that agreement is not always as strictly formal as often assumed. More specifically, lexicalized formal agreement features seem to be overruled in certain cases. A similar situation is seen in discourse ellipses, where no lexicalized formal features are present. Here, the agreement process must depend on an alternative feature construal based on information from the conceptual intentional interface.

To sum up, the analysis proposed entails that there are really no inherently valued features, since also traditionally inherent features must be valued externally, namely by the insertion of lexical items. Phi-features can be valued in two different ways: One way is external, from lexical items or in certain cases from the mental construal of these items, whether they are phonetically realised or not. The other way is internal, via the operation Agree, from the feature specifications of one structural position to another one inside the same sentence structure.

References

Akmajian, Adrian, and Frank Heny. 1975. *An Introduction to the Principles of Transformational Syntax*. Cambridge and London: The MIT Press.

Adger, David. 2003. *Core Syntax. A Minimalist Approach*. Oxford: Oxford University Press.

---

[5] A conceivable idea could be to postulate a twofold structure for the feature matrices, one for conceptual information and one for purely formal information. Then, syntax would only see the formal features, and the conceptual ones would be visible only at the interface. However, in order to see if this idea is fruitful, it would have to be further developed.

Bosque, Ignacio. 2006. Coordinated adjectives and the interpretation of number features. In *Studies in Spanish Syntax*, edited by L. Brugè, 47-60. Venezia: Libreria Editrice Cafoscarina

Chomsky, Noam. 1965. *Aspects of the theory of syntax.* Cambridge: The MIT Press.

—. 2001. "Derivation by phase." In *Ken Hale: A Life in Language*, edited by M. Kenstowicz, 89-155. Cambridge, MA: MIT Press.

Corbett, Greville G. 2000. *Number*. Cambridge: Cambridge University Press.

Den Dikken, Marcel. 2001. "'Pluringulars', pronouns and quirky agreement." *The Linguistic Review 18*: 19-41.

Haegeman, Liliane and Tabea Ihsane. 2001. "Adult Null Subjects in the non-*pro*-drop Languages: Two Diary Dialects. " *Language Acquisition 9(4)*: 329-346.

Haegeman, Liliane and Jacqueline Guéron. 1999. *English Grammar*. Oxford: Blackwell.

Harley, Heidi and Rolf Noyer. 1999. "Distributed Morphology." *GLOT International Volume 4 Issue 4.*

Hornstein, Norbert, Jairo Nunes and Kleanthes K. Grohmann. 2005. *Understanding Minimalism*. Cambridge: Cambridge University Press.

Jacobsen, Bent. 1986. *Modern transformational grammar*. Amsterdam, New York and Oxford: Elsevier Science Publishers B.V.

Josefsson, Gunlög. 2006. "Semantic and grammatical genders in Swedich – independent but interacting dimensions." *Lingua 116*: 1346-1368.

Merchant, Jason. 2004. "Fragments and Ellipsis." *Linguistics and Philosophy 27*: 667-738.

McCawley, James. 1998. *The syntactic phenomena of English*. Chicago: University of Chicago Press.

Napoli, Donna Jo. 1982. "Initial Material Deletion." *Glossa 16*: 85-111.

Nygård, Mari. 2004. "Talespråkssyntaks. En analyse av elliptiske konstruksjoner i talespråk." Master thesis. Norwegian University of Science and Technology.

Nygård, Mari, Kristin M. Eide and Tor A. Åfarli. 2008. "Ellipsens syntaktiske struktur." In *Språk i Oslo. Ny forskning omkring talespråk*, edited by Janne Bondi Johannessen and Kristin Hagen, 172-183.Oslo: Novus forlag.

Quirk, Randolph, Sidney Greenbaum, Geoffrey Leech and Jan Svartvik. 1985. *A Comprehensive Grammar of the English Language*. Longman.

Sauerland, Uli and Paul Elbourne. 2002. "Total Reconstruction, PF Movement, and Derivational Order." *Linguistic Inquiry, (*33) 2: 283-319.

Sigurðsson, Halldór Armann. "Conditions on argument drop."*Linguistic Inquiry*. (forthcoming).

Sigurðsson, Halldór Armann and Joan Maling. The Empty Left Edge Condition. In *Exploring Crash-Proof Grammars*, edited by M. Putnam. Amsterdam and Philadelphia: John Benjamins, forthcoming.

Stroumza, A. 1998. *Le journal de Bridget Jones*. Paris: Albin Michel.

NoTa Norwegian Speech Corpus. The Text Laboratory,ILN, University of Oslo. http://www.tekstlab.uio.no/nota/oslo/index.html

The Big Brother corpus: http://www.tekstlab.uio.no/talespraak/bigbrother/

Newspapers online

http://www.vg.no
http://www.dagbladet.no
http://www.aftenposten.no
http://www.adressa.no
http://www.guardian.co.uk
http://www.economist.com

SUBSECTIVITY, MEANING AND SYNTACTIC POSITION

JEFFREY PUNSKE
UNIVERSITY OF ARIZONA

Abstract

This paper argues that certain semantic features of adjectives (namely, intersectivity and subsectivity) are not lexical properties of the adjective but are assigned via syntactic position. Homophonous adjectives in three languages (Polish, French and English) are all shown to behave predictably with respect to these features based on syntactic position. Adjectives are shown to lack either feature when occurring in a high syntactic position, with various consequences discussed here.

1. Introduction

The relative position of elements within nominal structure is a major question within syntactic theory (Larson 1998/2007, Rutowski 2007, Valois 1991, Alexiadou 2001, Laenzlinger 2004, among many others). Many analyses have focused on the structural properties of adjective order (Valois 1991, Laenzlinger 2004). This paper focuses on a narrow aspect of adjective order within the DPs. Specifically it is concerned with the "classifier" position (Rutowski 2007) in Polish, the postnominal adjectival position. The analysis presented in this paper utilizes Rutowski's proposed Classifier Position to explain French prenominal adjectives and the behavior of the adjective "poor" and its Polish equivalent "*biedny*". These adjectives have different possible interpretations based on syntactic position. The different possible interpretations are shown to be a direct consequence of the syntax.

Most adjectives are assigned their subsective or intersective meanings by being under the scope of one of two generic quantifiers that assign either a subsective or intersective interpretation (modal adjectives are excepted because they enter the syntax with their own meaning postulates).

1) [ClassP [Γy [AP [Γx [AP N]]]]]
non-subsective subsective non-subsective (intersective)

This analysis departs from other proposals in that it does not make the typical stage-level/individual-level distinction (see Larson 1998/2007) but casts the distinction in terms of subsective vs. non-subsective (and the subtypes of non-subsective predication) (Montague 1970, Partee 2007, others). This paper shows that Larson's (1998/2007) and Larson's and Larson and Marušič's (2004) proposals concerning adjectival order based on a s-level/i-level distinction are not sufficient to account for all the data. For Larson et al., the critical ordering distinction is whether or not the adjective is s-level or i-level. S-level adjectives are predicted to always occur outside of i-level adjectives. The Classifier Position does not follow this general constraint so modifications to Larson et al. are required. The proposal given here recasts the distinction in terms of subsective/intersective distinctions, with s-level/i-level distinctions occurring within each. This proposal is akin to Truswell's (to appear) DP template:

2) $[_{DP}\ D^0\ [_{XP}\ AdjP^*_{subsective}\ X^0\ [_{NP}\ AdjP^*_{intersective}\ N^0]]]$
(Truswell, to appear)

The analysis presented here departs from Truswell in terms of the manner by which adjectives are assigned subsective or intersective interpretations, intersective adjectives being adjectives which generate sets which are intersections of the adjective set with the noun set. Subsective adjectives are adjectives which generate subsets of the noun (and not intersections). In Truswell's proposal adjectives enter the derivation with their subsective or intersective interpretations; in the proposal outlined here adjectives receive these interpretations based on their position.

There are two possible meaning postulates that the syntax can ascribe: intersective, which is assigned to adjectives within the scope of a generic quantifier, and subsective, which is assigned to adjectives outside the scope of the first generic quantifier but within the scope of another separate generic quantifier. The Classifier Position is outside of the scope of either quantifier and consequently receives neither a subsective nor an intersective interpretation.

The Classifier Position is also shown to require an overt NP to be licensed. This licensing is accomplished through Spec-Head checking through movement of the NP into the Specifier of ClassP. Differences in the relative order of adjectives and the noun are shown to be, in part, based on whether or not this movement is overt. Polish is the only language presented here that shows overt movement of the NP into $SPEC_{[ClassP]}$. As a consequence, the Polish adjectives in the Classifier position always occur postnominally. English does not have overt movement, so the Classifier adjective always occurs on the outermost adjectival position. The French order is derived by the lack of movement and the opposite directionality of adjectives within the NP (see Alexiadou 2001).

The final analysis given in this paper should be seen as an extension (and not a refutation) of Larson's discussion of s-level/i-level distinctions in adjectival modification and Truswell's semantic type distinction. The analysis given in this paper shows that both semantic type (intersective, subsective) and level are relevant to determining the order of adjectives. The analysis departs from Larson by showing that s-level/i-level distinctions are relevant within each semantic type and not the DP at large.

The organization of the paper is as follows: Section 2 presents an analysis of French prenominal, Polish postnominal and English adjectival modification. Section 3 defines the Classifier Phrase semantically, and shows that the differences in semantic meanings based on syntactic position are derivable from the syntax, and argues that most adjectives do not enter the derivation with semantic relationships present. These relationships are ascribed by the adjective‘s position. Section 4 gives syntactic justification for the movement analysis presented in section 2. Section 5 concludes the paper.

2. Adjectives and their places

This section is primarily concerned with the order of adjectives with respect to the nominal. It shows that the nominal-adjectives order found in Polish and French can be accounted for through Classifier projections and that this proposal can be extended to the English examples. This analysis is based on the Rutkowski (2007) analysis of postnominal adjectives in Polish.

2.1 Polish

The postnominal position in Polish is typically filled by an adjective that specifies the "type" of the noun (Swan, 2002; Rutkowski 2007; others)[1]. This property is best illustrated by the following examples.

---

[1] A reviewer notes that it is not the case that classifying adjectives are always found.

i. *wielki wybuch*

3a) zwykł-y kleszcz
Ordinary-NOM tick
"A common tick"

3b) kleszcz zwykł-y
tick ordinary-NOM
"The Common Tick"

4a) teatraln-y gest
Theatric-NOM gesture
"a theatrical gesture"

4b) gest teatraln-y
gesture theatric-NOM
"a gesture used in the theater" (3-4 Swan 2002)

This position can only be occupied by one adjective, whereas the prenominal position has no restrictions on the number of adjectives (Swan 2002). Swan (2002) also states that if more than one type-classing adjective occurs, then only one occurs in the postnominal position.

5) Państwowe Monopol Spirytusowy
state monopoly spirits
'state Liquor Monopoly" (Swan 2002)

Rutkowski (2007) notes in these cases that only the postnominal receives the type-class interpretation. Rutkowski (2007) analyzes this phenomenon through noun-movement into the head of Class P, leaving the adjective in the postnominal position.

---

great explosion
Big Bang
While this observation may pose a problem for some aspects of the analysis, the larger fact remains that only classifying adjectives are allowed postnominally in Polish. Cetnarowska, Pysz and Trugman (2008) use this fact to argue against Rutowki's ClassP analysis. In many ways, their analysis is close to the one presented here. Cetnarowska, Pysz and Trugman (2008) argue for iterated ClassAs, which may be a necessary future revision to the proposed analysis, but this data alone does not refute the analysis.

6) Rutkowski's (2007) N-movement proposal

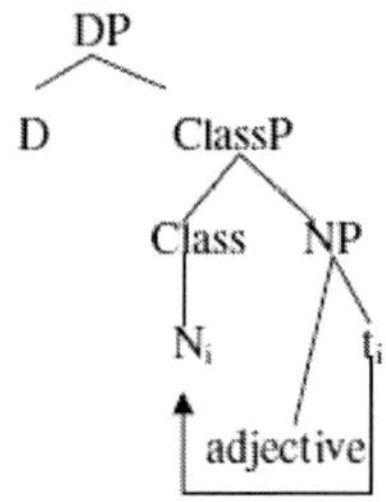

There are a number of structural issues with the N-movement proposal. First, there is no place within the structure for additional adjectives. For this proposal to work there would need to be two positions for adjectives to merge: one contained within the NP and one external to ClassP, which is essentially restating the problem. Given the geometry he proposes, however, all adjectives would be expected to occur postnominally when a type-class adjective is present because there is no other position where adjectives could occur. The data in (7) clearly show that this is not the case. Both Swan (2000) and Rutkowski (2007) note that more than one adjective cannot occur postnominally.

7a) mały pancernik olbrzymi
small armadillo giant
"a small giant armadillo" (small example of *Priodontes maximus*)

7b) olbrzymi pancernik mały
giant armadillo small
"a giant dwarf armadillo" (large example of *Zaedyus pichicy*)

7c) *pancernik olbrzymi mały
armadillo giant small

(adapted from Rutkowski 2007)

Both (7a) and (7b) are acceptable, while (7c) is ungrammatical. The NP-movement analysis incorrectly predicts 7c to be grammatical and 7a and 7b to be ungrammatical.

The other major drawback to Rutkowski's proposal is that adjectival semantics is left undiscussed. Under his proposal there is no way to derive the semantics of the adjective through the syntax. How the differences in meaning between (7a) and (7b) are derived is not shown at all.

Given the problems outlined above, this paper proposes a modified version of Rutkowski's geometry. The semantics of these constructions suggest strongly that the type-classing adjective is functioning as a classifier. Under the proposal given here the type-classing adjective is merged with the class-head. The NP moves into SPEC[ClassP] for semantic reasons discussed in section 4.

8) Preliminary Structure of Polish ClassP[2]

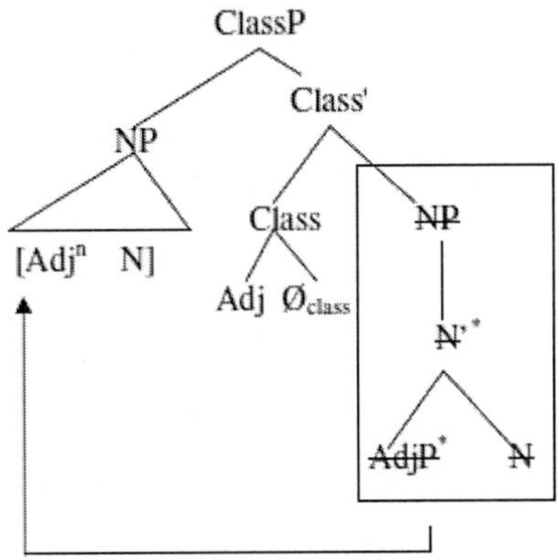

Further evidence for this analysis comes from the split NP/PP phenomenon where the adjective is separated through scrambling (Nowak 2000). Most adjectives are able to be scrambled away from the NP with exceptions that do not form a traditional natural semantic class (Partee 2003).

9) Do rozległ-ej weszlismy dolin-y
to large-GEN enter.PST.1.PL valley-GEN
"We entered a large valley"

10) * Z był-ym rozmawi-ała prezydent-em
with former-INSTR talk-PST.3.F.SG president-INSTR
'she talked with the former president"

(9-10 Partee 2003)

[2] Throughout this paper, all of the proposed ClassP trees have the NP as a direct complement. This is not a strong empirical claim but rather a move for presentational simplicity; without question there is a necessary functional structure which is elided in these structures.

Partee (2003) offers a semantic analysis of the adjectives that cannot be separated, based on whether or not the adjective involved is non-subsective, which is an unexpected result. However, Partee offers no syntactic reason for the lack of separation in these cases. There are two potential analyses of the basic surface order facts presented in (9) and (10). The first is a movement analysis of Nowak (2000) which requires two movements: first, movement of an adjective phrase out of the NP, then scrambling of the PP. The other is a base-generation analysis where the discontinuous constituents are generated in their surface positions. Regardless of which analysis is taken as correct, the Classifier-analysis is able to easily capture the ungrammaticality of (10). As section 4 will show, adjectives in the Classifier Position require the Spec-Head checking with the NP to be licensed. For both a movement analysis and a base-generation analysis the Classifier adjective would be unlicensed in (10), resulting in the ungrammaticality. Other adjectives have no such licensing restrictions, and are thus able to be separated under either analysis.

2.2 French

Some French adjectives must occur prenominally, some must occur postnominally and some are able to occur in either position as seen in examples 11-15 below (adapted from Laenzlinger, 2005). Alexiadou (2005) noticed that the adjectives that are unable to participate in the splitting phenomena in Polish are the same class of adjectives that must occur prenominally in the Romance language. A unified account of these phenomena is called for.

11a) la future mariée AN *NA
the future bride
"the future bride"
11b) *la mariée future
the bride future

12a) une voiture rouge NA *AN
a car red
"a red car"
12b) *une rouge voiture
a red car

13a) une voiture spendide AN NA
a car splendid
"a splendid car"
13b) une spendide voiture
a splendid car
"a splendid car" (11-13 taken from Alexiadou, 2005)

14a) un grand home AN NA
a great man
"a great man" (moral character)
14b) un homme grand
a man great
"a tall man"

15a) une maison petite AN NA
a house small
"a small house"
15b) une petite maison
a small house
"a seldom used house"
(14-15 adapted from Laenzlinger 2005)

The order of French adjectives has been a much discussed phenomenon in the literature (Valois 1991, Bouchard 1998, Alexiadou 2001, Laenzlinger 2004). Most of these analyses require each adjective class to have its own unique functional structure and for the noun to move through the specifiers of each adjective phrase that occurs postnominally (see Laenzlinger 2005). This set of analyses is highly stipulative, and a coherent case as to why the noun stops in the middle of this movement is rarely presented.[3]

Alexiadou (2001) argues against this position and for an explanation with multiple possible configurations for adjectival modification, one prenominally and one postnominally. The analysis proposed earlier for Polish is similar to Alexiadou's analysis of French. The major difference between Alexiadou's proposal and the one presented here is that the positions in Alexiadou's analysis are defined purely semantically whereas the analysis here explains the difference in terms of functional structure.

---

[3] Discussing these analyses in great detail is beyond the scope and aim of this paper. The major goal of most of these analyses is to explain the observed adjective orders within Kayne's (1994) Antisymmetry framework. Within that framework, the analyses are less stipulative, but if we do not assume Antisymmetry then a proposal like the one I have given here is much simpler.

This difference can again be derived through the analysis presented for the Polish data. The structure of the Polish and French Classifier phrases is identical. The major differences are in the facts that French adjectives occur postnominally within the NP and that the NPs do not overtly move.

16) Structure of French ClassP

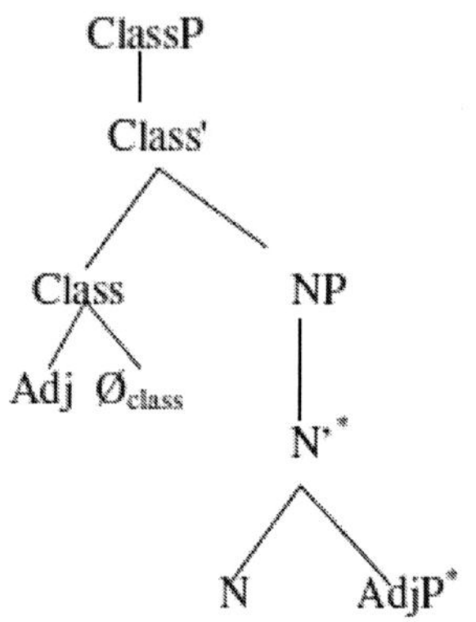

2.3 English

Compared to the other languages under study, English has a rigid order of elements within the determiner phrase. Determiners, demonstratives, possessives, etc. always precede the noun. Bare adjectives can occasionally occur after the nominal but in relatively few cases, as seen in examples (17) and (18) below.

17a) the visible stars
17b) the stars visible

18a) the responsible individuals
18b) the individuals responsible

(Larson and Marušič, 2004)

Modal adjectives[4] can also occur postnominally with slight differences in semantics (Larson 2007a/b, Schwarz 2007).

---

[4] "Modal adjectives, as their name implies, are adjectives which are linked closely to modals of the verbal systems. They differ in their relationship with the nouns they modify when compared to other adjectives. Instead of being defined in terms

19a) I interviewed every possible candidate.
19b) I interviewed every candidate possible.
19c) I interviewed every possible candidate possible. (Larson, 2007b)

In these cases there is a clear scope difference with relation between the order of "possible" and "candidate". The NP (19a) could be paraphrased as "every viable candidate. The NP in (19b) could be paraphrased as "every candidate for whom it was possible for me to interview." The NP in (19c) would be a combination of the two: "every viable candidate for whom it was possible for me to interview." It is important to note that the interpretation of 1b is crucially not a resultative (i.e. it is not by the act of interviewing that the candidate became possible). Resultative adjectives are external to the DP and are therefore not under discussion here.

20a) I interviewed every red candidate.
20b) *I interviewed every candidate red.
20c) *I interviewed every red candidate red.

By contrast, (20b) and (20c) are ungrammatical (again discarding any resultative reading). The examples related to those in (19) are discussed briefly in section 3. The examples in (18) are important as contrasts with the Polish and French data given in the previous sections.

Unlike Polish and French, there is no obvious syntactic distinction between Classifier and non-Classifier Adjectives[5] in English. To test the claims on English other examples must be considered.

Polish and French both differ in the interpretation of the adjective "poor" based on the position of the adjective.

21a) la francaise pauvre
the French.woman poor
"the impoverished French woman"

21b) la pauvre francaise
the poor French.woman
"the pitiable French woman"

---

of how they fit within the noun set, they are defined in terms of the probability of being a member of that set.

[5] The postnominally adjectives in section 1 seem like likely candidates for this position. Their status will be discussed in section 3.

Partee (2006) notes that the Polish adjective *biedny* (poor) can be split only under the impoverished interpretation and not under the pitiable interpretation. These characteristics are clearly accounted for through the analysis presented here. The difference in the meaning is a structural property. The "pitiable" reading is only possible when the adjective occupies the classifier position.

While this approach can explain the French and Polish data, it appears to fail to explain the English facts. In English, the adjective "poor" always occurs prenominally and ambiguously between a pitiable and impoverished interpretation. However, this is only true when the adjective occurs alone. Adding additional adjectives clarifies the interpretation of "poor".

22) The poor little rich girl *impoverished
23) The underweight geeky poor man *pitiable
"Poor" can even occur in both positions with a clear semantic difference between the two.
24) The poor little poor girl
The pitiable little impoverished girl
25) The poor underweight geeky poor man
The pitiable underweight geeky impoverished man

There are no adjectives that can occur to the left of the pitiable interpretation of "poor".

26) The little poor girl (*pitiable)

This suggests that in these cases the adjective "poor" is always highest structurally.

When the data from all three languages are considered it becomes clear that the structure proposed to explain the Polish cases can be extended to French and English. The differences in surface order are derived through the presence or absence of overt NP movement.

27) Proposed Structure of Class P

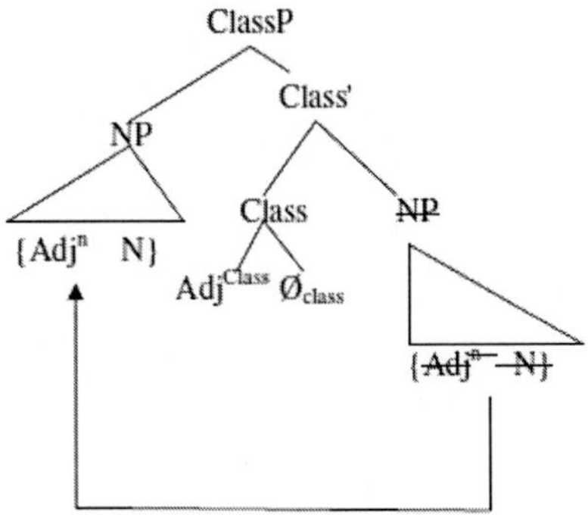

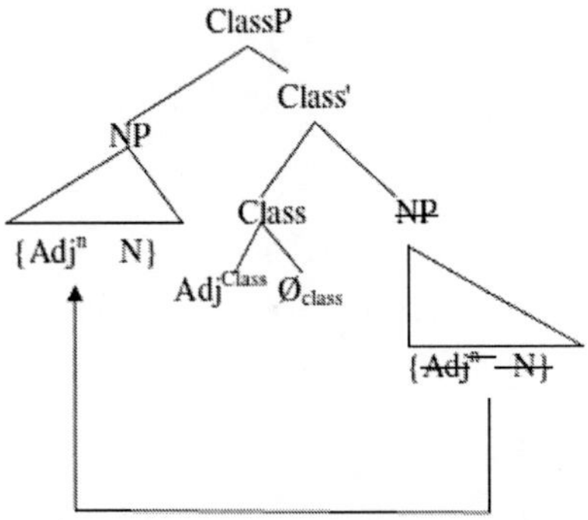

The differences between all three languages can be accounted for in the following ways. Polish has overt movement of the NP into SpecClassP. French and English both lack overt movement of the NP. French and English differ in the directionality of the adjunct adjectives within the NP. The different structures are presented in (28) – (30) below:

28) Polish Structure: *mały pancernik olbrzymi* ("a small giant armadillo")

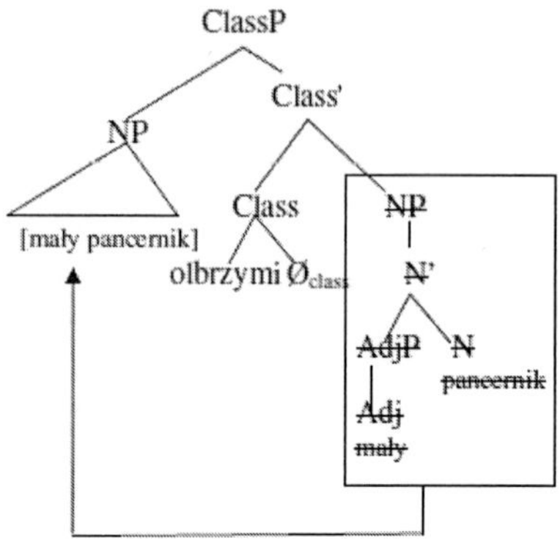

29) Modified French Structure: *la pauvre francaise* ("the pitiable French woman")

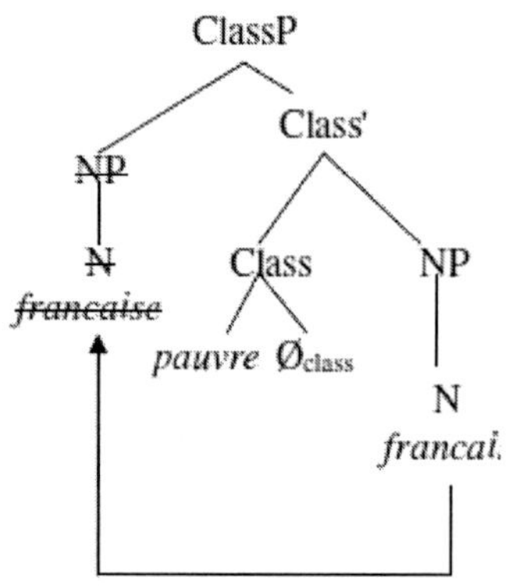

30) Modified English Structure: *poor sick man* ("a pitiable sick man")

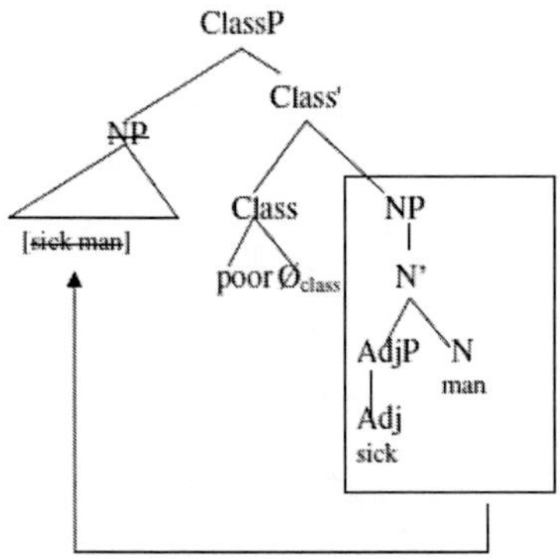

Each of these languages differs in which copy gets pronounced (see Chomsky 1993/95 for discussion of the Copy Theory of Movement). In Polish, the final product of the movement is pronounced. The NP and any remaining adjective are pronounced in SPEC[ClassP], while the classifying adjective is pronounced in the head of ClassP. For both French and English, the NP is pronounced in its premovement position. The reason for this movement is addressed in section 4.

3. Semantics of the Classifier position

This section examines the role of the Classifier position in the semantic interpretation and previous analyses of adjective distribution and their semantic differences in English (see Larson 1998, 2001). It will show that the previous analyses do not capture the correct generalization about the Classifier Adjectives. This section will also show that there is no unified *lexical* similarity between the adjectives that occupy the position, and that it is a property of the position which derives the semantics.

The adjectives in the Polish, French and English data do not form a straight-forward natural class. Very few adjectives are able to occupy the position in English[6]; in French, more are able to occur in this position, but Polish allows significantly more than both languages.

We are left with two very important and unanswered questions. What does this position contribute to the semantics? And what, if any, are the restrictions on this position?

[6] The adjective "poor" (under the pitiable interpretation) is the only one so far that has been demonstrated to unarguably occupy the position.

3.1 The Role of the Classifier Position

Larson (1998, 2001, 2007) and Larson and Marušič (2004) argue that the difference between stage-level (s-level) and individual level (i-level) adjectives is whether or not they modify the DP or the NP. DP- modifying, s-level adjectives occur higher in the structure. Larson and Marušič (2004) note that DP-level adjectives can occur both pre- and postnominally in English (examples (17) and (18) in section 1, repeated below). For Larson, following Chierchia (1995) i-level predicates are inherent generics bound by a generic quantifier Γ.

31) [AP [Γe [AP N]] AP]
s-level i-level s-level (Larson 2007)

Under this view, the quantifier Γ scopes over all the i-level adjectives, and s-level adjectives occur outside of its scope. (Examples 17-18 renumbered here as 32-33)

32a) the visible stars
32b) the stars visible

33a) the responsible individuals
33b) the individuals responsible

(Larson and Marušič, 2004)[7]

Under Larson's view, the "visible" in (32a) is ambiguous between an s-level reading and an i-level reading. The s-level interpretation is the standard "currently able to be seen," while the i-level interpretation means the inherently visible, regardless of the current visibility.

Larson and Marušič's analysis predicts that all Classifier Adjectives should be stage-level adjectives (which are semantically contradictory with the type-classifying nature of the position). Larson's analysis also predicts that adjectival modification order of [$ADJ_{i\text{-level}}$ $ADJ_{s\text{-level}}$ N] should be disallowed. However, if we reconsider example (24) (repeated here as 34) from the previous section, we see that this prediction is not borne out.

---

[7] Some speakers report difficulty with the (b) examples. Both (b) examples seem to improve greatly with contexts that make them seem more like their more complex cousins

i) the stars visible by night

ii) the individuals responsible for the crime

34) The poor little poor girl[8]
The pitiable little impoverished girl

The *pitiable* interpretation of "poor" is clearly an i-level adjective; it cannot be modified by temporal adverbs nor can it be used in when-constructions[9] (see Kratzer 1995 for more discussion). The *impoverished* interpretation, by contrast, can be modified temporally and used in when-constructions.

35) The occasionally poor woman was loved by many. *pitiable
36) When John is poor, his mother feels sorry for him. *pitiable[10]

These cases are a clear example of the [ADJ$_{\text{i-level}}$ ADJ$_{\text{s-level}}$ N] order—disallowed by Larson's analysis.

Larson and Marušič's analysis predicts not only that Classifier Adjectives should be stage-level as a property of being DP modifiers, but that these adjectives take the widest scope over all other adjectives. This is contrary to what the classifier adjectives are; they must be i-level since they represent permanent properties.

Postnominal adjectives in English offer a good test for this prediction. Larson (2007a) notes that these positions are also DP modifiers, and therefore stage-level adjectives. If the Classifier analysis is correct, the Classifier Adjectives should take wider scope than the postnominal adjective[11]. If the Classifier analysis is incorrect then there should be

---

[8] It may well be the case that the *impoverished* interpretation of "poor" is ambiguous between s-level and i-level reading. The distributional evidence seems to suggest that "poor" likes to be an i-level predicate. This initially suggests that 26 may not be a counter-example to Larson's proposal. Still, if we contrast 26 with an unambiguous use of *impoverished* "poor" as an s-level predicate, we see the same result.

i) the poor occasionally poor girl

[9] It is again interesting to note that this fact is not true of the actual adjective "pitiable", as seen by the following example:

i) The occasionally pitiable man was much more respected after winning the award.

[10] The lack of the *pitiable* interpretations in when-constructions is less convincing because *pitiable* "poor" cannot be used predicatively, nor can the actual adjective "pitiable" appear in such constructions.

i) *When John is pitiable, his mother feels sorry for him.

Nonetheless, the contrast with the *impoverished* "poor" is still relevant.

[11] There is some argument as to where postnominal adjectives are generated (see Larson and Marušič 2004). The proposal presented here is agnostic to either point

ambiguity in the scope relations. The example in 37 shows that the former is found.

37) The police rounded up the poor men responsible.
a. The police rounded up the impoverished men responsible.
poor < responsible, #responsible < poor
b. The police rounded up the pitiable men responsible
responsible < poor, #poor < responsible

The differences in the semantics are apparent in these two cases. In the (a) interpretation the group of rounded up men is not necessarily exhaustive. The police rounded up all of the impoverished men who were responsible (perhaps ignoring the rich who were also responsible). In (b) such a reading is disallowed. The group is exhaustive. There are no non-pitiable men responsible that the police failed to pick up. Simply stating that these adjectives are DP-modifiers does not capture all of the facts.

This result, however, is compatible with the Classifier analysis. When "poor" is interpreted with its non-Classifier *impoverished* meaning, the postnominal adjective "responsible" is interpreted with higher scope. With the Classifier-only interpretation, *pitiable*, the adjective "poor" takes wider scope over the postnominal adjective, as demonstrated by the exhaustive interpretation discussed previously.

Clearly, the Classifier Position is not a position of s-level modification compatible with Larson's example. However, we do not want to abandon this structure entirely because the general [$ADJ_{i\text{-level}}$ $ADJ_{s\text{-level}}$ N] generalization seems to hold, as demonstrated in the examples (38-39) below.

38) The invisible visible stars
39) #The visible invisible stars

Example 38 refers to a coherent class of stars which inherently have the property of being visible (i-level), but are currently obscured (by cloud cover, for example) (s-level). Example (39) refers to the incoherent class of stars that have the inherent property of not being visible (i-level) but are currently visible. For neither example is the other interpretation possible. These examples show clearly that the i-level adjective is the lower adjective. The *pitiable* interpretation of "poor" shows that this is not

---

of view. What is crucial about these examples is that the Classifier Adjective must have widest scope. This fact is captured by the analysis presented here, regardless of which analysis of postnominal adjectives is accepted.

always the case. To account for this, I maintain the heart of Larson's proposal, but with the additional Classifier Position added to it.

40) [ClassP [AP [Γe [AP N]] AP]
??[12] s-level i-level s-level

If Classifier Adjectives are the only class that does not pattern with Larson 's generalization, it would be a mistake to discard it[13]. The next natural question is where the Classifier Adjectives fit within Larson 's framework. The example of *pitiable* "poor" shows that the position must, at least, allow i-level adjectives. Is this an actual restriction or just an accident of the data? English will not provide a clear answer because of the relative paucity of Classifier Adjectives. If we reconsider the Polish data, it becomes much clearer that the Classifier Phrase is a level of i-level predication. The Polish examples (3-4) given earlier are repeated here as (41-42) for the reader's convenience.

41a) zwykł-y kleszcz
Ordinary-NOM tick
"a common tick"

41b) kleszcz zwykł-y
tick ordinary-NOM
"The Common Tick"

42a) teatraln-y gest
Theatric-NOM gesture
"a theatrical gesture"

---

[12] So far it is has not been demonstrated whether or not this position is required in either one of the interpretations or whether both are possible.

[13] Impoverished "poor" may yet still be a counter example. However, as noted previously it is possible that "poor" is most often an i-level adjective, but can also function as s-level predicate. The examples below distributionally support Larson's analysis.

i) The little poor girl
ii) *The poor little girl (under the "impoverished" interpretation)
iii) The occasionally poor little girl
iv) *The little occasionally poor girl (only possible as a parenthetical)

42b) gest teatraln-y
gesture theatric-NOM
"a gesture used in the theater" (41-42 Swan 2002)

Again, in these examples it becomes clear that the Classifier Adjective position is in fact a position of i-level modification. This still presents a problem for Larson 's analysis. Recall that the i-level nature of the lower adjectives was derived by the fact that they were under the scope of the generic quantifier Γ, but that the Classifier Adjective does not fall under the scope of the quantifier. The next natural question is what derives the facts that Larson has observed.

3.2 Three levels of adjective predication

Larson (2007) proposes two levels of adjectival modification. The facts about the Classifier Adjectives have shown that this is not sufficient. When we add the additional Classifier level, it becomes clear that the s-level, i-level distinction is not the only semantic distinction for the positions. The pattern with the Classifier level added is [$ADJ_{i\text{-level}}$ $ADJ_{s\text{-level}}$ $ADJ_{i\text{-level}}$ N].

We cannot assume that the generic quantifier Γ forces the i-level reading directly, but it is clear that adjectives below the quantifier are i-level adjectives. Since Montague (1970) (along with Kamp 1975 and Parsons 1970), semantic analyses of adjectives have argued that adjective meanings should be treated as "functions from properties to properties" (Partee 2003).

Partee (2003) notes that there are three to four basic adjective types: intersective, subsective, nonsubsective and privative[14]. These types are defined through their inference patterns. Intersective adjectives are adjectives which hold for any noun which can accurately replace the modified noun.

43) $\|\text{Adj N}\| = \|\text{Adj}\| \cap \|\text{N}\|$
44) $\|\text{carnivorous N}\| = \|\text{carnivorous}\| \cap \|\text{N}\|$ (Partee 2003)

Under this definition we can create the following valid inference:

[14] Partee (2003) argues against the privative class, explaining that this class is actually part of the subsective class and the meaning is coerced. This analysis is taken here and these examples will not be discussed.

45) Bucky is a carnivorous animal
Bucky is a seeing eye dog
∴ Bucky is a carnivorous seeing eye dog

The subsective class is defined as follows:

46) $\|ADJ\ N\| \subseteq \|N\|$
47) $\|skillful\ N\| \subseteq \|N\|$ (Partee 2003)

This can be shown through the invalid inference presented in Partee (2003):

48) Francis is a skillful surgeon
Francis is a violinist
Francis is a skillful violinist [not valid] (Partee 2003)

The non-subsective adjectives are defined as not being either intersective or subsective. According to Partee, "modal" adjectives such as "potential", "alleged" make up this class. These adjectives have no entailments and no meaning postulates are required (Partee 2003). Privative adjectives may be considered a subset of the non-subsective adjectives because they are neither subsective nor intersective. Privative adjectives also have the additional property of separating the noun from the noun set.

49) $\|Adj\ N\| \cap \|N\| = \emptyset$
50) $\|fake\ gun\| \cap \|gun\| = \emptyset$

If instead of casting the required ordering distinctions based on a purely i-level/s-level distinction, we look at the distinction in terms of intersective and subsective adjectives, what results will we generate?[15] Such an analysis is supported by Truswell's (to appear) Google-corpus-based observation that subsective adjectives precede intersective adjectives. With this in mind we can tentatively assign a new role to the generic

[15] The goal is not to refute Larson's analysis but to refine it. Consider again Larson 's example about visible stars (examples 42 and 43 earlier).

i) The invisible visible stars
ii) The visible invisible stars

These examples demonstrated the s-level/i-level distinction of Larson 's analysis, and these facts cannot be accounted for under a purely subsective/intersective analysis. The argument would have to be that the s-level/i-level splits occur within the subsective/intersective domains.

quantifier Γ. Instead of ascribing i-level interpretations to the adjectives, it ascribes intersective interpretations (this will be refined shortly). Adjectives occurring outside this position are subsective adjectives.

51) [ClassP [AP [Γx [AP N]]]]
?? subsective intersective

While these classes line up well, the match is not exact. The adjective "sick", for instance, is an intersective adjective but an s-level predicate. Under Larson's proposal this adjective should occur outside of all i-level predicates.

52) a tall sick man
53) ??a sick tall man

Under Larson's proposal, (52) should be disallowed because "sick" is an s-level predicate and "tall" is an i-level predicate. Under my proposal this adjective should occur within all subsective predicates. There should no problem with (53) because both adjectives are intersective. The questionable grammaticality is likely due to further, more fine-grained restrictions on adjective order (see Cinque (1994), Scott (2002) and Truswell (to appear) for more discussion of these restrictions).

54) a typical sick man
55) *a sick typical man[16]

The adjectives "typical" and sick are both s-level predicates, so both examples are fine under Larson's account. Under my account, (55) should be disallowed because "sick" is an intersective adjective and "typical" is a subsective adjective.

There is the added complication of the behavior of the non-subsective adjectives. These adjectives seem to pattern somewhat with the intersective adjectives, as seen in the examples below:

---

[16] Andrew Carnie (p.c.) notes that the judgment for (55) improves with an intonational break between the adjectives. The interpretation of the construction also changes greatly. "Typical man" behaves much more like a compound under such intonation. As will be shown in the coming pages, the improved grammaticality is accounted for by the analysis.

56a) a typical would-be politician[17]
56b) a would-be typical politician

57a) a typical potential politician[18]
57b) a potential typical politician

Surprisingly, these adjectives seem to be able to occur both within and outside the subsective adjectives. To account for the subsective internal non-subsective adjectives, the modified Larsonian account must be modified further. The generic quantifier Γ limits the adjectives under its scope to not being subsective, whether they are intersective or non-subsective.

The external non-subsective adjective must then be accounted for. These cases seem to be likely candidates for the Classifier position. Notice that when occurring outside the subsective adjective they scope over the entire complex phrase and do not just modify the nominal. A "would-be typical politician" may in fact already be a politician, where a "typical would be politician" cannot be. This is further supported by a co-occurrence restriction with the adjective "poor" under the *pitiable* interpretation.

58) *a poor would-be typical politician
59) * a would-be poor typical politician
60) a poor typical would-be politician
The apparent structure is the following:

61) [ClassP	[AP	[Γx [AP N]]]]
non-subsective	subsective	non-subsective[19]

There are two very important and unaddressed questions arising out of this structure. The first question is how the subsective readings of the adjectives in the middle position are forced. The second is what separates the non-subsective adjectives in the Classifier from the lower non-

[17] According to Partee (2003) "would-be" is a non-subsective, privative adjective. The privative nature of this adjective is questionable however. For our purposes this adjective will be treated as a non-subsective modal adjective.
[18] According to Partee (2003) "potential" is a non-subsective adjective.
[19] It is important to note that most of the adjectives in the lowest position will still be intersective. Only non-subsective adjectives which enter the derivation with their own meaning postulates (the relations between properties) can be in this position without being intersective. This fact will be explained shortly.

subsective adjectives. The answer to the first question will lead into the answer to the second.

Truswell (to appear) argues that intersective adjectives are adjectives within the NP and subsective adjectives occur within a higher undefined XP. The approach taken here is similar in some ways, but markedly different in others. Following the earlier analysis, a natural assumption would be that the subsective reading in the middle set of adjectives is created through the presence of a null quantifier, much like the lower adjectives. This quantifier could be viewed as equivalent to the licensing X^0 of Truswell. The analyses diverge after this initial similarity. For Truswell, adjectives are defined as subsective or intersective before entering the derivation. As is about to be shown, the same is not true for this analysis; for most adjectives their subsective/intersective nature is defined by their syntactic position.

62) [ClassP [Γy [AP [Γx [AP N]]]]]
non-subsective subsective non-subsective (intersective)

The template in (62) shows the different positions for subsective and non-subsective adjectives. The core idea here is that adjectives do not enter the derivation as subsective or intersective adjectives. An adjective becomes subsective by being under the scope of Γy and not Γx. Adjectives under the scope of Γy and Γx are intersective (except for the modal adjectives to be discussed shortly).

To explain the nature of the Classifier position, a few assumptions must be made. The first is that the modal adjectives enter into the syntax with their meaning postulates akin to the meanings of modals in the verbal system[20]. This is a natural assumption because there is no way to generate the required meaning postulates for each modal adjective. The second assumption is that the respective quantifiers force the intersective or subsective readings on all adjectives which lack their own meaning postulates (i.e. are not modal adjectives). This means that the Classifier, which is not under the scope of either quantifier, should not have any meaning postulate if it did not enter the syntax with one. This result is borne out clearly by the Polish and English data.

[20] Assuming that modal adjectives have meaning postulates is a departure from Partee (2003) but one that seems well founded by their semantics because the relationship between the adjective and the noun must be defined individually for each modal adjective. The set correspondence between "potential" politicians and "would-be" politicians can be different depending on context.

In English, the *pitiable* interpretation of the adjective poor is neither subsective nor intersective and does not have an independent meaning postulate. This result is even clearer in the Polish data. Consider again the data from (15a/b) (renumbered here 63a/b).

63a) mały pancernik olbrzymi
small armadillo giant
"a small giant armadillo" (small example of *Priodontes maximus*)

63b) olbrzymi pancernik mały
giant armadillo small
"a giant dwarf armadillo" (large example of *Zaedyus pichicy*)

In both examples the Classifier Adjective is neither intersective nor subsective. This is clearly visible in these examples because of the contrasting modifying adjective. It is not possible for both to be true in the way that subsective and intersective meaning postulates require at the same time (something cannot be both giant and small). Under the Classifier analysis presented here, this fact is easily captured. The prenominal modifier is within the scope of Γx and is ascribed an intersective reading. The Classifier adjective is outside of the quantifiers and does not receive a meaning postulate.

Notice that these examples from Polish seem to correspond with English adjective-noun compounds such like 'spare tire." The adjective "spare" is here also neither subsective or intersective. It does not imply that the tire is actually extra. Note the contrast in the following two dialogues:

64) A: Do you have a spare tire?
B: Yes, but I am driving on it.

65) A: Do you have a spare raincoat?
B: *Yes, but I am wearing it.

In the first example "spare" is not an intersective adjective, as shown by the fact that it can be contradicted but maintain a positive response. If we assume that the noun is not assigned a meaning postulate, then this result is also easily predicted. The adjective "spare" is projected within the noun and therefore invisible to the quantifier and not assigned an intersective meaning. This results in the same semantics for adjectives in nominal compounds and adjectives in the Classifier Position, because both positions result in non-subsective adjectives. This result is also supported by the fact that the *pitiable* interpretation of "poor" can be found in the otherwise disallowed nominal adjacent position in complex phrases containing the compound "poor bastard".

66) the tall poor bastard

Here the interpretation of "poor" is only the *pitiable* reading, unless the noun "bastard" is taken literally as *a man without a father*. This result is only expected if the two positions share the same semantic relationship, which is shown by the analysis given.

Polish and English vary parametrically in where these types of adjectives occur. In English, non-modal adjectives (with the exception of "poor") must occur within the nominal to receive the non-subsective reading. In Polish, all non-subsective adjectives occur in the Classifier Position.

To sum up, this section has shown that adjectives do not enter the derivation with a meaning postulate but derive one through the syntax. There are two possible meaning postulates that the syntax can ascribe: intersective, which is assigned to adjectives within the scope of the generic entity quantifier; and, subsective, which is assigned to adjectives outside the scope of the generic quantifier Γx but within the scope of a different generic quantifier Γy. The Classifier Position and noun do not receive meaning postulates. As a consequence, adjectives that occur within the Classifier Projection or within the noun projection must be non-subsective and can only have meaning postulates if they entered the derivation with them.

4. Syntax of Classifiers Revisited

Now that the semantics of the position is understood, the reason for the proposed NP-movement given in section two becomes much easier to understand.

67) Proposed Structure of Class P

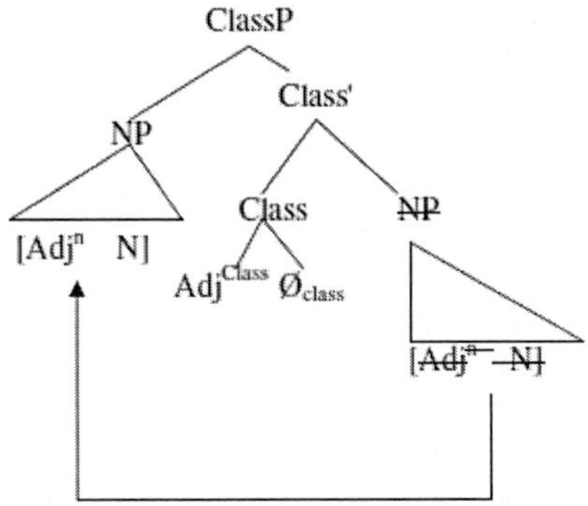

Under the semantic proposal given in the previous section, the adjectives in the Classifier Phrase are deficient. All other adjectives fall under the scope of a quantifier to license them. The Classifier Adjectives, however, are not licensed by any quantifier. For the Classifier Adjective to be interpreted it must be licensed by the NP through Spec-Head checking. It is still unclear what if any meaning postulate is derived from this. The need for the Classifier Adjective to be licensed by an NP can be shown by the impossibility of non-subsective interpretations of adjectives in bare Determiner-Adjective constructions[21] and the lack of predicative use.

68) The poor should be treated well (*pitiable)
69) John is poor (*pitiable)

This fact is readily explained if Classifier Adjectives require NPs to be licensed. To derive this licensing arrangement the Classifier and the NP must enter into an agreement relationship, hence the movement.

5. Conclusion

The analysis argues for a Classifier Projection to explain the relative ordering of adjectives cross-linguistically. In French, prenominal adjectives

[21] These types of constructions seem to be able to show up for the adjective of some adjective-noun compounds.

i) The spare also went flat.

This is only possible when the noun is contextually relevant and is therefore a likely candidate for ellipsis and separate from the other case discussed previously.

occupy this position; in Polish, it is the postnominal adjectives; and in English, it is the leftmost position. This difference is derived through a movement analysis of the NP into SPEC[ClassP]. In Polish, the final product of the movement is pronounced. The NP with any other adjectives is pronounced in SPEC[ClassP], while the classifying adjective is pronounced in the head of ClassP. For both French and English, the NP is pronounced in its premovement position.

The semantic analysis showed that adjectives that do not enter the derivation with a meaning postulate derive one through the syntax. As a consequence, adjectives that occur within the Classifier Projection or within the noun projection must be non-subsective and can only have meaning postulates if they entered the derivation with them. Because the adjectives in this position are unlicensed by any quantifier, NP movement is required to license the Classifier.

The analysis presented here also makes some predictions which have yet to be tested. The first is that N-to-D movement (see Delsing 1993) should be blocked by the presence of a Classifier adjective because of restrictions on head movement (see Rizzi 1990). Because none of the languages discussed here have N-to-D movement, it is unclear what the restrictions are. There are some promising observations from Embick and Noyer (2001), which show that Swedish N-to-D movement is blocked by the presence of an adjective. This, however, is far from conclusive.

The analysis also predicts that in languages in which all adjectives occur postnominally, the Classifier adjective should always be the last adjective. Such a language would have the French ordering of adjectives within the NP with overt NP movement like Polish. "Mirror image" results of postnominal adjective orders have been discussed throughout the literature (see Scott 1998, Sproat and Shih 1991). Because of this, it would be very surprising if such a result were not found.

The next natural extension of this work is to see what if any relationship these Classifier Adjectives have with the grammatical class Classifier. Are these the same elements, filled with different lexical items, or is the term "Classifier Adjectives" perhaps a misnomer? The fact that only one Classifier Adjective can occur in a given phrase suggests that the former may be correct, but needs considerable more work.

References

Alexiadou, A. 2001. "Adjective Syntax and Noun Raising: Word Order Asymmetries in the DP as the Result of Adjective Distribution." *Studia Linguistica* 55 (3), 217–248.

Alexiadou, A. 2005. Patters of adjectival modification. Handout of talk at the University of Venice: May 20-21, 2005.

Bouchard, D., 1998. "The distribution and interpretation of adjectives in French: a consequence of Bare Phrase Structure." *Probus* 10, 139–183.

Cetnarowska, B. A. Pysz and H. Trugman. 2008. "Accounting for some flexibility in a rigid construction: On the position of classificatory adjectives in Polish." *GLiP*-6, Warsaw, Poland.

Chierchia, G. 1995. "Individual-level Predicates as Inherent Generics." In *The Generic Book*, edited by G. Carlson and J. Pelletier, 176-223. University of Chicago Press: Chicago.

Chomsky, N. 1993/95. *A minimalist program for linguistic theory*. Reprinted in *The Minimalist Program,* Chomsky, N. 167-218 The MIT Press: Cambridge.

Cinque, G. 1994. "On the evidence for partial N movement in the Romance DP." In *Paths toward universal grammar,* edited by G. Cinque, J. Koster, J-Y. Pollock, L. Rizzi and R. Zanuttini, 85-110. Georgetown: Georgetown University Press.

Delsing, L.O. 1993. "The internal structure of noun phrases in Scandinavian languages." PhD dissertation, University of Lund.

Embick, D. and R. Noyer. 2001."Movement operations after syntax." *Linguistic Inquiry*: 32-4, 555-595.

Kayne, R.S., 1994. *The Antisymmetry of Syntax*. MIT Press: Cambridge, MA.

Kratzer, A. 1995. "Stage-level and Individual-level Predicates." In *The Generic Book*, edited by G. Carlson and J. Pelletier, 176-223. University of Chicago Press: Chicago.

Laenzlinger, C. 2005. "French adjective ordering: perspectives on DP-internal movement types." *Lingua*: 115, 645-689.

Larson, R.K. 1998. "Events and modification in nominals. " In *Proceedings from Semantics and Linguistic Theory (SALT) VIII,* edited by D. Strolovitch and A. Lawson Cornell University, Ithaca, NY.

—. 2007a. ACD in AP? Ms., Stony Brook University.

—. 2007b. Parametric Variation in the Indo-Iranian DP. University of Arizona Linguistics Colloquium: March 22, 2007.

Larson, R.K. and F. Marusic. 2004. "Indefinite pronoun structures with APs." *Linguistic Inquiry 35:* 268-287.

Longobardi, G. 1994. "Reference and Proper Names: A Theory of N-Movement in Syntax and Logical Form. " *Linguistic Inquiry* 25 (4): 609-665.

Montague, R. 1970. "English as a Formal Language." In *Linguaggi nella Società e nella Tecnica,* edited by Bruno Visentini et al. 189-224. Milan: Edizioni di Comunità.

Parsons, T. 1970. "Some problems concerning the logic of grammatical modifiers." *Synthèse* 21:320-334.

Partee, B. 2007. "Privative adjectives: subsective plus coercion." Ms., University of Massachusettes at Amherst.

Rizzi, L. 1990. *Relativized Minimality*. The MIT Press: Cambridge

Rutkowski, P. 2007. "The Syntactic Properties and Diachronic Development of Postnominal Adjectives in Polish." Ms., Warsaw University and Yale University.

Rutkowski, P. and Progovac, L. 2005. "Classification and projection in Polish and Serbian: the position and shape of classifying adjective." In *Formal Approaches to Slavic Linguistics 13: The South Carolina Meeting*, edited by Steven Franks, Frank Y. Gladney and Mila Tasseva-Kurktchieva, 289-299. Ann Arbor, MI: Michigan Slavic Publications .

Schwarz, B. To appear. Modal superlatives. *Proceedings of Salt XV*.

Swan, O. 2003. *A Grammar of Contemporary Polish*. Slavica: Pittsburgh

Scott, G.-J. 1998. "Stacked adjectival modification and the structure of nominal phrases." *SOAS Working Papers in Linguistics and Phonetics* 8: 59-89.

—. 2002. "Stacked adjectival modification and the structure of nominal phrases." In *Functional structure in the DP and IP: the cartography of syntactic structures volume I,* edited by G. Cinque, 91-120. Oxford: Oxford University Press.

Sproat, R. and C. Shih. 1991. "The cross-linguistic distribution of adjective ordering restrictions." In *Interdisciplinary Approaches to Language. Essays in Honor of S. Y. Kuroda.* Dordrecht: Kluwer Publishing.

Truswell, R. "Attributive adjectives and nominal templates." *Linguistic Inquiry* (forthcoming)

Valois, D., 1991. "The internal syntax of DP and adjective placement in French and English." *NELS* 21: 367–382.

INSTANCES OF POSTHEAD MODIFICATION IN RUSSIAN NPS*

HELEN TRUGMAN
HOLON INSTITUTE OF TECHNOLOGY

Abstract

This paper argues that postnominal adjectival modification (N-Adj) in unmarked Russian signals kind-referring nominals, and proposes a non-movement analysis of such adjective placement grounded in Bouchard's (2002, 2005) representational theory. Specifically, it is claimed that a non-canonical word order stems from the modification of a non-atomized noun, which yields a complex nominal predicate, or a taxonomic kind term. This accounts for non-argumental uses of N-Adj constructions in Russian. Argumental uses of N-Adjs are derived by a type-shifting operation (Chierchia 1998). This approach is extended to account for other cases of postnominal modification, such as NP-appositives and Type Genitives.

1. Introduction

This paper examines a number of nominal constructions in Russian that exhibit a non-canonical word order between a noun (N) and its modifier (Adj). Adopting the representational model developed in the recent works by Denis Bouchard (2002, 2005) I claim that such word order permutations are attested in cases of modification at the level of non-atomized NPs where the N, together with the Adj, form a complex kind-referring NP. I will refer to such constructions as *inverted NPs or inverted nominals* and discuss several environments where they are found—kind-

* The author would like to thank the audience at SLS-4, Madeleine Halmøy and anonymous reviewers for helpful comments and suggestions on the former version of the paper. All errors remain my own responsibility.

referring NPs (1a) and nominal (re)categorizing predicates,[1] (1b); various expressives, such as exclamations and vocatives,[2] (2); names/ labels of industrial products and scientific terminology, (3):[3]

---

[1] I use the terms categorizing and recategorizing after Bouchard (2002, 276) and Halmøy (2010) to refer to non-atomized nominal predicates (determinerless in French and Norwegian) that do not refer and only indicate that the referent of the subject belongs to the category denoted by the nominal predicate N-Adj. In contrast, NP predicates accompanied by a determiner refer either to a non-specific individual in characterizing sentences; or to a specific or a definite one in identity predicates. (See Halmøy (ibid.) and references cited therein for more discussion).

[2] Expressives refer to a type of speech acts that express the speaker's emotional attitude towards some situation, fact or person. Exclamations are taken here to be forms of indirect address, whereas vocatives are forms of direct address to some salient referent in the discourse. Vocatives can co-occur or alternate with exclamations, but this fact is of no relevance here. Many expressives are idiomatized forms both in English and in Russian, and the most common syntactic structure used for this speech act is a nominal sentence, or a noun phrase of the form: (Adj)N! What (Adj) N!, N of N! (see Frolova 1991 and references cited therein).

[3] Even though some inverted expressions can easily occur in all the syntactic environments presented in (1)-(3), as demonstrated in (i)-(iv) below; others cannot do so. This is true for names of natural kinds (animal and plant species); names of industrial products, artifacts, and scientific terms, which are generally limited to scientific or technical prose. Yet, some may give rise to expressives with a humorous effect, as illustrated in (v) with a Type Genitive modifier (see section 6):

(i) Èto naš novyj vid rabotnika—*"durak stoerosovyj"*. *label for a person*
"This is our new kind of worker—'the clot-head."

(ii) Ej, *durak stoerosovyj*, kuda preš'? *expressive (vocative)*
"Hey, clot-head, where are you barging?"

(iii) *Durak stoerosovyj* široko rasprostranjen. *kind-referring argument*
"The clot-head is widespread."

(iv) Vas'ka—*durak stoerosovyj*. *categorizing predicate*
"Vas'ka is a clot-head."

(v) Ej, ty, tupaja *lošad' priževal'skogo*, doumničalas'? *expressive (vocative)*
"Hey, see what you got by playing smart, you, stupid Przewalski's horse?"

Inverted epithets, as in (i-iv), possess a number of properties distinct from other inverted expressions. For instance, they easily combine with referential elements to produce object-referring NPs, as in (29), and can co-occur with numerals in some contexts. However, the core properties of various inverted NPs seem to be consistent across all categories, which justifies their uniform semantic account. For the lack of space I do not discuss peculiarities of inverted epithets in this paper.

(1) a. Panda *gigantskaja* skoro isčeznet s lica zemli.
panda gigantic soon will-disappear from face Earth
"The giant panda will soon disappear from the face of the Earth."
b. Petr byl čelovekom *molodym, porjadočnym.*
Peter was man young, decent
"Peter was a decent young man."

(2) a. Durak *bezmozglyj*!
fool brainless
"Brainless idiot!"
b. Ej ty, pugalo *ogorodnoe*, idi sjuda!
hey you scarecrow vegetable-garden$_{ADJ}$ come here
"Hey you, scarecrow, come here!"

(3) maslo *podsolnečnoe*
oil sun-flower$_{ADJ}$ "sun-flower oil"

In section 2 I demonstrate that such expressions share a number of properties with kind-referring nominals.[4] Section 3 presents predicative uses of inverted NPs, which invalidate the former account of such NPs put forth in Trugman (2007). Section 4 explicates a competitive account couched within the representational model by Bouchard (2002, 2005), and section 5 provides support for the analysis of inverted NPs as unatomized properties underspecified for semantic Number. In section 6, I discuss mechanisms of their atomization in several environments and extend the analysis to other cases of post-N modification in Russian in section 7.

The present discussion does not apply to the following environments with post-N modification:

- cases of stylistic postposition of adjectives attested in poetic use, and various scrambling phenomena triggered by the Information Structure requirements, as in (4a), discussed in Kovtunova's (1969) seminal work and more recently in Baylin (1995), King (1995), Sekerina (1999), among many others;

[4] I follow Chierchia (1998) and references cited therein in the interpretation of "natural kinds", which are taken to encompass not only biological species and "well-established" kinds but also artifacts, and complex things (like intelligent students or spots of ink) that exhibit sufficiently regular behavior. "What counts as kind is not set by grammar, but by the shared knowledge of a community of speakers." (Chierchia ibid., 348). See also Šmelev (1996) for a similar idea.

- split-NP phenomena or Split Scrambling illustrated in (4b) after Pereltsvaig (2007, (9c));
- phrasal modifiers of N, whose canonical position is postnominal, as shown in (4c), modified after Babby (1975, 186), his (4.35e):

(4) a. Pticy *pevčie* na vetkax, i ne vidno rož *sovetskix*…
birds song$_{ADJ.PL}$ on branches, and not seen faces$_{GEN.PL}$ Soviet$_{GEN.PL}$
"There are song birds on branches, and Soviet faces are not seen around…"

b. Ox kakix ja sebe blinov segodnja nadelala *vkusnyx*.
oh what I to-self pancakes today CUM-made tasty
"Ah, what tasty pancakes I made for myself today."

c. On čelovek [*dostojnyj velikoj ljubvi*].
he man worthy great love
"He is a man worthy of great love."

I limit my discussion wherever possible to singular inverted NPs in subject function. The majority of the data cited in the paper come from online and published sources.

2. Inverted NPs as kind-referring expressions

In Trugman (2007) I discussed the inverted word order in product labels and scientific terminology, as in (3), and argued for their kind-referring nature based on tests from Krifka et al. (1995). In particular, it was argued that inverted NPs are determinerless counterparts of definite singular generics in English, or names of kinds. Other types of inverted NPs discussed in the present paper appear to conform with these criteria as well.

2.1. Well-established kinds

First, it is often claimed that a singular nominal predicate yields a kind-referring NP when linked to a well-established kind and fails to do so otherwise. Carlson's (1977) famous example of bottles (attributed originally to Barbara Partee) shows that while *a Coke bottle* is a proper kind, *a green bottle* is not. This requirement seems to hold for all the inverted constructions discussed here:

(5) a. Student *nesposobnyj* / **nizkij* — razdražitelen.
Student ungifted/ short is irritable
"A mediocre/ *short student is irritable."
b. Puškin — poèt *liričeskij*/ **ljubimyj.*
Pushkin is poet lyrical/ loved
"Pushkin is a lyrical/ beloved poet."
c. Durak *nabityj*/ **simpatičnyj*!
idiot full/ good-looking
"Complete/ *Good-looking idiot!"
d. tort *šokoladnyj*/ **vkusnyj*
cake chocolate/ tasty
"a chocolate/ tasty cake"
((5d) is modified from Trugman 2007, (9a) and (10a))

However, the inverted word order can also be used to designate a novel kind, which is not well-established in the speaker's and listener's universe, yet can be easily perceived as such. Then a humorous effect may arise, as in (6) from the Internet (cf. Kovtunova 1969, 27-28). The example in (6) explicitly demonstrates that the inverted word order is directly associated with the kind name, as attested by the overt use of the word *vid* "kind":[5]

(6) Skul'ptor Eduard Dolkart vyvel novyj vid pandy—"panda *gigantskaja bul'varnaja ašdodskaja*".
"Sculptor Edward Dolkart bred a new kind of panda—'the Ashdodian boulevard giant panda'."

2.2. Restrictions on modifier type

Inverted constructions seem to tolerate only individual-level modifiers, which describe inherent, permanent properties of N, and are ruled out with stage-level modifiers (see Carlson 1977 for classification of modifiers).

[5] Dayal (2004, 425) also argues against restricting singular definite generics to well-established kinds and demonstrates that context manipulation may render them grammatical. Cf. with Schmitt and Munn (1999, 7), who distinguish between novel types expressed by bare singulars in Brazilian Portuguese and "canonical" types, i.e. well-established kinds, such as animal species or common artifacts, realized by singular definite generics.

(7) a. Ženščina *molčalivaja/ *molčaščaja* — javlenie redkoe.
woman taciturn/ silent is phenomenon rare
"A taciturn woman/*A woman who is silent is a rare phenomenon."
b. A vorona — ptica *pevčaja/ *pojuščaja*?
and crow is bird $song_{ADJ}$/ *singing?
"And is the crow a song bird/ *a singing bird?"
c. Ej, čučelo *goroxovoe/ *stojaščee*, ty menja slyšiš'?
Hey, stuffed-man pea_{ADJ}/ standing you me_{ACC} hear
"Hey, scarecrow/ *standing scarecrow, can you hear me?"
d. vetčina *rublennaja/ *porezannaja* (Trugman 2007, (14))
cold-meat chopped/ sliced
"cold meat made from chopped meats"/ "sliced cold meat"

2.3. Compatibility with true kind predicates

There is no firm consensus in the literature (see Chierchia 1998, Krifka et al. 1995, Halmøy 2010, and references cited therein) about which predicates count as true kind-predicates accepting only kind-referring NPs as arguments, and which ones are generic or quantificational predicates that tolerate other nominal arguments, such as generic NPs and taxonomic kinds. Nevertheless, it can be shown that the inverted NPs under discussion are compatible with *unambiguous* kind-predicates. Such predicates as *vymeret'* "die out, become extinct"; *naxodit'sja na grani vymiranija* "be on the edge of extinction" take kind-referring subjects, and *izobresti* "invent" takes kind-referring objects.[6] Names of natural kinds, artifacts and scientific terms were shown to be grammatical with such

---

[6] Chierchia (1998, 361) observes that Russian prefers bare plurals for kind reference, as in *Dinozavry/ *Dinozavr vymer(li).* "Dinosaurs/ *Dinosaur got extinct." Dayal (2004, 401), on the other hand, presents evidence in support of bare singulars used for kind reference with such predicates as *proizojti* "to get evolved", *zaščiščaetsja zakonom* "to be protected by law" and *izobresti/ pridumat'* "to be invented". I believe that Chierchia's contention holds for bare Ns denoting superkinds, such as dinosaurs, fishes, monkeys, whales, which denote a diverse group of animals with several taxonomic types. A taxonomic kind realized as a singular N-Adj or Adj-N nominal is grammatical with kind predicates, as illustrated in this paper. If a kind cannot be further subdivided into sub-kinds, a bare singular N is also grammatical in kind reference, as in *Dront vymer.* "Dodo is extinct."; or in *Čelovek proizošël ot obez'jany.* "Man has evolved from apes." (cited from Dayal ibid., (15a)).

predicates (Trugman 2007). Other types of inverted NPs are also grammatical in such contexts:

(8) a. Podsnežnik i kuvšinka *bolotnaja* naxodjatsja na grani
snowdrop and lily marsh$_{ADJ}$ are-found on edge
vymiranija.
extinction$_{GEN}$
"The snowdrop and marsh lily are found on the edge of extinction."

b. Audiokasseta *cifrovaja* byla izobretena v 1987 godu.
audiocassette digital was invented in 1987 year
"The digital audiocassette was invented in 1987."

c. Suxoj zakon v Finljandii uničtožil pjan'
dry law in Finland exterminated drunkard
podzabornuju (kak vid).
under-the-fence$_{ADJ}$ (as species)
"Prohibition in Finland has exterminated the lying-in-the-gutter drunkard (as a species)."

2.4. Lack of object reading with dynamic predicates

Dayal (2004, 402-403) claims that bare nominals in Russian, both singular and plural, can function as genuine kind terms and genuine definites. This dual behavior is best illustrated with episodic (also called dynamic, non-characterizing or object-level) predicates. For instance, (9a) can be understood as a generic statement about the elephant as a species—all elephants eat grass; or as an episodic statement about a particular elephant salient in the discourse (see Carlson 1977, 38-39 for English). Canonical Adj-N constructions in Russian are also ambiguous between the kind and definite object-referring readings, as illustrated in (9b). In contrast, inverted NPs do not preserve the object reading in such contexts, and (9c) can be interpreted only as a generic statement about a species—the individuated reading is ruled out.

(9) a. Slon est travu.
Elephant eats grass
"The elephant eats grass/ is eating grass."

b. *Afrikanskij* slon est travu.
African elephant eats grass
"The African elephant eats grass/ is eating grass."

c. Panda *gigantskaja* est bambuk.
panda gigantic eats bamboo
'The giant panda eats bamboo/*is eating bamboo."

This behavior of N-Adj constructions buttresses the present claim that they are kind-referring NPs—the latter are taken to be compatible with dynamic predicates, such as progressive and perfect sentences in English (Krifka et al. 1995, 12 and 63), yet the resultant statement must apply to the whole species, as shown in (10a) and (10b) for Russian:

(10) a. Na Evropejskij continent cixlazoma *glazčatja* byla
On European continent cichlasoma eye_{ADJ} was
zavezena iz Južnoj Ameriki.
brought from South America
"*Cichlasoma octofasciata* was brought to the European continent from South America."

b. Durak *stoerosovyj* prodolžaet rasprostranjatsja po miru.
fool utter continues to-spread around world
"The clot-head continues to spread around the world."

With episodic predicates that cannot produce a generic statement, i.e. whose argument is necessarily interpreted as object-denoting, inverted NPs are rendered ungrammatical (cf. Dayal ibid., 430 for English). This is illustrated in (11); (11b) is cited after Trugman (2007), her (12b'):

(11) a. *Čelovek *bol'noj* sidit v priëmnoj.
man sick is-sitting in reception-room
"A sick man is sitting in the reception room."

b. *Tigr *ussurijskij* byl ubit včera brakon'erami.
tiger $\text{Ussurijsk}_{\text{ADJ}}$ was killed yesterday $\text{poachers}_{\text{INSTR}}$
"An Ussurijsk tiger was killed by the poachers yesterday."

c. *Durak *stoerosovyj* dejstvuet mne na nervy uže čas.
fool utter working me on nerves already hour
"A clot-head has been driving me crazy for an hour."

2.5 Similarity of behavior with proper names

Trugman (2007), following Krifka et al. (1995, 65-67), showed that inverted labels and scientific terminology exhibit a similarity of behavior with proper names, which was taken as further support for the claim that inverted NPs function as names of kinds.[7] First, both proper names and kind-referring terms are often analyzed as definite, referring expressions. Moreover, the class of kind-referring expressions includes some proper names, such as scientific Latin terminology—e.g., *cichlasoma octofasciata* in (10a) above. Many Russian scientific terms are translations of traditional Latin terminology (see Kovtunova 1969). In addition, kind and proper names are grammatical in the *so-called* constructions discussed in Carlson (1977). This similarity is further strengthened by the existence of proper names hosting post-nominal adjectives. Such inverted proper names can participate in all types of inverted constructions discussed here—as recategorizing predicates, (12a), as expressives, (12b), as kind-referring arguments, (12c), as well as in picture captions, i.e. label counterparts:

(12) a. Pet'ka — nu prosto Koščej *Bessmertnyj*!
Pet'ka is well simply Koshchei Deathless
"Pet'ka looks just like Koshchei the Deathless!"
b. Ej, ty, Vasilisa *Premudraja*, idi sjuda!
hey you Vasilisa Wisest come here
"Hey you, Vasilisa the Wise, come here!"
c. Narodnaja mudrost' izobrela Vasilisu *Premudruju*.
Folk wisdom invented Vasilisa Wisest
"Folk wisdom invented Vasilisa the Wise."

To conclude, the above tests appear to unambiguously support the kind-referring status of the inverted NPs in Russian.

3. Previous account of N+Adj and its inadequacies

3.1 Movement analysis of inverted terms in Trugman (2007)

Based on these and other tests, Trugman (2007) proposes an analysis of the N-Adj order in labels and scientific terminology couched in Chomsky's Bare Phrase Structure framework (1995 and later works). Specifically, relational adjectives, which participate in inverted terms, are analyzed as multiple non-branching and non-projecting $Adj^{min}=Adj^{max}$

[7] Krifka et al. (1995, 67) treats the definite determiner in English singular definite generics as a formal marker of definiteness, hence, compatible with the names of kinds. Such generics are analyzed by analogy with proper names bearing a definite determiner, such as *the Sudan*.

specifiers of N (due to their denominal nature[8]). It is argued that N in such constructions raises out of NP and moves to D, which is phonetically null in Russian, to license the latter and acquire definiteness and kind interpretation, akin to the N-to-D movement proposed for Romance names in Longobardi (1994, 1999) (see Trugman 2007, 418-419). The N-raising does not proceed as a regular head movement, however, since it would fail to derive the mirror image ordering of postnominal adjectives in cases of multiple modification, as in (13a), borrowed from Trugman (ibid., (23)). The postnominal position of adjectives is derived via the adjunction of N to Adj merged as a specifier. In cases of multiple post-N modification, as in (13a), a successive movement of N-Adj_1 to the higher specifier Adj_2 with obligatory "pied-piping" of adjectives is assumed. The last step in the derivation moves the complex head N-Adj_1-Adj_2...Adj_n to the null D to license the latter and derive the definite kind name.

(13) a. solod *pyvovarennyj jačmennyj svetlyj*
malt brewing barley$_{ADJ}$ light
"light barley beer-brewing malt"

b. [$_D$ N-A_1-A_2-A_3 + D [$_{N3}$ N-A_1-A_2 (solod–pivovarennyj–jačmennyj)+ A_3 (svetlyj) [$_{N2}$ N-A_1 (solod–pivovarennyj)+ A_2 (jačmennyj) [$_{N1}$ N (solod)+ A_1 (pivovarennyj) [$_N$ solod]]]]]

Though this mechanism provides a neat account for the mirror image order of adjectives in post-N position, it seems to be somewhat *ad hoc*—there is no clear trigger for the initial N-to-Adj movement and subsequent "pied-piping" of adjectives in cases of serial modification.

Besides this conceptual problem, the account in Trugman (2007) makes several predictions which cannot be sustained empirically. Specifically, if Russian inverted nominals are definite names of kinds parallel to English singular definite generics, they are expected to be felicitous as predicative nominals only in the kind-oriented mode of speaking, as in (14), similar to their English counterparts (see Dayal 2004, 431 and Krifka et al. 1995, 85-88 for discussion of such structures in English).

[8] This contention is supported by such properties of relational adjectives as their inability to derive comparative and superlative forms, to have corresponding adverbs, to take degree words as modifiers, to form abstract nouns or antonymous pairs among other things (see Trugman 2007, 418 and references cited there). Such adjectives are merged as $X^{min}=X^{max}$ specifiers of functional projections, FPs, and license the latter, thus precluding the realization of the functional head (Giusti 2002, 70).

(14) Posmotrite, deti, èto — panda gigantskaja.
look kids this is panda gigantic
"Look, kids, this is the giant panda."

However, inverted NPs allow for a much broader predicative use, as illustrated by their use as characterizing predicates and expressives herein. If we assume that the inverted order arises due to the obligatory N-to-D movement to license D, we would be unable to account for various predicative uses of such expressions. The derivational account would need to resort to an additional mechanism preventing N from raising as high as D to ensure the predicative nature of inverted NPs. Yet, this would undermine the whole idea of N-to-D movement, since attraction of N by the null definite D triggers the noun-adjective inversion in the first place. If Ns can also precede Adjs in predicative constructions we are left with the question—what causes such inversion in the absence of D?[9] In other words, we end up concluding that inversion is independent from the presence or absence of D in the structure. Trugman (2007) does not discuss predicative uses of inverted NPs; therefore, in the following section I first demonstrate that such NPs used predicatively are indeed nominal properties rather than object-referring NPs, and then proceed to spell out an alternative analysis for these constructions.

3.2. Inverted NPs as property-denoting NPs

As illustrated in (1b), (5b), (7a) and (7b), inverted NPs are felicitously used as characterizing nominal predicates predicated either of object-referring arguments, (1b) and (5b), or of kind-referring ones, (7a).[10]

[9] Certainly, one can argue that in such cases N raises to license an indefinite null D. Yet, then it will be unclear why this movement does not occur across-the-board in all kinds of nominals. One would be forced to assume at least two types for both definite and indefinite null determiners in Russian: a kind-taking and an object-taking D, with only the former type triggering overt N-to-D movement in kind-referring expressions. Though expletive definite Ds in proper names and kind-taking determiners have been proposed for other languages (see Vergnaud and Zubizarreta 1992, Longobardi 1994, Krifka et al. 1995, Chierchia 1998, among others), postulating such an ambiguity within a realm of null determiners seems to be *ad hoc* at the moment.

[10] Inverted NPs predicates in Russian seem to correspond to several types of nominal predicates in other languages. For instance, categorizing/ generic predicates, as in (1b), are parallel to English singular indefinite NP-predicates, as in *Peter was a young man*. On the other hand, expressives used as predicates, as in *Petja—osël uprjamyj*. "Peter is an obstinate donkey." seem to recategorize the

Several tests below demonstrate that they function as property-denoting rather than individual-denoting NPs in such cases.

First, inverted nominals are ungrammatical in identity nominal predicative constructions, which require two object-referring nominal arguments (see Arutjunova 1976 as cited in Padučeva 1985/2002, Ivanova 2005, Testelets 2006 for the discussion of identity predicates in Russian; Rothstein 2004 for Hebrew, Citko 2006 for Polish, among many others). Such binominal identity predicates in Russian are often signaled by the presence of an overt pronominal copula, such as demonstratives *èto* "this", *tot samyj* "that same", or a double pronominal and verbal copula *èto i jest'* "and this is", as shown in (15) below ((15a) is cited from Ivanova 2005):[11]

(15) a. Nadja byla ta samaja podruga, s kotoroj devočki
Nadja was that same friend with whom girls
vmeste fotografirovalis'.
together photographed$_{\text{REFL}}$
"Nadja was that same friend with whom the girls took pictures of themselves."
b. Petr — èto molodoj čelovek iz našego pod'jezda.
Peter is this young man from our entrance
"Peter is the young man from our block of flats."

Note, however, that the presence of the copula renders (16a) ungrammatical, wherein the predicative nominal is inverted. It shows that the latter fails as an identity predicate, hence cannot be an object-referring nominal.

(16) a. Petr — (**èto*) čelovek *molodoj/ porjadočnyj.*
Peter is this man young/ decent.
"Peter is a young/ decent man."

---

argument, inducing a shift of meaning, as happens in French determinerless NP-predicates: *Il est rat/ chien/ vache/ chameau.* "He is rat/ dog/ horse/ camel." (Bouchard 2002, 177, (12a)), which have indefinite NPs in English counterparts: *He is a rat/ dog/ horse.* Eliciting exact conditions on licensing N-Adj expressions as various NP-predicates is a topic for future research.

11 Testelets (2006) shows that binominal identity sentences in Russian may also have a null copula, as in *Ubijca—Stapleton.* "The murderer is Stapleton." Such identity structures may be distinguished from characterizing nominal predicates with null copulas with the help of a Case test suggested in Citko (2006): While characterizing nominal predicates can bear instrumental case, identity ones obligatorily host both NPs in nominative: *Ubijca byl Stapleton/ *Stapletonom.* "The murderer was Stapleton$_{\text{NOM}}$/ *Stapleton$_{\text{INST}}$."

b. Pet'ka — *(*èto*) moë pugalo *ogorodnoe*.
Pet'ka is this my scarecrow vegetable-garden$_{ADJ}$
"Pet'ka is my unkempt fellow."

This contention gets additional support from the cases of inverted expressives accompanied with referential determiners, such as possessive pronouns, as in (16b). The presence of a possessive turns the inverted expressive into an individuated, object-referring nominal. Thus, it becomes grammatical in an identity predicate hosting the *èto* copula, as predicted. The same contrast between determinerless and referential nominal predicates holds in Haitian Creole (Deprez 1995) and French (Bouchard 2002, 276), as illustrated in (17), which further buttresses the contention that inverted NP-predicates in Russian are property-denoting bare nominals that only categorize the subject according to this property:

(17) a. Un éléphant est *une* bête.
"An elephant is a beast."
b. Un éléphant est bête.
"An elephant is stupid." (from Deprez ibid., (40))

Next, inverted nominal predicates cannot pronominalize (18) or relativize (19) by an individual-variable anaphora (see Padučeva 1985/2002 and references cited therein). They pronominalize by a *type*-anaphor *takoj*, as shown in (18a and b). Compare this with French determinerless predicates (Bouchard 2002, 277) that are replaced by the pronoun *le*, which pronominalizes property-denoting elements, as shown in (18c).

(18) a. Pet'ka — [kozël vonjučij]$_i$, i ty *on_i-že/ $takoj_i$-že!
Pet'ka is goat stinking, and you him-PART/ such-PART
"Pet'ka is a stinking goat, and so are you!"
b. Lou Shen — [panda gigantskaja]$_i$. Naš zoopark tože
Lou Shen is panda gigantic Our zoo also
*eje_i / $takuju_i$ priobrel.
her/ such acquired
"Lou Shen is a giant panda. Our zoo has also acquired *it/ one like that."
c. La fillette devint cheinne et ses soeurs *le* devinrent aussi.
"The little girl became a bitch and her sisters became one too." (Bouchard ibid., (15b))

(19) *Moj brat — [paren' molodoj]$_i$, kotorym$_i$ ja goržus'.
My brother is fellow young, who I am-proud-of
"*My brother is a young fellow, who I am proud of."

Moreover, the property-denoting status of inverted NP-predicates follows from their use as Type Genitives, discussed in Trugman (2004a/b). Such genitives serve as property-denoting attributes of N (cf. Kolliakou's 1999 proposal for French and Greek), which is confirmed by a series of semantic and syntactic tests. They can co-occur with referential arguments/complements of N bearing the same thematic/ semantic role and are always found N-adjacent; they never pronominalize or relativize by an individual-denoting pronoun, nor do they possessivize or participate in possessor ascension. In other words, such genitive NPs are analyzed as bare nominals forming with the head noun a compound-like structure, akin to English N_2N_1 compounds (see Trugman 2004a/b for more details).[12] Interestingly, Russian scientific literature abounds in Type Genitives expressed as inverted NPs, as shown in (20):

(20) a. cvetki [romaški *aptečnoj*]
flowers chamomile$_{GEN}$ pharmacy$_{ADJ.GEN}$
"flowers of pharmaceutical chamomile"
b. koren' [barbarisa *obyknovennogo*]
root barberry$_{GEN}$ common$_{GEN}$
"the root of common barberry"
c. list'ja [mjaty *perečnoj*]
leaves mint$_{GEN}$ pepper$_{ADJ.GEN}$
"pepper mint leaves"

Note that if Type Genitives are incorporated NPs, their kind-referring status follows straightforwardly (cf. Mithun 1984, as cited in Krifka et al. 1995, 87). Such NPs do not introduce a discourse referent and must be syntactically simple (they do not project any functional structure above NP), as shown in Trugman (ibid.). Therefore the grammaticality of inverted

[12] In Trugman (2004a) I proposed that TypeGens undergo lexical incorporation into the head noun and form a complex noun head [$_N$N+N$_{GEN}$]. The incorporation into N is made possible by the bare NP status of TypeGens and enables the latter to be Case-marked by N by default: N being an inherent case licenser discharges its genitive Case onto the TypeGen, which becomes structurally indistinct from the complement of N after incorporation. This incorporation analysis is consistent with the kind-referring nature of TypeGens proposed herein (see section 7 and fn. 22).

NPs as Type Genitives seriously falsifies the N-to-D raising analysis in Trugman (2007).

Finally, the use of inverted NPs as vocatives and exclamations also runs counter to their analysis as definite DPs. Such expressions are often argued in linguistic literature to be nominals realizable without the DP-layer, hence, bare NPs (see Longobardi 1999, Curat 1999, and section 6 for more discussion). Note that proper names with postnominal Adjs discussed in section 2.5 are also legitimate as expressives, as in (12b), as well as in canonical predicative positions, (12a). Consequently, a comprehensive analysis of inverted NPs and names must account for the dual behavior of such expressions. It is important to emphasize that the ability of inverted NPs to act as predicates in no way falsifies their analysis as kind terms. This kind of behavior, i.e., type shifting from properties to kinds, is considered meaning-preserving, for instance, in Chierchia (1998, 374) as it "...merely changes the type of its argument, leaving the information associated with it otherwise unchanged."[13]

Since the proposal in Trugman (2007) does not seem to extend elegantly to accommodate predicative uses of inverted NPs, an alternative analysis of such expressions is called for, which will provide mechanisms for both uses of inverted NPs in Russian. In view of the limitations of the movement account of the phenomenon, I propose a semantically based analysis that offers a uniform mechanism accommodating their dual nature. This alternative analysis is grounded in the representational theory of Denis Bouchard (2002, 2005).

4. Alternative analysis of inverted nominals

Bouchard (2002, 2005) develops a neo-saussurean approach to language that accepts arbitrariness not only for the relation between a sign and what it signifies, but also for relations that hold between different items:[14]

---

[13] "A property P is a function from worlds into characteristic functions true of individuals. The corresponding kind $^{\cap}$P (when there is one) is a function from worlds into the largest individual (i.e. set) of which P is true. This is like changing (world by world) from characteristic functions to sets, which are two different ways of coding the same information." (Chierchia 1998, 374)

[14] Saussure (1967) regards language as a system of signs holding an arbitrary relation between a signifié and a signifiant ("[T]here is nothing common, in the essence, between a sign and what it signifies.", from Saussure 1967 as translated in Bouchard 2002). Therefore language variation is expected not only regarding the

> Not only must meaning *units* be paired with a form, but the *relation* between these units (which carries its own meaning) must also be provided a perceptual form. (Bouchard 2002, 37)

He recognizes four major ways of giving meaning to a linguistic form: linear order, tone marking, Case marking of the Dependent, and Head marking, with each way being as good a signifiant for the signifié of a relation as the other.[15] Though Russian seems to employ not only the word order between items but also Dependent Marking as signifiants, for the purposes of this paper I focus exclusively on the use of word order, or juxtaposition, within the nominal domain as a means of conveying a particular meaning. To put it simply, I argue that the non-canonical linear order of NP constituents can function as an unambiguous marker of kind reference in Russian.[16] Due to the space limit I present just a synopsis of Bouchard's model in the following section, referring the interested reader to his works for details.

4.1. Synopsis of Bouchard (2002, 2005)

Each language sets the relation between Head and Dependent so that Head either precedes or follows Dependent. This setting is called the Central Linearization Parameter. The parameter is set, e.g., in English and French so that Head precedes Dependent, where "Dependent" generalizes over arguments and modifiers. Bare Dependents within the nominal domain (i.e., bare or non-phrasal adjectives discussed in this paper) that are found in an isomorphic whole-to-whole relation with the Head and participate in determining the extensity of the nominal expression combine

---

choice of conceptual categories that are grammaticalized and/or lexicalized in a language, but also regarding the way these categories are expressed.

[15] Bouchard (2002) recognizes four major ways of giving meaning to a form:

i. *Juxtaposition:* A and B are ordered temporally next to one another, deriving the structural relation of sister and immediately contain.

ii. *Superimposition:* B is a modulation superimposed on A, such as intonations to express grammatical functions in tone languages.

iii. *Dependent Marking*: the dependent gets a marking, such as Case marking.

iv. *Head Marking*: the head is marked, as in predicate marking (polysynthetic languages).

[16] The idea that kind reference in Russian might require special marking does not run against the universal trend, since kind-referring nouns tend to be marked in some way across languages (see Gerstner-Link 1988).

with it in accordance with the Linearization Parameter.[17] Any modifier that relates to a sub-part of N (i.e., any one of the functions in the network of N) cannot do this in the canonical word order and has to merge in the opposite direction to signify a different semantic relation with N—whole-to-part. This is referred to as an Elsewhere application of the Linearization Parameter. This model is illustrated in (21) for French: in (21a), the adjective modifies the whole network of N and yields the meaning "a man that is poor, not rich"; in (21b), on the other hand, the adjective modifies only the characterizing function *f* of N, hence appears prenominally and gets a different interpretation.

(21) a.	homme	*pauve*	*whole-to-whole relation with N*
	man	poor	"a poor (not rich) man"
b.	*pauvre*	homme	*whole-to-part relation with N*
	poor	man	"a poor (pitiful) man"

In English, on the other hand, both readings are available in the pre-N position. This follows from the distinct locus of semantic Number encoding in both languages. Semantic Number (Num, henceforth), which is taken to be a minimal means of identifying an actant, or an argument, is coded directly on N in English, while in French, the semantically meaningful Num is found on the determiner (see Bouchard 1998, 2002 for argumentation[18]). Consequently, in French, a bare Adj in postposition stands in a whole-to-whole relation with a bare N, whereas in English a postnominal Adj cannot establish a whole-to-whole relation with N alone because N bears Num. For Adj to establish a whole-to-whole relation with N alone, it has to appear prenominally, in accordance with the Elsewhere application of the Parameter. The whole-to-part relation with N (i.e., when

---

[17] To establish the extensity of an expression implies assigning properties to the whole network of N—the characteristic function *f,* the variable assignment function *g*, the time interval *i*, possible world *w*, etc., as a set.

[18] "Bouchard (2002), following an observation by Lamarche (1990, 1991), shows that it is the Det which bears the semantic expression of Number in French, whereas semantic Number is borne by the Noun in English. Det can appear alone in French, it can be a clitic-marking which identifies an actant, because it bears Number, which provides it with the minimum content required for atomization, hence for identification of an actant. By using the Number-bearing element alone, without an N range, as in *Paul le/la/les voit*, the speaker indicates that the referent of the direct object actant is part of the shared background of the speaker and addressee: the Number bearing element functions anaphorically. In English, Det does not bear Number, but rather the N does, so Det does not have the minimum required to function anaphorically." (Bouchard 2005, 1692)

Adj modifies one of the sub-functions of N) is established in pre-N in the Elsewhere fashion in both languages, (21b). Consequently, *a poor man* is ambiguous in English, permitting both interpretations of *poor* in pre-N position.

4.2. Modifying the representational model for Russian

In Trugman (2010) I showed that Russian exhibits mixed behavior with respect to tests for semantic Number encoding proposed in Bouchard (2002). Specifically, Russian nouns obligatorily marked for number morphology do allow for post-N Adjs, just as French Numberless Ns do, as amply illustrated above. I argued that such post-N bare Adjs should be analyzed as dependents of bare Ns, despite the latter's overt number marking, since such Adjs do not combine with N as adjectival predicates with an atomized actant (as do phrasal modifiers of N[19]). To account for this paradox, I proposed that Russian Ns in inverted NPs carry semantically vacuous number morphology, with precise cardinality of N being dependent upon other linguistic and extra-linguistic factors. This semantic Number underspecification is obfuscated by the unavoidable number morphology in Russian, which is part of a portmanteaux nominal morpheme signifying number, Case and gender of the noun simultaneously (cf. Deprez 2005). Following this rationale, a Semantic Number Encoding Parameter in Russian (SNEPR) was proposed (Trugman 2010, (15)):

[19] Several properties of post-N Adjs point to this conclusion. First, as discussed above, inverted NPs are grammatical as Type Genitives (i), which are bare property-denoting NPs, hence, unsaturated nominal predicates. In addition, Adjs in inverted NPs do not have relative clause counterparts (ii), do not scramble out of NPs without a meaning loss (iii); and lack meaning-preserving clausal predicate rephrasals, (iv):

(i) jagody [maliny sadovoj]
berries raspberry$_{GEN}$ garden$_{ADJ.GEN}$
"berries of garden raspberry"

(ii) *jagody maliny, kotoraja javljaetsja/ byla sadovoj
berries raspberry$_{GEN}$ which is/ was garden$_{ADJ.GEN.INSTR}$

(iii) *Sadovoj on nasobiral jagody maliny.
garden$_{ADJ.GEN}$ he picked-up berries raspberry$_{GEN}$

(iv) *$^{?}$Malina byla sadovoj.
raspberry was garden$_{ADJ.GEN}$

> *Semantic Number Encoding Parameter in Russian (SNEPR)*
> Unavoidable morphological number marking in Russian does not necessarily signify semantic Number encoding and can signal morphologically default number realization of a non-atomized N.[20]

This parameter challenges the one-to-one correspondence between morphological and semantic Number on Russian Ns, and allows them to be semantically Number-less in the presence of overt morphological number marking (cf. Bouchard 2002 for attributive Ns in French and English; Doron 2003 for bare singulars in Hebrew, Halmøy 2010 for Norwegian indefinite singular NPs; as well as Zweig 2008 for English plural NPs being unspecified for multiplicity).

The SNEPR Parameter allows for an elegant account of Russian postnominal adjectives illustrated above. Post-N Adjs combine with N in accordance with the Central Linearization Parameter, which is presumably set in Russian as in English and French, with Head preceding Dependent. The N-Adj ordering relation signals a whole-to-whole relation between a non-atomized N and its adjectival modifier, which results in a complex nominal predicate N-Adj denoting a natural class or kind. In other words, an inverted NP defines a single set of individuals exhibiting two properties (one denoted by the nominal predicate and the other by the adjective) as necessarily linked.

I follow Bouchard's (2002) contention that both singular and plural Number markings can express *the sort* of individual involved rather than a singular atomized individual or a plurality of such individuals. Therefore, singular Russian inverted NPs are treated here as corresponding to an unatomized singularity, whose referent is instantiated as a non-individuated mass with the complex property of N+Adj (cf. Bouchard, ibid., 305). Note that this treatment of inverted NPs as mass-like is consistent with their kind-referring behavior since mass nouns are often taken to be kind-denoting (Chierchia 1998 and references cited there). Furthermore, semantically vacuous number morphology of inverted NPs allows them to be conceptually plural, while morphologically singular, akin to mass nouns and singular definite generics (cf. Chierchia ibid., Dayal 2004). This line of reasoning predicts that N-Adj constructions will exhibit behavior similar to mass nouns. Firstly, as illustrated in sections 2 and 3, N-Adj expressions resemble mass nouns in being used as both kind

[20] Morphologically default number can be realized as either singular or plural depending on pragmatic factors (see Šmelev 1996): while some kind terms are conventionalized as singular NPs, others are used in the plural form. I will leave this topic for future research.

terms and predicates—mass nouns freely occur in both functions without any additional markings (see Quine 1960, Ter Meulen 1980, 1981, among many others). In the following section, I discuss several additional properties of such expressions that support their mass-like behavior.

5. Evidence for Number underspecification of N-Adjs

5.1. Impossibility of direct counting

First, on a par with ungrammatical **tri wody* "three waters", **pjat' mjas* "five meats", N-Adjs constructions seem to resist direct association with quantifiers and numerals and require a measure phrase or a classifier to be counted. Otherwise, the canonical Adj-N order must be used, as shown in (22) and (23) respectively:

(22) a. Postupili v prodažu kostjumy *mužskie*, desjat' par.
arrived in sale suits men's ten pairs
"Ten men's suits arrived for sale."
b. Najdena pjan' *podzabornaja*, v količestve pjati čelovek.
found drunkard under-the-fence, in quantity five men
"There have been found five lying-in-the-gutter drunkards."

(23) a. Pjat'desjat butylok *suxogo* vina/ *vina *suxogo*
fifty bottles dry wine/ wine dry
byli dostavleny v magazin.
were delivered to store
"Fifty bottles of dry wine were delivered to the store."
b. Petja i Vasya byli dva *vospitannyx* parnja/
Petya and Vasya were two well-mannered fellows/
*dva parnja *vospitannyx*.
two fellows well-mannered
"Petya and Vasya were two well-mannered fellows."

5.2. Number mismatches in characterizing sentences

It is well known that with kind and generic predicates the morphological number of the argument does not necessarily correspond to its semantic interpretation: a singular form of the noun can refer to a plurality, a whole class of entities (see Chierchia 1998, 351ff, Corbett 2000, 19). It was shown above that inverted NPs in Russian are felicitous both as arguments and as nominal predicates of characterizing sentences.

When used as arguments of kind predicates, singular inverted NPs denote the whole class rather than a singular individual, despite singular morphology, as in (24):

(24) Žavoronok *polevoj* isčez iz
lark$_{SG}$ field$_{ADJ.SG}$ disappeared$_{SG}$ from
srednej polosy Rossii.
middle region Russia.gen
"The field lark died out in the middle region of Russia."

Likewise, singular inverted NPs used as characterizing predicates can easily predicate of bare plurals, as shown in (25). Both subject and predicate NPs in (25) are kind-referring, yet their morphological number markings exhibit disagreement.[21] This supports the conceptual plurality of inverted NPs akin to mass terms.

(25) a. Studenty — narod *vesëlyj/ mnogočislennyj.*
Students (are) people$_{SG}$ merry$_{SG}$/ numerous$_{SG}$
"Students are a merry /numerous people."
b. Lisy — zver' *umnyj.*
foxes (are) animal$_{SG}$ smart$_{SG}$
"Foxes are smart animals."
(cited after Babby 1975, 222, (4.114f&e))

5.3. Generic anaphora and collective predicates

Inverted NPs allow for both singular and plural generic anaphora and satisfy the agreement principle with both of them (cf. Krifka et al. 1995, 106), as shown in (26a). Though with a semantically plural predicate a plural anaphora might be preferred by some speakers, as in (26b), a singular anaphora is also grammatical. Russian singular inverted NPs also felicitously associate with semantically plural *collective* predicates, such as *razmnožat'ja* 'reproduce', as in (26c) (cf. Krifka et al. 1995, 90). This

[21] Certainly, both the argument and its NP predicate in (25) can surface as morphologically singular while referring to the whole class of entities:
(i) a. Student — narod vesëlyj.
student$_{SG}$ is people$_{SG}$ merry "Students are a merry people."
b. Lisa — zver' umnyj.
fox$_{SG}$ is animal$_{SG}$ smart "The fox is a smart animal."
Such facts were cited in support of the idea that nominal and adjectival predicates in Russian do not agree with the subject in φ-features; and agreement in such cases is semantically based (see Babby 1975).

behavior further underscores the mismatch between their semantic Number and morphological number, which resembles that of mass nouns.

(26) a. Panda *gigantskaja* vymiraet, poètomu *ona* oxranjaetsja/
Panda$_{SG}$ gigantic is-dying-out, therefore she is-protected/
oni oxranjajutsja zakonom.
they are-protected law$_{INSTR}$
"The giant panda is dying out therefore it is/ they are protected by the law."

b. Panda *gigantskaja* vymiraet, poètomu $^{?}$*eje/ix* pytajutsja
panda$_{SG}$ gigantic is-dying-out, therefore her/ them are-trying
razmnožat' metodom iskusstvennogo oplodotvorenija.
to-reproduce method artificial fertilization
"The giant panda is dying out; therefore efforts are being made to have it/them reproduce by methods of artificial insemination."

c. Panda *gigantskaja* v nevole ne razmnožaetsja.
panda$_{SG}$ gigantic in captivity not reproduce$_{SG.REFL}$
"The giant panda does not reproduce in captivity."

5.4. Scope effects

Russian inverted NPs possess peculiar scopal properties, which draws a further parallel between them and other kind terms, such as mass nouns, bare plurals and nouns overtly referring to kinds. Chierchia (1998, 368-374) adopting a neo-Carlsonean approach uses scopal differences between bare plurals and indefinite NPs in English to argue that the former refer unambiguously to kinds. Applying similar tests to Russian inverted NPs, it can be shown that their scope is similar to that of bare plurals and mass terms in English. The four properties demonstrated in (27) below are constructed after Carlson's (1977) tests and highlight the obligatory narrow scope of singular inverted NPs in various syntactic constructions:

(27) a. *Property 1: Opacity with intensional verbs*
Petja iščet ženščinu molčalivuju vot uže tri goda.
"Peter is looking for a taciturn woman already for three years."

b. *Property 3: Narrow scope with respect to negation*
Petja ne vstrečal ženščinu molčalivuju v našix krajax.
"Peter didn't meet a taciturn woman in our area."

c. *Property 2: Differentiated scope*
Petja vstrečal ženščinu boltlivuju neodnokratno.
"Peter met a talkative woman several times."

d. *Property 4: Anaphora test*
Petja iščet ženščinu molčalivuju i Vasja iščet takuju/*eje tože.
"Peter is looking for a taciturn woman and Vasya is looking for one/ *her too."

In all the sentences above, the inverted NPs does not presuppose the existence of some specific taciturn or talkative woman, whom Peter is seeking for or met some time ago. In other words, the inverted NPs appear to have an obligatory opaque reading and, hence, a narrow scope with respect to other sentential quantifiers. In contrast to Adj-N strings that are ambiguous between the opaque and transparent readings (akin to English indefinites), inverted NPs in Russian share scopal properties with various types of kind names in English (such as mass nouns, singular definite generics, and NPs referring overtly to kinds, such as "this kind of X", as in (6) and (8c)). All the aforementioned properties support the present contention that inverted NPs in Russian are kind-referring NPs underspecified for semantic Num, which may undergo atomization/ individuation under certain conditions discussed in the following section. Their Number underspecification allows them to appear in contexts that require either singular or plural kind terms in other languages.

6. Atomization of inverted NPs

If inverted NPs originate as unatomized entities (complex nominal predicates where the adjectival dependent combines with the noun head in a whole-to-whole manner), they have to acquire referential potential in one way or another in order to function as arguments, or actants of verbal predicates. However, inverted NPs are often used in non-propositional structures as well. In this section I discuss possible ways of atomization of inverted NP used in several syntactic and pragmatic contexts.

6.1. Atomization due to extra-linguistic conditions

Curat (1999), as cited in Bouchard (2002), discusses various determinerless constructions in French, such as labels, invectives and interpellations (which are inherently predicative in Bouchard's system since Num is encoded on Det in French, and in its absence the NP is non-atomized). Curat claims that such nominals may acquire their referential import from some restricted semantic or pragmatic conditions rather than from syntactic atomization by Det. When labels and expressives are found in direct contact with the referent or its graphic representation, there is no need to atomize N "...in order to pick out a particular referent from the class of the N: the direct contact already identifies a referent" (see Bouchard, ibid., 290).

This claim was extended in Trugman (2010) to Russian product labels, scientific names, and names of artifacts with inverted word order. It is empirically supported by the examples in various encyclopedias or catalogues, wherein visual images of objects are accompanied by corresponding picture captions exhibiting the N-Adj order.

The same is claimed to be true when an inverted NP is used in direct contact not with the graphic image but with the referent present in the discourse situation, as happens with various expressives, such as exclamatory constructions, vocatives, interpellations that may describe a person either derogatorily, like insults and invectives, or positively, like praises (though the latter are rarer and are found mainly in poetry or prayer). Russian expressives used in the presence of the referent cannot bear any markers of referentiality, as shown in (28), similarly to such expressions in French.

(28) a. Tak vot ty kakaja, (*èta/ *moja) panda gigantskaja!
So here you what, this my panda gigantic
"That's what you look like, you giant panda!"
b. (*Ètot/ *Kakoj-to) Durak nabityj! Na sebja posmotri!
this/ some fool filled on self look
"Stupid head! Look at yourself!"

In contrast, when used in the absence of the referent or indirectly, they obligatorily require a referential marker, either definite or indefinite, in order to become object-referring. In French, as well, all insults directed at a third person require the presence of a determiner (Curat 1999, 203).

(29) a. *(Tvoj) čërt rogatyj vsex raspugal!
your devil horned everyone scared-away
"Your horned devil scared everyone away!"
b. *(Kakoj-to) kozël vonjučij pocarapal mne mašinu!
some goat stinking scratched me_{DAT} car
"Some stinking goat scratched my car!"

This demonstrates that when atomization of inverted NPs by pragmatic means is unattainable it must be achieved by other linguistic means. However, in direct contact with the referent or its image syntactic atomization is not required.

6.2. Atomization of sentential arguments

When, on the other hand, inverted NPs function as kind-referring arguments of full-fledged sentences, they have to undergo the process of atomization (in Bouchard's terminology) or "nominalization" in Chierchia's. Kinds are regarded by the latter as individuals denoting the maximal set, the sum of all instances of the kind (ibid., 349). Therefore, inverted (predicative) NPs have to undergo a type shifting operation from properties to corresponding nominalizations. Yet, this mapping presupposes a plural kind term since sets are plural entities; which explains why bare plural kind names are quite common across languages. In contrast, a bare singular form of N cannot function as kind-referring in many languages and requires an additional marking, such as the article *the* in English, to do so. Chierchia (ibid.), for instance, proposes that in English singular definite generics a count noun is first recategorized as a mass noun by applying a massifying function MASS, which neutralizes the singular-plural distinction. Then, the definite article composes with such a massified noun to denote the totality of objects (the group *g* containing all objects). A singular definite generic, thus, is similar to mass expressions in having singular morphology yet denoting a collective. When such singular generics occur with kind-level predicates (as in "*The dog is common*"), *the dog* refers to a class-as-one (a collective, which is reconstructed as an atom) (Chierchia, ibid., 381-382).

Dayal (2004) also recognizes the mismatch between a singular morphology and a plural interpretation of singular definite generics across languages and proposes to consider such kind-terms as taxonomic kinds. In her approach, common nouns are ambiguous between properties of ordinary individuals and properties of sub-kinds. The definite determiner, both in singular and plural NPs, can combine with either—properties of individuals or properties of kinds. This approach to singular definite generics as quantifying over a domain of taxonomic entities brings even closer the parallelism between Russian inverted NPs and singular definite generics in English: Russian inverted NPs represent sets of taxonomic NPs that share the same generic name, hence are *bona fide* taxonomic noun phrases. If we adopt Dayal's analysis of singular definite generics as a kind of taxonomic noun phrases their similarity with inverted Russian nominals follows straightforwardly.

I claimed here that Russian inverted NPs are underspecified for Num, and resemble mass nouns in neutralization of the singular/plural distinction. Therefore, Russian inverted NPs can get singular kind reference similarly to English singular definite generics, yet they do not need to undergo the massifying operation, in contrast to their English counterparts, since they are underspecified for number (cf. neutralized singular properties in Brazilian Portuguese discussed in Schmitt and Munn 1999; number-neutralized "singular" indefinite kind names in Hebrew in Doron 2003; number- and definiteness-neutralized Norwegian bare nouns used as kind names in Halmøy 2010). Following this rationale, Russian inverted NPs functioning as arguments can be regarded as nominalizations of complex N-Adj predicates, i.e. their corresponding kinds, derived by the "down" cap operation proposed in Chierchia (1998), which is assumed to be free in languages without overt determiners.[22] Though Chierchia (ibid., 361) assumes that this operator should be restricted to plurals in Russian; in principle, he allows for singular generics in Russian by analogy with the English singular definite generics. The argumentation presented in this paper cogently shows that Russian inverted nominals are very close counterparts to English singular definite generics.

7. Extending the approach to other modifier types

This analysis of N-Adj expressions easily extends to other cases of post-N modification attested to in Russian. Russian nouns exhibit two additional types of postnominal modifiers—attributive nouns in various appositive constructions and attributive genitive phrases called Type

[22] As mentioned at the beginning of the paper, I restricted discussion of argumental inverted NPs mainly to subject arguments. However, in (27), inverted nominals function as objects of the main predicate and have scopal properties akin to bare plurals and mass terms. I do not claim that inverted NPs are counterparts of singular definite generics in such contexts. Inverted NPs functioning as objects of verbal predicates may be analyzed as incorporated into the verbal predicate. Incorporation of inverted NPs is a feasible option in the present analysis due to their syntactic status as bare nominals, as well as their kind-referring nature (see Mithun 1984 as cited in Krifka et al. 1995, 87, and van Geenhoven and McNally 2005 for the analysis of incorporated objects as kind-referring). In the incorporation analysis there will be no need for atomization of inverted NPs in such contexts.

Genitives (see Trugman 2004a/b for details). They are illustrated in (30a) and (30b) respectively:

(30) a. Kreslo-*krovat'* bylo izobreteno v dvadcatom veke.
armchair-bed was invented in twentieth century
"The convertible armchair was invented in the 20th century."
b. ego velikodušie *genija*
his magnanimity $genius_{GEN}$
"his magnanimity of a genius'

Several tests can be provided in support of the unatomized/ predicative nature of both the attributive NP, *krovat'*, and the attributive TypeGen *genija*, in the two constructions (see also Trugman 2010 and references cited there).

(31) *Common properties of NP-attributes:*
- They do not refer to and resist modification by referential elements.
- They resist pronominalization by an individual variable pronoun and allow for pronominalization only by *type*-pronouns *takoj, tak.*
- They resist relativization and possessivization.
- They form questions with *kakoj/ kakov* 'what kind' question words.
- They do not function as controllers of verbal or adjectival clausal predicates.
- Nominal attributes may disagree with the head noun in φ-features (such as gender, number, and sometimes Case)

Based on these and additional tests, Trugman (2004a/b) proposes that N-TypeGen constructions in Russian form a complex noun head $[_N N+N_{GEN}]$ in a fashion similar to English N_2N_1 compounds (cf. Bouchard 2002 for the analysis of *N de N* constructions in French). The incorporation into N is made possible by the bare NP status of TypeGens, which makes them property-denoting modifiers (parallel to the non-head of the compound). Such N-TypeGen combinations are taken to designate *types* of individuals rather than their specific *tokens* (cf. Vergnaud and Zubizarreta 1992, Givón 2001, Halmøy 2010). This analysis has been extended to post-N nominal dependents in appositive N-N constructions in Trugman (2010) following the similarity of their behavior. In sum, in both constructions the NP-dependent forms with the N-head a syntactic structure in which the NP-dependent is shielded from independent Semantic Number encoding.

Semantic Number is interpreted simultaneously on both members of the nominal construction. This process yields a semantic output akin to English N_2N_1 compounds.[23]

This analysis of nominal dependents as non-atomized Ns makes them similar to adjectival dependents of inverted NPs and allows us to treat N-N and N-TypeGens structures in Russian as complex noun predicates as well. This automatically yields all the properties of nominal and TypeGens attributes discussed in previous works: their obligatory adjacency to N; their property-denoting nature and incompatibility with referentiality markers. The validity of this analysis is supported by the similarity of behavior of N-N and N-TypeGens constructions to inverted NPs in the environments discussed here. For the lack of space I cannot fully demonstrate all aspects of their behavior but provide only some examples that illuminate their kind-referring properties. In (32), nominal attributes of appositives are illustrated in (a) through (f); whereas their TypeGen counterparts—in (a') through (f'):

(32) *scientific names/labels*

a.	kabačok *cukini*	a'. lošad' *priževal'skogo*
	courgette zucchini	horse Przewalski$_{GEN}$
	"a courgette zucchini"	"a Przewalski's horse"

arguments of kind-selecting predicates[24]

b. Kamen' *pesčanik* široko rasprostranen.
stone sand wide spread
"The sand stone is widespread."

---

[23] Note the similarity between N_2N_1 compounds and "associative Adj-N" combinations in English, like *a musical clock* or *an electric engineer* discussed in Giegerich (2005) and references cited there. Giegerich puts forth an intriguing claim that some associative Adj-N structures may be the product of the lexicon, whereas others may be created in the syntax. Though I do not extend this claim for Russian N-N, N-GenP, N-Adj combinations in this paper, it does not seem to be inconceivable since many of such combinations are highly conventionalized and may easily be analyzed as lexemes. I leave this issue for future research.

[24] In the literature, such predicates as *byt' široko rasprostranennym* "be widespread" are usually treated as kind-selecting, on a par with *be extinct*, *be invented*, *evolve from* (see Carlson 1977). However, some authors make a more fine-grained distinction and treat them as different from real kind predicates, assigning them to a separate group of quantificational predicates (see for instance, Krifka et al. 1995, Halmøy 2010). Yet the predicate *be widespread* cannot apply to individuals; thus, the claim that the examples in (32b&b') host kind-referring nominals seems to be valid.

b'. Ambicii *Napoleona* široko rasprostraneny.
ambitions Napoleon$_{GEN}$ wide spread
"Napoleonic ambitions are widespread."
c. Ptica dront vymerla.
bird dodo become-extinct
"The dodo is extinct."
c'. Losad' *priževal'skogo* davno vymerla.
horse Przewalski$_{GEN}$ long-ago become-extinct
"The Przewalski's horse became extinct a long time ago."

arguments of episodic predicates
d. Ryba-*xameleon* byla zavezena v 1905 godu iz Indii…
fish-chameleon was brought in 1905 year from India
"The fish-chameleon was brought from India in 1905."
d'. Krivaja *Koxa* byla opisana v 1904 godu.
curve Koch$_{GEN}$ was described in 1904 year
"The Koch curve was described in 1904."

expressives
e. Žadina-*govjadina*!
cheapskate beef
"Cheapskate!"
e'. Ej, ty, tupaja lošad' *priževal'skogo*, doumničalas'?
hey you stupid horse Przewalski$_{GEN}$ philosophized
"Hey, see what you got by playing smart, you stupid Przewalski's horse?"

characterizing predicates
f. Petja — student-*otličnik*.
Peter is student student-of-honors
"Peter is a student of honors."
f'. Petja — kladez' *mudrosti*.
Peter is well wisdom$_{GEN}$
"Peter is a well of wisdom."

The examples in (32) show that N-N appositives and N-TypeGen constructions are close counterparts of N-Adj constructions. In this way, all modificational structures hosting postnominal modifiers appear to lend themselves to a uniform analysis, which significantly enhances the credibility of the present proposal.

8. Conclusion

In this paper I claimed that the unorthodox ordering relation between N and Adj in Russian can signify a particular semantic meaning, specifically, a kind-referring term or its corresponding predicate. Adopting the representational approach by Bouchard (2002, 2005) I argued that inverted NPs in Russian signify adjectival modification of a non-atomized N, which accounts for the post-nominal position of the adjective. In this way, inverted NPs were analyzed as complex nominal predicates denoting kinds; and a series of tests were provided to illustrate their kind-referring nature in both argumental and predicative uses. It was proposed that inverted nominal predicates can acquire referential import in several ways: either by direct contact with the referent in the discourse (Curat 1999) or by the semantic type-shifting convention proposed in Chierchia (1998). The ability of *singular* inverted NPs to undergo "nominalization" in Chierchia's terminology follows from their semantic Number underspecification, which makes them similar to mass nouns and allows for singular generic interpretation. This analysis was extended to two other types of postnominal modification in Russian—nominal attributes in appositives and TypeGens. Though some residual issues remain, it seems that the present account succeeds at providing a uniform analysis to seemingly disparate modificational phenomena in Russian.

References

Babby, Leonard, H. 1975. *A Transformational Grammar of Russian Adjectives*. Mouton: The Hague.

Baylin, John. 1995. A Configurational Approach to Russian "Free" Order. PhD dissertation, Cornell University.

Bouchard, Denis. 1998. “The distribution and interpretation of adjectives in French: A consequence of Bare Phrase Structure.” *Probus* 10 (2): 139-83.

—. 2002. *Adjectives, Number and Interfaces: Why Languages Vary*. Amsterdam, Boston, London: North Holland.

Bouchard, Denis. 2005. “Exaption and linguistic explanation.” *Lingua* 115: 1685-1696.

Carlson, Gregory. 1977. Reference to Kinds in English. PhD dissertation, University of Massachusetts, Amherst, Mass.

Chierchia, Gennaro. 1998. “Reference to kinds across languages.” *Natural Language Semantics* 6 (4): 339-405.

Chomsky, Noam. 1995. *The Minimalist Program.* Cambridge, Mass.: MIT Press.

Citko, Barbara. 2006. "Copula sentences reconsidered." In *Annual Workshop on Formal Approaches to Slavic Linguistics. The Princeton Meeting*, edited by James E. Lavine et al, 83-97. Ann Arbor: Michigan Slavic Publications.

Corbett, Greville G. 2000. *Number*. Cambridge University Press.

Curat, Hervé 1999. *Les déterminants dans la référence nominale et les conditions de leur absence*. Geneva-Paris: Librairie Droz.

Dayal, Veneeta. 2004. "Number marking and (in)definiteness in kind terms." *Linguistics and Philosophy* 27 (4): 393-450.

Deprez, Viviane. 2005. "Morphological number, semantic number and bare nouns." *Lingua* 115: 857-883.

Doron, Edit. 2003. "Bare singular reference to kinds." *SALT* 13: 73-90

Farkas, Donka F. and Henriëtte de Swart. 2007. "Article choice in plural generics." *Lingua* 117: 1657-1676.

Frolova, Irina. 1991. "English/Rusian nominal sentences-expressives: Contrastive analysis." *PSiCL* (*Poznań Studies in Contemporary Linguistics*) 26: 155-156. Available at: http://ifa.amu.edu.pl/psicl/files.

Gerstner-Link, Claudia. 1988. Űber Generizität. Generische Nominalphrasen in singulären Aussagen und generischen Asusagen. PhD dissertation, University of Munich, Munich.

Givón, Talmy. 2001. *Syntax: An Introduction.* Amsterdam: John Benjamins Publications.

Giegerich, Heinz. 2005. "Associative adjectives in English and the lexicon-syntax interface." *Journal of Linguistics* 41: 571-591.

Giusti, Giuliana. 2002. "The functional structure of Noun Phrases: A Bare Phrase Structure approach." In *Functional Structure in DP and IP: The Cartography of Syntactic Structures*, Vol. 1., edited by Guglielmo Cinque, 54-90. Oxford: Oxford University Press,

Halmøy, Madeleine. 2010. The Norwegian Nominal System—A Neo-Saussurean Perspective. PhD dissertation, University of Tromsø.

Ivanova, Yelena. 2005. "Predloženija identifikacii v russkom i bolgarskom jazykax." In *Aspekti na kontrstivnoto opisanie na ruskija i b'lgarskija ezik*. Šumen: Universitetsko izdatelstvo "Episkop Konstantin Preslavski". Available at:
http://www.russian.slavica.org/ article2581.html.

King, Tracy, H. 1995. *Configuring Topic and Focus in Russian.* Stanford University: CSLI Publications.

Kolliakou, Dimitra. 1999. "De-phrase extractability and individual/ property denotation." *Natural Language and Linguistic Theory* 17: 713-81.

Kovtunova, Irina, I. 1969. *Porjadok slov v russkom literaturnom jazyke XVIII— pervoj treti XIX veka*. Moskva: Nauka.

Krifka, Manfred, Francis J. Pelletier, Gregory N. Carlson, Alice ter Meeurlen, Godehard Link, and Gennaro Ghierchia. 1995. "Genericity: An Introduction." In *The Generic Book*, edited by Gregory N. Carlson and Francis J. Pelletier, Chicago: The University of Chicago Press.

Longobardi, Giuseppe. 1994. "Reference and proper names." *Linguistic Inquiry* 25 (4): 609-665.

—. 1999. "Some Reflections on Proper Names." Ms., Università di Trieste.

Padučeva, Elena V. 1985/2002. *Vyskazyvanie i ego sootnesennost' s dejstvitelnostju (referencialnye askpekty semantiki mestoimenij).* Moskva: Nauka.

Pereltsvaig, Asya. 2007. "On the universality of DP: A view from Russian." *Studia Linguistica* 61(1): 59-94.

Quine, Willard van Orman. 1960. *Word and Object.* Cambridge, Mass.: MIT Press.

Rothstein, Susan. 2004. *Predicates and their Subjects*. Dordrecht: Kluwer.

Sekerina, Irina A. 1999. "On-line processing of Russian scrambling constructions." In *Annual Workshop on Formal Approaches to Slavic Languages. The Seattle Meeting 1998*, edited by Herbert Coats, Katarzyna Dziwirek, and Cynthia M. Vakareliyska, 397-412. Ann Arbor: Michigan Slavic Publications.

Šmelev, Aleksei. 1996. *Referencialnye mexanizmy russkogo jazyka.* Slavica Tamperensia IV. Tammerfors: University of Tampere.

Schmitt, Claudia and Alan Munn. 1999. "Against the nominal mapping parameter: Bare nouns in Brazilian Portuguese." *NELS* 29.

Ter Meulen, Alice. 1981. "An intensional logic for mass terms." *Philosophical Studies* 40 (1): 105-125.

Testelets, Yakov, G. 2006. "K tipologii predloženij s nevyražennoj svjazkoj." In *Problemy tipologii i obščej lingvistiki*, edited by V. S. Xrakovskij, S. Y. Dmitrenko and N. M. Zaika, 151-153. Saint Petersburg: Nestor-Istoria.

Trugman, Helen. 2004a. "More puzzles about postnominal genitives." In *Possessives and Beyond: Semantics and Syntax,* edited by Ji-yung, Kim, Yury A. Lander and Barbara H. Partee, University of Massachusetts Occasional Papers in Linguistics 29. Amherst, MA: GLSA Publications, 217-240.

—. 2004b. Syntax of Russian DPs, and DP-internal Agreement Phenomena. PhD dissertation, Tel-Aviv University.

—. 2007. "Rudiments of Romance N-to-D movement in Russian." In *Potsdam Linguistic Investigations: Linguistic Investigations into Formal Description of Slavic Languages*, edited by Kosta, Peter et al., 411-426. Frankfurt am Main: Peter Lang.

—. 2010. "Modifiers of bare nouns in Russian." In *Current Issues in Formal Slavic Linguistics* [Contributions from the 7.5 European Conference on Formal Description of Slavic Languages held in Moscow, 6-8 December 2008], edited by Zybatow, Gerhild, Philip Dudchuk, Serge Minor, Ekaterina Pshehotskaya, Peter Lang Publishers.

Van Geenhoven, Veerle and Louise McNally. 2005. "On the property analysis of opaque complements." *Lingua* 115: 885-914.

Vergnaud, Jean-Roger and Maria-Luisa Zubizarreta. 1992. "The definite determiner and the inalienable constructions in French and English." *Linguistic Inquiry* 23: 595-652.

Zweig, Eytan. 2008. Dependent Plurals and Plural Meaning. PhD dissertation, New York University. Available at http://www-users.york.ac.uk/ ~ez506/ downloads/Zweig2008Plurals_Thesis.pdf.

DISTRIBUTION OF CLASSIFICATORY ADJECTIVES AND GENITIVES IN POLISH NPS *

BOŻENA CETNAROWSKA,
UNIVERSITY OF SILESIA
AGNIESZKA PYSZ,
HØGSKULEN I VOLDA
AND HELEN TRUGMAN
HOLON INSTITUTE OF TECHNOLOGY

Abstract

Using the framework of Bouchard (2002, 2005) the present paper investigates the competition between classificatory adjectives and genitive noun phrases for the head-adjacent position of the postmodifier of N. Two distinct word order patterns are discussed: one—exhibiting the obligatory adjacency between N and its genitive satellite; and the other—allowing the classificatory adjective to intervene between the two; and mechanisms of conflict resolution are proposed. In particular, we claim that head-adjacent genitive NPs, referred to as Type Genitives, are property-denoting satellites, which allows them to compete with classificatory adjectives for the postnominal placement. The proposed classification of genitive satellites coupled with the semantic hierarchy of modifiers accounts for the (un)grammaticality of various word orders within the nominal phrase.

1. Introduction

As the title of this paper suggests, it deals with the two kinds of noun modifiers in Polish: Classificatory Adjectives (ClassAs) and Genitive NPs.

* The authors of the paper would like to thank the audiences of PLM-2009 and SLS-4, Bożena Rozwadowska, Madeleine Halmøy and anonymous reviewers for helpful comments and suggestions. All errors remain our own responsibility. The names of the authors are given in alphabetical order.

The term "classificatory" is used here in contradistinction to the term "qualifying", with ClassAs restricting the denotation of the noun they modify, as opposed to Qualifying Adjectives (QualAs) describing a non-defining feature of the head noun (e.g. Warren 1984, Willim 2000b). Since the majority of the ClassAs fall within the class of relational adjectives, they tend to exhibit a particular morphosyntactic behavior, such as non-gradability, lack of adverbial modification, infelicity in predicative position, lack of deadjectival nominalizations, etc. (see, for instance, Townsend 1975 for Russian, Giegerich 2005 for English, Szupryczyńska 1980, Topolińska 1984, Nowakowska 1998, CP&T 2010 for Polish). In this vein, some researchers contrast QualAs with relational adjectives instead (e.g., Bosque and Picallo 1996), with ClassAs and thematic adjectives being two sub-classes of the latter category. However, the term ClassAs is used in this paper in a broader sense than relational (or denominal) As proper. Specifically, we use the term to encompass all As that stand in a particular *semantic relation* with the head noun, irrespective of their morphological nature. In doing so, we follow the tradition by Willim (2000b), who gives both relational and non-derived adjectives as examples of ClassAs; or/and by Szymańska (2000), who writes that ClassAs include "various semantic types of adjectives providing that they serve for distinguishing classes of objects" (ibid., 184).[1]

Following our previous analysis of ClassAs (CP&T, to appear), which is grounded in the semantic theory by Denis Bouchard (1998, 2002 and later works), ClassAs are taken to modify a bare N predicate (or a non-atomized N), forming with the latter, what we called, a "tight unit"—a complex nominal predicate defining a single set of individuals by the two properties simultaneously, those of N and A. Such adjectives, thus, participate in establishing the extensity of N and stand in a whole-to-whole relation with it (see Bouchard 2002, 170-175, CP&T, in press, p.9, Trugman, this volume). A tight semantic link between ClassAs and the head noun is also mentioned in Willim (2000b, 157); and the ability of an

[1] The term 'ClassAs' used here is somewhat similar to 'associative adjectives', such as *feline behavior, dental decay*, discussed in Giegerich (2005, 579) for English, which "may express an argument-predicate structure inherited from a predicate contained in the noun; or they may express the less structured relationship of 'associated with', 'to do with' (which is then often augmented by encyclopedic knowledge on the speaker's part)". As mentioned in fn. 4, the property of associativeness is encoded in the adjective's lexical semantics and does not presuppose the existence of a semantically related noun (e.g., *foreign policy, arable farmer*).

adjective to establish such a semantic link with N serves as a criterion for labeling it a ClassA. See section 3.1 for more details.

In contrast, some other approaches to adjectival modification propose a uniform analysis of adjective classes based on the A position within the nominal projection. For instance, classificatory interpretation is claimed to be linked to a unique postnominal (post-N) position within Polish NPs in Rutkowski and Progovac (2005) (R&P henceforth), Rutkowski (2007, 2009). In this approach, any A can acquire either classificatory or qualifying interpretation depending on its place of merge within the nominal projection. The postnominal position of ClassAs is achieved after N moves out of NP to the higher Classificatory projection.[2] This approach yields a very strong empirical prediction that any element merged as a non-iterative Spec, NP (which is claimed to be the locus of merge of ClassAs) will get a classificatory interpretation, and a qualifying interpretation otherwise.

We have shown in our previous work (CP&T, in press) that this syntactic approach to ClassAs suffers from several empirical and conceptual problems. For instance, As occupying a prenominal (pre-N) position may and sometimes must be interpreted as ClassAs; and more than one ClassAs can be hosted by the same NP, yielding N-ClassA-ClassA or ClassA-N-ClassA strings. In the present paper we explore additional conditions that might force ClassAs to migrate to a pre-N locus. Specifically, we examine the mutual distribution of ClassAs and various Genitive satellites[3] (GenPs) within the nominal projection and propose a mechanism accounting for the resolution of their competition for post-N placement.[4]

---

[2] This movement is open for parametrization across languages—while in Polish it is claimed to be overt, in Serbian it is taken to be covert. If one considers Romance languages, where some types of ClassAs appear post-N, while others—pre-N, one is forced to further assume the optionality of overt N-to-Class movement. This claim seems rather stipulative since there is no well defined trigger for N movement besides a need to derive the postnominal position of ClassAs. Additionally, it is invalided empirically by Polish ClassAs that often alternate between pre-N and post-N position (see examples in (2) and (3)).

[3] The term "genitive satellite" is used here as an umbrella term to cover all kinds of Genitive NPs accompanying all kinds of nominal heads.

[4] An anonymous reviewer mentions that the syntactic model by R&P (2005) can account for the pre-N position of ClassAs in case a GenP is present in the nominal: it is the GenP that is merged in Spec, NP in such cases and surfaces post-N after N^0-to-$Class^0$ movement. Yet, this treatment of ClassA-N-GenP strings presents a grossly oversimplified picture, since it (i) allows for ClassA merge outside the NP, which *a priori* excludes its classifying interpretation in R&P model; (ii) assumes

Examples in (1) and (2) exemplify respectively multiple post-N ClassAs, and lone migrating ClassAs, appearing either in pre-N or post-N position, which invalidate the claims put forth in R&P (2005) and Rutkowski (2007) that only one ClassA is allowed per NP, and that it must be post-N[5]:

(1) *multiple postnominal ClassAs* (cited after CP&T, in press, (8))

a. drukarka atramentowa kolorowa
   printer *ink-jet*$_{ADJ}$ *color*$_{ADJ}$
   "a color ink-jet printer"

b. msza święta żałobna
   mass *holy* *memorial*
   "a memorial holy mass"

(2) *lone migrating ClassAs*[6] (cited after CP&T, in press, (43))

a.	nocny	dyżur	b.	naftowa	lampa
	night$_{ADJ}$	*duty*		*oil*$_{ADJ}$	*lamp*
a'.	dyżur	nocny	b'.	lampa	naftowa
	duty	*night*$_{ADJ}$		*lamp*	*oil*$_{ADJ}$

GenP merge in Spec, NP irrespective of the semantic and syntactic nature of such satellites; and (iii) leads to a false claim that all post-N GenPs are found in a similar semantic and syntactic relationship with N, which is invalidated by a classification of GenPs proposed in this paper.

[5] Noun phrases with two postnominal classificatory adjectives have been judged by an anonymous reviewer as only marginally acceptable, and "limited to a very unnatural genre of product labeling". A similar view is expressed in Linde-Usiekniewicz (2010). We judge N-ClassA-ClassA phrases to be acceptable in a broader range of contexts. Our judgments have been confirmed by the results of a questionnaire study conducted with native speakers—the majority have found such phrases acceptable. For instance, out of 42 Polish undergraduates who completed a written questionnaire, the phrase *mundur policyjny galowy* 'uniform police$_{ADJ}$ parade$_{ADJ}$' was recognized as fully acceptable by 17 informants, and as acceptable, though not perfect, by 12 speakers.

[6] According to the anonymous reviewer, the adjective *naftowa* is acceptable prenominally in (2b) *naftowa lampa* only when it refers to a non-defining feature of the lamp. This does not seem to be a correct observation, however, since it is difficult to interpret the adjective in question as denoting an accidental property of the lamp in the phrase *piękna naftowa lampa* 'a beautiful oil lamp' (taken from an ad). See also Willim (2000b, 2001), where no difference is observed between the interpretation of *lampa naftowa* and *naftowa lampa*.

While some ClassAs seem to freely alternate between pre-N and post-N position in the absence of any other dependents of N, as in (2), yielding stylistic distinctions only (cf. Willim 2000a, 2000b, 2001; Buttler, Kurkowska and Satkiewicz 1973, 392, 395), ClassA migration may also be attested when N hosts two or more ClassAs, as in (3):[7]

(3) *ClassA migration in the presence of another ClassA*
(cited after CP&T, in press, (12))
a. pasażerskie przewozy lotnicze[8]
passenger$_{ADJ}$ transport aerial
a'. lotnicze przewozy pasażerskie
aerial transport passenger$_{ADJ}$
"passenger air transportation/ air passenger transportation"

ClassA migration is also found when N hosts a Genitive satellite in addition to a ClassA, as illustrated in (4):

(4) a. neolityczne narzędzie pracy
Neolithic$_{ADJ}$ tool work$_{GENP}$
"a Neolithic work tool"
b. galowy mundur policjanta
parade$_{ADJ}$ uniform policeman$_{GENP}$
"a/the policeman's parade uniform"
c. molekularna struktura wody
molecular$_{ADJ}$ structure water$_{GENP}$
"the molecular structure of water"

It appears that Polish Ns hosting multiple satellites have to resolve the competition between the latter. In the present paper we investigate mechanisms involved in conflict resolution and its outcome in various nominal types. Before explicating the analysis we want to mention a number of syntactic environments that are excluded from the present discussion:

---

[7] This "more balanced" word order is often preferred to multiple post-N strings by both speakers of the language and traditional grammarians (see Gębka-Wolak 2000 for more discussion).

[8] Since *przewozy* is a deverbal result nominal, its modifier *pasażerskie* may be analyzed in some frameworks as a thematic adjective, rather than a classifying one (Bosque and Picallo 1996, Linde-Usiekniewicz 2010). Yet, as mentioned in the introduction, we treat such modifiers as ClassAs as well due to the similarity of the semantic link they establish with the head noun.

(5) *Environments excluded from discussion*

✓ strings of post-N satellites created by contrastive focal stress, with the contrast to be either explicitly mentioned or implied:

a. Giełda papierów wartościowych *warszawska* osiąga obecnie lepsze wyniki niż giełda papierów wartościowych *nowojorska*.
"Warsaw Stock Exchange shows better results these days than that in New York."

✓ strings of post-N satellites in which the final one can be analyzed as a reduced relative clause (either restrictive or appositive), even though the adjective might be classificatory:

b. Matka bliźniaków, *chora*, została zabrana do szpitala.
"Mother of the twins, (who was) ill, was taken to hospital."
(modified from Buttler et al. 1973, 393)

✓ instances of poetic speech or of any other stylistically marked register of the language:

c. Chleba *naszego powszedniego* daj nam dzisiaj.
$bread_{GEN}$ our_{GEN} $daily_{GEN}$ $give_{IMP}$ us_{DAT} *today*
"Give us today our daily bread."

Following these limitations, all examples that can be felicitous under the conditions in (5), yet ungrammatical otherwise, are marked with an asterisk. The data in the paper come from the Internet and were also checked with native speaker informants. For the latter purpose, a questionnaire has been used to test the acceptability of seventeen Polish noun phrases exhibiting various modification patterns— involving (i) a replacement of a GenP by a Classificatory Adjective and (ii) changes in word order, such as *mundur galowy policjanta* (lit. uniform $parade_{ADJ}$ $policeman_{GEN}$), *mundur policjanta galowy* (lit. uniform $policeman_{GEN}$ $parade_{ADJ}$) , *mundur policyjny galowy* (lit. uniform $policeman_{ADJ}$ $parade_{ADJ}$), *mundur galowy policyjny* (lit. uniform $parade_{ADJ}$ $policeman_{ADJ}$) "a policeman's parade uniform". This amounted to 53 test items. Native speakers of Polish were asked to assess the acceptability of those test items, using a 5-point scale, ranging from * (absolutely wrong) to √ (fully acceptable). Five informants were interviewed orally and provided comments on their judgments. Further 42 informants filled in the written questionnaire. The judgments given in the present paper are based on the results of our questionnaire, as well as on our native speaker judgments[9].

2. Word order patterns

Mutual distribution of ClassAs and GenPs involves two major word order patterns, with several additional patterns being attested with a limited number of lexical items, as discussed in section 4:

(6) *Pattern A:*	a.	ClassA-N-GenP	*Pattern B:*	a.	ClassA-N-GenP
	b.	**N-ClassA-GenP*		b.	*N-ClassA-GenP*
	c.	*N-GenP-ClassA		c.	*N-GenP-ClassA

Both patterns readily allow for the so-called "balanced" word order in (a), while excluding the word order in (c) in stylistically and pragmatically neutral contexts. The crucial distinction between the two patterns lies in the word order in (b): Namely, in Pattern B, a ClassA can intervene between N and its Genitive satellite, whereas in Pattern A it is ruled out.

The two patterns seem to be sensitive to the type of the noun heading the nominal phrase. We follow Rozwadowska's (1997, 68) classification of Polish nominal types and distinguish between *plain nouns* (*stół* "table", *mistrz* "champion"), *simple event nominals* (*pożar* "fire"), *derived result nominals* (*prezentacje* "presentations"), *derived event/ process nominals* (*zakupy* "shopping"), and *verbal nouns* (*zaprezentowanie* "presentation" and *prezentowanie* "presenting"). In our discussion we ignore simple event and verbal nouns. In addition, we recognize the ambiguity of some derived Polish nominals that have both non-process and process counterparts, such as *interpretacja* "interpretation", *ocena* "grade, mark", *spotkanie* "meeting", *zakup* "a buy", *zakupy* "shopping", etc. Pattern A is illustrated in (7) and (8), while Pattern B—in (9-11):

---

[9] The results of our questionnaire study differ from the results of the study carried out by Paweł Rutkowski and reported in his 2009 talk at the SLS-4 meeting in Zadar. As observed by the reviewer, most informants in Rutkowski's study found the N-ClassA-ClassA order to be far more infelicitous than ClassA-N-ClassA strings. We believe the results differ due to the wrongly constructed context in which multiple post-N ClassAs were used in Rutkowski (2009). Specifically, the sentence *Let's talk about N-ClassA-ClassA!* used by Rutkowski to check the test items is typical of a colloquial register and is not an appropriate context for N-ClassA-ClassA phrases that tend to appear in a more formal register of the language (mostly in its written mode).

Pattern A:

(7) *plain NPs*

a.	żużlowy	mistrz	Europy
	speedway$_{ADJ}$	*champion*	*Europe*$_{GENP}$
b.	*mistrz	żużlowy	Europy
c.	*mistrz	Europy	żużlowy

"a/the European speedway champion"

(8) *result NPs*

a.	coroczne	transmisje	Polskiego	Radia
	every-year$_{ADJ}$	*broadcasts*	*Polish*$_{GEN}$	*Radio*$_{GEN}$
b.	*transmisje	coroczne	Polskiego	Radia
c.	*transmisje	Polskiego Radia	coroczne	

"annual Polish Radio broadcasts"

Pattern B:

(9) *plain NPs*

a.	galowy	mundur	(policjanta/	kadeta/	strażaka)
	parade$_{ADJ}$	*uniform*	*policeman*$_{GENP}$/	*cadet*$_{GENP}$/	*firefighter*$_{GENP}$
b.	mundur	galowy	policjanta/	kadeta/	strażaka
c.	*mundur	policjanta	galowy[10]		

"a policeman's/ cadet's/ firefighter's parade uniform"

(10) *result NPs*

a.	fizyczna	aktywność	(nastolatków)
	physical$_{ADJ}$	*activity*	*teenagers*$_{GENP}$
b.	aktywność	fizyczna	nastolatków
c.	*aktywność	nastolatków	fizyczna

"teenagers' physical activity/teenage physical activity"

(11) *event/process NPs*

a.	hurtowa	sprzedaż	*(gazu)	(przez firmę Statoil)
	wholesale$_{ADJ}$	*trade*	*gas*$_{GENP}$	*(by firm Statoil)*
b.	sprzedaż	hurtowa	gazu	(przez firmę Statoil)
c.	*sprzedaż	gazu	hurtowa	(przez firmę Statoil)

"wholesale trade of gas by the Statoil company"

---

[10] In our questionnaire study, the word order N-GenP-ClassA in (9c) *mundur policjanta galowy* was judged as 'absolutely wrong' (*) by 20 informants; as 'varying from ungrammatical to marginal' (*??) by 10 informants; as 'marginal' (??) by 3 informants; and as 'acceptable yet not perfect, slightly deviant' (?) by 8 native speakers. Only 1 informant deemed it fully acceptable.

3. Accounting for the word order patterns

3.1 Common word orders for both patterns

As examples (7-11) show, (a)-orders are grammatical while (c)-orders are ungrammatical in both patterns. The major difference between the two patterns lies in the (b)-order.

As mentioned above, native speakers seem to prefer the (a)-order, with both the ClassA and the GenP found adjacent to N. This distribution of satellites of N has been accounted for in traditional grammars as an attempt to get a more symmetrical NP (see Gębka-Wolak 2000, 135, who refers to such a phenomenon as a balance between the string on the left and right side of the head—"równowaga długości ciągu lewo- i prawostronnego"). Noun phrases which conform to this principle are claimed to sound more natural than those which violate it. Note that NPs with pre-N ClassAs, as in the (a)-order in both patterns, would fail to get classifying interpretation in the model proposed by Rutkowski and R&P (ibid.) for they would be merged outside the NP boundaries, with the Spec, NP being taken by the genitive satellite.

CP&T's (in press) proposal, based on the representational theory by Bouchard (2002), accounted for pre-N instances of ClassAs by taking them to modify atomized N+Num combinations, in contrast to post-N ClassAs that modify non-atomized, bare Ns and form with the latter complex nominal predicates denoting individuals by a set of properties assigned by both N and ClassA. We called such N-ClassA combinations "tight units" and claimed that semantic Number is interpreted on such N-ClassA units bearing morphological number as a whole. In other words, the interpretive system simultaneously interprets the number morphemes and the N-ClassA "tight unit", in a fashion similar to the interpretation of complex lexemes, such as compounds. While we do not claim here that N-ClassA "tight units" are lexical compounds, it is not inconceivable that some might originate in the lexicon while others in the syntax on a par with "associative AdjNs" constructions in English (see Giegerich 2005).[11]

---

[11] Relational adjectives, being denominal, are often analyzed as parallel to attributive nouns in N-N compounds (see Babby 1975 for Russian, Spencer 1998, Giegerich 2005 and references cited there for English). Spencer (ibid.) writes, "To call something an *atomic bomb* is to claim some relationship between the property of being that bomb and the property of being an atom, rather than attributing "atomicity" to *bomb*. But this is exactly the pragmatically determined relation ρ used to define the constructional meaning of compounds." The relational adjective is, thus, taken to be derived from N at the level of argument-structure and is

Migrating pre-N ClassAs, on the other hand, combine with atomized Ns.[12] In other words, they actually combine with complexes of N and semantic Number (i.e. N+Num), for Number is taken to be the minimal means of atomization of actants, or arguments, in any language. Therefore, when an atomized N is modified by a bare adjective, the latter establishes a whole-to-whole semantic relationship with N+Num in post-N position, in accordance with the Linearization Parameter. This relation yields a predicative adjective modifying the N. In order to establish the whole-to-whole relation between the adjective and N alone, the former has to appear in pre-N position by the Elsewhere application of the Linearization Parameter.[13] Consequently, both post-N and pre-N ClassAs may establish a semantically similar relation with N, with the only difference: no "tight unit" formation is attested in cases of pre-N modification, hence less scientific flavor of pre-N ClassAs ensues. In principle, CP&T's model accounts for the (a)–order in both patterns without any additional adjustments.

Now let us consider the ungrammaticality of the (c)-order in both patterns. At first glance, it seems to stem from GenP intervening between N and ClassA (irrespective of GenP's precise semantic or syntactic status). This also follows straightforwardly from our proposal—no "tight unit" formation with ClassA is possible after N has been modified or saturated by GenP. Even though GenP can hold distinct relationships with N (as we discuss in the following section), this head-dependent relation always

---

interpreted in the same way as the attributive noun in a compound. The meaning of *atomic bomb* is essentially the same as that of *atom bomb*. Our mechanism of "tight unit" formation assumes a complex property of being a bomb and related to an atom at the same time, which later gets atomized as one whole.

[12] One should not confuse ClassAs that may appear pre-N with or without another ClassA being present in post-N position, as in (2)&(3), with those that *must* appear pre-N in various real lexical idioms, such as *lwia paszcz*, lit.: lion_{ADJ} jaw, "a snapdragon" or *boża krówka*, lit.: God_{ADJ} cow_{DIM},"a ladybird". In such phrases a ClassA combines with a non-atomized N in a *whole-to-part* fashion modifying the characteristic function of the nominal predicate. Consequently, the adjective appears in pre-N position in accordance with the Elsewhere Condition of the Linearization Parameter (see CP&T, in press, section 5.1).

[13] We take the Linearization Parameter to be set in Polish so that the Head precedes its Dependents, with Dependents being indistinguishable between arguments and modifiers (see Bouchard 2002, 64-8 for the discussion of the Linearization Parameter and its arbitrary setting in each language).

precludes "tight unit" formation with the following ClassA,[14] even though reiteration of GenPs in one nominal is not ruled out, as shown in (12):

(12)	a.	narzędzie	pracy	naszego	menadżera
		tool	*work*$_{GENP}$	*our*$_{GEN}$	*manager*$_{GEN}$
		"our manager's work tool"			
	b.	narzędzie	pracy	każdego	rządu
		tool	*work*$_{GENP}$	*every*$_{GEN}$	*government*$_{GEN}$
		"every government's work tool"			
	c.	skuteczne	narzędzie	pracy	przedsiębiorcy
		effective	*tool*	*work*$_{GENP}$	*businessman*$_{GENP}$
		"a businessman's effective work tool/ an effective businessman's work tool"			

The claim that it is the presence of an intervening GenP that interferes with "tight unit" formation is further supported by examples in (13): when ClassA is separated from N by two GenPs, ungrammaticality increases dramatically:[15]

(13)	a.	*narzędzie	pracy	podstawowe	
	a'.	**narzędzie	pracy	spekulanta	podstawowe
		tool	*work*$_{GENP}$	*speculator*$_{GENP}$	*basic*
		"a basic work tool of a speculator"			

[14] As mentioned in the introduction, some pragmatic conditions can override this restriction and a non-adjacent ClassA becomes felicitous, as happens, for instance, under the contrastive focus in (5a). We take this possibility to be limited to intervening GenPs that are *Typing Attributes* (see section 3.2.4.). Such TypeGens are claimed to form compound-like units in Russian (Trugman 2004a/b) hence they form with the N complex predicates akin to "tight units" in Polish N-ClassA constructions. Both "tight unit" formation and Genitive modification are iterative operations (see (3) and (12)), since both create a new nominal predicate without saturating/atomizing the noun. We propose that focal stress facilitates iterative complex predicate formation with *morphosyntactically heterogeneous* (TypeGen vs. ClassA) yet *semantically homogeneous* (both are Typing Attributes) satellites of N, yielding the N-GenP-ClassA word order. Thus, under contrastive focal stress the examples in (13a&b) with two Typing Attributes would be acceptable.

[15] The examples in (13a&b) are less serious violations not only due to the number of intervening GenPs, but also due to the semantic nature of the intervening phrase. We discuss violations of semantic hierarchy below in section 3.2.4.

b. *krzywe Béziera wielomianowe
b'. **krzywe Béziera trzeciego stopnia wielomianowe
curves *Bézier*$_{GENP}$ *third*$_{GEN}$ *degree*$_{GEN}$ *polynomial*
"polynomial cubic Bézier curves"

3.2 Identifying the triggers of distinction

Now we are left with the crucial distinction between Patterns A and B: the (b)-word order, repeated in (14):

(14) Pattern A: b. *N-ClassA-GenP
Pattern B: b. N-ClassA-GenP

Why does Pattern A rule it out, while Pattern B rules it in? Note that the ClassA occupies the prescribed post-N position, and must be grammatical in both patterns according to the ClassP model proposed in Rutkowski and R&P (ibid.). If, as an anonymous reviewer suggests, in such cases as (14) the GenP occupies the Spec, NP and hence blocks the ClassA from being merged there, we encounter another conundrum: what mechanism then allows for both a ClassA and a GenP in Pattern B, while excluding this in Pattern A? And what is the locus of ClassA merge in both cases? Once again we witness the inadequacy of the model allotting a unique fixed position to either a ClassA or a GenP. In reality, the picture appears to be much more complex and varied.
Consider examples in (15), which involve the *ungrammatical* (b)-order—*N-ClassA-GenP—exhibited by Pattern A:

(15) *Pattern A: *N-ClassA-GenP*
a. *narzędzie neolityczne pracy
tool *Neolithic*$_{ADJ}$ *work*$_{GENP}$
"a Neolithic (work) tool"
b. *mistrz żużlowy Europy
champion *speedway*$_{ADJ}$ *Europe*$_{GENP}$
"a/the European speedway champion"
c. *giełda warszawska antyków
exchange *Warsaw*$_{ADJ}$ *antiques*$_{GENP}$
"Warsaw Antique Market"

Pattern A requires obligatory adjacency between N and its GenP, which resembles the obligatory adjacency between N and the ClassA required in both patterns in the (c)-order. In other words, in Pattern A, the GenPs in

(15) seem to fail to establish a proper semantic relation with N across an intervening ClassA, just as a ClassA cannot establish a proper semantic relation with N across an intervening GenP in the (c)-order in both patterns. This stands in a sharp contrast with the *grammatical* (b)-order of Pattern B illustrated in (16):

(16) *Pattern B: N-ClassA-GenP*

a.	mundur	galowy	(policjanta)
	uniform	*parade*$_{ADJ}$	*policeman*$_{GENP}$
b.	gospodarstwo	domowe	(Polaka)
	estate	*house*$_{ADJ}$	*Pole*$_{GENP}$
c.	struktura	molekularna	(wody)
	structure	*molecular*$_{ADJ}$	*water*$_{GENP}$
d.	aktywność	fizyczna	(nastolatków)
	activity	*physical*$_{ADJ}$	*teenagers*$_{GENP}$
e.	badania	podstawowe	(krwi)
	analyses	*rudimentary*$_{ADJ}$	*blood*$_{GENP}$

Pattern B seems to freely allow for the lack of adjacency between N and its optional GenP satellite. What is at work here?

We propose to account for this distinction by adopting for Polish a finer classification of Genitive satellites put forth in Trugman (2004a/b) for Russian. Trugman (ibid.) claims that some GenPs in Russian do not function as individual-denoting complements/arguments of the head noun, but rather serve as property-denoting attributes of N (cf. Kolliakou's (1999) proposal for French and Greek). She refers to such Genitive satellites as Type Genitives (TypeGens for short) and supports her claim with a series of semantic and syntactic tests.[16]

Following Trugman's analysis, we claim that some GenPs in Polish are also *property-denoting* and are better analyzed as TypeGens.[17] It can be

[16] Cf. *types* of individuals vs. their specific *tokens* discussed in Vergnaud & Zubizarreta (1992), Givón (2001), as well as in Halmøy (2010).

[17] TypeGens can be associated with various semantic and/or thematic roles. We distinguish between (i) TypeGens that function as plain attributes naming the type of N, without any thematic relation between N and TypeGen implied, as in *mistrz Europy* "a champion of Europe"; (ii) TypeGens that are associated with the external argument of non-eventive N, such as creators, agents, and possessors, as in *mundur policjanta* "a policeman's uniform"; and (iii) TypeGens associated with the internal argument of eventive Ns or with the complement of result Ns (both presumably related to the theme), as in *wyprzedaże końcówek serii* "odds-and-ends

easily demonstrated that such GenPs in Polish possess a set of similar properties with TypeGens in Russian, which supports their predicative nature. For space limitations we cannot discuss all the tests in detail. The reader is referred to Trugman (ibid.) for discussion. The following section briefly demonstrates that, when applied to Polish, these tests yield similar results.

3.2.1 Tests for Polish Type Genitives being property-denoting

Trugman (2004a) analyzes Russian TypeGens as predicative, or property-denoting NPs. In our present terminology (adopted from Bouchard 2002) it amounts to saying that they are non-atomized dependents of NPs. Some Polish GenPs, as in (15), appear to exhibit similar properties to Russian TypeGens. The following tests, cited after Trugman (2004a), demonstrate their predicative nature.

A. TypeGens can co-occur in one NP with atomized satellites of N, such as the referential possessors *jego* "his" in (17b) and *naszego menadżera* "our manager$_{GENP}$" in (12a), and are always found closer to N than atomized satellites:

(17) a. Przyjechał on w towarzystwie swojego ojca ubranego
came he in company his father$_{GEN}$ dressed
w galowy mundur oficera marynarki.
in parade$_{ADJ}$ uniform officer$_{GEN}$ Navy$_{GEN}$
"He came accompanied by his father dressed in a parade uniform of a Navy officer."

b. jego galowy mundur oficera marynarki
his parade$_{ADJ}$ uniform officer$_{GEN}$ Navy$_{GEN}$
"his parade uniform of a Navy officer"

B. Animate TypeGens do not possessivize (18a) or relativize (18b) and form questions with *jaki* "what kind" question words rather than *czyj* "whose" (18c). The possessive pronoun *jego* "his" in (18a) and the relative pronoun *którego* "whose" in (18b) are not ungrammatical as indicated by #, but rather get a reading different from that denoted by the TypeGen

sales". In addition, we recognize that various sub-classes of TypeGens are mutually hierarchically ordered, with plain modifiers and themes being lower than the possessor/agent TypeGen. See Trugman (2004b) for arguments in favor of these ordering relations.

oficera marynarki—they can only refer to another person who is the possessor of the uniform, not to the type of uniform:

(18) a. Piotr kupił galowy mundur oficera marynarki, i Paweł także kupił #jego galowy mundur/ taki galowy mundur/ galowy mundur tego typu.
"Peter bought a parade uniform of a Navy officer, and Paul also bought #his parade uniform / such a parade uniform/ a parade uniform of this type."
b. #Nie lubię policjanta, którego mundur galowy kupił Piotr.
"I don't like the policeman whose parade uniform was bought by Peter."
c. Piotr kupił galowy mundur policjanta/ strażaka.
"Peter bought a parade uniform of a policeman/ firefighter."
Jaki /#Czyj mundur galowy kupił Piotr?
what kind/ whose uniform parade bought Peter
"What kind of /whose parade uniform did Peter buy?"

C. TypeGens do not permit either backward or forward pronominalization (19a&b) or possessivization by an individual variable pronoun (19c&d). The *property* anaphora, on the other hand, is possible, as shown in (19d):

(19) a. *backward pronominalization*
*Ponieważ *on*$_i$ ma brudną pracę, fartuch *rzeźnika*$_i$ wykonany jest z nieprzemakalnego materiału.
"*Since he$_i$ has a dirty work, a butcher's$_i$ apron is made of waterproof material."
b. *forward pronominalization*
*Ojciec przyszedł ubrany w galowy mundur *oficera*$_i$ *marynarki*, ponieważ *on*$_i$ / *ten*$_i$ pozwolił mu go założyć dziś wieczorem.
"*Father came dressed in a parade uniform of a Navy officer$_i$, because he$_i$ /that one$_i$ allowed him to put it on for this evening."
c. *backward possessivization*
*Ponieważ *jego*$_i$ praca jest brudna, fartuch *rzeźnika*$_i$ wykonany jest z nieprzemakalnego materiału.
"*Since his$_i$ work is dirty, a butcher's$_i$ apron is made of waterproof material."
d. *forward possessivization*
Ojciec przyszedł ubrany w galowy mundur *oficera*$_i$ *marynarki*$_i$, ponieważ *taki* mundur galowy / **jego*$_i$ mundur galowy sprawił że ojciec wyglądał bardziej dystyngowanie.

"Father came dressed in a parade uniform of a Navy officer because such a parade uniform/*his parade uniform made father look more dignified."

D. TypeGens fail to participate in "possessor ascension" constructions. Possessor ascension can be defined as a process in which an NP-internal possessor rises to occupy an argument role in the clause (see Chappell and McGregor 1996, 6-7). It turns out that atomized/individual-denoting Genitive possessors can be substituted for the dative object, (20a&a'), while TypeGens denoting possessors fail to do so, as in (20b&b'):

(20) a. Piotr przekreślił rysunek **Marka.**
Peter crossed-out $drawing_{ACC}$ $Marek_{GENP}$
"Peter crossed out Mark's drawing."
a'. Piotr przekreślił **Markowi** rysunek.
Peter crossed-out $Marek_{DAT}$ *drawing*

b. Piotr przekreślił krzywą **Béziera.**
Peter crossed-out $curve_{ACC}$ *Bézier*$_{GENP}$
"Peter crossed out a Bézier's curve."
b'. *Piotr przekreślił **Bézierowi** krzywą.
Peter crossed-out *Bézier*$_{DAT}$ *curve*

E. Russian TypeGens are grammatical with a group of inherently predicative *evaluating nouns*, such as *molodec* "a good guy", *balbes* "dummy", *negodjaj* "scoundrel", *mošennik* "swindler", etc. (see Padučeva 1985/2002, 103). Such nouns allow for argumental use only with an accompanying overt determiner, such as an indefinite pronoun or a demonstrative. Used with the definite determiner they function as anaphoric epithets (see Dubinsky and Hamilton 1998 and references cited therein for the discussion of English anaphoric epithets). When used as bare Genitive satellites of Ns, they function as property-denoting predicates, i.e. TypeGens. In Polish, GenPs expressed by such nouns also function as TypeGens, as shown in (21a&b). In the presence of an overt determiner they acquire an individual-denoting/ atomized reading, similar to their Russian counterparts, which yields ungrammaticality in (21a'&b'):

(21) a. On ma duszę łajdaka
he has $soul_{ACC}$ $scoundrel_{GENP}$
"He has a scoundrel's soul."

a'. *On ma duszę tego łajdaka.
he has soul$_{ACC}$ this$_{GEN}$ scoundrel$_{GEN}$
"He has this scoundrel's soul."

b. Jego życie hulaki skończyło się pewnego dnia.
his life reveller$_{GENP}$ ended REFL *one day*
"His life as a playboy ended one day."

b'. *Jego życie jakiegoś hulaki skończyło się pewnego dnia
his life some$_{GEN}$ reveller$_{GEN}$ ended REFL *one day*
"His life as some playboy ended one day."

3.2.2 Semantic hierarchy of multiple modifiers

The tests above point to the conclusion that some Genitive NPs in Polish may function as TypeGens. Trugman (2004a/b) analyzes Russian TypeGens as forming a complex noun head with the head noun: $[_N N+N_{GEN}]$. This incorporation process is made possible by the bare NP status of TypeGens and enables the latter to be Case-marked by N by default: N being an inherent case licenser discharges its Genitive Case onto the TypeGen, which becomes structurally indistinct from the complement of N.[18] Extending Trugman's analysis of TypeGens to Polish yields the following prediction: TypeGens combine with Ns in a compound-like structure, not unlike "tight units" that Ns form with ClassAs. Thus, we assume that the relationship between N and its dependents in N-ClassA and N-TypeGen structures is semantically similar, with both requiring obligatory adjacency between the head and its dependent.[19] Interestingly, just as ClassAs can reiterate within one NP (see (1a-b)) so can property-denoting Genitive satellites, such as TypeGens and Genitive modifiers called Third Term Genitives.[20] Multiple instances of

---

[18] A similar mechanism of Case-licensing by N to its athematic complement was proposed in Engelhardt (1998) for activity nominals in Hebrew: in such nominals the absence of D forces N to license Genitive on its complement which is actually an argument of the embedded V head.

[19] The notion of adjacency should not be understood as a simple juxtaposition between the head and its dependent. We assume that the adjacency requirement is also satisfied in cases of iterative ClassAs or GenPs, since they involve multiple instances of complex predicate formation with each subsequent modifier being adjacent to the preceding complex predicate and forming another complex predicate with it.

[20] The name Third Term Genitive in Trugman (2004a/b) is borrowed from Borschev and Knorina (1990), who proposed it for genitive modifiers that host an obligatory parameter word, which they call "a third term", such as *stopnia* "order" in (22).

Genitive property-denoting dependents in Polish are demonstrated in (22). In (22a), a TypeGen co-occurs with a Third Term Genitive, whereas in (22b), a TypeGen is followed by another TypeGen denoting a possessor:

(22) a. *wielomianowe* krzywe Béziera trzeciego stopnia
polynomial *curve* *Bézier*$_{GENP}$ *third*$_{GEN}$ *degree*$_{GEN}$
"polynomial cubic Bézier curve"
b. *skuteczne* narzędzie pracy przedsiębiorcy
effective *tool* *work*$_{GENP}$ *businessman*$_{GENP}$
"an effective businessman's work tool"

CP&T (in press) show that the mutual order of multiple ClassAs in one NP is semantically governed, (23a&b):

(23) *multiple ClassAs* (from CP&T, in press, (35c&d))
a. *msza żałobna święta
mass *memorial* *holy*
"a memorial holy mass"
b. *ustawa skarbowa karna
regulations *fiscal* *criminal*
"fiscal criminal regulations"

Likewise, Trugman (2004a/b) argues for tight ordering restrictions on multiple GenPs in Russian, derived from their distinct loci of merge: TypeGenP—3TermGenP—Possessor GenP.[21] Polish GenPs obey the hierarchy as well, as shown in (24a&b)—when it is violated the NP is ruled out:

(24) *multiple GenPs*
a. *krzywa trzeciego stopnia Béziera
curve *third*$_{GEN}$ *order*$_{GEN}$ *Bézier*$_{GENP}$
"a third-order Bézier's curve"
b. *narzędzie spekulanta pracy
tool *speculator*$_{GENP}$ *work*$_{GENP}$
"a speculator's work tool"

The hierarchy of modifiers was proposed by many linguists to account for ordering of multiple adjectives, as well as adverbs in Cinque (1999, 106)

[21] Trugman (2004a/b) uses the term "Possessor GenP" for referential GenPs functioning as possessors or external arguments of N.

(e.g., Dixon 1982, Sproat and Shih 1988, Cinque 1994, Androutsopoulou 1996, Giusti 1997, Bouchard 1998, Scott 2002, Pereltsvaig 2007, among many others). The hierarchy in (25) is modified after the universal hierarchy of AP-related Functional Projections (FPs) for non-complex and result nominals proposed in Scott (2002, 114). We use the term "TYPING ATTRIBUTE" instead of his "COMPOUND ELEMENT" (cf. Pereltsvaig 2007), though the latter term is quite consonant with the compounding hypothesis put forth for Russian TypeGens in Trugman (2004a/b) and with the "tight unit" formation proposed for Polish ClassAs in CP&T (in press). Note that the term "TYPING ATTRIBUTE" encompasses all sub-classes of TypeGens (see also fn. 8).

(25) SUBJECTIVE COMMENT>SIZE>SPEED>WEIGHT>TEMPERATURE> WETNESS > AGE> SHAPE>COLOUR>NATIONALITY/ORIGIN> MATERIAL>TYPING ATTRIBUTE>NOUN HEAD

While this hierarchy was suggested for pre-N modifiers of N, with their post-N order being derived by successive N/ NP movement to higher FPs (Cinque 1994, 2009; Scott 2002, Laenzlinger 2005), we propose it holds for direct merge of both pre-N and post-N modifiers of N in Polish in the spirit of Bouchard (1998, 2002). Thus, we take the order of post-N modifiers to be a mirror image of the hierarchy in (25). However, this bidirectional merge of modifiers is not entirely free and several restrictions operate to constrain it.

3.2.3. Restrictions on modifier merge

A. Bidirectionality of modifier merge does not entail a possibility of simultaneously merging two modifiers in pre-N and post-N position that hold identical semantic relation with N. Such structures are generally excluded irrespective of the directionality of adjective merge (cf. (26b') from Spanish):

(26) a.	*futrzarski	przemysł		futer	*Polish*
	fur$_{ADJ}$	*industry*		*fur*$_{GENP}$	
a'.	*pusnoj	promysel		pusniny	*Russian*
	fur$_{ADJ}$	*industry*		*fur*$_{GENP}$	
b.	*molekularna	struktura		molekuł	*Polish*
	molecular	*structure*		*molecules*$_{GENP}$	
b'.	*estructura	molecular	de	moléculas	*Spanish*
	structure	*molecular*	*of*	*molecules*$_{GENP}$	

B. On the other hand, bidirectional merge is possible when synonymous pre-N and post-N satellites can be interpreted as holding *distinct* semantic relations with N. In (27), the GenPs are interpreted as individual-denoting possessors, while the ClassAs get property-denoting, or *type*, interpretation and function as Typing Attributes specifying the type of poles or uniform:

(27) a. narciarskie kijki narciarza
ski$_{ADJ}$ *poles* *skier*$_{GENP}$
"a skier's ski poles"
b. górniczy mundur górnika
miner$_{ADJ}$ *uniform* *miner*$_{GENP}$
"a miner's miner's uniform"

In (28), on the other hand, it is the GenPs which are interpreted as Typing Attributes, while the ClassAs get other interpretations—NATIONALITY in (28a) and SUBJECTIVE COMMENT (a qualifying adjective) in (28b):[22]

(28) a. europejski mistrz Europy
European champion Europe$_{GENP}$
"a/the European champion of Europe"
b. piękna miss piękności
beautiful miss beauty$_{GENP}$
"a/the beautiful Beauty Queen"

Note that in all the cases above the two satellites cannot be interpreted as belonging to the same semantic group. In other words, *europejski* in (28a) cannot be interpreted as the type of champion together with the TypeGen *Europy*. Neither can *narciarza* and *górnika* in (27) be interpreted as TypeGens in the presence of ClassAs Typing Attributes *narciarskie* and *górniczy*. These readings are excluded.

C. In cases of parallel modification, when two non-synonymous modifiers belonging to the same semantic type co-occur in one NP, the former have to form a *compound,* as shown in (29) (cited after CP&T, ibid., (36); cf. R&P 2005), or a *conjoined structure*, as shown in (30). This also indicates that the semantic hierarchy governs the distribution of post-N modifiers.

---

[22] This example in English and in Russian is also interpretable with two classifying adjectives as in *evropejskij evropejskij čempion* "a European European champion", with the first one being necessarily interpreted as the nationality modifier and the noun adjacent one as the Typing Attribute (cf. Cinque 2006).

(29) a. filologia rosyjsko-angielska
philology *Russian*$_{ADJ}$-*English*$_{ADJ}$
b. przemysł owocowo-warzywny
industry *fruit*$_{ADJ}$-*vegetable*$_{ADJ}$

(30) *conjoined ClassAs*
a. filologia rosyjska i angielska
philology *Russian*$_{ADJ}$ *and* *English*$_{ADJ}$
b. przemysł owocowy i warzywny
industry *fruit*$_{ADJ}$ *and* *vegetable*$_{ADJ}$
conjoined GenPs
c. były mistrz świata i Europy
former *champion* *world*$_{GEN}$ *and* *Europe*$_{GEN}$
"the former champion of Europe and the world"
d. Szkoła Biznesu i Języków Obcych
school *business*$_{GEN}$ *and* *languages*$_{GEN}$ *foreign*$_{GEN}$
"the School of Business and Foreign Languages"

In principle nothing should prevent conjoining parallel modifiers even if they are structurally distinct, as shown in (31) from English and Russian: in (31a) a genitive modifier is conjoined with an adjective; while in (31b) a noun hosts a postnominal conjoined phrase consisting of a ClassA and a GenP.

(31) a. a husband of good birth and prosperous *English*
b. car' Moskovskij i vseja Rusi[23] *Russian*
tzar *Moscow*$_{ADJ}$ *and* *all*$_{GEN}$ *Russia*$_{GEN}$
"the Tzar of Moscow and All Russia"

3.2.4 Violations of semantic hierarchy as a source of ungrammaticality

We argued above that GenPs and ClassAs can denote various semantic relations and can reiterate in one projection under certain conditions. Since both GenPs and ClassAs can realize the Typing Attribute, they are predicted to compete for adjacency with N. This competition is elegantly

[23] This Russian example was provided by Gil Rappaport (p.c.). However, such cases are not frequently attested, presumably due to the existence of adjectival or Genitive counterparts for both modifiers, which allows for coordination of structurally similar modifiers.

resolved by a possibility of a symmetrical merge of modifiers on both sides of N, as demonstrated in the (a)-order in both patterns. Whereas the GenP is constrained to the post-N position due to its being marked for Case by N,[24] the ClassA is more mobile since it can establish a proper semantic relation with N in two different ways (see CP&T, in press).

Recall that a striking contrast was found between the (b)-orders in Patterns A and B. While in Pattern A, a noun followed by a ClassA and then by a GenP yields an ungrammatical expression—*N-ClassA-GenP, in Pattern B, the same order is grammatical. This contrast, however, seems to be triggered by the violation of the semantic hierarchy in Pattern A as well. Specifically, in Pattern A, the Genitive satellite is a TypeGen, i.e. a Typing Attribute, which must be adjacent to N; hence an intervening ClassA (of a higher semantic class) leads to ungrammaticality. In Pattern B, on the other hand, it is the ClassA that is a Typing Attribute, while the GenP is higher on the semantic hierarchy. Hence, the reverse word order N-ClassA-GenP is required. Consider again the examples of the (b)-order in (32) and (33) repeated after (15) and (16) respectively:

(32) *Pattern A: *N-ClassA-GenP (Typing Attribute)*

a. *narzędzie neolityczne pracy
   tool Neolithic$_{ADJ}$ work$_{GENP}$
   "a Neolithic (work) tool"

b. *mistrz żużlowy Europy
   champion speedway$_{ADJ}$ Europe$_{GENP}$
   "a/the European speedway champion"

c. *giełda warszawska antyków
   exchange Warsaw$_{ADJ}$ antiques$_{GENP}$
   "Warsaw Antique Market"

(33) *Pattern B: N-ClassA (Typing Attribute)-GenP*

a. mundur galowy (policjanta)
   uniform parade$_{ADJ}$ policeman$_{GENP}$

[24] The marking of N dependents by Case assignment seems to be also contingent on the Central Linearization Parameter in a language, with case-assigned dependents following the head if it is the basic setting of the Linearization Parameter. Thus Genitive NPs in English appear postnominally as other dependents. Genitive possessives, on the other hand, show up prenominally in accord with the Elsewhere application of the parameter since they are found in two relations simultaneously: one "thematic" with N and the other functional with Det. Hence the Genitive possessive does not establish a whole-to-whole relation with N alone and has to appear before N (Bouchard 1998).

b.	gospodarstwo	domowe	(Polaka)
	estate	*house*$_{ADJ}$	*Pole*$_{GENP}$
c.	struktura	molekularna	(wody)
	structure	*molecular*$_{ADJ}$	*water*$_{GENP}$
d.	aktywność	fizyczna	(nastolatków)
	activity	*physical*$_{ADJ}$	*teenagers*$_{GENP}$
e.	badania	podstawowe	(krwi)
	analyses	*rudimentary*$_{ADJ}$	*blood*$_{GENP}$

It appears that in both Patterns all ungrammatical word orders but one can be subsumed under violations of the semantic hierarchy of modifiers.

(34) *Pattern A:*	a.	ClassA-N-GenP$_{TA}$	*Pattern B:* a.	ClassA$_{TA}$-N-GenP
	b.	*N-ClassA-GenP$_{TA}$	b.	N-ClassA$_{TA}$-GenP
	c.	*N-GenP$_{TA}$-ClassA	c.	*N-GenP-ClassA$_{TA}$

In all the word orders in (34) ungrammaticality ensues only when a Typing Attribute (of any syntactic type) is non-adjacent to N, i.e. dislocated from its lowest position in the semantic hierarchy. The only word order that runs counter to this generalization is the one in (c) in Pattern A: c.*N-GenP$_{TA}$-ClassA. Above, we accounted for its ungrammaticality by assuming that the ClassA cannot create a "tight unit" across the Genitive satellite, even though the latter does not saturate N. We take this to be the consequence of the Case-licensing mechanism involved in this structure: N modified by a TypeGen cannot form a complex nominal predicate with the following ClassA. This structure, however, might be saved by contrastive focus intonation, as shown in (34b)-(35b). Hierarchical misplacements, as shown in (34c)-(35c), cannot:

(34) a.	międzynarodowe	*mistrzostwa*	*Australii,*	w	tenisie
	international$_{ADJ}$	*championship*	*Australia*$_{GENP}$	*in*	*tennis*
b.	??mistrzostwa	Australii	MIĘDZYNARODOWE	w	
c.	*mistrzostwa	międzynarodowe	Australii	w	tenisie

"international tennis championship of Australia"

(35) a.	wielomianowe	krzywe	Béziera
	polynomial$_{ADJ}$	*curves*	*Bézier*$_{GENP}$
b.	??krzywe	Béziera	WIELOMIANOWE
c.	*krzywe	wielomianowe	Béziera

"polynomial Bézier's curves"

Note that contrastive focus cannot license the (c)-word order in Pattern B: c.*N-GenP-ClassA$_{TA}$, since any intervening GenP higher on the hierarchy will lead to its violation, as illustrated in (36):

(36)	a.	*mundur	tego	policjanta	galowy
		uniform	*this*$_{GEN}$	*policeman*$_{GEN}$	*parade*$_{ADJ}$
	b.	*gospodarstwo	mojego	sąsiada	domowe
		household	*my*$_{GEN}$	*neighbor*$_{GEN}$	*home*$_{ADJ}$
	c.	*struktura	tego	związku	molekularna
		structure	*this*$_{GEN}$	*compound*$_{GEN}$	*molecular*$_{ADJ}$

4. Other resolutions of multiple modifier clusters

4.1. Avoiding ambiguity

Besides the two patterns discussed above, there exist several other ways of resolving the competition for adjacency with N between two typing attributes expressed by distinct morphosyntactic forms. First, if there is a need for multiple modification of N, and one of the Typing Attributes can be expressed either as ClassA or as TypeGen, an adjectival form will be preferred over a Genitive satellite for the following reasons: (i) to avoid ambiguity of GenP interpretation, as (37a&b), where the referential reading of the GenP prevails; and (ii) to avoid problems with the "tight unit" formation (between N and ClassA) across a GenP, as shown in (37c). In other words, existence of a synonymous ClassA will block using a GenP as a Typing Attribute (cf. (38)) so as to avoid ambiguity and to facilitate establishing proper relations with N.

(37)	a.	#bambusowe	kijki	narciarza[25]
		bamboo$_{ADJ}$	*poles*	*skier*$_{GENP}$
	b.	#kijki	bambusowe	narciarza
	c.	*kijki	narciarza	bambusowe
		"bamboo ski poles"		

[25] The sign # intends to demonstrate the felicitousness of these examples under the possessor reading of the GenP, while signaling their infelicitousness under the Typing Attribute reading of the GenP.

(38) a. bambusowe kijki narciarskie
bamboo$_{ADJ}$ *poles* *ski*$_{ADJ}$
b. kijki narciarskie bambusowe
"bamboo ski poles"

4.2. Substantivization of ClassAs

Another conflict resolution mechanism is attested with obligatorily non-migrating ClassAs. Such ClassAs are excluded in pre-N position since they acquire a qualifying reading there. This is illustrated in (39):

(39) *'non-migrating' ClassAs* (cited after Rutkowski (2007), (4); and R&P (2005), (7), respectively):
a. krzywa linia *qualifying reading*
curved line
"a curved line" (a line that happens to be curved)
a'. linia krzywa *classificatory reading*
line curved
"a curve" (a type of line)
b. komiczny actor *qualifying reading*
comic actor
"a comic actor" (an actor we describe as comic)
b'. aktor komiczny *classificatory reading*
actor comic
"a comedy actor" (a type of actor)

Consequently, such ClassAs cannot migrate to pre-N position and establish a balanced word order when they co-occur with TypeGens, as in (40a). They must appear in post-N position, together with the GenP (40b), and their mutual ordering is also semantically governed (40c). The only correct word order in (40b) is often replaced by another descriptive mechanism that has the same semantic import yet achieves it with a simplified structure. Specifically, some non-migrating ClassAs undergo substantivization, as shown in (40d):

(40) a. *krzywa linia Béziera
b. linia krzywa Béziera
c. *linia Béziera krzywa
d. krzywa Béziera
"Bézier's curve"

Such substantivized adjectives are found both in Polish and Russian, and they seem to be formed from ClassAs or from participles (the latter often acquire a generic reading under substantivization, as discussed in Spencer 2002 for Russian).[26] This phenomenon indirectly supports the "tight unit" formation proposed for post-N ClassAs in CP&T (in press): a tight semantic relationship between N and ClassA allows the complex nominal predicate (i.e. a "tight unit") to fit, by analysis, as a predicate which is morphologically adjectival yet semantically a noun. Some parallel examples of substantivized adjectives in Russian and Polish are given in (41):

(41)	*Polish*	*Russian*	
a.	krzywa	krivaja	"a curve"
b.	prosta	prjamaja	"a line"
c.	zmienna	peremennaja	"a variable"
d.	chory	bolnoj	"a sick person/patient"

4.3. Pragmatics-driven migration of non-migrating ClassAs

As mentioned above, some ClassAs seem to be fixed postnominally, since they acquire a non-classificatory interpretation in pre-N position, as illustrated in (39) and more examples are given in (42):

(42) a. pracowník kulturalny
employee cultural
"an employee in the cultural sector"
a'. kulturalny pracownik
"a well-mannered employee"

b. widowisko historyczne
spectacle historical
"a historical spectacle"

[26] Spencer (2002) distinguishes between 4 different classes of substantivized adjectives (adjectives modifying zero anaphora; adjectives with (apparently) elided head nouns, as in (40) above; surnames; and deadjectival converted nouns that include participles, substantivized adjectives, pronominal adjectives, such as *každyj* "each", *vsjakij* "any, every", *ljuboj* "any", *svoj* "one's own", and the demonstratives *ètot* "this" and *tot* "that"). Excluding the first type, which results from an elliptical structure with an empty nominal head being easily reconstructable, the other three types of substantivized adjectives exhibit nominal properties and constitute an instance of de-phrasal word formation (ibid.).

b'. historyczne widowisko
"historic (i.e. memorable) spectacle"
(cited after Buttler et al. (1973, 395-396)

However, the presence of a GenP in the same noun phrase might force even a non-migrating ClassA to migrate to pre-N position, apparently for the sake of creating a balanced NP, with two modifiers found head-adjacent. This behavior of non-migrating ClassAs, which is quite unexpected and unaccountable in the ClassP model by R&P (2005) and Rutkowski (2007), does not pose problems for the present account: a ClassA can establish a proper semantic relation with N in the pre-N position, and pragmatics, our knowledge of the world, will help to disambiguate between a qualifying and a classificatory reading of the adjective. Multiple examples of such cases, wherein an adjective gets a classificatory reading in the pre-N position, are found on the Internet. Some of them are given in (43a) and (44a):

(43) a. dyplomatyczna służba Watykanu
diplomatic service $\textit{Vatican}_{GENP}$
b. służba dyplomatyczna Watykanu
c. *służba Watykanu dyplomatyczna
"the Vatican's diplomatic service"

(44) a. dramatyczny Teatr imienia Marii Zańkowieckiej
$\textit{drama}_{ADJ}$ *theatre* $\textit{name}_{GEN}$ $\textit{Maria}_{GEN}$ $\textit{Zańkowiecka}_{GEN}$
b. Teatr dramatyczny imienia Marii Zańkowieckiej
c. *Teatr imienia Marii Zańkowieckiej dramatyczny
"the Drama Theatre named after Maria Zańkowiecka"

In (43) the adjective *dyplomatyczna* is found pre-N in the presence of the referential possessor *Watykanu*, and gets a proper classificatory reading there; whereas in (44) the adjective moves to pre-N in the presence of a Third Term Genitive modifier.

We predict that a ClassA will not appear prenominally if it cannot unambiguously acquire a classificatory reading there. In such contexts, it will stay in postposition to indicate its classificatory interpretation, as shown in (45):

(45) a. jego dyplomatyczne zabiegi *qualifying reading*
"his diplomatic (i.e. tactful) steps"

b. jego zabiegi dyplomatyczne *classificatory reading*
"his diplomatic steps"

5. Conclusion

This paper presented a multi-faceted distribution of Classificatory Adjectives and Genitive satellites in Polish nominal phrases and discussed their mutual distribution within one NP. Two major patterns of the distribution were discussed and explained in a fairly parsimonious way. We have shown that the representational account of ClassAs proposed in CP&T (in press) can accommodate both patterns if a finer classification of Polish Genitive satellites is recognized. Following Trugman's (2004a/b) proposal for Russian GenPs, we distinguished between Type Genitives, or property-denoting Genitive modifiers, and individual-denoting Genitive arguments/complements/possessors of N. This classification of GenPs coupled together with a semantic hierarchy of modifiers, whose universal nature has been independently proposed in linguistic literature, accounts for the (un)grammaticality of various word orders in both Patterns. It was shown that ungrammaticality may also stem from the structural distinction between GenPs and ClassAs, when an intervening GenP precludes "tight unit" formation with the subsequent ClassA. Yet, this restriction may be overridden by some pragmatic conditions, such as a contrastive focus. It was demonstrated that pragmatics seems to play an important role in ClassA placement in Polish (cf. Willim 2000b, 2001) and can overrule some grammar conventions in proper contexts.

References

Androutsopoulou, Antonia. 1996. “The licensing of adjectival modification.” In *Proceedings of the Fourteenth West Coast Conference on Formal Linguistics (WCCFL),* edited by Camacho, Jose, Lina Choueiri and Maki Watanabe, 17-32. Stanford, CA: CSLI,

Babby, Leonard, H. 1975. *A transformational grammar of Russian adjectives*. The Hague: Mouton.

Borschev, Vladimir B. and Lidia V. Knorina. 1990. “Tipy realij i ix jazykovoe vosprijatie.” In *Voprosy kibernetiki: Jazyk logiki i logika jazyka*, edited by Vjačeslav Vsevoldovič Ivanov, 106-134. Moskva: Akademija Nauk SSSR.

Bouchard, Denis. 1998. “The distribution and interpretation of adjectives in French: A consequence of Bare Phrase Structure”. *Probus* 10: 139-183.

—. 2002. *Adjectives, number and interfaces: Why languages vary*. Amsterdam, Boston, London: North Holland.

Buttler, Danuta, Halina Kurkowska and Halina Satkiewicz. 1973. *Kultura języka polskiego. Zagadnienia poprawności politycznej*. Warszawa: PWN.

Cetnarowska, Bożena, Agnieszka Pysz and Helen Truman. in press. "Accounting for some flexibility in a rigid construction: On the position of classificatory adjectives in Polish." In *Generative investigations: Syntax, morphology, and phonology*, edited by Piotr Bański, Beata Łukaszewicz, Monika Opalińska and Joanna Zaleska, Newcastle: Cambridge Scholars Publishers.

Cetnarowska, Bożena, Agnieszka Pysz and Helen Truman. 2010. "Where movement fails: Problems with movement-based accounts of adjective placement". Poster presented at GLOW-33, Wrocław, Poland, April 13, 2010.

Chappell, Hilary and William McGregor. 1996. *The grammar of inalienability: A typological perspective on body part terms and the part-whole relation*. Berlin: Mouton de Gruyter.

Cinque, Guglielmo. 1994. "On the evidence for partial N-movement in the Romance DP." In *Paths towards Universal Grammar. Studies in honor of Richard S. Kayne*, edited by Guglielmo Cinque, Jan Koster, Jean-Yves Pollock, Luigi Rizzi and Raffaella Zanuttini, 85-110. Washington D.C.: Georgetown University Press.

Cinque, Guglielmo. 2005. "The dual source of adjectives and phrasal movement in the Romance DP." Unpublished manuscript, University of Venice.

—. 2009. *The syntax of adjectives: A comparative study*. http://hdl.handle.net/10278/1179.

Dixon, Robert M. W. 1982. *Where have all the adjectives gone?* The Hague: Mouton.

Dubinsky, Stanley and Robert Hamilton. 1998. "Epithets as antilogophoric pronouns". *Linguistic Inquiry* 29: 685-692.

Engelhardt, Miriam. 1998. "The syntax of nominalized properties." PhD dissertation, The Hebrew University, Jerusalem.

Gębka-Wolak, Małgorzata. 2000. *Związki linearne między składnikami grupy nominalnej we współczesnym języku polskim*. Toruń: Wydawnictwo Uniwersytetu Mikołaja Kopernika.

Giegerich, Heinz. 2005. "Associative adjectives in English and the lexicon-syntax interface." *Journal of Linguistics* 41: 571-591.

Giusti, Giuliana. 1997. "The categorial status of determiners." In *The new comparative syntax*, edited by Liliane Haegeman, 95-123. London: Addison Wesley Longman.

Givón, Talmy. 2001. *Syntax: An introduction*. Amsterdam: John Benjamins.

Grimshaw, Jane. 1990. *Argument structure*. Cambridge, Mass.: MIT Press.

Halmøy, Madeleine. 2010. "The Norwegian nominal system—A neo-saussurean perspective." PhD dissertation, University of Tromsø.

Kolliakou, Dimitra. 1999. "De-Phrase extractability and individual/ property denotation". *Natural Language and Linguistic Theory* 17: 713-781.

Laenzlinger, Christopher. 2005. "French adjective ordering: Perspectives on DP-internal movement types". *Lingua* 115: 645-689.

Linde-Usiekniewicz, Jadwiga. 2010. "A position on classificatory adjectives in Polish." Unpublished manuscript, University of Warsaw.

Padučeva, Elena Viktorovna. 1985/2002. *Vyskazyvanie i ego sootnesennost s dejstvitelnostju (referencialnye aspekty semantiki mestoimenij)*. Moskva: Nauka.

Pereltsvaig, Asya. 2007. "On the universality of DP: A view from Russian". *Studia Linguistica* 61(1): 59-94.

Rozwadowska, Bożena. 1997. *Towards a unified theory of nominalizations: External and internal eventualities.* Wrocław: Wydawnictwo Uniwersytetu Wrocławskiego.

Rutkowski, Paweł. 2007. "The syntactic properties and diachronic development of postnominal adjectives in Polish.", In *Formal Approaches to Slavic Linguistics: The Toronto Meeting 2006*, edited by Richard Compton, Magdalena Goledzinowska and Ulyana Savchenko, 326-345. Ann Arbor, MI: Michigan Slavic Publications.

—. 2009. "Let's talk about postnominal adjectives!" Talk given at The 4th Annual Meeting of the Slavic Linguistics Society, Zadar, Croatia, September 3, 2009.

Rutkowski, Paweł and Ljiljana Progovac. 2005. "Classification Projection in Polish and Serbian: The position and shape of classifying adjectives." In *Formal Approaches to Slavic Linguistics: The South Carolina Meeting*, edited by Steven Franks, Frank Y. Gladney and Mila Tasseva-Kurktchieva, 289-299. Ann Arbor, MI: Michigan Slavic Publications.

Scott, Gary-John. 2002. "Stacked adjectival modification and the structure of nominal phrases." In *Functional structure in DP and IP*, edited by Guglielmo Cinque, 91-122. Oxford: Oxford University Press,

Spencer, Andrew. 1998. "Relational adjectives and the redundancy of lexical categories." In *Proceedings of the First Mediterranean*

Conference of Morphology 1997, edited by Booij, Geert, Angela Ralli and Sergio Scalise, 19-29. Patras: University of Patras.

—. 2002. "Gender as an inflectional category". *Journal of Linguistics* 38 (2): 279-312.

Sproat, Richard and Chilin Shih. 1988. "Prenominal adjectival ordering in English and Mandarin." In *Proceedings of the 18th Annual Meeting of the North Eastern Linguistics Society*, 465-489.

Szupryczyńska, Maria. 1980. *Opis składniowy polskiego przymiotnika*. Toruń: Wydawnictwo UMK.

Szymańska, Izabela. 2000. "On the adjectival modification in Polish noun phrases—from the X-bar theory towards a functional explanation". *Acta Universitatis Lodziensis. Folia Linguistica Anglica* 2: 175-192.

Topolińska, Zuzanna. 1984. "Składnia grupy imiennej." In *Gramatyka współczesnego języka polskiego. Składnia,* edited by Zuzanna Topolińska, 301-389. Warszawa: PWN

Trugman, Helen. 2004a. "More puzzles about postnominal genitives." In *Possessives and beyond: Semantics and syntax,* edited by Kim Ji-yung, Yury A. Lander and Barbara H. Partee, 217-240. University of Massachusetts Occasional Papers in Linguistics 29. Amherst, MA: GLSA Publications.

—. 2004b. "Syntax of Russian DPs, and DP-internal agreement phenomena." PhD dissertation, Tel-Aviv University.

—. This volume. "Instances of posthead modification in Russian NPs."

Vergnaud, Jean-Roger and Maria-Luisa Zubizarreta. 1992. "The definite determiner and the inalienable constructions in French and English." *Linguistic Inquiry* 23: 595-652.

Warren, Beatrice. 1984. *Classifying Adjectives*. Göteburg: Acta Universitatis Gothoburgensis.

Willim, Ewa. 2000a. "Analiza zestawień z przymiotnikiem w minimalistycznym modelu gramatyki generatywnej". *Polonica* 20: 37-70.

Willim, Ewa. 2000b. "Some aspects of the grammar and interpretation of adjectival modification." In *Proceedings of Generative Linguistics in Poland 1*, edited by Piotr Bański and Adam Przepiórkowski, 156-167. Warszawa: IPI PAN.

—. 2001. "On NP-internal agreement: A study of some adjectival and nominal modifiers in Polish." In *Current issues in formal Slavic linguistics*, edited by Gerhild Zybatow, Uwe Junghanns, Grit Mehlhorn and Luka Szucsich, 80-95. Frankfurt/Main: Peter Lang.

TRANSITIVITY AS A MARKER OF VALUATION

MACIEJ KIELAR
ADAM MICKIEWICZ UNIVERSITY, POZNAŃ

Abstract

The process of valuation is assumed to be a discursive phenomenon. Considering Puzynina's (1992) ideas, which Krzeszowski (1997: 16) characterises as '[p]ragmatics of axiological terms,' one may notice that valuation may also be realised in language on the level of the grammatical structure. Therefore, the aim of the analysis in the present paper is to show the link between grammatical structures and their functions in expressing valuation. Achieving this goal seems possible, taking into consideration (1) the integration of assumptions of functional grammar, (2) the idea that valuation is present in every linguistic production, and (3) the fact that Critical Discourse Analysis (henceforth CDA) views discourse as a collection of socially constructed values.

The focus is on the idea of 'transitivity', which in the current paper is understood according to Halliday's (1978: 46) and Fowler's (1991: 70) definitions. Hence, according to Wodak's (1995: 207-210) outline of CDA modes, 'social semiotics', or in other words the 'functional school' of CDA, appears to be best suited for the present study, as it focuses on the relation between the grammatical system and the purposes it serves to its users.

To exemplify the use of 'transitivity' in the expression of valuation in journalistic discourse, it has been decided to investigate the Press discussion of the 2004 EU enlargement in ten British and Irish national daily newspapers. Therefore, the corpus of the press releases consisting of some 30,000 words has been gathered. It encompasses articles published between 15 April and 7 May 2004 which represent such journalistic genres as press note, report, commentary, report with elements of commentary and coverage. In the course of this analysis, expressions introducing valuation have been divided into active sentences with the agent as grammatical subject and active sentences with other roles as grammatical subject. Consequently, the significance of transitivity as a linguistic mechanism used by journalists for the purpose of introducing valuation is presented and discussed with reference to selected examples.

1. Valuation, ideology and language

In analysing the linguistic means of expressing valuation, which according Krzeszowski (1997, 22–24) is a process of ascribing values constituting a part of our knowledge and determining our perception of reality, one would intuitively look at semantics. However, scientists working on this issue show at least two different views of how language embraces this issue. Krzeszowski (1997, 17), by blurring the division into semantics and pragmatics, advocates the idea of axiological semantics in which values are seen as an integral part of any linguistic expression whose nominal aspect is subject to valuation. The second view is presented by Puzynina (1992, 111–115) who suggests that valuations may take place on two levels. On the first level, valuation may be expressed by the systemic properties of language and would be called semantic valuation. On the second, valuation may depend on the textual use of particular lexical elements. In such a case, one has connotative valuation. It must be said that it may be rather difficult to distinguish between these two types. As the author suggests, if the valuation performed by means of words such as 'good – bad,' 'pretty – ugly,' etc., is quite obvious, expressing valuation by means of syntax, morphology, phonetics, or even paralinguistic features is not so. Therefore, particular syntactic constructions, in which certain verbs are used, may include the speaker's/writer's valuation of an action.

Looking at Puzynina's ideas, one may come up with a conclusion that they are closely related to, if not the same as, the idea of transitivity. As Halliday (1978, 46) says, transitivity marks a type of a process and the roles of participants associated with this process. In other words, one could say that transitivity refers to the differences in meaning between different types of verbs, rather than to the structure in which they are involved, i.e. the way people organise their expressions of the surrounding world. Therefore, transitivity should not be treated as identical with the terms of traditional grammar. Fowler (1991, 71; 76–77) says that the analysis of transitivity can be perceived as a semantic perspective in which ideas are expressed in a clause; that is, about what is said about the surrounding reality, events, people involved in them, and their relations with each other.

Because of the subject of the study, that is transitivity, in the present paper it will be Puzynina's proposal of expressing valuation in language that will be followed. As for the method of the study, van Dijk's (1998, 43, 74–77, 314–318) ideas can be helpful because of two reasons. First, Van Dijk explains that values belong to the sphere of culture, which is more general than the sphere of ideology. Therefore, values enter the construction of ideologies from a higher level and govern them through their evaluative dimension. Second, people acquire, share and change ideologies in the course of social interaction, such as language use. These views are repeated by Verschueren (1999, 238) who points out that ideology can be seen as a conglomerate of commonsense, basic, and often normative beliefs that are manifested in discourse. As Fairclough (1989, 2; 84–85) says, the notion of commonsense is crucial to an understanding of the link between ideology and language, firstly, because commonsense assumptions, are ideological and are manifested in all kinds of social behaviour, and secondly, because language is the most common form of social behaviour based on commonsense assumptions.

Consequently, a correlation of Puzynina's, van Dijk's, Verschueren's and Fairclough's ideas hints at the use of Critical Discourse Analysis (CDA) as the investigative approach, as according to indications made by Kress and Hodge (1979, 4–9), Fairclough (1989, 17–26, 1995, 131), Fowler (1991, 4), Schiffrin (1994, 39–40), Wodak (1995, 204–207, 2000, 187–192), Wodak and Busch (2004, 105–122) and Widdowson (2000, 156), it is CDA which treats the perception of discourse both as a social practice, such as the contextually determined language use, and as a collection of socially constructed values. Therefore, it might be said that transitivity can be treated as a means of expressing valuation, while CDA might be seen as the best suited method for its investigation.

In the present study, we focus on the use of transitivity for the purpose of expressing valuation in journalistic discourse, whose main topic is the 2004 EU enlargement. As Wojtaszczyk (2006, 14–16) describes its significance, it was the biggest enlargement that took place in the EU history. Ten countries, eight of which belonged to the former Soviet block – Latvia, Lithuania, Estonia, Poland, the Czech Republic, the Slovak Republic, Hungary, Slovenia, and two 'Mediterranean' countries Malta and Cyprus – joined the EU. This paved the way for the 2007 EU enlargement, when another two countries of the former Soviet block, Romania and Bulgaria, became full-fledged members, as a result, within fifty years of its history the organisation had expanded from six to twenty-seven members

2. Investigating transitivity as a marker of valuation

2.1. The data

The corpus prepared for the purposes of the present study of valuation in journalistic discourse with respect to the ideology of the enlargement of the European Union consists of some 30,000 words. It comprises texts which have been selected from the U. K. and Irish national daily newspapers. All of these texts have been published and have since been stored in archives on the web pages of the following titles: Belfast Telegraph (B.T.), Daily Mirror (D.M.), Daily Telegraph (D.T.), The Independent (I.), The Sunday Times (S.T.), the Guardian (G.), The Times (T.), Irish Independent (I.I.), Sunday Irish Independent (S.I.I.) and The Irish Times (I.T.). The search through the web archives of these newspapers was conducted in December 2005 and January 2006. As a result of this, forty articles which belong to five different journalistic genres were selected.

These genres may be labelled: the press note (P.N.), report (R.), commentary (C.), report with elements of commentary (R.-C.), and coverage (Cov.). It is important to notice here that, as McQuail (2005, 370), Bauer (2004, 143–145) and Mrozowski (2001, 323) say, the concept of a journalistic genre is constantly evolving. Hence, genre distinctiveness as such is here understood as a continuum rather than as indicating one in a set of clearly identifiable classes. In other words, the genres of the Press do not possess a set of easily identifiable distinctive features characteristic of one particular genre and not of any other. It is also suggested that it is mainly the impression of the reader which enables any such divisions. In accordance with these assumptions, the distinction presented here could be characterised as impressionistic. The distribution and frequency of use of a particular genre could be characterised as follows. Commentary, (C.), is the genre most frequently used. It has 11 attestations in 7 out of 10 titles. Report with elements of commentary, (R.-C.), is the second most often used genre label, as it appears 12 times in 6 out of 10 newspapers. Then, there is the coverage, (Cov.), which is found 8 times in 4 titles. The press note (P.N.) appears 4 times in 4 titles and report (R.) has 5 attestations in 5 titles out of 10. However, it needs to be recognised that each of the ten titles has its own 'favoured' genres which are exploited more often than others.

Table 1. The list of genres in selected newspapers

	TITLES OF THE SELECTED NEWSPAPERS									
Genre	*B. T.*	*D. M.*	*D.T.*	*I.*	*S. T.*	*G.*	*T.*	*I. I.*	*S. I. I.*	*I. T.*
P. N.	*1/25%*	*1/33%*	*1/20%*	-----	-----	-----	-----	*1/33%*	-----	-----
R.	*2/50%*	-----	*2/40%*	*1/20%*	-----	-----	-----	-----	-----	-----
C.	*1/25%*	-----	*1/20%*	-----	-----	*2/66%*	*1/25%*	*1/33%*	*2/100%*	*3/33%*
R.-C.	-----	*2/66%*	-----	*3/60%*	*2/100%*	*1/33%*	-----	*1/33%*	-----	*3/33%*
Cov.	-----	-----	*1/20%*	*1/20%*	-----	-----	*3/75%*	-----	-----	*3/33%*
Total	*4/100%*	*3/100%*	*5/100%*	*5/100%*	*2/100 %*	*3/100%*	*4/100%*	*3/100%*	*2/100 %*	*9/100%*
Words	*1718*	*1718*	*2623*	*4902*	*3158*	*3853*	*3870*	*1817*	*1568*	*6722*

Abbreviations:
(1) Newspapers Titles: D. M. – Daily Mail; D. T. – Daily Telegraph; I – Independent; S. T. – Sunday Times; G. – The Guardian; T. – The Times; B.T. – Belfast Telegraph; I. I. – Irish Independent; S. I. I. – Sunday Irish Independent; I. T. – The Irish Times
(2) Genres: P. N. – Press Note; R. – Report; C. – Commentary; R.-C. – Report with elements of commentary; Cov. – Coverage;

2.2. Instances of transitivity used as a valuating mechanism

In this section, we shall move to a presentation of a sample of analysis of 6 examples featuring instances of transitivity used for the expressing valuation. The total number of analysed extracts was 140.

> [1] Today *the European Union celebrates* the accession of ten new member states, bringing the membership of the EU to 25. Mary Fitzgerald looks at the background to today's *historic enlargement* (Belfast Telegraph, 01 May 2004).

In example [1] "the European Union" is assigned the role of agent rather than causer, which suggests that it is being ascribed people's powers and abilities with respect to making decisions or taking action. Here, the expression "the European Union" may also be seen as representing both the people who live in the member states and the European government. In other words, the EU might be seen either as the citizens of all the member states or as the invisible force that guides, or even directs, the life and actions of its citizens. Looking at the predicate "celebrates" and the adjective "historic" which modifies the noun "enlargement", one may infer that these words indicate the successful accomplishment of political and economic negotiations with the accession states and assign a huge importance to the event for the future of the continent, since the adjective "historic" used in such a context points to two facts. Firstly, the EU has never expanded so rapidly and, secondly, eight of ten accession countries used to belong to the Soviet bloc.

Example [2] illustrates some problems that appear in the course of European integration. Here, the author discusses the issues from the immediately post-war times, when the Cold War order was introduced to Europe.

> [2] *The Czechs* have had a *long-running row* with *Germany* over *the Benes Decrees*, the post-war declarations which *deprived the Sudetenland Germans* of citizenship and property rights. Relations with Austria have been only a little easier because of Vienna's safety fears about the Temelin nuclear power plant (Independent, 30 April 2004).

The participants here are "the Czechs" and "Germany." At first sight, one may notice that it is the members of the nation confronted, not with the members of another nation, but rather with the government of another state. What is more, positioning "the Czechs" as the grammatical subject of this sentence and giving them the role of actor by using "had" as a verb of action presents them as instigators of the "row." The very noun "row" indicates that the process that has been taking place for some time was far from the standards of European debate. It seems that by ascribing the role of an agent to one group, the author of item [2] values it negatively. Also, by using the adjective “long-running” the author presents the members of the nation as being unable to act responsibly and in accordance to some standards that are present within EU debates. In this light, it is the Czechs who are the only negative characters in this situation.

While the EU enlargement causes problems and controversy, it could also be seen as bringing an end to a period of time known as the Cold War, just as in the following example.

> [3] *EUROPE's leaders* today *will put the final seal* on *the reunification of a continent divided* by *the Cold War*, as the EU finally expands to 25 nations, becoming the world's biggest free trade area (Irish Independent, 01 May 2004).

In extract [3], it is the politicians, or, as the author calls them, “Europe’s leaders” who are the grammatical subject in this example and at the same time they play the role of the agent. This results in presenting them as the force responsible for the actions that will take place on the 1st of May. The verb and the object – “will put the final seal” – may be seen as a way of signing documents of great importance and significance in history. Referring to the declaration of the European enlargement signed by all the community members to create “the reunification of the continent”, the author magnifies the importance of this moment in European history. The very noun “reunification” suggests a positive evaluation, as it is contrasted with the “Cold War division.” It is natural that “unity” is perceived as a desired state, while “division” modified by “the Cold War” cannot be seen as such. However, the noun “reunification” suggests that Europe must have been united in the past. As a matter of fact, it is impossible to indicate a period of time in European history without wars, divisions or with completely voluntary unions. Therefore, one may say that the use of “reunification” introduces an image of a desired state of affairs.

In the next example, the writer mentions a crucial factor supporting and sanctioning the existence of the EU. This is the principle of the solidarity which results in the EU’s assistance with respect to the social and economic development of member states, especially those that are poorer in comparison to other members.

> [4] The *entry* of new and less well off countries to the European Union will result in much of the Structural Funds *support that we received in the past*

> *to help bring our economy closer to the European average being needed elsewhere* (Belfast Telegraph, 27 April 2004).

Quotation [4] features the role of theme assigned to the noun "entry". By formulating the sentence in this way, the writer wants readers to focus on what "entry" involves with reference to the Irish. This is indicated by the use of the pronouns "we" and "our". The author points to the fact that one of the main EU objectives is to help its member states in social and economic development. There is a suggestion that the Irish economy has already benefited from the help expressed in "support that we received in the past to help bring our economy closer to the European average." At that time, on the basis of the value solidarity, EU assistance is 'being needed elsewhere,' i.e. in the new member states. In this way, the author positively characterises the role of the EU in Northern Ireland's development.

In quotation [5], the journalist points at issues related to the entire social sphere. Hence, we find echoes of such matters as migration and politics, but also history. As a matter of fact, the author starts his writing with a reference to history in order to move on to the social matters.

> [5] *The barriers* are coming down, but cultural and language differences will persist. In addition, the *affluence of well-off countries* such as Britain and France will contrast with *the poverty of new entrants* such as Latvia and Lithuania (Belfast Telegraph, 01 May 2004).

The writer wants the readers to focus on an event. Therefore, we may notice a sentence without an agent but with a semanto-syntactic theme which is used in order to mark the significance of the occurrence. The verb "coming down" selects the role of the theme for the noun phrase "the barriers", which cease to exist; however, the readers may wonder who is removing them. The next two sentences hint at an answer. If culture and economy remain as differences, this means that what becomes common to some extent is economy and politics. Hence, these could be recovered as the factors responsible for beginning to unite Europeans. In this way, one may point to the politicians as the ones responsible for these changes.

> [6] *The biggest expansion in Europe's history* is only two days away when some relatively poor and struggling countries from central and eastern Europe will be *ushered* into what's been known as a "*rich man's club*" (Daily Mail, 29 April 2004).

In quotation [6], one may notice the presence of two clauses which display two different grammatical constructions. However, the first being the main clause serves as the basis for the analysis. This is an active sentence in which the enlargement, which the author refers to as "the biggest expansion in Europe's history," is given the role of theme by the verb "is". Being the subject, it is found in the initial position of the clause. Therefore, it attracts the reader's focus instantly, which is the way it assumes the valuating role. Within this phrase, the author also expresses valuation by means of lexical elements such as the adjective "biggest" and the prepositional phrase functioning as the adverb of time "in Europe's history." Indeed, in the course of the 2004 enlargement ten new countries joined the organisation. The scale of the enlargement was an unprecedented event in fifty-year-long history, which is signalled by the adverb of time "in Europe's history." Moreover, these two valuating expressions may also reflect the quality of the change happening to the EU. The adjective "biggest" may suggest not only the scale, but also the effort which has been invested in the preparations of the 'old' and especially 'new' states, most of which are former communist countries, whose policies and economies had to be adjusted to the standards of the European Union. The adverb phrase also suggests that this enlargement is a unique event for the whole continent, not just the EU, because it marks a definite end to the era known as the Cold War.

3. Conclusions

The issue of transitivity and the related notion of semantic roles have been the central organising principles for the analysis. English favours SVO sentence order, where it is usually the subject which is ascribed the role of agent or causer of an action described by the verb. This order reflects the order of things as they happen in extra-textual reality.

With reference to the material analysed, it is usually 'the EU' which is presented as the 'mighty' part causing various happenings regardless of whether it appears in the position of the subject. This is the natural order of things bearing in mind the general topic of the texts investigated. Hence, it is the organisation which is assumed to take the responsibility. Only in some cases is it politicians, or 'the people', who also appear as another possible agent. It seems clear that the EU itself functions thanks to politicians and not on its own; however, this distinction may also be of a valuating significance. In this way the EU may be presented as an entity which seems not to be linked to the politicians whom we, as the European society, may often perceive as those who tend to forget their role as representatives of the society. Therefore, the EU will not be valued through the actions of particular officials, which in turn, may suggest a common or, even, to some extent blurred responsibility.

The so-called 'other role' that most frequently appears in the subject position is 'theme' and it designates the topic of clauses. These are usually the copula verb constructions, so that the verb phrase 'describes' the given topic. In this case, it is the noun 'enlargement' which most often appears in such clauses. Again, as in the just discussed 'the EU' phrase acting as the agent, bearing in mind the general topic to which the analysed material is devoted, such a situation is perfectly understandable. The role of the verb phrase is to value this subject, but this usually happens by means of valuating adjectives. However, if verbs other than a copula verb are selected, then the valuation may be expressed by means of the relation of the subject and the lexical verb.

With the respect to the significance of transitivity used for the process of valuation in general, one may notice that the use of an agent or causer in the subject position introduces the valuation of the situation presented as natural, stemming from the order of things that can generally be recognised in the environment. The entity that performs or causes the action is assumed to be the 'mighty' one and its importance is highlighted by the initial position in the sentence. It is immediately recognised as such by the addressee of the message and leads to the fact that the responsibility can be easily and instantly ascribed to that entity.

When the sentence is active and follows the SVO order, but the subject is of a role other than the agent or causer, one may observe a purposeful departure from the presentation of reality in the way it is or seems to be. The order of things is distorted. One cannot see at once who or what did or caused something to happen, as what appears at first in such a clause is the effect or affected. The responsibility is shifted to another part of the clause. In this way, the author of the message values the outcome of the process or the described process as more important than its cause.

References

Primary Sources

The Belfast Telegraph (http://www.belfasttelegraph.co.uk/search/index) (DA: 19 Dec. 2005)

The Daily Mail (http://www.dailymail.co.uk/ pages/dmsearch) (DA: 19 Dec. 2005)

The Daily Telegraph (http://www.dailytelegraph.co.uk/search/index) (DA: 6 Jan. 2006)

The Guardian (http://browse.guardian.co.uk/search) (DA: 16 Dec. 2005)

The Independent (http://www.indeoendent.co.uk/index) (DA: 16 Jan. 2006)
The Irish Independent (http://www.independent.ie/search/index.jsp) (DA: 20 Jan. 2006)
The Irish Times (http://www.ireland.com/search) (DA: 16. 12. 2005)
The Sunday Irish Independent (http://www.independent.ie/search/index.jsp) (DA: 20 Jan. 2006)
The Sunday Times (http://www.timesonline.co.uk/tol/sitesearch.) (DA: 14 Dec. 2005)
The Times (http://www.timesonline.co.uk/tol/sitesearch.) (DA: 14 Dec. 2005)

Secondary sources

Bauer, Zbigniew. 2004. „Gatunki dziennikarskie" [Journalistic genres]. In *Dziennikarstwo i świat mediów* [Journalism and the world of media], edited by Zbigniew Bauer, Edward Chudziński, 143–173. Kraków: Universitas,
Fairclough, Norman. 1989. *Language and power.* London: Longman.
—. 1995. *Critical discourse analysis: The critical study of language.* London: Longman.
Fowler, Roger. 1991. *Language in the news: Discourse and ideology in the press.* London: Routledge.
Halliday, Michael, A., K. 1978. *Language as social semiotic: The social interpretation of language and meaning.* Baltimore: University Park Press.
Kress, Gunther – Robert Hodge. 1979. *Language as ideology.* London: Routledge – Kegan Paul.
Krzeszowski, Tomasz, P. 1997. *Angels and devils in hell. Elements of axiology in semantics.* Warszawa: Energia.
Luke, Allan. 2001. "Ideology." In *Concise encyclopedia of sociolinguistics*, edited by Rajend Mesthire, 559–563. Amsterdam: Elsevier.
McQuail, Denis. 2005. *Mass Communication Theory. An Introduction.* 5th edition London: Sage.
Mrozowski, Maciej. 2001. *Media masowe: władza, rozrywka i biznes* [Mass media: Power, entertainment and business]. Warszawa: Oficyna Wydawnicza ASPRA-JR.
Puzynina, Jadwiga. 1992. *Język wartości* [Language of values]. Warszawa: Państwowe Wydawnictwo Naukowe.
Schiffrin, Deborah. 1994. *Approaches to discourse.* Oxford: Blackwell.

Van Dijk, Teun, A. 1998. *Ideology: A multidisciplinary approach.* London: Sage Publications.

Verschueren, Jef. 1999. *Understanding pragmatics.* London, New York, Sydney, Auckland: Arnold.

Widdowson, Henry. 2000. "Critical practices: on representation and interpretation of text." In *Discourse and Social Life,* edited by Srikant Sarangi and Malcolm Coulthard, 155–169. *Harlow*: Pearson Education.

Wodak, Ruth. 1995. "Critical linguistics and critical discourse analysis." In *The Handbook of Pragmatics,* Jef Verschueren, Jan-Ole Östman and Bloomaert, 204–210. Amsterdam; Philadelphia: John Benjamins.

—. 2000. "Recontextualization and the transformation of meanings: a critical discourse analysis of decision making in EU meetings about employment policies." In *Discourse and Social Life,* edited by Srikant Sarangi and Malcolm Coulthard, 185–206. Harlow: Pearson Education.

—. 2002. "Aspects of critical discourse analysis." *Zeitschrift für Angewandte Linguistik* 36: 5–31

Wodak, Ruth – Brigitta Busch. 2004. "Approaches to media texts." In *The Sage Handbook of Media Studies*, edited by John D. H. Downing, 105–122. Thousand Oaks, London, New Delhi: Sage Publications.

Wojtaszczyk, Konstanty, A. 2006. „Istota i formy integracji europejskiej" [The core and forms of the Eurpoean integration]. In *Integracja europejska: wstęp* [European integration: An Introduction], edited by Konstanty A. Wojtaszczyk, 13–23. Warszawa: Wydawnictwa akademickie i profesjonalne.

TO INHERIT EVERYTHING: VARIATION IN QUANTIFIER RESTRICTION[1]

KONRAD SZCZESNIAK
UNIVERSITY OF SILESIA

Abstract

This study focuses on variation in the interpretation of quantifiers used in sentences with multiple verbal arguments. Quantifier restriction will be analyzed as being resolved through a process whose first step is the identification of so called ascription, which is the association of the quantifier with a concrete verbal argument present in the sentence. The interpretation of quantifiers is calculable with reference to all the verbal arguments, overt or covert. In the process of quantifier ascription, a number of interpretive mechanisms are in operation. These include syntactic and semantic constraints as well as pragmatic considerations. It will be argued that the quantity expressed by a quantifier depends on whether it can be regarded as being possessed by the participant named in a sentence. It will also be shown that the syntactic position that the participant occupies in the sentence plays a role in interpreting a quantifier. Once possible interpretations of a quantifier emerge through a process of syntactic and semantic evaluation, the intended meaning is selected based on a pragmatic evaluation of context in which a given utterance is made. The selection is made from a range of semantically different interpretations, of varying degrees of likelihood ranging from preferred, through disfavored, to unlikely readings.

1. Introduction

Universal quantifiers like 'everything' or 'everybody' have been recognized in the literature as a special category of expressions. They serve

[1] I am grateful to my anonymous reviewers whose keen observations and valuable suggestions helped improve this contribution.

to express the entirety of a given quantity, but exactly how large a quantity is under consideration depends on context and the speaker's intention. Determining just how much is meant by 'everything' is a complex operation known as quantifier domain restriction. Unlike fixed-reference expressions, universal quantifiers are free to convey really any quantity at all. The quantifier 'everything' can mean anything from a handful of objects to infinity. It is equally capable of expressing abstract and concrete quantities. Furthermore, the notions expressed by universal quantifiers are abstracted away from any detailed considerations of magnitude, which makes 'everything' equally felicitous when referring to quantities of microscopic dimensions ("everything in the living cell") as well as to those of cosmic proportions ("everything in the Milky Way"). In other words, the lowly word 'everything' used in two different sentences may assume two completely different meanings. But even within the same sentence, in one specific context, universal quantifiers can have varying interpretations, as in the joke about a Buddhist monk at a hot-dog stand who says "Make me one with everything."

Yet despite this interpretive freedom and potential for ambiguity and vagueness, universal quantifiers are used consistently most of the time, and rarely lead to misunderstanding. One reason why interpreting universal quantifiers is possible at all is because of regularities guaranteed by a number of factors, both linguistic and extra-linguistic, constraining the number of potential interpretations that a quantifier may entail.

Universal quantifier domain restriction has been looked at from many different angles. Some of the approaches adopted in the literature include the situation semantic approach motivated by the deictic nature of quantifiers (von Fintel 1994, Kratzer 1986, 2002). It has also been pointed out that quantifier restriction is a special case of anaphora resolution that involves associating a quantity with the topic of a sentence (von Fintel 1994). Restriction of quantifier domains has featured especially prominently in a debate centering on the issue of whether truth-conditional effects of extra-linguistic context are traceable to context or logical form (Perry 1986, Stanley 2000, Carston 2008). The debate revolves around a wide range of questions, but briefly, as far as quantifier resolution is concerned, the issue is whether the interpretation of quantifiers is conditioned by the linguistic elements present in a sentence or by non-linguistic elements supplied by context. I will address this debate later in the paper.

An unfortunate outcome of the confrontation of such conflicting accounts of quantifier restriction is that it is easy to conclude that interpreting quantifiers should ideally involve a single mechanism wholly responsible for restricting the domain of a quantifier. Claims that quantifier domains are always restricted in one fashion only, across the board, with each author insisting on a different restriction mechanism, bring to mind the familiar fable of blind men studying an elephant, each inspecting a different part of the animal. Given the amount of variation inherent in interpreting a quantifier, it should be uncontroversial to allow the possibility of there being a number of constraints that, depending on occasion, come into play individually or in conjunction with other constraints.

Some such constraints will be sketched in the present contribution, and they will involve the notion of possession and the syntactic position of verbal arguments. It will be argued that the quantity expressed by a quantifier depends on whether it can be viewed as being possessed by the participant represented by a verbal argument and on what syntactic position that argument occupies in the sentence. Traditionally, the role of context will also be acknowledged. It is important to stress that these factors may often be in conflict, the main claim being that none of them are absolute or inviolable, and none seem to take precedence over the others. Instead, they apply alternately, probably depending on the type of predicate complemented by the universal quantifier in question. If correct, this view of alternating constraints would account for the attested variability in the interpretation of universal quantifiers shown below.

2. Quantifier ascription

In what follows, a case of alternating quantifier readings will be presented. Sentences (1a-b) are descriptions of the same situation. They differ in terms of the perspective they take.

(1) a. I inherited a million dollars from Dad.
b. Dad bequeathed a million dollars to me.

The two sentences are mutually entailing logical equivalents linked by a converse relation. However, that equivalence disappears when the theme argument of the verb is not a concrete value but a universal quantifier.

(2) a. I inherited everything from Dad.
b. Dad bequeathed everything to me.

The interpretation of the quantifier is different in each case. In (2b), the quantifier is interpreted as 'everything that Dad owned'; in (2a) the quantifier can mean either 'everything that Dad owned' or 'everything that I own now'. The readings of (2a) can be represented formally as

$$\forall x[C(x)](\text{inherited}'(I,x,\text{Dad}'))$$
where $C(x)=\text{owned}(\text{Dad},x)$
or $C(x)=\text{own}(I,x)$.

A similar relation holds between sentences (3-4) below. In these pairs, the sentences containing a RECEIVE-type verb have a potential for ambiguity which is not normally found in the GIVE-type sentences: $\forall x[C(x)]$ $(\text{bought}'(\text{we},x,\text{B\&S}'))$, where $C(x)=\text{offered}(\text{B\&S},x)$ or $C(x)=\text{own}(\text{we},x)$. It is not my intention to explain the variation in terms of the distinction between GIVE-type and RECEIVE-type verbs. This correlation is not perfect and can be made to disappear under special contextual conditions.

(3) a. We bought everything from Bell and Spencer Co.
  b. Bell and Spencer Co. sold us everything.
(4) a. I've learned everything from Dad.
  b. Dad has taught me everything.

2.1 Ascription vs. restriction

This interpretation of the quantifier is not exactly a case of the familiar question of quantifier restriction (Kratzer 1986; von Fintel 1994), where "everything" is taken to refer to the quantity brought into focus in a given context. Rather, the main question is which participant in the sentence is associated with the quantity expressed by the quantifier. This new sense will be referred to as quantifier ascription, as is represented in angle brackets in (5).

(5) a. I inherited everything from Dad, <everything associable with the recipient>.
$C(x)=\text{own}\ (I,x)$

It should also be emphasized that quantifier domain restriction and ascription are not separate questions. Ascription is part and parcel of restriction—the exact value arrived at in the course of ascription serves as input for restriction resolution. There may be doubts as to whether ascription is a real separate process, apart from restriction. As one anonymous reviewer pointed out, associating the value of a quantifier with a participant is something that restriction can do. This skepticism seems perfectly warranted, especially in light of the fact that ascription cannot exist in isolation. However, I am not arguing for ascription as a process independent of or competing with restriction, but as its subcomponent. What I suggest is that in quantifier domain restriction it is useful to consider the role of the participants named in a sentence, which is something that, to the best of my knowledge, has not been done before in the literature. No account of restriction makes an explicit assumption that the restriction of quantifiers has an orientation toward a specific verbal argument[2]. This orientation is evident in any given sentence with multiple participants: the interpretation of the quantifier involves an express effort to bind with a single participant; a quantifier cannot ascribe to two participants at the same time. Further, there are clear patterns as to what ascriptions are entertained—verbs seem to have default preferences for specific participants. I think these observations justify postulating ascription as a subroutine of restriction, as it provides an explicit descriptive tool for a phenomenon that otherwise might be (and has been) left out of the analysis of restriction. The role of ascription in restricting quantifier domains can be represented schematically as

> ascription + restriction within a participant = quantifier domain restriction

This is intended to mean that quantifier domain restriction is determined jointly by ascription and restricting the quantity carried by the

---

[2] There are similar accounts that capture quantifier interpretation in terms of binding. For example, Stanley (2007, 49) studies the relationship between quantifying expressions within a sentence and shows that the semantic interpretation of one quantifier will depend on the value introduced by the other. My account is more general in that it proposes relationships between quantifiers and *any* verbal argument present in the sentence. Another important point about ascription is that it does not rely on binding in its classic Government and Binding sense: ascription is not confined by the binding constraints that the interpretation of personal pronouns is subject to. Specifically, possessive pronouns are constrained more tightly. Whereas "everything" could be ascribed both to the giver and the recipient in (i), there is less freedom in the case of possessive pronouns: In (ii), "his" is only co-referential with the subject "Jack", but cannot refer to the oblique object "Dad".

(i) Jack$_i$ inherited everything$_{i/j}$ from Dad$_j$.

(ii) Jack$_i$ inherited his$_{i/*j}$ house from Dad$_j$.

The overlap is only partial which means that ascription involves more than just binding constraints. It will be shown that ascription resolution is governed not only by syntactic but also semantic and pragmatic considerations.

participant ascribed. The relationship between ascription and restriction within a participant depends on the meaning of the verb. In the case of the 'bequeath' scenario in (2b), the ascriptive input <everything associated with the agent/source argument> is fed into the restriction stage. Then restriction proceeds to establish what part of the quantity associated with the agent is meant, which in this particular case is likely to be "everything owned by the agent". On the other hand, in example (6), it is unlikely that the agent sent all her possessions to the recipient. Although in both (2b) and (6), the quantity conveyed is carved down to a value associable with the agent, the verb 'send' makes that value much smaller than the wholesale "everything she owned".

(6) She sent everything to her son.
$\forall x[C(x)](sent'(she,x,son'))$
$C(x)=owned(she,x)$

The resulting quantity established by the interaction of restriction and ascription is what is normally recognized in the literature as quantifier domain restriction. In this context it is important to acknowledge that, within the framework of situation semantics, quantifier domain restriction has been shown to rely heavily on specific situations which a given statement describes (Barwise and Perry 1983, Kratzer 2002). Situation semantics is a powerful alternative to possible worlds, because quite simply the interpretation of a quantifier from a general world-level proposition is an impossible task. At a coarse-grained scale of an entire world, the quantifier may refer to widely differing quantities, ranging from a few objects in the closest vicinity of the agents mentioned in a sentence to precisely all objects in the universe. This indeterminacy is captured in the joke mentioned before, where a Buddhist monk at a hot-dog stand orders "one with everything." In a common hot-dog transaction, "everything" will be interpreted as "all available condiments", but the presence of a Buddhist monk—normally imagined as a meditative figure reflecting upon the transcendental connections with the entire universe—affects the interpretation of the quantifier by assuming a de facto infinite domain. To specify the quantity intended, it is necessary to use a specific situation as envisioned by the speaker. In the examples reviewed so far and in the remainder of this paper, topic situations undoubtedly play an important role too. For example, the quantity expressed in (6) will depend on which specific situation the sentence refers to. The sentence will be true with reference to tons of priceless archeological relics, and it ill be equally true if all that the sentence refers to are three unsold items left over from a garage sale. The implications of situation semantics are even more dramatic, as a sentence with a quantifier may have conflicting truth values depending on its context and a specific situation. As Barwise and Perry's (1983, 160) sleeping experiment example shows, the quantifier "no one" in "No one is asleep" can be used with reference to differently demarcated sets of people. It can be used to mean "no people in the room" or "no assistants watching the sleepers." The sentence "No one is asleep" may be false if it refers to the former situation and true if it refers to the latter. Clearly, it is impossible to provide an accurate description of a quantifier in a sentence without taking into account the details of a concrete situation.

However, notwithstanding the appeal and importance of the situation-semantic approach, it also carries a danger of the impression that the restriction of a quantifier is a free-choice decision constrained only by the imagination of the speaker who sets down the specifics of the intended situation. As will be argued below, the kinds of quantities expressed by quantifiers are also constrained by linguistic factors in the form of overt and hidden variables to which quantities are ascribed. Some hypothetical ascriptions are either extremely unlikely or plain impossible, regardless of the preferences of their topic situations, especially when the interaction of ascription and restriction would yield readings involving potential contextual constituents violating the semantic nature of overt or hidden arguments. However, before details of these limitations are presented, it is important to review some properties of ascription.

2.2 Ascription is an implicature

The value negotiated between ascription and restriction can actually be part of the utterance expressed overtly as an afterthought (7a), or as a relative clause following the quantifier (7b).

(7) a. I inherited everything from Dad, <everything that I own >.
b. I inherited everything <that I own> from Dad.

The fact that quantifier ascription-restriction can be expressed overtly is a sign that it is reinforceable, a typical characteristic of an implicature. What lends further support to this possibility is that quantifier ascription also passes another classic test for implicature, namely cancelability (8a). When the first implicature is canceled, it passes on to the next available argument. In this context, the inheritance comprises the totality of the speaker's father's possessions; the speaker herself probably owns possessions of her own apart from what she inherited.

(8) a. I inherited everything from Dad, but not everything that I own.
b. I inherited everything from Dad, but not everything that I own, <so probably everything that Dad owned>.

Ascription is an example of a generalized conversational implicature (GCI). Example (9) shows that it does not require a specific context to arise. Whereas particularized conversational implicatures (PCIs) depend on the question A asks and will vary from context to context, the GCI is constant across various situations. No matter what background assumptions are held by the speakers, a predictable GCI arises defining which of the participants will be associated with the value of "everything". This consistency makes ascription similar to conjunction buttressing (Levinson 2000), scalar quantity implicatures (Horn 1972, Ariel 2008), and other instances of GCIs identified in the literature.

(9) A: Were you and Dad close?
B: I learned everything from Dad.
GCI: Everything that I know.
PCI: Dad and I were very close.

Ascription may not be a typical example of an implicature, the reason being as one anonymous reviewer has pointed out, it does not pass one test for implicatures. Specifically, ascription does not vanish in downward entailing contexts. For example, the exclusive interpretation of the disjunctive *or* in *Mary or Jane will come to the party* disappears in *I don't think Mary or Jane will come* (meaning *both* Jane and Mary will not show up). In the case of ascription, a downward entailing verb does not produce the same effect. According to the reviewer, in a sentence like *I didn't inherit everything from Dad,* the quantifier is still interpreted as "everything Dad owned", as in the non-negated example.

I think it is not entirely clear that the ascription in a negated sentence is the same as in a non-negated one. A negated sentence will involve the counterfactual hypothetical scenario *I inherited everything from Dad* that the negative sentence denies, but the counterfactual itself involves an elusive shifting ascription that is not entailed clearly one way or another and therefore impossible to establish with certainty. It is impossible to know for sure that the original ascription remains the same in a negated sentence if we have no fix on what the original ascription is in the first place.

What is true, however, is that ascription is a peculiar example of an implicature that cannot be canceled for good. Once canceled, it moves on to attach to another argument, as illustrated in example (8), so it cannot vanish definitively. This happens because although the quantifier is free to express any conceivable value, it must represent some value larger than zero, and that value must be associated with some argument. A quantifier not associated with any argument would describe an empty domain, which would defeat the whole purpose of a quantifier.

3. Ascription mechanisms

In what follows, it will be assumed that the implicature of quantifier ascription results from the operation of linguistic constraints which make some readings more likely than others. Some ascriptive interpretations will go through as preferred readings, while others will be either disfavored, very unlikely or even impossible. The generalizations discussed below will include syntactic and semantic constraints. However, a note of caution is in order here. The ascriptions generated by the constraints are not necessarily the only options possible for a given sentence, but rather candidates with varying degrees of likelihood. As a result, even an unlikely interpretation may very well be selected as the intended ascription if sufficient contextual clues militate in its favor. Ascription resolution will normally involve a number of mechanisms, both linguistic and extra-linguistic contextual ones. It is certainly not the case that context alone should select an interpretation to the exclusion of linguistic elements found in the sentence or vice versa.

3.1 Unarticulated constituents vs. hidden variables

These two positions are assumed by the two opposing camps in the debate mentioned in the introduction. On the one hand, an interpretation of a quantifier can be accounted for in terms of what John Perry (1986, 206, 1998) called unarticulated constituents. These are elements derived from context and are not conveyed by any morpheme present in the utterance. Stanley (2000, 410) summarizes the idea thus:

(10) *x* is an unarticulated constituent of an utterance *u* iff (1) *x* is an element supplied by context to the truth-conditions of u, and (2) x is not the semantic value of any constituent of the logical form of the sentence uttered.

Under this analysis, known as the free enrichment account, the meaning of a quantifier is specified or "enriched freely" by unarticulated constituents coming from context. In other words, the meaning of "everything" is whatever makes sense in a given context. An alternative to unarticulated constituents is an account, championed by Jason Stanley, involving hidden variables, also referred to as covert indexicals, which are saturated by reference to context, but the variables themselves are slots carried by logical form. Sentence (11) is a typical example adduced to compare the relative merits of the two competing accounts.

(11) In every room in John's house, he keeps every bottle in the corner. (Stanley 2000, example 22b)

According to Stanley, the quantifier in this example comes with a hidden variable in the form of <every, i>, where 'i' signifies a specific location, which in this case is "John's house". What this means is that the value of "every bottle" is set to something like "every bottle in John's house", since this value is with the semantic value of the constituents of the logical form of the sentence. Stanley argues that the restriction of quantifier domain in this example cannot be a matter of an unarticulated constituent introduced on the force of contextual salience only—it cannot be taken to mean "every bottle" in any context where the utterance is produced. Although this interpretation cannot be ruled out completely, the restriction of the quantifier is constrained by the considerations of logical form of the first clause, and that interpretation takes precedence over a contextually salient reading which may arise only in given special circumstances.

Stanley's account makes it possible to define quantifier ascription in more formal terms: Ascription is the saturation of the variable <i> of the quantifier with a value supplied by one of the arguments found in a sentence. In Stanley's account, the value for <i> is a physical location, for instance "in the house", where a quantity is found. Such locations are often overtly conveyed or implicated in the sentence, but the choice of locations that can saturate the variable <i> is not limited to physical locations. Other locations available include metaphoric locations, such as "in somebody's possession". These are associated with verbal arguments and are distinct from the physical location that serves as a background in a sentence. This way, the hidden variable <i> can also refer to a metaphoric location if its value comes from a verbal argument, as will be shown in section 3.2 below. But the crucial point to make is that the variable cannot be filled with a value from an unarticulated constituent if that constituent is only contextually relevant without being represented as one of the verbal arguments. This point will be demonstrated in section 3.3.

My goal here is to demonstrate that ascription relies on hidden variables and its behavior is dictated by the logical form of the sentence. Ascription does not lend much support to the free enrichment account, as it is hard to find convincing examples of restrictions of quantifiers which cannot be traced back to some verbal argument through ascription.

3.2 Thematic roles as key to ascription

An important point to be borne in mind is that ascription is not really a free-association decision. The hidden variable <i> will be saturated by values provided by many sources, and in a sentence with multiple arguments, each argument can in theory supply a value for the variable, but there is an order in which the values are considered. Depending on the verb and the syntactic frame it imposes, some arguments will have first dibs on the quantifier association, whereas other arguments are considered following cancellation of the first ascription. If ascription to a given argument is indeed an example of a GCI characterized by interpretive preferences in the sense of Levinson (2000), it could be suspected to be strongly controlled by logical form. This seems to be the case in the examples reviewed so far, where RECEIVE-type sentences allowed for the first ascription to be canceled and shifted to the next available participant. This smooth flexibility did not obtain in GIVE-type situations. In the "bequeath" scenario (2b above), only one interpretation is possible ("everything the giver owned"). If it is canceled, the next available interpretation will involve a different restriction (but within the same ascription), e.g. "everything that Dad kept in his tool shed". The ascription <everything that I own now> does not arise if the quantifier is used without modifiers or explicit contextual elements.

At this point, it would be interesting to consider possible generalizations to account for the varying patterns of ascription. I do not think it is possible to propose a clear-cut formula that could be used to predict the ascriptive preferences for each sentence, as ascription is a question of variable statistical tendencies rather than absolute outcomes. That is, while most listeners would entertain ascription A in a given sentence out of context, some other listeners might very well assume ascription B. Although A may be the first choice for most people, B may be only slightly less attractive an ascription.

If a tentative generalization can be sketched here, it would have to do with which argument can be viewed as a possessor of the quantity expressed by the quantifier. Consider the sentence *The pickpocket snatched everything from me.* Here, although the verb does describe an event where something is seized by force, there is a sense in which the pickpocket is not a legitimate possessor of what he has stolen, and it is the source (the owner) that is viewed as more of a possessor than the goal is. In other words, arguments are compared in terms of which one is a better example of an owner. But ownership is not always available as a measure of comparison. If none of the arguments is an owner in a strict legal sense, then the notion of possession is used. (Possession is not the same thing as ownership. Briefly, possession as a linguistic relation is a notion broader than ownership as a legal institution. For example, the teacher-student relation is one of possession, not ownership. One can use possessive pronouns in this case, as in *my student,* even though the student is not owned.)

The selection of the possessor will depend on how strongly the verb entails a successful change of possession. Change of possession is conceptualized as a transfer event from a source to a goal. These two thematic roles coexist in an unequal relationship in that the source is always a presupposed inevitable part of any transfer of possession event, whereas the goal is an unknown, as it may or may not be reached (an offer can be turned down, teaching may not result in learning, etc.) This asymmetry explains why in most cases, ascription tends to be oriented toward the source: the source is always guaranteed to possess whatever is being transferred. However, if a verb entails a successful change of possession, as in *inherit*, *regain*, *learn*, *buy* or *earn*, and if the goal is a true recipient and possessor, then the likelihood of a goal ascription increases.

Another contributing factor may be the syntactic position of the verbal arguments. In most sentences, the ascription is on the subject. This may be because the argument in this position is presupposed as a given.
Also, as is well known, the subject encodes the sentence topic, a "matter of [already established] current interest which a statement is about and with respect to which a proposition is to be interpreted as relevant" (Lambrecht 1994, 119). Because the subject serves to contextualize the remaining elements in the sentence, it is the first to provide a value for the hidden variable <i> in the course of ascription.

The entailment of transfer of possession and the syntactic position of the argument are just two possible factors that may steer the process of ascription, but of course there may be more. When multiple factors converge, as in *I inherited everything from Dad,* where the verb entails a change of possession and the possessor is in the subject position, the goal ascription seems strong enough. But they may well be in conflict, as in the above example *The pickpocket snatched everything from me.* Here, the goal is in the subject position, but as pointed out above, the verb *snatch* does not entail a change of possession event as strongly as the verb *inherit.* In such cases, the ascription is less decisive and may rely more on context.

Although I cannot adduce psycholinguistic evidence to bear on this issue, it is quite likely that parallel interpretations are entertained while a sentence with a quantifier is processed. Various ascriptions may be selected, their respective restrictions calculated and then compared against context to determine which one is the most likely one. A parallel processing is a possibility especially plausible in situations where the ascription factors clash. For example, in a sentence like *We heisted everything from the museum* (goal in the subject, but weak entailment of change of possession), there could be two ascriptions "everything in the museum" and "everything we now have", both activated in parallel. They are competing ascriptions in an optimality theoretic fashion, one of which will be rejected following evaluation against context and the other will emerge as the intended interpretation. The ascription "everything we now have" may turn out to be the intended interpretation in a situation where the speaker utters the sentence while pointing at a collection of coins and paintings.

This shows that ascription can be force-fitted to any argument, even one which is not regarded as a likely candidate out of context or in a neutral context. For example, it was argued above that the recipient argument of the verb *teach* is not normally ascribed the value of the quantifier (no entailment of successful learning[3], and the goal is not in the subject). But consider a situation where two speakers are discussing their knowledge of some academic field and one of them, surprised at how much the other knows, asks "How do you know all that?" If the other picks up an encyclopedia and says "This encyclopedia taught me

[3] Disputing claims that transfer of possession verbs in the double object construction treat the indirect object as a possessor, Levin & Rappaport-Hovav (2005, 210) argue that "double object sentences do not necessarily involve the [commonly recognized] entailment of successful change of possession." They demonstrate that the change of possession in question is only implicated, and not entailed by the verb.

everything", the ascription will be with the recipient complement of the verb, not the source argument. (The source ascription is not very plausible, as an encyclopedia contains much more material than an average reader would care to go through.)

What is noteworthy is that when little contextual information is available, some ascriptions are more attractive than others, and that is clearly dictated by logical form. Even though ascription regularities may be hard to capture in neat formulae, there are clear preferences associated with concrete scenarios. An event conveyed by a specific verb will evoke presumptive interpretations of ascription.

Perhaps more importantly, no matter which arguments are considered for ascription first, all ascription-restriction interpretations in all these cases coincide with *the arguments in the sentence*. Even when a given interpretation is not ascribable to an overt argument, an argument responsible for that interpretation can be easily pointed out as a covert argument. It is the syntax and semantics of a sentence that guide ascription-restriction resolution; restriction is not an extra-linguistic calculation based on common sense.

3.3 Possible and impossible ascriptions

Why should this fixation with verbal arguments be so important? Because they are what constrains free enrichment which then does not enjoy absolute freedom. If it did, any ascription would be possible as long as it made sense or were relevant in a given context. In what follows, examples of hypothetical but impossible ascriptive interpretations will be shown, and it will be argued that where ascription loses touch with verbal arguments, it overgenerates by yielding interpretations which cannot be justified by contextual factors. Consider the following example.

(12) We loaded everything into the trunks.

Here all the possible interpretations can be shown to hinge on the arguments present in the predicate. Two obvious interpretations are either "everything that is in the trunks" or, more likely, "everything we had to load" or "everything that was sitting next to the car". In other words, the ascription is associated with the goal argument ("the trunk"), the agent or an implicit (hidden argument) location where the things expressed as "everything" were pre-stored. The goal ascription <everything in the trunk> may be problematic, but is not impossible: (12) could be a natural thing to say in a situation where the interlocutors are inspecting the contents of the trunks of the cars in front of them, and one says (12) with stress on "we".

What is definitely not likely is "everything" being interpreted as "the cars". Such an interpretation would go against some properties of the arguments of this predicate. As an initial approximation, let us assume that an ascriptive interpretation is impossible if it involves a quantity larger than the argument that quantity is ascribed to. But before the rationale behind this limitation is explained, it is important to first address more obvious causes behind the oddness of interpreting "everything" in (12) as "the cars". After all, this situation could be argued to be a banal case of the physical impossibility of putting a car into its own trunk. However, similar quantity-larger-than-argument interpretations are odd even in situations where the laws of physics do not get in the way. For example, (13a) can be interpreted as clearing the front seat of the things on its surface (13b); or it could even mean unscrewing some bizarre devices secured to it for whatever mysterious reasons (13c), or indeed any other fancy scenario one might invent. But what (13a) cannot mean is something like (13d), where the quantifier is intended to refer to the whole car. Theoretically, one could imagine removing a seat from a car and frame such a scenario as (13). From the situation-semantic perspective, this state of affairs could be taken as a specific unique situation carrying implicit domain restriction 13d. However, that situation would not support the restriction in question, even if the speaker made it clear that that is the intended reference, because for reasons of possession properties outlined in the next section, that would not be an acceptable way of expressing this situation.

(13) a. Remove everything$_C$ from the front seat.
b. C = anything scattered on the seat.
c. C = things screwed to the seat.
d. C ≠ all the other parts of the car.

3.4 Possession in ascription

An ascriptive link between a quantifier and a given argument determines the value of that quantifier through a relation of possession. Specifically, the value must be subject to possession by that argument. Once the quantifier is ascribed to an argument, the participant expressed by that argument should be capable of possession of the value captured by the quantifier. In example (13), the seat can be said to possess whatever is scattered on its surface, so ascription to the argument "the front seat" can sanction this interpretation of "everything". At the same time, the possession requirement makes (13d) unacceptable, because the seat cannot be conceptualized as a possessor of the car.

Exactly what is meant by "possess" is a potential point of contention. Possession is normally associated with animate participants, naturally the best candidates capable of possession in the first place. But this sense is too narrow for many situations relevant to the present problem and it will be extended here to allow more possessor types, including non-human animate possessors and inanimate possessors. This extended approach to possession is adopted by Barker and Dowty (1993) who show that wholes made up of parts are automatically treated as possessors of those parts. They are realized as genitive arguments. To take (13) as an illustration, the car is the possessor and is realized either as the object of the relational preposition *of,* as in *the front seat of [the car]* or as a prenominal possessor, as in *[the car]'s front seat.* Further instances of such an extended view of possession can be drawn from studies of the syntactic properties of structures involving possession. For example, Rappaport and Levin (2008, footnote 10) show that "possessors and, thus, recipients can be inanimate in certain instances of inalienable possession, as in *give the house a coat of paint* or *give the page a number.*" In this broadened conception of possession, a possessor-possessum relation arises in meronymic combinations. Thus, the "number" can be thought of as a possessum of the "page" because it is part of the page. From the linguistic point of view, possession covers a much wider range of relations than the concept of ownership.[4]

While in my analysis the quantity conveyed by the quantifier is represented as being possessed by one of the participants in a sentence, under Stanley's formal analysis, the quantifier is restricted by the saturation of its variable <i> with the value coming from a location. These two apparently different positions can be shown to be perfectly compatible if it is demonstrated that there is a link between the concepts of possession and location. In fact, there is ample evidence that the proximity of entity A relative to entity B is an instance of possession of A by B, as in Benveniste's (1966) view of the verb "to have" as an inverted version of the expression "to be at". Such evidence comes from the literature on the grammaticalization of possessive constructions, where the link is postulated through the following argumentation. Possession is an elusive abstract concept; it cannot be observed directly the way motion or location can. A stolen apple doesn't look any different from any other apple (Snare

[4] A comprehensive treatment of the various types of possession can be found in works produced within the Cognitive Grammar framework, such as Langacker (2008) or Šarić (2002).

1972, 200). It is therefore not surprising to find that to express possession, various unrelated languages exapt constructional formulae which serve to convey concepts such as location, goal or companion (Heine 2001, 316, 1997, 91-94). In many languages, possessive constructions were grammaticalized out of locative constructions, as in Russian, where the possessum and the possessor are subject and oblique object respectively, and the possessive relation between the two is conceptualized as the location of the possessum relative to the possessor.

(15) U menya brat.
At me brother.
'I have a brother'

One can assume a metaphoric association between possession and location based on the following facts. The abstractness of possession is conveyed in concrete spatial terms. It is noteworthy that the constructions found in language after language represent the possessor and the possessum as being located near each other. Whatever the exact form or original meaning of the possessive constructions in question, they all ultimately involve some type of location, where both these arguments are situated and it is their proximity that serves as an indication of a possessive relationship between them.

One conclusion that can be drawn from typological research is that there is an intuitive equal sign between possession and location, or more precisely between possession and proximity. Put simply, if the quantity represented by the quantifier is located near a participant, that participant can automatically be viewed as the possessor of that quantity.

But there is one more requirement that a potential possessor must meet if it stands in a meronymic part-whole relation to the quantity. One property of meronymic pairs is that the relationship between the part and the whole is strictly one-way. "The number of the page" is acceptable, but "the page of the number" is odd. Similarly, the possessive link between a car and its trunk is a one-way irreversible relationship, one can say "the car's seat", but not "the seat's car". This is why the ascription (13d) above does not go through. The ascription of a quantity to an argument is awkward when that quantity cannot be conceptualized as a possible possessum. This limitation can be formalized as follows.

(14) Holonymy Blocking Constraint
Restriction cannot include in its scope a quantity which would be a holonym for the argument that the quantifier is ascribed to.

Put another way, this requirement is a consequence of Barker and Dowty's (1993) part and whole proto-roles. Simply, the whole is always realized as the possessor of its part, not vice versa.

What should be clear from the above discussion is that while constraints on restriction are imposed both by logical form and considerations of context, some interpretations are impossible if they conflict with the semantic constraints associated with logical form. Holonym interpretations of quantifiers do not go through, even if they are shown to make sense in a given context, precisely because they are filtered out by the arguments that ascription binds with. Because ascription is directed toward arguments, regardless of whether they are overt arguments or covert elements capable of being realized as arguments, the semantics of those arguments determines the possible restrictions of a quantifier. Without this screening influence of arguments, any contextually-justifiable restriction would be possible.

4. Conclusions

Because of their inherent semantic underspecification, quantifiers can be relied on to exhibit considerable variation in terms of their interpretive properties. The present paper looked at how language selects from among various interpretations made available by the use of universal quantifiers. I hope to have shown that the linguistic form of a sentence plays an important role in shortlisting the most likely interpretations which are then compared against the peculiarities of a particular context.

Stanley's assertion that all extra-linguistic contextual effects on truth-conditional content are traceable to logical form may be a very strong claim, but its validity is confirmed at least in the case of quantifier domain restriction. While interpreting quantifiers involves a number of mechanisms, both linguistic and extra-linguistic, the latter are allowed as long as they do not seriously violate semantic or syntactic constraints like the requirement that the quantity ascribed to an argument should be subject to possession by that argument. Conversely, any verbal arguments, including covert ones, can be interpreted as controlling the interpretation of a quantifier, as long as they can be thought of as capable of possessing the quantity expressed by that quantifier. The ascription of a quantifier depends on whether the quantity it represents can be possessed by a given participant and on what syntactic position that participant occupies in the sentence. These constraints ensure that the potentially confusing variety of interpretations is reduced to a manageable set of candidate meanings, making it possible to interpret quantifiers in practice.

References

Ariel, M. 2008. *Pragmatics and Grammar*. Cambridge University Press, Cambridge.

Barwise, J. and Perry, J. 1983. *Situations and Attitudes*. Cambridge, MA: The MIT Press

Barker, C. and Dowty D. 1993. "Nominal Thematic Proto-Roles." Unpublished Manuscript. Ohio State University

Benveniste, E. 1966. "'Être' et 'avoir' dans leurs fonctions linguistiques." In *Problèmes de linguistique générale*, 176-186. Paris: Gallimard.

Carston, R. 2008. "Optional pragmatic processes or optional covert linguistic structure?". *UCL Working Papers in Linguistics* 20: 143-156.

von Fintel, K. 1994. *Restrictions on Quantifier Domains*. PhD thesis, University of Massachusetts, Amherst.

Horn, L. R. 1972. *On the semantic properties of the logical operators in English*. Mimeo: Indiana University Linguistics Club.

Kratzer, A. 1986. "Conditionals." *Chicago Linguistics Society* 22(2): 1-15.

—. 2002. "Facts: Particulars or Information Units?" *Linguistics and Philosophy*, 25: 655–70

Langacker, R. 2008. *Cognitive Grammar. A Basic Introduction*. Oxford University Press, Oxford.

Lambrecht, K. 1994. *Information Structure and Sentence Form*. Cambridge: Cambridge University Press.

Levinson, S. 2000. *Presumptive Meanings. The theory of generalized conversational implicature*. MIT Press, Cambridge, MA.

Perry, J. 1986. "Thought without representation." *Supplementary Proceedings of the Aristotelian Society* 60:137-52.

—. 1998. "Indexicals, Contexts and Unarticulated Constituents." In *Computing Natural Language,* edited by Aliseda, van Gabeek and Westerståhl, 1–11. CSLI Publications, Stanford,

Rappaport Hovav, M. and Levin B. 2008. "The English dative alternation: The case for verb sensitivity." *Journal of Linguistics 44:129-167.*

Šarić, L. 2002. "On the meaning and prototype of the preposition *pri* and the locative case." *Rasprave Instituta Za Hrvatski Jezik i Jezikoslovlje* 32:225–248.

Snare, F. 1972. "The concept of property." *American Philosophical Quarterly* 9, 200-206.

Stanley, J. 2000. "Context and Logical Form." *Linguistics and Philosophy* 23:391-434.